Rewriting the First World War

Rewriting the First World War

Lloyd George, Politics and Strategy 1914–1918

Andrew Suttie

First published 2005 by
PALGRAVE MACMILLAN
Houndmills, Basingstoke, Hampshire RG21 6XS and
175 Fifth Avenue, New York, N.Y. 10010
Companies and representatives throughout the world

PALGRAVE MACMILLAN is the global academic imprint of the Palgrave Macmillan division of St. Martin's Press, LLC and of Palgrave Macmillan Ltd. Macmillan® is a registered trademark in the United States, United Kingdom and other countries. Palgrave is a registered trademark in the European Union and other countries.

ISBN-13: 978-1-4039-9119-5
ISBN-10: 1-4039-9119-7

This book is printed on paper suitable for recycling and made from fully managed and sustained forest sources.

A catalogue record for this book is available from the British Library.

Library of Congress Cataloging-in-Publication Data
Suttie, Andrew, 1959–
    Rewriting the First World War : Lloyd George, politics and strategy 1914–1918 / Andrew Suttie.
        p.   cm.
    Includes bibliographical references and index.
    ISBN 1-4039-9119-7 (cloth)
    1. Lloyd George, David, 1863–1945. War memoirs of David Lloyd George.   2. World War, 1914–1918—Historiography.   3. World War, 1914–1918—Personal narratives, British—History and criticism.   I. Title.
    D522.42.S88 2005
    940.3'41—dc22   2005047611

10   9   8   7   6   5   4   3   2   1
14   13   12   11   10   09   08   07   06   05

Transferred to Digital Printing 2007

Contents

List of Tables

Preface and Acknowledgments

It seems that the further the First World War recedes into history, and as gradually but inevitably all personal memory of the conflict disappears, interest grows on all levels. More people are attending and observing commemoration ceremonies such as Armistice Day and Anzac Day at Gallipoli; books are being published by academic and independent historians at an increasing rate (at least it seems so), and the history of the war is being taught in all its facets in universities in many countries. There is even now a specialised Master of Arts in British First World War Studies being offered at the University of Birmingham.

The First World War was, arguably, the seminal event of the twentieth century, shaping even more than the Second World War the Europe we know today, the way we view war, and even changing the language we use. For Britain, as for most of the major belligerents, it was a cataclysm: the casualties were unprecedented and a national trauma which is felt to this day. Lloyd George's *War Memoirs* played an important role in helping to shape what became the popular view of the war, as one of military incompetence, waste and futility. His portrayal of the British generals as blinkered and strategically inept, and of their negligence regarding the lives of the men under their command, made for powerful reading, and reinforced the message of other more literary war – or rather anti-war – books which were beginning to appear in the late 1920s and early 1930s. Lloyd George's message could only be given added *gravitas* by his status as a former Prime Minister and by the inclusion in his memoirs of masses of official documents. Given these factors, it is perhaps to be wondered that a book-length study of Lloyd George's *Memoirs* has not until now been published.

I could not have successfully completed the thesis upon which this book is based without the help of many people. Thanks are due first and foremost to my thesis supervisor, Associate Professor Robin Prior, who suggested this topic, pointed me in the right direction for sources and offered sound advice drawn from his great fund of knowledge of the First World War. I am grateful that he was able to maintain his confidence, when my own was faltering, that the project would one day be completed. No graduate student could hope for a better supervisor.

I would also like to thank the academic and administrative staff in the School of History (now part of the School of Humanities and Social Sciences), University of New South Wales, Australian Defence Force Academy for their friendship, support and encouragement, in particular Professor Peter Dennis, Dr Elizabeth Greenhalgh, Debbie Lackerstein, Christine Kendrick and Elsa Sellick. In addition my thanks are due to the Academy for its financial support during the research stage of this project, which assisted me to carry out archival research in the United Kingdom.

I am grateful for the hospitality extended to me by the late Mr John Grigg and his wife Patricia. All 'Lloyd Georgians' are indebted to John for his insights into Lloyd George's life and the challenges he faced during the First World War. The last volume of his wonderful biography of Lloyd George, taking the story up to 1918, alas, appeared too late to be fully utilised in the writing of this book.

My thanks to the following libraries and archives: the Australian Defence Force Academy Library; the Curators of the Bodleian Library, Oxford; the Syndics of the Cambridge University Library; the British Library; Clerk of the Records, House of Lords Record Office; Keeper of the Department of Documents, Imperial War Museum; Churchill Archive Centre, Churchill College, Cambridge; Trustees of the Liddell Hart Centre for Military Archives, King's College, London; and the Master and Fellows of Trinity College, Cambridge. Copyright material from the Ramsay MacDonald papers in the Public Record Office, Kew, is reproduced by permission of the grand-daughter of the late Malcolm MacDonald, and extracts from the Sylvester papers are reproduced by kind permission of the National Library of Wales, Aberystwyth.

I am grateful for support and encouragement to, among others in Melbourne my parents, Lionel and Cecile, my brother Timothy, and Ying Wei, Perry Dwyer, Anne Unger and Rob Stowell, in Canberra, Mary Venner and Jenny Rafferty, and in London, Malcolm Rose and Jenny Mackay. Some of them became almost as familiar with Lloyd George as I did. Special thanks should also be extended to the examiners of my doctoral thesis, Professor R.J.Q. Adams, Professor David French and Professor David Dutton, for their constructive, learned and positive comments. I would finally like to thank the staff at Palgrave Macmillan who have been of such assistance in the preparation of this book. Needless to say, all remaining faults, omissions and shortcomings in this volume, whether of fact or interpretation, are entirely my own.

Introduction

Historian Anniker Mombauer noted in her recent study of Helmuth von Moltke, Chief of the German General Staff in 1914, that the origins of the First World War have been the object of debate continually since August 1914.[1] It is not only the origins of the war, however, which have been debated since 1914–18. The strategy and conduct of the war have also been intensely controversial issues. For Britain the big questions have been not only whether Britain was right to intervene in support of its Entente partners, but also was the political and military leadership correct to raise a mass army and fight the main German forces on the Western Front and could some other, cheaper way, to defeat the Central Powers have been found?

The British Government's decision to intervene in August 1914 was publicly justified by the German violation of Belgian neutrality: in reality, it was based on the Government's assessment of where British national interests lay, and this was not necessarily concerned only with the defence of a small nation's independence and neutrality. Some have seen this decision to intervene as a mistake, and one which helped turn a localised war into a European and world war.[2] But others, beginning with the British Foreign Secretary in 1914, Sir Edward Grey, have argued that Britain had little choice but to intervene. The traditional and overriding British interest was to maintain the balance of power in Europe, and a German defeat of France and Belgium (and probably Russia) would hardly serve that interest. British intervention was, therefore, a necessity.

Once committed to intervention and war against the Central Powers, policy makers made decisions according to the plans drawn up for just such an eventuality. The British Expeditionary Force (BEF) of four infantry divisions and one cavalry was quickly sent to France to stand on the left flank of the French army. Over the following four years Britain's military commitment in France alone grew to nearly 60 divisions. The BEF, the largest army ever fielded by Britain, there confronted, alongside the French and Belgians, the main force of the main enemy. This together with the static nature of the warfare as it had developed by December 1914, and the fairly evenly matched forces during 1915–17, explains to a large extent the horrendously high casualty rate during the period 1915–18. Was there, however, an alternative?

Critics have suggested yes. On the one hand, there was the option of fighting the war according to what was seen by some as the British tradition, that is principally with the Royal Navy and financial support for allies. This, of course, would have left the costly land fighting to Britain's allies. The Navy would have blockaded the enemy (which it did even so) so that its trade was cut off: slowly, if it was not defeated on the battlefield, Germany would be starved into defeat. This did not take into account the probability that without British assistance France would have been defeated in 1914 as it was in 1870, with far-reaching consequences for British security.

Acceptance of the necessity to raise a large army does not of course imply agreement with the way it was actually deployed. Thus a further argument is that the concentration on the Western Front was wrong. After the front in the west had become static by the end of 1914, a 'way around' should have been sought, it was argued. Attacks on Germany's allies Austria-Hungary and Turkey would have knocked away the 'props' and thereby led to Germany's collapse. However a defeat of Turkey in the deserts of the Middle East or of Austria in the Balkans would not have done much to curb a massive German army in the process of defeating and occupying France. It ignores the logistical and strategic reality: that the German army had invaded Britain's Entente partner France, and that the closest and most appropriate theatre in which to deploy British forces in France's defence was in that country. It also ignores the fact that throughout the war, Germany's allies were more a drain on its resources rather than strategic assets.

The final criticism was that Britain's generals displayed a lamentable lack of imagination in their conduct of the war. They were blinkered, eyes fixed on the shell torn landscape of northern France and Belgium, where their tactics were to bludgeon the enemy into defeat through ghastly and futile frontal attacks against impregnable positions, in the vain hope they would break the enemy defences and the cavalry would come pouring through. The first point here is that enemy positions were quite definitely not impregnable. Even before the war of movement resumed in 1918, breaches in the enemy lines, by both sides, were achieved. The problem was how to maintain the momentum, to exploit the break *in* and turn it into a genuine break *through*.[3] The second point is that such criticisms of the generals are to some extent at least justified, particularly when applied to the campaigns of 1916–18. By 1917 at the latest, some at least of the Allied generals had gained sufficient experience to reach the conclusion that, in the circumstances of trench warfare, a breakthrough on the scale envisaged by Sir Douglas Haig, Commander-in-Chief of the BEF in 1916 and 1917, that is one which would result in a decisive victory, was just not possible, and that a different method was called for. Instead of offensives with distant objectives, designed to win a decisive victory, but never doing so, they proposed more limited operations with achievable objectives which, while they might not win the war on their own, would have a significant, and ultimately decisive, cumulative effect.

II

On the above points, David Lloyd George had quite decided views as expressed after the war in his *War Memoirs* and elsewhere. *Prima facie*, of course, Lloyd George was an unlikely critic of British strategy and conduct of the war. He was, after all, the only senior British politician (and probably the only one in most if not all of the belligerent powers) who saw the war through holding office at or near the top of government. As he put it in the *War Memoirs*, 'I was the only Minister in any country who had some share throughout the whole of the war in its direction. . . . No other Minister in any of the belligerent countries held an official position from the 1 August, 1914, to the 11 November, 1918.'[4] He began the war as Chancellor of the Exchequer, established the Ministry of Munitions in June 1915, moved to the War Office one year later and ascended finally to the Prime Ministership in December 1916. All these offices gave him influence and increasing power over the strategic and political conduct of the war. The last, of course, also gave Lloyd George the ultimate responsibility for the conduct of the war.

It is certainly ironic, therefore, that by the publication of the *War Memoirs* in the 1930s, Lloyd George became one of the best known and fiercest critics of the British conduct of the war. It is even more ironic that he reserved his most vitriolic criticisms for those operations which occurred under his Prime Ministership, in particular the series of engagements given the official title of Third Battle of Ypres, or more popularly Passchendaele.

Lloyd George's broadsides were largely reserved for Britain's generals, and two in particular, Haig and Sir William Robertson, Chief of the Imperial General Staff (CIGS).[5] Their lack of imagination, obstinacy, and obsession with the muddy battlefields of Flanders, according to Lloyd George, led to the needless slaughter of masses of fine British troops and brought the Allies no closer to victory. Even Haig's performance in the final months of 1918 brings no greater praise from Lloyd George than that he was a good second in command. Robertson and his successor as CIGS, Sir Henry Wilson, and many other British and Allied generals were attacked with varying degrees of ferocity.

Many of Lloyd George's political colleagues also come in for attack. In this sphere, the main targets were those Liberal political figures such as Herbert Samuel, Reginald McKenna, Edward Grey and Walter Runciman who were either political antagonists during the war or long after it, during the period of infighting which characterised Liberal politics as its fortunes declined in the later 1920s and early 1930s. Many of these figures, of course, had also refused or had not even been considered for inclusion in the wartime coalition headed by Lloyd George formed in December 1916. Yet it is fairly clear that a good deal of the venom on display in the *War Memoirs* relates not to pre-war or wartime events but to those political events well after the war. Lloyd George's treatment of Sir Edward Grey is perhaps the best example of this.

There are thus two main points to make regarding his attacks on British strategy and the conduct of the war. First, they were certainly not directed at himself or those who were close to him during the war such as Lord Milner or Andrew Bonar Law. Lloyd George declines to accept any responsibility for the disastrous episodes of the Somme, Passchendaele, or the British defeats of March–April 1918.[6] He points to the generals, who deceived the politicians, and mishandled their troops and the operations in which they were engaged, and those politicians who were in the generals' pockets, and indeed the press, who aided and abetted in the great deception, as bearing the responsibility for the great cost of the war. The second point is that, despite this disclaimer, his determined attempt to avoid all responsibility for wartime disasters, he cannot escape the fact that, as he so proudly proclaims, he was the only statesman to see it through from beginning to end in a position of power and responsibility. His relentless attacks on the politicians, generals and their strategy and conduct of the war and military operations ultimately rebounds to his own discredit and cannot fail to detract from his own significant and genuine wartime achievements.

III

In the *War Memoirs*, Lloyd George deals with issues ranging from military policy and strategy, the qualities of the Allied generals, wartime politics, to the very un-military and less obvious education reform and the vexed issue of 'drink' (an evil that, in 1915, Lloyd George characterised as more dangerous to the Allied cause than the Germans). The wide range of issues discussed in the *War Memoirs* clearly reflects the central role in the British and Allied war effort Lloyd George played from the beginning to the end of the conflict. I cannot hope, for reasons of space, to address more than a selection of what I consider some of the more important issues. Therefore there had to be a fairly rigorous selectivity at work here. What then has been the basis for the selection of the topics I have chosen?

Apart from Chapter 1, 'Writing the War Memoirs' (to which I shall return), and the partial exception of Chapter 9 (on Russia), all chapters in this book deal with what were unarguably both major episodes in the history of the Great War and in Lloyd George's wartime career. The outbreak of war, the discussions on strategy early in 1915, the establishment of the Ministry of Munitions, Lloyd George's translation to the Prime Ministership, the Nivelle and Passchendaele offensives of 1917, the introduction of the convoy system, the great battles in France in 1918 and finally the manpower issue which came to a head in 1918 were all major turning points in the war *and* in Lloyd George's career. Consequently, Lloyd George's discussions of these episodes in the *War Memoirs* are full and in many ways form the substantive core of the books. Not only is a great deal of space in the six volumes devoted to these episodes, but clearly they were all events about which Lloyd George felt passionately at the time, and indeed, still did when it came to writing the *Memoirs* in the 1930s. To briefly take one example, arguably the most important section of the *Memoirs* is that dealing with the Third Battle of Ypres, or Passchendaele.

More than any other battle, perhaps more than the Somme, even by the 1930s Passchendaele had come to symbolise all that was wrong and wasteful about the way the war was fought on the Western Front. B.H. Liddell Hart, by the 1930s both a fierce critic of the British generals of the Great War and Lloyd George's key military advisor for the *War Memoirs*, regarded Haig's handling of Passchendaele as criminal. Lloyd George, as we shall see, held very similar views. In his account in the *War Memoirs*, Lloyd George is relentless in his condemnation of Haig, Robertson and their allies, reaching a level of vituperation which must, as I argue, have sprung from a deep sense of guilt at not having stopped the carnage. Indeed, Lloyd George, in order to reach a wider audience and to emphasise his points further, published the Passchendaele chapters as a separate pamphlet.[7] In the 1930s, his account clearly struck a chord and helped shape the perception of the Western Front as an example of waste, futility and horror that must never be repeated.

In fact, what holds true for the treatment of Passchendaele largely holds true for the treatment of the other episodes which make up the core of the *War Memoirs* and of this book. They form a continuous and interconnected thread of, on the one hand, defence of his own actions, and on the other, condemnation of the people who Lloyd George held responsible in large measure for the outbreak of the war, for Britain being so ill-prepared for modern war on a continental scale, and for the enormous and unprecedented losses which the British forces suffered through an ill-conceived and incompetently conducted strategy. And it is precisely those elements of the *War Memoirs*, from Grey and his responsibility for the outbreak of war, through to the debate between 'Westerners' and 'Easterners', to the concept of attrition, and to Haig's faulty dispositions on the Western Front which almost led to defeat in 1918, which have proved the most influential. They have powerfully supported and reinforced a widely held and enduring perception that Britain's intervention in the war was a catastrophic mistake and that the fighting on the Western Front was an exercise in futility and waste led by incompetent, bungling, even criminally negligent senior officers.

As noted above, in this book there are two exceptions to this 'master' narrative. Chapter 1 examines the writing of the *Memoirs*, and Chapter 9 looks at some of the issues discussed by Lloyd George regarding Russia in the *War Memoirs*. An examination of the writing of the *War Memoirs*, while it has been undertaken before,[8] I felt necessary to include to show how Lloyd George wrote the *War Memoirs*, who helped him, and indicate some of the more important influences upon the finished work. He was apparently always at pains to emphasise that nobody was responsible for the writing of the books but himself, but it is clear that, while perhaps there was not the same level of assistance that Churchill utilised, for example, in the writing of his histories, the *War Memoirs* would not have been published with the same degree of authority without the help of such people as A.J. Sylvester and Liddell Hart.

The second exception is the chapter on Russia. Although the key difference between many of the passages on Russia and those on events in the west is that Lloyd George was not directly involved in the events he discusses (this is one of the reasons I have included Russia), the main reason for its inclusion is that in some senses Russia was indeed an integral part of Lloyd George's 'master narrative'. Many chapters in the *War Memoirs* are devoted to the Russian role in the war, then later the revolution which saw the monarchy fall and Russia withdraw from the war. Russia, in Lloyd George's eyes, was the lost opportunity of the Allied war effort: if a real attempt had been made to supply Russia with the armaments it so badly needed in the first years of the war, he argued, then Allied victory might well have come sooner and the Russian Revolution averted. But western political and military leaders were almost without exception fixated on the Western Front, and Russia was allowed to fall through lack of support. Only when Lloyd George became Prime Minister, we are told, was a serious and concerted effort made to ascertain Russia's needs and coordinate the Allied military effort, but by then it was too late. The Russian Front, along with the Balkans, Italy and the Middle East, was the much needed alternative to the carnage on the Western Front, for 'if only' the Allies had concentrated more resources on bolstering the Russians (and/or the Italians, Romanians, Serbs and so on) countless lives would have been saved through a shortening of the war. I need only state here that even during Lloyd George's tenure at the Ministry of Munitions, the first priority remained, quite properly, the supply of munitions to the BEF. Finally, the section on the failure to rescue the Imperial family from imprisonment and death at the hands of the Bolsheviks has been included because it is one section which was substantially changed due to pressure from royal and political quarters.

There are other topics discussed in the *War Memoirs* which deserve to be addressed in a study such as this, but which for reasons of space have had to be omitted. Two mentioned above, are of sufficient importance to deserve brief comments here. The war at sea in most accounts focuses on two aspects, the contest between the capital ship fleets culminating in the Battle of Jutland, and the introduction of convoys to protect Allied merchant ships. On the former Lloyd George has little to say, but on the latter we have the famous passage of Lloyd George descending on the Admiralty and taking 'peremptory action' to impose convoys on reluctant Admirals. As historians have argued, however, while the sequence of cause and effect is far from clear, Lloyd George over stresses his own role in the adoption of the convoy system and rather downplays the processes already at work in the Admiralty towards the adoption of convoys prior to his visit.[9]

Manpower centres on two issues: the conscription controversy in 1915–16, and whether in 1918 Lloyd George was withholding men from Haig's command for fear of another Passchendaele. Initially, it seemed that Britain would not need compulsory service in the armed forces, as hundreds of thousands of men responded to Lord Kitchener's call for volunteers in the first months of the war. As casualties mounted, however, and volunteering slowed, new means were sought. Lloyd George had expressed support for a form of conscription as early as 1910.[10] And he supported conscription when it was introduced in 1916.[11] The question of whether Lloyd George was keeping Haig's BEF below establishment in 1918 for fear of more casualties on the scale of Third Ypres was (and is) more controversial. Wartime controversy resulted in a Commons debate in May 1918 over whether the BEF was weaker or stronger in manpower than the year before, sparked by the former Director of Military Operations' letter to the press alleging that it was in fact weaker and that the Government had lied about it. It was resolved in firmly in favour of the Government. This was a confused and complicated affair. In the *War Memoirs*, Lloyd George paints it as another attempt of the military cabal and its press allies to overthrow his Government. And, indeed, there was something in this. Whatever the rights and wrongs concerning the details of the charges brought by General Maurice, the result of the debate was to destroy the credibility of Asquith, the leader of the Opposition, the forced retirement of Maurice on half pay and the consolidation of parliamentary support for the Government.[12]

IV

The core, then, of this book has a common theme. While whether Lloyd George was merely 'pamphleteering' is debatable, there was a purpose in the *War Memoirs* apart from contributing to the historical record (though of course he hoped that his version would help shape the wider perception of his role in the conduct of the war and become an accepted part of the historical record, as indeed it did for so long). His main purpose was, on the one hand, to correct the record and condemn those political and military figures who either since the war had denigrated Lloyd George's conduct of the war or, later, his political machinations in the 1920s (for example, Edward Grey, Herbert Samuel, and a myriad of army officers), and, on the other, to damn those senior military figures responsible for the war on the Western Front (primarily Douglas Haig and the CIGS William Robertson). In this latter purpose, in particular, he tapped successfully into a popular mood of disillusionment and disenchantment, and in turn helped reinforce some of the central myths of the First World War. A critical look, then, at some of the key sections of the *War Memoirs* is perhaps overdue.

The *War Memoirs* were a popular and overall a critical success. Lloyd George's account of the war remains influential to the present day. Yet in each of the episodes under discussion in this book, problems abound. In order to illustrate this, I have used the vast array of documents contained in the Lloyd George papers in the House of Lords Public Record Office. These papers have been supplemented by use of the Cabinet Papers in the Public Record Office, various official publications, and the private papers of many of Lloyd George's wartime colleagues or protagonists. I have also made great use of the published diaries, memoirs and autobiographies of various public figures of the period. And of course there is a vast array of secondary literature dealing with various aspects of this study. Details are given in the Notes and Bibliography.

Despite the enormous number of studies of the First World War in its various aspects, it is unfortunate that, to my knowledge, only one historian has attempted to provide an analysis of selected elements of Lloyd George's *War Memoirs as history*; that is, to make some attempt to compare Lloyd George's arguments with the historical record. George Egerton, for example, in his important article was more concerned with outlining the writing process and examining the role of memoir in how we perceive historical events. Such insights are valuable, but his approach is quite different to this book. Only historian Trevor Wilson has provided an extended critique from an historical perspective, but as a journal article its scope is necessarily limited.[13]

I make no claim to be exhaustive or to say the last word on Lloyd George's *War Memoirs*. There is room for much further work, on, for example, the war at sea, the manpower question (as noted above), or war finance. And almost any of the following chapters could become a full-length study in itself. Neither is this book a startlingly original study on a completely new area: the First World War is, after all, well trodden ground. What I do offer is a new and original angle on familiar events, examined through the prism of the recollections of the most prominent political leader of the period.

1
Writing the *War Memoirs* 1931–36

I

Few political memoirs of the Great War have been as influential or as controversial as Lloyd George's *War Memoirs*. Over the years these volumes have made a significant contribution to shaping the historical and popular perceptions of the key events and especially the personalities of the 1914–18 conflict. When the *Memoirs* first appeared in 1933–36 the responses of critics and the reading public testify to the passionate reaction to his arguments and criticisms.[1] In particular, many were outraged by the attacks on the generals, some praised the literary style and many the extensive documentation. It is no surprise that the *Memoirs* stirred controversy. The public and private memory of the war was still fresh in the minds of the adult population, and Lloyd George was an important figure in British politics even after his resignation in 1922.

This chapter examines how Lloyd George wrote his memoirs, what assistance he had in the research and writing and the role of his principal advisers, Sir Maurice Hankey and B.H. Liddell Hart, in the research and writing process. They were particularly important; the first, in the factual details of important wartime events and with advice on what Lloyd George could and should publish in terms of official documents; the latter with advice on military matters. While the end product is unmistakeably Lloyd George's, Hankey's and Liddell Hart's influence can be clearly discerned.

II

The publication of the *Memoirs* was awaited with anticipation for several reasons. Lloyd George was the last of the major figures of the war to publish his account. He was a most controversial Prime Minister, and he alone had retained high office throughout the war, and crucially also remained a key member of the Cabinet's war policy directing committees.[2] In terms of continuity of tenure of high office during the war, Lloyd George's record was unique. He was thus in the position of being able to reveal the inner workings of the wartime government and decision-making process at the highest levels better than anyone. In contrast, that other great war memoirist, Winston Churchill, produced memoirs as voluminous, but they suffer from his exclusion from office and power for much of the war. He left the Government under a cloud late in 1915 and did not return until 1917, and even then was not a member of the War Cabinet. He thus had significantly less direct experience of political developments and wartime policy making than Lloyd George.[3] The same applies to Asquith, Grey and most other senior Liberals, who were in opposition from December 1916, while the Unionist leaders only entered government in May 1915. Lloyd George was thus the best placed of all his contemporaries in Government to produce an account of wartime decision-making at the highest level for the entire period 1914–18.

There are other factors which help explain the *Memoirs'* popularity and their enduring influence. Those close to him during the writing of the *Memoirs* testify to his energy, enthusiasm and vigour in dealing with the mass of material at his disposal.[4] This is all the more remarkable as he began the serious work at the age of 70, and the sixth and final volume was not published until late 1936, when he was 73.[5] He wrote quickly; he pointed out to his secretary A.J. Sylvester in 1934 that while Arnold Bennet had written 275,000 words in a year, he had written 400,000 in eight months. As Sylvester noted, Lloyd George became at one point concerned at the effect of such exertions upon his health, and on occasions took to his bed 'rundown' with a temperature.[6]

This energy is reflected in his narrative. While some critics then and more recently were less than complimentary regarding Lloyd George's literary ability,[7] the *War Memoirs* have remained a classic of the genre due to their readability, extensive documentation and the vigour of Lloyd George's arguments. As George Egerton has observed, 'it became apparent... that the skills of an unsurpassed political orator and an accomplished journalist had been translated successfully to the medium of memoir'.[8] Or as the reviewer for the *Times Literary Supplement* commented:

almost every line of [the *War Memoirs* is] impressed with his rich, confident, aggressive personality...it is easy to imagine some historian of the future telling his pupils that, if they wished to understand how it was that Lloyd George came to the front as the War situation darkened and how it was that he alone among the statesmen of Europe stood the strain of it all right through from the week of ultimatums to the signature of the Peace Treaties, they only have to read half a dozen pages of his memoirs – any half-dozen will do.[9]

Whether the work can be regarded as history, however, is another question. Churchill's judgement was that the *War Memoirs* 'may not be Literature, but [are] certainly History'.[10] The *Memoirs* did attract considerable praise from a number of historians.[11] There is little doubt that many were impressed with the documentation Lloyd George utilised to support his arguments. These documents, of course, were at the time inaccessible to historians and would not be opened up until the 1960s. Lloyd George himself, however, commented to H.A.L. Fisher, 'I am not writing history as a historian...but as a solicitor in possession of the documents.'[12] His primary concern was *not* to produce a scholarly history of the war years, but to vindicate his wartime leadership and reputation.[13]

The *Memoirs*, far from 'unread' were a considerable sales success, particularly in the condensed two-volume edition. They were first published in lots of two volumes in 1933, 1934 and 1936, with the cheap two-volume edition appearing in January 1938.[14] As the volumes were published, excerpts were serialised in the *Daily Telegraph* (serialisation rights sold for £25,000). By February 1937 sales of the British six-volume edition stood at 12,707 for volume one, 10,720 for volume two, 8971 for volume three, 9413 for volume four, 6607 for volume five and 5819 for volume six. Demand for the volumes can perhaps be gauged by the fact that, as the publisher noted at the time of the publication of the fifth volume, distribution extended to 500 bookshops throughout Britain, 'nearly every European country' except the Soviet Union:

> 12 towns in South Africa, 11 towns in New Zealand, about 15 towns in India and practically the same number in Australia, while copies will also be available in Japan, China, Shanghai, Cairo and Muritius, and, of course, through the Ryerson Press of Toronto, throughout Canada. It is safe to say that no other book which we have published has ever received such a world-wide distribution on publication.

The book also went on sale at the Dorchester, Russell, Langham, Regent Palace and Strand Palace Hotels, and the National Liberal and Royal Automobile Clubs in London.[15]

Respectable as the sales of the six-volume edition were, the later cheap edition was a best seller. Both volumes had sales of over 100,000 by May 1938, and by October 1944 sales stood at 145,146 for the first volume, and 141,283 for the second.[16] It is clear, then, that through serialisation in the press and healthy sales, his arguments and criticisms of former political colleagues and especially of the military leaders of the 1914–18 conflict reached a wide audience.

III

Lloyd George first turned to the business of memoir writing in the early postwar period. Part of his motivation even at this early stage was undoubtedly that he had been the target of criticism in much of this early war literature. Another incentive, of course, was money. Contracts were signed with publishers in both Britain and the United States, and Major-General E.D. Swinton was engaged to carry out the basic research and generally 'devil' for the Prime Minister. This was, according to Sylvester, a 'clever' move on Lloyd George's part, for Swinton had 'marvellous contacts and was trusted by the Fighting Services; he knew all the secret archives and what is more, had access to them. So popular indeed was he that a room was allocated to him in the offices of the Cabinet at 2, Whitehall Gardens'.[17]

The financial aspects of these contracts, however, scandalised the press and public in the economically straitened circumstances of the immediate postwar period. It was, moreover, a population in which scarcely a family had escaped completely unscathed from the ravages of the war and the unprecedented sums which he secured for his memoirs – up to, according to one estimate, £132,000 – gave the appearance that he was profiting from tragedy. This raised such a storm of protest in the press that he was forced to declare that all proceeds would be donated to war charities.[18] Swinton, however, continued working, writing to J.F.C. Fuller in late 1922: 'I am at present devilling for a great book, the greatest book in the world.'[19] A.J. Sylvester noted: 'Swinton and his Secretary, Mrs Reynolds, worked for years . . . he read and carefully sifted all the official and private documents of all kinds in an endeavour to write the skeleton of L.G.'s War Memoirs. Swinton's own conception of his task was to build the trunk of the tree as he described it and the main branches.'[20]

Soon, however, Lloyd George began to lose interest in the project. Swinton recalled that Lloyd George's 'heart was not in the job. . . . Clearly the time was not ripe for leisured thinking and writing. That must await retirement from office.'[21] After his fall from office, and most importantly robbed of his windfall, Lloyd George, requiring additional income, discovered that journalism was much more lucrative than memoir writing, and instead of writing about the past he could comment on current problems and issues. He was, after all, still an active and ambitious politician. According to Sylvester, Lloyd George's mind was not on the job and Sylvester lacked clear directions: 'In the end Swinton was expected not only to build the trunk and the branches but to put on the twigs and all the leaves as well! – a mighty task especially with no clear or definite instructions.'[22] Suggestions that Swinton undertake a scholarly history of Lloyd George's role in the war came to nothing, and he prophetically wrote to Lloyd George in January 1924:

> To continue devilling for your Memoirs I am quite willing. But I do not feel competent to attempt a book on your activities during the war, or to take the responsibility for the views and opinions which would be expressed in it. As you know many people are waiting for the appearance of your book with guns and clubs.[23]

The memoirs were put on hold. Instead throughout the 1920s Lloyd George concentrated on writing syndicated articles on politics and international affairs which earned him large sums of money.[24]

In the preface to Volume I of the *War Memoirs* Lloyd George writes that two events persuaded him to revive the memoirs. The first was a sudden illness and a painful operation. This released him from the 'burden' of leadership of the troubled Liberal Party.[25] His prostate troubles did remove him from the political scene at a crucial moment, for Ramsay MacDonald was in the process of forming a 'National Government', and it is almost certain that despite his ambivalent feelings about the coalition Lloyd George would have been offered and felt himself bound to accept a post in that Government.[26] As it was he was forced into a protracted convalescence, and after the 1931 General Election there was little prospect of a return to office.[27] These momentous events would have a significant impact on aspects of the *War Memoirs*.

The second event was a visit from a wartime colleague who urged Lloyd George to give his account of the war. Lloyd George had, after all, a unique perspective: 'It was', he wrote, 'pointed out to me that I was the only person in authority who was in Mr Britling's position. I saw it through.'[28] As Lloyd George put it later to Hankey:

General [J.C.] Smuts urged me very strongly a year ago to write my Memoirs. He pointed out that unless I did so, judgement might go against me in default on the vital issues of war management raised by [other books on the war]. He urged very properly that these books constituted the material from which the future historian of the War would draw. It was his plea that determined me to take in hand immediately the writing of my memoirs.[29]

The decision to write the memoirs can be further explained by the fact that by 1931 many of the leading participants – Lloyd George's ex-colleagues – had published their reminiscences and recollections, many of which contained strong criticisms of Lloyd George. Memoirs had appeared by, among others, the former Chief of the Imperial General Staff (CIGS) Sir William Robertson,[30] former Prime Minister H.H. Asquith,[31] Foreign Secretary Sir Edward Grey[32] and the former First Lord of the Admiralty (among other offices) Winston Churchill.[33] In addition, major works on Secretary of State for War Lord Kitchener,[34] Robertson's successor as CIGS Sir Henry Wilson[35] and Commander-in-Chief of the British Expeditionary Force in France Field Marshal Douglas Haig[36] which utilised their private and/or public papers appeared during this period. And Sir Frederick Maurice, former Director of Military Operations in the War Office under Robertson, revived the manpower controversy of May 1918 with his series of press articles, later published as *Intrigues of the War*.[37] As many of these works were either critical of Lloyd George or did not, in his view, give credit where credit was due, it was clearly time to 'supplement and corrrect' the record.[38] As he wrote to Sir Maurice Hankey, the long-serving Secretary to the Cabinet:

for 15 years I have borne a stream of criticism polluted with much poisonous antagonism...My shelves here groan under their muti-lated bowdlerised, distorted quotations. I must in all justice not to myself but to public and posterity, tell the whole truth.[39]

To prepare himself for the task, he took advantage of his convalescence after his illness and operation to read many of these accounts. He sailed to Ceylon and, as Sylvester relates, took with him 'masses of books written on the war, and a selection of archives. L.G. who was a prodi-gious reader, read the whole lot'; elsewhere, Sylvester noted that Lloyd George 'took with him a huge trunk of every book that had ever been written on the War by anyone of importance. These he read, marked and annotated.'[40] He was highly critical of many of these books. On

Churchill's *World Crisis*, for example, he commented to Frances
Stevenson: 'I have read marked and annotated Winston's four volumes.
You might have thought the central figure throughout was W.S.C
himself. He is not always fair to me. He glides over my Munitions
achievement with one sentence.'[41] He complained that John Buchan's
and – ironically in view of their later association – B.H. Liddell Hart's
accounts, as well as Churchill's

> Either from prejudice or ignorance . . . pass by my share in the war as
> if it were trivial. A good deal of this is deliberate. Munitions – unity
> of command – submarine campaign – my keeping up the spirit of the
> nation by rousing appeals. All this is not altogether suppressed but
> dismissed perfunctorily.[42]

Sylvester recorded in his diary that Lloyd George thought Churchill
'tremendously conceited . . . regarding his own efforts in the War'.
While the book was entitled *The World Crisis*, Churchill was solely
concerned with explaining his own actions and defending himself.[43] He
was particularly aggrieved at Churchill's neglect of his achievements at
the Ministry of Munitions; he said:

> it was clear that there was only one man who had won the war and
> that was Winston himself. He said nothing at all about the Ministry
> of Munitions which LG had set up from nothing; but he devoted
> pages to the Ministry of Munitions when he, Winston, was Minister
> of that Department.[44]

There is a clear sense of resentment and rivalry here. (Of course, too,
some of the sentiments that Lloyd George expressed regarding
Churchill's *World Crisis* could equally, and would be, expressed when
the *War Memoirs* appeared.)

Lloyd George also complained that writers of what were claimed to be
'impartial histories of the war' never bothered to ask him for information or explanations of events in which he took a leading role; again the
leading culprits were Buchan, Churchill and Liddell Hart. He was
annoyed that they ignored the importance of his 'keeping up the
morale of the nation' during the war. Germany, he noted, 'failed largely
because it had no one who could discharge this function'.[45]

Lloyd George, however, could take some satisfaction from the fact
that he was paid many times more the amount that Churchill received
for *his* memoirs. As Sylvester recorded: 'Winston came by to see L.G. by

appointment at 6.45. He was staggered at the amount L.G. had made. It is the one thing he talks about at the moment – that Winston made £5,000 for his book and yet at a time of unparalleled depression L.G. has made 5 times as much.'[46]

By 1931–1932 Lloyd George was out of office with little immediate prospect of return, and had the financial, personal and political incentive to devote his considerable energies to writing his 'inside' account of the war in which he had played so vital a part. The writing of the *War Memoirs* he kept firmly in his control, but the research, utilising his own personal archive, those of government departments and other individuals, was largely conducted by members of his personal staff.[47]

IV

All six volumes bear the stamp of Lloyd George's personality; as Egerton has put it: 'Discretion and dignity had never been allowed to impede Lloyd George's career; neither would they inhibit his writing.'[48] From beginning to end he was firmly in control of the writing process;[49] he began by dictating passages to Sylvester. As Sylvester noted, 'This morning Gwilym and Megan were all ready to go out; so was L.G. when in he rushed in true L.G. style to dictate to me. He dictated about 400 odd words on the book. In the evening he dictated just under 3,000.'[50] After this beginning, however, Lloyd George wrote everything by hand, in his own 'higgledy-piggledy handwriting which was murder to read', as Sylvester notes, and it was then typed out and returned to Lloyd George for amendments. To Sylvester it became clear with the passage of time why Lloyd George decided to write it all himself: 'it was, that he, and he alone, was the fellow who had written, in his own hand, all his War Memoirs. Nobody ever helped him.'[51]

Some chapters he clearly thought to be of the utmost importance in presenting his case; for example, according to Sylvester Lloyd George worked 'incessantly' on the chapters dealing with Third Ypres. They were

> written, re-written and re-re-written time after time...L.G. had himself many talks with high-ranking officers: he had masses of secret documents from the CIGS and other Generals at home and abroad, including Haig, from French sources, and from information given daily to the Cabinet about our losses. Moreover he had had a lot of material privately from an official German source.[52]

For certain sections Swinton's drafts provided the basis for new drafts. Lloyd George, even so, was heavily dependent on secretarial and research assistance provided by his staff. In this capacity his secretaries, A.J. Sylvester, Frances Stevenson, and to a lesser extent Malcolm Thomson, played key roles.[53]

Frances Stevenson had been in Lloyd George's employ since 1911. In addition to being his efficient secretary, she was also his mistress and would become, in 1943, his second wife. Her invaluable contribution to the *War Memoirs* lay in her detailed diary of the war years and beyond, crucial in providing a chronology of events.[54] The diary was later edited by A.J.P. Taylor and published in 1971. Malcolm Thomson, for his part, wrote summaries of issues based on the hoard of documents in Lloyd George's own archive and the available secondary material, which, however, according to Sylvester, in the end proved to be of little use to Lloyd George.

Of the three it was A.J. Sylvester who was most closely involved and played the biggest part in the research for the *Memoirs*. Sylvester was a champion typist and shorthand writer who was hired by Hankey's office in 1915.[55] He was the first person to take a shorthand note at a Cabinet meeting. When the Cabinet Secretariat was established in December 1916, Sylvester became Hankey's private secretary, and in 1921 he became a private secretary to Lloyd George. After the latter left office in 1922, Sylvester stayed on under Bonar Law and Baldwin, but in 1923 he accepted an offer to become Lloyd George's 'principal' private secretary.[56] Sylvester carried out all the research in the Whitehall archives and also interviewed Lloyd George's former colleagues for the *War Memoirs*.[57] From 1931 Sylvester kept a diary and it contains frequent references to the interviews with political and military figures and his painstaking searches for documents in the archives.[58]

As noted above, two key 'outsiders' also played an important advisory role in the writing of the *Memoirs*: Sir Maurice Hankey and B.H. Liddell Hart. Hankey's main role, as Secretary to the Cabinet since 1916, Secretary to the Committee of Imperial Defence and Clerk of the Privy Council, was to protect Cabinet secrecy.[59] He was also concerned, however, with maintaining a 'suitable respect, decorum and discretion' with regard to the events and leaders of the past.[60] As he wrote, in response to Lloyd George's criticisms of various former colleagues,

> I ask myself whether it is really to the public advantage that our national heroes should be hauled off their pedestals. It has somewhat of the same effect as would be produced in the churches if some

distinguished churchman were to marshal the historical evidence against the saints! I also deprecate the possibility of a public controversy between the persons concerned in these events, with a competition of attack and counter-attack, involving extensive search in the official records for material.[61]

Lloyd George, however, was 'really the judge'. Lloyd George promised to do his 'best to tone down the acerbities of truth'.[62]

Hankey told Lloyd George that he had two options in seeking authorisation for the use of Cabinet records. He could seek permission to publish from the King, which meant, in effect, applying to the Prime Minister, Ramsay MacDonald, for authority. But Hankey conceded that this procedure had not always been followed. Churchill and General E.D. Swinton, for example, had passed their manuscripts to Hankey for unofficial vetting, while others had not sought permission at all from the Prime Minister or, less officially, from Hankey, including Sir George Arthur (for his biography of Kitchener), Lord French, Sir William Robertson, Lord Beaverbrook and Lord Grey.[63] Rather than be placed in a potentially awkward position, Hankey wrote, Lloyd George would be well advised

> to go through the correct procedure and write to the Prime Minister. You could mention that I have read the book unofficially and that you have adopted my suggestions...The Prime Minister and Lord President know that I have read the book and could call for my report and, provided my advice is accepted, your position would be absolutely secure. An alternative would be to write to Mr. Baldwin on the ground that you realise that the Prime Minister is overburdened owing to his early departure for Washington.[64]

In the event, Lloyd George chose the second course, justifying his decision to Hankey by noting that he was 'the very last of the prominent figures of the War, except yourself, to give an account of what took place', and that most of those who had already published had not dealt fairly with the material at their disposal, with the result that they reflected 'adversely' on his conduct of the war.[65] He pointed out that of all the cases Hankey cited, only one went through the official channels and sought authority from the Prime Minister, and only one submitted their manuscript to Hankey as Clerk of the Privy Council: 'Winston seems to have been the only one who placed the whole of his MS to you before it was sent to the printer. I adopted the same proceeding.'[66] If there were going to be problems with publishing Cabinet documents, Lloyd George vowed he would publish in America, 'and in England he would publish it with blank pages where the quotations should have been printed. In the case of men like Runciman, whom he was going for, he would put a tiny little photograph on one corner of the blank page.'[67]

Lloyd George's use of Cabinet memoranda and other documentation generally met with Hankey's approval. When he wrote officially to Lloyd George on Baldwin's behalf on 21 April 1934 regarding the use of official documents in volumes III and IV, he noted that Lloyd George had followed the same practice as in the first two volumes: there was considerable 'textual quotation of documents that were written solely for official purposes'. The war years were, however, treated as exceptional and a 'wide latitude' was given to memoirists of that period.[68] The issue that aroused some concern was the quotation of War Cabinet minutes. While it was appreciated that there was a significant difference between the War Cabinet and normal peace-time Cabinets, direct quotation from the minutes should be kept to a minimum. It should be, he wrote:

> confined to cases where it is indispensable to the historical presenta-
> tion of the facts, and the least possible resort should be made to such
> devices as quotation marks, the indenting of the passages, special
> type, etc.... the extracts from War Cabinet Minutes are not very
> numerous, but Mr Baldwin hopes that when they are examined you
> will find little or no difficulty in reducing them within very narrow
> limits. He suggests also that you should, as far as possible, confine
> quotation to cases where persons other than members of the War
> Cabinet were present.[69]

Quotations from Cabinet committees also raised concerns about 'Hansardisation' of particular ministers: this would provide an 'undesir-able and highly inconvenient precedent'. All Foreign Office telegrams, in addition, should be paraphrased.[70]

Hankey was cooperative in giving Sylvester access to the official files, often assisting him in searches for information.[71] Moreover he consulted his own diary on certain questions, for example on the adop-tion of the convoy system. Here he sent Lloyd George his diary extract from 13 February 1917, when Lloyd George had invited certain colleagues to breakfast to discuss the question.

Tuesday February 13 [1917] Your breakfast, attended by [First Lord] Carson [Admirals] Jellicoe, Duff and myself. My recollection, which is confirmed by Duff, is that my memorandum was read aloud. The only note I have in my diary is as follows:- 'They resisted a good deal, but I think the discussion did good. They admitted that they were already convoying military transports, and agreed to enquire about the results of a big convoy of eight military transports coming from Australia'.[72]

Hankey carefully read each chapter and made detailed notes, and while many of the remarks raised merely a question of accuracy or wording, occasionally a more serious problem arose. In these cases, he sent offending passages to the appropriate departments of state or other individuals for a second opinion and further comment. For example, chapters or sections touching on potentially sensitive foreign policy matters would be sent to the Foreign Office, and chapters on the military or naval effort would be sent to the War Office, the Admiralty or the appropriate area in the Committee of Imperial Defence (CID) Historical Section. Thus in April 1934 Hankey wrote to Lloyd George:

The Submarine Chapter is wonderful. May I show it to the man in our historical section who 'devilled' for this part of the Official History? You needn't fear he is pro-Jellicoe! We had horrid rows with J. at the time and I had to intervene myself! But he might pick up something that wants altering or make a constructive suggestion.[73]

Hankey's influence over the writing of the *War Memoirs* was beneficial in terms of factual accuracy and in toning down some of Lloyd George's more barbed comments on some of his ex-colleagues. Generally, he had a high opinion of the *Memoirs*: the volumes were a

unique contribution to history, which will be read for years to come.... I do not recall a parallel case to this, where the Statesman who directed with success the British effort in a major war – perhaps the greatest war in history – in its decisive stages, has given a full documented account of the way he discharged his responsibility.[74]

In his 'private' opinion, it was a 'very great' book.

The role that Hankey played in advising Lloyd George was crucial both in terms of factual accuracy and from the 'official' viewpoint. The role B.H. Liddell Hart undertook was as a private paid adviser and military 'expert'. Lloyd George engaged Liddell Hart, on Hankey's recommendation, as an adviser on the military aspects of the book early in 1933. Liddell Hart had briefly served on the Western Front and, since being invalided out of the army in 1924 had achieved distinction as a writer and commentator on military affairs. His position as military correspondent for the *Daily Telegraph* since 1925 had provided him with a platform from which to disseminate his views on military policy. Hankey told Lloyd George that Liddell Hart would give good value as he was very familiar with the 'writers of the Western Front school' with whom he was in 'more of less continuous controversy'.[75]

Liddell Hart's focus in his books on the war was the issue of command.[76] Liddell Hart was initially a fulsome admirer of the British generals of the 1914–18 war and their strategy; writing in September 1916, he described Haig as the 'greatest general Britain had ever owned', and asserted that Britain had produced in the war 'fully a hundred first rate generals'.[77] If Liddell Hart's view of British generalship had continued in this vein, then neither Hankey nor Lloyd George would have thought him suitable as an adviser. After the war, however, his views began to change. Closer contact with many of the 'brasshats' who had been responsible for 1914–18 operations resulted in a more negative, even contemptuous view of Britain's wartime military leadership. As he wrote, his views changed 'through close contact with the *best* of them . . . they depended on a novice like me to show them the lessons of war'.[78] By the time from 1932 to 1933 his increasingly critical views of the generals coincided with those of Lloyd George and, inevitably, they tended to confirm and reinforce each others' views and prejudices.[79] They also shared the assumption that the individual was of prime importance in historical events.[80] This empathy, indeed, extended to their views on the Second World War. Frances Stevenson's comments in a letter to Lord Beaverbrook in 1950 could equally apply to their views on the earlier war: 'L.G. and Liddell Hart were very much of the same mind on many aspects of the war, & L.G. liked to see L.H. because the latter *confirmed* his own opinions, when others were critical of L.G.'s attitude.'[81]

Two others had the opportunity to read all or part of the draft *Memoirs*. By virtue of his position as Prime Minister, Ramsay MacDonald was sent drafts of particular chapters for comment. In theory, the Prime Minister had the last word on what material could or could not be published, but as Lloyd George disliked MacDonald because he was 'so pretentious and ineffectual – except perhaps with women' he would not ask any favours of him.[82]

Lloyd George's treatment of MacDonald in the *Memoirs* is less than flattering. A particularly critical passage on the labour unrest in 1917 in Britain aroused MacDonald's scorn:

> It is clear that the spectacle of Russia had inspired both Mr Ramsay MacDonald and Mr [Philip] Snowden with a vision of themselves sweeping into power, like another Lenin and Trotsky, upon a great wave of popular enthusiasm. The vision, it is true, was eventually fulfilled after a fashion, but not till more than fourteen years had passed, and the red in their paint-pot had been all used up.[83]

This and other passages provoked MacDonald to comment that the book was:

> one of the most collossal confessions of ignorance of the situation that ever I have read...As I told you yesterday, I do not wish to interfere with anything said in any of those books. I think it most reprehensible that that kind of writing should be indulged in without a full and balanced knowledge...I have no intention of entering into any of these controversies, but when I do tell the story it will be told with such care that it will stand.[84]

The Palace was also concerned at Lloyd George's treatment of MacDonald. The King's Private Secretary, Sir Clive Wigram came to see Sylvester in late April 1934, hoping that the derogatory references to MacDonald and his Labour colleague Phillip Snowden would be deleted:

> Sir Clive said that L.G. was a big man and he did not want him to make himself small. He could afford to be magnanimous. Sir Clive did not like the idea of L.G. being vindictive towards people like these, who were holding high office. I talked to L.G. on the telephone immediately afterwards. He said he would not alter it.[85]

According to Frances Stevenson, Lloyd George was 'furious' and felt that the King had no right to make this request. Asquith and Kitchener, who, after all did their best to help the war effort, were not spared, he 'is therefore not going to spare one who, like Ramsay, did his best to thwart and hinder every effort to prosecute the war vigorously'.[86] The passages on MacDonald remained highly critical, for example:

> British Socialism was . . . divided in opinion, the majority supporting the War, while the pacifist minority, strongly represented in the Independent Labour Party, whose leading figure was Mr Ramsay MacDonald, devoted itself to criticising and creating difficulties and generally weakening the morale of the nation.[87]

Stanley Baldwin, Lord President of the Council, read the memoirs in their entirety, and as Sylvester noted, 'made not one alteration'.[88] Of an early draft, Baldwin commented, 'I thought the Bonar [Law] chapter admirable and fair . . . it'll sell, and on its merits'.[89] A year later, Sylvester recorded a meeting with Baldwin:

> I asked him how much he had read. He replied: 'I have read it all.' I was surprised. He said: 'I am a very quick reader.' He went on: 'It is wonderfully well written. He (L.G.) fairly skins some of them. I cannot say that I agree with all of it, but then it is not my function to criticise. It is very well written and I can see what an enormous amount of work it has meant for you.[90]

Baldwin's complimentary tone was reciprocated by Lloyd George: he was grateful for Baldwin's relaxed approach to the use of official documentation. Lloyd George thought that Baldwin 'behaved like a brick'. Baldwin had said, 'You are the last of the lot to write: you are entitled to produce your case and any document which enables you to prepare it, you may have. . . . He has behaved like a gentleman.'[91]

Throughout the writing of the *Memoirs*, Lloyd George, in addition to the advice and assistance provided by Liddell Hart, Hankey, Baldwin and MacDonald, also utilised the memories of many of his ex-colleagues in government, his counterparts from Allied Governments, and even figures from the former enemy countries. Peter Bark, the former Russian Finance Minister, now in exile was able to help Lloyd George with the Russian chapters. Sylvester recorded one conversation in September 1933 which ranged widely over the personality of the Tsar and Tsarina, members of the Imperial court and the causes of the Revolution,[92] while earlier that year at the Reform Club General Smuts, Hankey, Lloyd George and his son Gwilym shared their memories, again recorded diligently by Sylvester.[93] General Hubert Gough, former commander of the Fifth Army and sacked in the wake of the German advances in March

1918 was able, in two meetings arranged by Liddell Hart at the end of 1935 and the beginning of 1936, to give Lloyd George his impressions of the men and events involved in that drama.[94] Others interviewed by either Lloyd George himself or more usually Sylvester (some more than once) included Lord Lee of Fareham (wartime Tory MP, personal military secretary to Lloyd George at the War Office and Director-General of Food Production, 1917–18), Sir Glynn West (at the Ministry of Munitions during the war), Sir William Beveridge (civil servant at the Ministry of Munitions), Sir John Davies (wartime private secretary to Lloyd George), Sir Eric Geddes (Ministry of Munitions, 1915–16, inspector-general of Transportation in all theatres of war, 1916–17 and first Lord of the Admiralty, 1917–18), Sir Herbert Creedy (private secretary to successive secretaries of State for War, 1913–20, including Lloyd George, later permanent under-secretary at the War Office) and again General Smuts.[95] Thus in addition to published historical accounts of the war and his mass of official documents, Lloyd George was able to call upon a range of former politicians, officials and generals for their first-hand reminiscences.

V

The *War Memoirs* were a resounding, though not completely unqualified success with reviewers, as with the public. They welcomed the documentation, were impressed with the literary style, and while some deplored the attacks on the generals, it was generally felt that the *Memoirs* revealed much of the vigour, energy and combativeness of the man himself. The question of whether the *War Memoirs* was good 'history' was addressed by some reviewers, with widely different answers. Some were impressed with the historical skills Lloyd George displayed, others accused him of mere pamphleteering.[96] The following chapters will explore, in some detail, a selection of the more important issues addressed in the *War Memoirs* relating to the conduct of war and politics in 1914–18 in an attempt to arrive at a properly considered and informed assessment of whether the *War Memoirs* can be regarded as a work of 'history' or merely a self-serving defence of Lloyd George's controversial wartime record.

2
'Pandemonium let Loose': The Outbreak of War 1914

At the outbreak of war in August 1914, Lloyd George occupied the second place in the government. He had been Chancellor of the Exchequer for six years, and while he remained the most important 'Radical' member of the Cabinet, in the realm of foreign policy there was, at least from 1911, in reality little dividing him from his Liberal 'Imperialist' colleagues such as H.H. Asquith and Sir Edward Grey. Like them he was determined to maintain the strength of the Empire, convinced of the need for a strong navy to protect it, and aware of and determined to resist any German ambitions for dominance in Europe at the expense of Britain's Entente partners. This was underlined in particular by his intervention in the Agadir crisis of 1911 and would be again by his eventual support for British entry into the war in August 1914.

Lloyd George opens his account of the Great War by explaining how it came about. The key element in this is his relentless criticism of Sir Edward Grey. It was Grey, according to Lloyd George, who must bear a substantial burden of responsibility for the catastrophe of August 1914. It was he who entered into dangerous commitments to France, and he who withheld this information from the Cabinet. Indeed, this was part of a wider pattern of secrecy and refusal to submit to Cabinet or parliamentary control on the part of the foreign affairs 'clique' headed by Grey. It was Grey, too, who dithered ineffectually when the crisis came in July 1914; his 'half-hearted proposals' met with no success when a more decisive and statesmanlike approach might have prevented war.

For Lloyd George, Grey was but one of the mediocre statesmen who held the important leadership positions throughout Europe before the war. There was, alas, no Bismarck, Palmerston or Disraeli able to arrest the slide into war or even limit its extent.[1] None of them wanted war, but none knew how to stop it; as a consequence, the Powers of Europe 'slithered over the brink'. The Great War, in short, was the result of 'accident and confusion'.[2] There *were*, however, some leaders who were quite prepared to risk a general conflagration, whether it be to defend their country's status as a Great Power or as a product of a 'better now than later' mentality.

Lloyd George's account veers between seeking to distance himself from Grey and Britain's pre-war policies, and seeking to present himself as the war leader who even before the war was aware of the German threat and did his utmost to prepare the nation. Or, as Trevor Wilson has argued:

> In one version [Lloyd George] writes as a political radical or a 1930s revisionist, for whom war is folly and accident and waste, the product of a failure of statesmanship to which Britain's foreign minister was a significant contributor. In the other Lloyd George writes as a great war leader who has rallied his nation in a crusade against arrogance and aggression and a deadly challenge to British liberty and independence.[3]

Needless to say, these two versions are hardly compatible.

II

The first of Lloyd George's 'character sketches' is devoted to the Liberal Foreign Secretary Sir Edward Grey since 1905. In Lloyd George's view it was:

> a mistaken view of history to assume that its episodes were entirely due to fundamental causes which could not be averted, and that they were not precipitated or postponed by the intervention of personality. The appearance of one dominating individual in a critical position at a decisive moment has often altered the course of events for years and even generations. A gifted and resolute person has often postponed for centuries a catastrophe which appeared imminent and which but for him would have befallen. On the other hand a weak or hesitant person has invited or expedited calamity which but for him might never have happened or which at least could have been long deferred.[4]

It is soon apparent in his character sketch in which category Lloyd George placed Grey (indeed, it is soon clear in which category he placed *himself*). Lloyd George proceeds, in Hankey's words, to tear Grey 'rather ruthlessly from his pedestal'.[5]

Sir Edward Grey, according to Lloyd George, possessed those qualities in 'appearance, manner and restraint' which gave the impression of the 'strong, silent man'; one was led 'to expect imperturbable strength in an emergency'. When Grey spoke, there were no fireworks, but he possessed 'to perfection that correctitude of phrase and demeanour which passes for – and sometimes is – diplomacy, and that serene flow of unexceptional diction which is apt to be reckoned as statesmanship until a crisis comes to put these urbanities to the test'. His mind was not made for prompt action; he lacked that 'quality of audacity which makes a great Minister'. He was also the most insular of statesmen, and 'knew less of foreigners through contact with them than any Minister in the Government'. He rarely, if ever, left English shores; Northumberland 'was good enough for him'.

Grey's appeals for a conference in July 1914 were not heard, or if they were they were not heeded. His 'dislike of leaving England' was a grave handicap. His 'egotistic insularity' and lack of 'audacity' led to failure in his attempts at mediation; later he failed in his half-hearted attempts to keep Turkey and Bulgaria out of the war, and Asquith had to step in to save the negotiations with Italy in early 1915. Grey lacked the 'knowledge', the 'vision', 'imagination', 'breadth of mind and that high courage, bordering on audacity, which his immense task demanded'. The 'ideal' Foreign Secretary, Lloyd George concludes, would be a 'cross between a recluse and a tramp, e.g. between Sir Edward Grey and Mr Ramsay MacDonald'.[6]

More specifically Lloyd George accuses Grey of concealing information from the Cabinet on vital aspects of British foreign policy. Before the war, a 'ridiculously small percentage' of the Cabinet's time was devoted to foreign affairs; even on those occasions when Grey reviewed the international situation for the benefit of Cabinet members and visiting Dominion Prime Ministers, what was left out of his presentation was often more important than what was divulged. Nothing, for example, was said about Britain's military commitments and obligations on the continent in the event of war.[7] Routine papers were circulated to ministers, which Lloyd George read 'with the greatest care and interest', but these 'informed you of nothing essential to judgement on vital issues'. Press baron Lord Northcliffe asserted 'that he knew more than any Cabinet Minister as to what was really happening', doubtful, but Lloyd George appeared to agree.[8]

The best-known example of Grey's reluctance to share information with his colleagues is the Anglo-French staff discussions initiated by the previous Unionist administration and continued by the Liberals. Their purpose was to ensure effective cooperation in the event that both countries found themselves at war with Germany. When Grey finally informed the Cabinet in 1911, the reaction was, according to Lloyd George, something 'akin to consternation'. Grey assured ministers that there was no binding commitment involved, but suspicions remained, and Lloyd George argues that this made Cabinet unity so difficult to achieve in July 1914. He himself, he writes, was satisfied that the only obligation Britain was under was to uphold Belgian neutrality.[9]

In fact Lloyd George was not an unimportant figure in relation to foreign affairs and was closer to Grey than might appear from the pages of the *War Memoirs*. As Paul Guinn has noted, all governments 'have their key figures; all Cabinets have their inner circles of power'; it is clear that by the latest 1911 Lloyd George, as the second man in the Government, was for all intents and purposes part of this inner circle.[10] Even before 1911, as Chancellor of the Exchequer he was obliged to take more than a passing interest in defence and in particular the annual naval estimates, intimately linked with the naval rivalry between Britain and Germany and easily the single most contentious issue between the two Powers.[11] His interest led on one occasion to a foray into personal 'diplomacy', much to the annoyance of Grey and the Foreign Office.[12] Yet three years later, Lloyd George was sufficiently in tune with Grey and Asquith during the Agadir crisis to act as the spokesman of the Government and in a famous speech warned the German Government not to ignore Britain and its legitimate interests, thereby raising the diplomatic temperature such that many thought war imminent.[13] In the aftermath of his speech he was one of the small group of ministers who attended the important meeting of the Committee of Imperial Defence during which Sir Henry Wilson, the Director of Military Operations, explained the arrangements agreed with the French in the event of war with Germany. As Esher later told Scott:

> The Defence Committee, other than members of the cabinet, were mostly away on their holidays, and the whole business was carried through by a small junta of cabinet members of the Committee. . . . It consisted in fact of the Prime Minister, Lloyd George, Churchill, Grey, General French and Lt. Gen. Ewart and two admirals, I think Admiral Seymour and Prince Louis of Battenberg.[14]

Lloyd George himself told Scott in 1911 that Grey was very good at showing him *everything*.[15]

It is clear, from Lloyd George's *own account*, that Grey *did* lay before the Cabinet the details of the Anglo-French discussions. Moreover, these arrangements were 'not at all vital'; they were not binding commitments.[16] Lloyd George himself accepted Grey's assurances. Whatever Grey's personal feelings on the matter (and they would become clear in July 1914), British intervention remained *prima facie*, at least, contingent on an attack on Belgium.

Lloyd George's criticisms of Grey become more strident in his discussion of the July crisis and the outbreak of war. Of one thing about Grey Lloyd George was sure: he 'failed calamitously in his endeavours to avert the Great War'. This of course begs the question: was it really ever in Grey's power to avert the outbreak of war? Lloyd George's answer is yes:

> Had he warned Germany in time of the point at which Britain would declare war – and wage it with her whole strength – the issue would have been different. I know it is said that he was hampered by divisions in the Cabinet. On one question, however, there was no difference of opinion – the invasion of Belgium. He could at any stage of the negotiations have secured substantial unanimity amongst his colleagues on that point...in the name of a united people he could have intimated to the German Government that if they put their plan of marching through Belgium they would encounter the active hostility of the British Empire. And he could have uttered this warning in sufficient time to leave the German military authorities without any excuse for not changing their dust-laden plans.[17]

In the crucial days of July–August 1914, however, Grey's hand 'trembled in the palsy of apprehension, unable to grip the levers and manipulate them with a firm and clear purpose'. In the 'din' of the Powers' preparations for war, his appeals were 'barely heard'. Grey prevaricated, hesitated and feebly proposed impractical diplomatic solutions. Grey first proposed that Russia and Austria 'talk it out amongst themselves'; then suggested that Germany act as mediator with Austria, France with Russia and Russia with Serbia. Then when these proposals failed to win support, he proposed a conference of Ambassadors be held in London but without the representatives of Austria and Serbia. Grey's proposal was:

> not wisely framed, and it was not put forward with conviction; it was not pressed home and it was finally dropped; in fact it was dropped at the first objection. It was a timid and half-hearted approach,

and at the first difficulty it encountered it was abandoned by its distracted author.[18]

Could Grey have averted war by warning Germany that British intervention would certainly follow a German violation of Belgium's neutrality? It is doubtful. By the time Grey felt he could issue such a warning – Belgium's insistence upon its neutrality and its need to avoid even the appearance of compromising this before a threat was apparent meant considerable delay – it was too late to have any effect.[19] For Grey the real issue was France: Lord Riddell noted on 2 August that Asquith and Grey thought it 'vital to support France' and if the Cabinet did not agree, he threatened resignation.[20] Insisting on support for France, would have split the Cabinet. On the notion that Grey should have stated at the outset that Britain would regard a violation of Belgium as its *casus belli* perhaps Lloyd George is on firmer ground. Yet what would have been the effect? German plans, as senior British ministers knew, necessitated passing through Belgium to attack France in a massive assault, whether the Belgians agreed to their passage or not. German planners were counting on a decisive blow against France to knock it out of the war quickly; then Germany would be free to deal with the Russians. Britain could at most initially support France with only six divisions. Would the threat of intervention of this small force, at *any* stage of the crisis, have induced the Germans to alter their plans? It is highly unlikely. It is clear that from at least 1912 Germany expected Britain to intervene if the Schlieffen Plan was implemented.[21] British forces were just not significant enough in the calculations of German policy makers and strategists in a war which was expected to be over in a matter of months if not weeks. A British Expeditionary Force supporting the French would perhaps reduce the Germans' chances of a quick victory, and therefore some in Berlin sought to keep Britain neutral. But German leaders did not believe that British intervention would 'preclude victory' in the end.[22]

In Lloyd George's account of the descent into war Grey is clearly, if not the only villain, then one of the more important. The vehemence of Lloyd George's attacks[23] can be explained not only by reference to Grey's conduct of foreign policy and diplomacy before the war (indeed, this offers but little explanation of Lloyd George's ferocity by itself) but also through an examination of Liberal politics during the 1920s and the early 1930s. Grey, of course, remained loyal to Asquith in December 1916. Until the end of his life, Grey remained highly critical of Lloyd George, and not just because of the sense of betrayal created by the events of December 1916. Grey – and many others – resented above all Lloyd George's personal control of sizeable funds, accumulated originally during his premiership largely through the sale of honours and augmented through the sale of the *Daily Chronicle* in 1926.[24] Grey said in a speech in December of that year:

> It was a new thing, unprecedented in the politics of this country, that one man should be in possession of an enormous fund at his own disposal for political purposes. It was the Liberal Party today, but it might be the Conservative Party tomorrow or the Labour Party some other day, which might be agitated about the matter, or the fund could be used for an entirely new policy initiated by the person who controlled it. That was a very disturbing element, not merely in the Liberal Party, but in the politics of this country altogether.

It appeared to the Asquithians, Grey among them, that Lloyd George was buying the Liberal Party.[25]

Hostility towards Lloyd George on the part of the Asquithians continued throughout the 1920s, exacerbated by different views within the leadership group of the party on the General Strike in 1926.[26] From that year, with the departure of Asquith from the leadership, anti-Lloyd George sentiment was centred mainly within the Liberal Council established and chaired by Grey. The latter's animosity towards Lloyd George – then the leader of the Liberal Party – was such that in January 1930, he told the Council that he would not recognise Lloyd George as the leader of the Liberal Party and that it was 'totally wrong' for it to be 'dependent' upon Lloyd George's Fund.[27]

Lloyd George himself admitted privately that postwar politics had influenced his portrait of Grey in the *War Memoirs*, while still maintaining he had been a 'calamitous' Foreign Secretary. To his brother William George, he wrote:

> You say he was a colleague of mine. I would be bound to take that into account had he behaved in a true spirit of comradeship. Instead of that he was one of the bitterest of those who assailed me when I was made chairman of the Party. I therefore owe him nothing on the score of friendship or camaraderie.[28]

He was not bound, he told his brother, to 'praise everybody, but rather to tell the truth'. His treatment of Asquith he considered to be 'indulgent' and he had softened criticisms of his 'failures and defects'. He wrote, however, that 'the charlatans and skunks I deal faithfully with. Grey certainly belongs in my opinion to the first category.'[29]

III

By the time the final crisis broke in late July and early August 1914, Lloyd George was a pivotal figure in the deliberations which led to the Cabinet entering the war essentially united. Beaverbrook argued in his famous account that in the circumstances of a potentially and disastrously divided Cabinet, 'practically everything depended on the attitude of Mr Lloyd George'.[30] While that may be something of an exaggeration, his attitude was important. Personally, the July crisis was, in the words of one historian, a '"monumentally emotional experience for Lloyd George. In the course of it he weighed evidence and yet grasped at improbabilities; he temporised and then acted decisively. Finally, he joined in the Cabinet consensus", ... made possible by the violation of Belgian neutrality'.[31]

Readers of the *War Memoirs* expecting a detailed insider account of those dramatic days from Lloyd George, however, must have been sorely disappointed. His account of the July crisis is brief and uninformative, reflecting, no doubt, his later mixed feelings regarding British participation in the war. Certain of his arguments, however, have remained highly influential. The central point is his insistence that the German invasion of Belgium was the reason he decided to support intervention, and that it was a decision on Britain's part based on morality and the defence of small nations. Was Belgium, however, rather the heaven-sent pretext to enable Lloyd George and his colleagues to decide on British intervention with the support of a unified Cabinet and country? Or was it a decision in reality based on calculations of national interest and the maintenance of the balance of power? And did the Great Powers, in Lloyd George's memorable phrase, 'back their machines over the precipice', or, alternatively 'slither over the brink' into war? Was this a war which, as Lloyd George contends, nobody wanted and began by accident rather than design?

Lloyd George states in the *War Memoirs* that he was never in any doubt that 'if the Germans interfered with the integrity and independence of Belgium, we were in honour bound to discharge our treaty obligations to that country'.[32] If Germany had respected Belgian neutrality, then his view – which he put to his colleagues – was that Britain should remain neutral, use the opportunity to rearm, and when the combatants had exhausted themselves, intervene to impose 'saner counsels'.[33]

This idea, of course, is based on the assumption that France would *not* be quickly overrun by the German armies. Lloyd George argues that France would not be quickly defeated; this view found little favour then and finds little favour today. In any event, there is little direct evidence that this is what he was putting to his colleagues at the time, although Scott recorded on 27 July that Lloyd George thought that 'there could be no question of our taking part in any war in the *first instance*. Knew of no Minister who would be in favour of it.' Lloyd George's emphasis in the early days of the crisis was first, predictably, upon efforts to preserve peace, but second, and tellingly, upon the need to protect France: 'he admitted [Scott wrote] that a difficult question would arise if the German fleet were attacking French towns on the other side of the Channel and the French sowed the Channel with mines'.[34] One idea was to 'pair' with Italy as a way of helping France. He told Riddell on 31 July that he was 'fighting hard for peace',[35] and Asquith wrote on 1 August that Lloyd George was 'all for peace', though he also wrote that he was in favour of keeping Britain's options open.[36] (Oddly, the next day Asquith described Lloyd George as one of the unconditional *neutralists* in the Cabinet, along with Morley, Harcourt and others. This Lloyd George *never* was.[37])

In various accounts of a dinner that evening with C.F.G. Masterman, Sir John Simon and Ramsay MacDonald (the last two non-interventionists), at Riddell's house, a more accurate picture emerges of Lloyd George's position. In a long discussion on the 'rights and wrongs of the situation' Lloyd George told the company that the Government

> had determined to tell Germany that England would remain neutral if Germany undertook not to attack the coast of France or to enter the English Channel with a view to attacking French shipping. He said that if the Germans gave this undertaking in an unqualified manner and observed the neutrality of Belgium, he would not agree to war but would rather resign. He spoke very strongly, however, regarding the observance of Belgian neutrality.[38]

He thus clearly saw that German naval activity in the Channel would be a potential threat to British interests; that there was some obligation on Britain's part to protect France's northern coast (due to the naval arrangements agreed to two years before by the two Governments); and there was also an obligation to maintain Belgian neutrality. On this last point, however, he suggested that if it was only a technical violation, then Britain might escape the necessity of intervening. If the Germans only marched through the southern tip of Belgium, rather than invading and occupying Belgian territory and thereby destroying Belgian independence, and if Germany agreed to pay costs after the war, Britain should remain neutral and he himself would not support British intervention. The Cabinet itself seemed to express this view when on 2 August it decided that a *substantial* violation of Belgian neutrality would place Britain in the situation regarded as possible by Gladstone in 1870, when an attack on Belgian independence was considered as forcing Britain to take action.[39] This was a line which Lloyd George presented to many of his interlocutors, particularly those in the 'radical' wing of the party. Thus Scott recorded on 4 August that:

> He [Lloyd George] had gone so far, however, as to urge that if Germany would consent to limit her occupation of Belgian territory to the extreme southerly point of Belgium – the sort of nose of land running out of Luxembourg – he would resign rather than make this a *casus belli*.[40]

By 3 August, however, the German ultimatum to Belgium and King Albert's plea for help clarified matters; Belgium would indeed be overrun and Belgium would resist. Riddell wrote that now the issue was 'fairly plain'. Lloyd George told him that 'the action of Germany regarding Belgium had made his decision quite clear, and that he could now support Grey without any hesitation'.[41] Scott wrote on 4 August that Lloyd George told him that 'Up to last Sunday [2 August] only two members of the Cabinet had been in favour of our intervention in the War, but the *violation of Belgian territory* had completely altered the situation. Apart from that it would have been impossible to draw us into war now.'[42]

It should be stated at this point that Lloyd George (and other senior ministers) was well aware that a German attack on France would almost certainly involve a German violation of Belgian neutrality, although, as noted above there were doubts as to whether this would mean the extinguishing of Belgian independence or only a minor infringement of its sovereignty, and as to whether the Belgian Government would resist. Three years before at the CID meeting of 23 August 1911, the Director of Military Operations (DMO) Sir Henry Wilson, himself long convinced that Germany would invade through Belgium, expounded to senior ministers, including Lloyd George, British arrangements to meet that invasion, and argued that a British military contribution would tip the balance against Germany.[43] Soon after, Lloyd George wrote to

Churchill, proposing that the BEF be sent to Belgium rather than France in the event of a German invasion (this would be, of course, contingent upon whether Belgium resisted).[44] On 27 July 1914, while the infringement of Belgian neutrality was – *ostensibly* – not at all certain, he also predicted to Scott that Germany would seek to strike hard at France and cripple her in the first instance, then swing back and strike at Russia. By sea she might use her superiority in order to land a force behind the French force advancing to meet *the German invasion across Belgium*.[45] If he was aware of the threat to Belgium, then all his prevarications and speculations and hesitations in the few days prior to 4 August were, if not a sham, then something less than what they seemed.[46] He knew that Britain, bound to Belgium by legal obligation and self interest, would enter the war once Germany had implemented its plan. The dramatic scene portrayed by Lloyd George in the Cabinet room when the assembled ministers sat around the Cabinet table waiting to learn whether Germany would 'honour their bond' to protect Belgium's neutrality was not quite the 'cliffhanger' in the way Lloyd George would have us believe.[47]

Some of his contemporaries held doubts about Lloyd George's declared position. Thus Ramsay MacDonald, at the dinner at Riddell's house referred to above, later observed that while Lloyd George indeed 'harped on the exposed French coast & Belgium...I gathered that excuses were being searched for'.[48] Frances Stevenson, the closest to Lloyd George of all, was convinced that Lloyd George's position was that his

> mind was really made up from the first, that he knew we would have to go in, and that the invasion of Belgium was, to be cynical, a heaven-sent excuse for supporting a declaration of war. He was fully aware that in taking the side of the pro-war party in the Government he would offend a large section of his supporters.[49]

As it turned out, however, in taking the side of the pro-war party *over Belgium*, he did not alienate any significant section of his support, in the Cabinet, the House of Commons or among the Liberal press, because Belgium was an issue on which all but the most extreme pacifist could agree. Only two Cabinet Ministers, John Morley and John Burns, both by 1914 of only marginal importance,[50] resigned; the others who threatened resignation stayed on after the invasion of Belgium became fact. In the Commons, a small band of Labour MPs around Ramsay MacDonald opposed the war, and they remained the only significant grouping in the House to do so. The political truce in Britain occasioned by the outbreak of war, while imperfect, was firmly in place at least in this early period. Much of the Liberal and pacifist press, including C.P. Scott's *Manchester Guardian* and Robertson Nicoll's *British Weekly*, were convinced, albeit reluctantly, of the necessity for British intervention once the German invasion of Belgium became known.[51] And in the event, even after Lloyd George had put on his 'war paint' and in a speech in September declared unequivocally his support for the war and the destruction of German militarism, he retained the support, though sometimes shaky, of most of his usual supporters.[52]

The truth is that there were competing instincts in Lloyd George's mind.[53] His first instinct was, naturally enough, for peace. Despite his reputation, however, Lloyd George was not a 'peace at any price' man. He recognised that Britain had a clear interest in the maintenance of France's independence and power. German hegemony in Europe would be as intolerable for Britain as Napoleon's had been (or Germany's would be again, under Hitler, in 1939, although ironically Lloyd George in the late 1930s would on occasions be at least equivocal on the possibility or the necessity of effectively resisting and defeating Hitler). He recognised too that a victory for Russia and France in a European war without British participation – perhaps even with – would pose problems for Britain.[54] In effect, then, Lloyd George recognised the need for the maintenance of a balance of power.

France, too, as the only other Great Power Liberal democracy, had a greater pull on Lloyd George's loyalties and affection than the pseudo-democracy that was the *Kaiserreich*, let alone the Russia of Bloody Sunday, pogroms and absolutism. Favouring war in support of France, however, would have alienated a great deal of Lloyd George's support, and quite probably split the Cabinet. Belgium, however, would provide that 'unifying *casus belli*' that France could not: for there 'would be far more sympathy for a small country bullied and trodden down by a mighty neighbour than for a country which was not only large but also, until very recently, Britain's historic enemy'.[55] While Lloyd George's attitude during the days prior to the declaration of war could be construed – cynically – as a tactic designed merely to maintain or even advance his own position, it could also be interpreted, more generously, as one of a politician torn between his natural aversion to war and his realisation, on the other hand, that with France threatened by Germany, Britain's vital national interests were at stake, and that there-fore whatever means were necessary to bring the Cabinet and the country into the war united were justified. Rather than describe

Lloyd George as a man without convictions, whose behaviour throughout the crisis was dominated by his 'eye to the main chance, as he perceived it in terms of political possibilities and public opinion', it is more appropriate – while acknowledging some degree of political self interest, as is the case with practically *every* politician – to view his behaviour in the light of this conflict.[56]

IV

Were the statesmen of Europe in July and August 1914 as blind to the consequences of their decisions as Lloyd George implies when he describes the nations of Europe 'backing their machines over the precipice' into war?[57] Nobody wanted war, Lloyd George writes, or expected it. Perhaps if there had been a Bismarck in Germany, or a Palmerston in London, or a Clemenceau in Paris, the outcome may have been different, but the statesmen in control of affairs in 1914, while all 'able, experienced, conscientious and respectable', lacked the drive, the vision and imagination needed to avert a catastrophe. Operative here, of course, is the assumption that Europe's statesmen actually wanted to avoid a European war, and research into the causes of the First World War over the past few decades would seem to lay this myth to rest, in particular with regard to that country which was the key to the entire diplomatic situation in July and August 1914: Germany. Indeed, it now appears that the German decision for war had little to do with the immediate diplomatic crisis which ensued after the assassination of the Austrian heir to the throne in Sarajevo. Rather, after the abortive Haldane mission to Berlin in 1912 which attempted to reach an understanding in naval armaments between Britain and Germany, British policy hardened towards Germany. Britain was determined to stand by its Entente partners, France and Russia, in an effort to 'prevent Germany from achieving its goal of *"Weltherrschaft"* – world domination'.[58] In response Germany became convinced that its position as a Great Power would continue to deteriorate relative to its rivals – France and especially a Russia rapidly recovering from its defeat by the Japanese in 1905 – unless 'drastic action' was taken. This could take one of two forms – either an alliance with Britain, in effect a diplomatic revolution in Europe (which would also involve the moderation or abandonment of German naval ambitions) or a European war. The former was unacceptable to the Kaiser (and Britain, given Germany's naval ambitions) but the second option was increasingly attractive, given Russia's military recovery after the Russo-Japanese War. War, it was felt, was bound to come with Russia in any case, so sooner rather than later was better for Germany.[59] This was clearly the sentiment expressed by the Chief of the Great General Staff, von Moltke, at the 'War Council' of 8 December 1912. At that same meeting the Kaiser envisaged that Austria's quarrel with Serbia would, if Russia supported the Serbs (as was likely), certainly bring about general war, which he regarded with something akin to enthusiasm.[60]

The German Government's decisions in July–August 1914 were not then the result of blunder or incompetence or accident. Germany did not 'back her machine over the precipice' but knew full well what the consequences of its decisions would be, and felt the results would be well worth the risks of a full-scale European conflict. The assassination in Sarajevo and the subsequent Austrian ultimatum to Serbia provided the German statesmen and military the opportunity to wage that 'preventative war they had been recommending for years'.[61] For other belligerents, too, it is clear that their leaders knew the risks they were taking, and that a major Europe-wide war was the likely consequence of their decisions. Yet in that pre-1914–18 world, war was still an accepted course of action for the Great Powers. The willingness and ability to enter into major hostilities was a defining trait of a Great Power, and all the major belligerents entered that war because they felt that their status as a Great Power was under threat. Thus far from the Powers entering the First World War by 'backing over a precipice', through blunder or incompetence, each state entered the war for quite rational reasons and in the full knowledge (though Austria-Hungary *hoped* that it would be localised) that it was possible, even probable, that a Europe-wide conflict would ensue.

V

In his discussion of pre-war foreign policy and the outbreak of the war, Lloyd George's aim is clear. It is to dissociate himself as far as possible with Grey's foreign policy which, when it came to the test in July and August of 1914, so clearly could not prevent Britain and Europe from descending into the most destructive war that the world had yet experienced. Yet Lloyd George cannot escape all responsibility. From 1908 he was Chancellor of the Exchequer, and therefore responsible for the Government's budgetary policy including for the two services. He must therefore share in the responsibility for the unreadiness of British arms for a continental war. Perhaps he can be forgiven for this, as very few foresaw the type of war which came to pass in 1914–18 and the demands which it came to make on the British population and economy.

More importantly, from 1911 at least he was much more of an insider in foreign policy terms than he professes; Grey, it will be remembered, showed him 'everything'. Grey and indeed the Foreign Office were delighted with Lloyd George at the time of Agadir in 1911, and if relations between Grey and Lloyd George did not continue with quite the same closeness in 1912–14, this was due mainly to demands from other spheres on Lloyd George's time and interest. And finally, in the great crisis of 1914, he underplays his key role in bringing the Cabinet to favour intervention as the leading 'radical'. He also perpetuates three of the great myths of the July crisis – that first, Belgium was the reason rather than the pretext Britain went to war, second, that Grey committed the fatal error in not making Britain's position clear, and third, that the Great Powers blundered blindly into a war that no one wanted. It is clear that if a balanced and accurate account of the outbreak of the war is required, one must look elsewhere than Lloyd George's *War Memoirs*.

3
Strategic Dilemmas: 1914–15

Following his account of the outbreak of war, Lloyd George provides a critique of several aspects of British strategy in the first weeks of hostilities. He first argues that the decision to deploy the BEF on the left wing of the French was wrong and instead that BEF would have been better placed to inflict a severe, even decisive blow against the German advance by concentrating in Antwerp and joining forces with the Belgians. He then describes his proposal to circumvent the developing stalemate in France with an audacious Allied attack on Austria-Hungary in alliance with the Balkan states. This was rejected by the Cabinet, however, in favour of an attack on Turkey in the Dardanelles, initially with naval forces alone and later with substantial land forces, with well-known results. Allied forces were later deployed in Salonika at the end of 1915, but rather than launching a powerful attack on Austria as Lloyd George wanted, they were too weak in numbers and equipment to be anything but an irritant to Austria and Bulgaria until the last months of the war.

II

An *ad hoc* War Council consisting of Asquith, Haldane, Grey and Churchill, together with the senior military and naval leaders, met on 5 August 1914 and decided, after some deliberation, to deploy the BEF in France as per arrangements in place. Commander-in-Chief of the BEF Field Marshal Sir John French suggested, however, that the BEF be concentrated in Antwerp on the Germans' flank.[1] Lloyd George argues in the *War Memoirs* that the five British divisions 'would have provided the necessary stiffening for the Belgian militia', and the Germans would not have dared to strike so far into French territory as they did 'without clearing their flank from the redoubtable menace. They would thus have lost valuable time, and time was the essence of their plan.'[2]

In the War Council, French argued that the original destination of the BEF was no longer safe, but by landing in Antwerp the BEF could cooperate with the Belgians and the Dutch:

> The three forces would form a considerable army, and would necessarily contain a large German force, and they might be able to advance southward. The feasibility of this plan, however, was largely a naval question. As an alternative to a landing at Antwerp, he proposed a landing in France and a movement to Antwerp by the coast route.[3]

Others in attendance strongly objected. Churchill pointed out that the passage of the BEF to Antwerp depended to a great extent upon the attitude of the Dutch, 'owing to the necessity of navigating the Scheldt, the mouth of which was wholly in Dutch territory'. And the Dutch, as Grey pointed out, showed no sign of abandoning their neutrality. Moreover the security of the transport from attack could not be guaranteed because of the longer distance, although he did not address the question of an alternative land route. Sir Charles Douglas, Chief of the Imperial General Staff (CIGS) stressed the dislocation and disruption, especially to railway timetables, which would result from the much longer voyage to Antwerp. Two senior generals, Douglas Haig and Henry Wilson, were contemptuous of French's proposal, though in the privacy of their diaries. Haig wrote that he 'trembled at the reckless way Sir J. French spoke about "the advantages" of the BEF operating from Antwerp against the powerful and still intact German Army!'; while Wilson described the plan as 'ridiculous'.[4]

Grey's observation that the Dutch were 'very firm' in their intention to remain neutral should have put an end to the proposal once and for all, for both Sir John French *and* Lloyd George, as it appeared to depend on the participation of the Dutch. While the War Council decided to adhere to the original plan of embarking for northern France – after all, 'well-laid plans existed for this course and...no plans existed for any other'; the 'logic of the situation' dictated the plans of deployment[5] – Lloyd George, supported by Liddell Hart and others, continued to argue in the *Memoirs* as if it were a realistic option in the circumstances of August 1914.

The idea had, it must be said, a history. A proposal to transport the BEF to Belgium rather than France first arose prior to the Anglo-Belgian staff talks of 1906.[6] DMO Major-General J.M. Grierson wrote in a memorandum in January 1906 that as it was probable that the Germans would invade through Belgium and that the Belgian army would resist, a British force based at Antwerp, combined with the Belgians, would produce an army of over 200,000 and would be 'advantageously placed to operate against the communications of the Germans endeavouring to turn the line of the French eastern fortresses'.[7] The War Office, however, soon came to the conclusion that:

> whether Germany in a war with France violates Belgian territory or whether she does not, our wisest course will be not to commit ourselves to independent operations in that country but to land in France; to support the French left rather than the Belgian right.[8]

The 'Belgian option', however, remained attractive to some senior ministers. Lloyd George, after the August 1911 CID meeting, wrote to Churchill and argued that British participation should be in Belgium:

> 150,000 British troops supporting the Belgian army on the German flank would be a much more formidable proposition than the same number of troops extending the French line. It would force the Germans to detach at least 500,000 men to protect their lines of communication. The Anglo-Belgian army numbering 400,000 would pivot on the great fort at Antwerp. The command of the sea would make that position impregnable. Is there no way open to us to sound Belgium?[9]

Churchill agreed and wrote to Grey on 30 August, 'We should, if necessary, aid Belgium to defend Antwerp' and to Lloyd George the next day, 'I think there is no doubt your view is sound that we should get hold of the Belgians; and I think yr phrase "pivoting on Antwerp" is much more correct than "based on Antwerp" wh I had rather loosely employed.'[10]

Lloyd George held the same views over twenty years later when writing the *War Memoirs*, as did Liddell Hart. The latter argued that the plans agreed upon in the years before 1914 between the two general staffs amounted to an acceptance of a role for the BEF as an 'appendix to the French left wing' and neglected the possibility of exploiting the mobility offered by sea power. The latter factor would have enabled French's Antwerp plan to proceed with every prospect of success; it 'would have stiffened the Belgian resistance'[11] (note the similarity in the language used by Liddell Hart and Lloyd George) and 'by its mere situation threatened the rear flank of the German armies as they advanced through Belgium into France'.[12] Liddell Hart pointed to the great moral effect 'phantom forces' – British and even Russian forces supposedly landing on the Belgian coast threatening the German flank – had on the German command in 1914, and concluded that 'the balance of judgement would seem to turn heavily in favour of the strategy which Sir John French had suggested at the outset. By it the British Expeditionary Force might have had a...decisive influence on the struggle.'[13]

Neither in Liddell Hart's nor Lloyd George's arguments, however, is there any reference to the neutrality issue, the increased danger to the transports while *en route*, nor to the disruption and dislocation that would have been likely from such an improvised plan. Perhaps most importantly, they ignored the fact that the small BEF, even if fighting alongside the Belgian Army, was no match for the larger German forces and the heavy artillery that the Germans could – and later did – use to pound Antwerp into surrender. And they did not consider the possibility that the Germans could quite simply bypass a 'contained' Antwerp and proceed to destroy the main enemy in the West, France, weakened by the lack of British support. Schlieffen had foreseen this and had written that if the BEF were to land at Antwerp and link up with the Belgians it 'would be more securely billetted in that fortress than on their own island, and present even less of a threat'.[14] The BEF, in short, had little choice but to act as an 'appendix' of the much larger French Army in 1914, and in the event played a crucial role in helping to halt the German advance at the Battle of the Marne.

Lloyd George's views were reinforced by discussions with the former Imperial German Foreign Minister Richard von Kuhlmann. In 1933, von Kuhlmann asserted that if the British had 'occupied Antwerp in force (in August 1914) we couldn't have advanced through Belgium'.[15] The loss of time caused by the abandonment of the move through Limburg (the Netherlands) as intended by Schlieffen had already caused considerable anxiety in the German General Staff.[16] A British force in Antwerp, cooperating with the Belgian forces, would have caused more delay and created further difficulties for the German forces on their way through Belgium. Another German, however, and one who was in a better position to know than the civilian von Kuhlmann, in 1936 – too late for inclusion in the relevant chapter – told Lloyd George that the BEF, if deployed in the defence of Antwerp:

would not have prevented us because we would have put our special two or three corps in ... The danger to the French would have been much bigger.... Without any doubt, if the British Army had not been there [alongside the French] it would have been terrible for the French. LG. They would have scuppered up the French. W[etzell] Yes.[17]

In other words, not only would the BEF most likely have been destroyed, but the Germans may well have inflicted a decisive defeat upon the French, which in turn would have severely restricted Britain's ability to continue the war effectively.

In the light of this it is noteworthy that in the final volume of the *War Memoirs*, in a chapter entitled 'Some Reflections on the Functions of Governments and Soldiers Respectively in a War', Lloyd George chose to disregard his old strictures about the great mistake in deploying with the French rather than in Antwerp, and instead described the actual deployment of the BEF in August 1914 as the saviour of the French army:

One of the ablest of the German Generals told me recently that but for the force of four highly trained British divisions placed on the Belgian frontier the German Army would have outflanked and Sedanised the whole of the French Fifth Army and thus brought the War to a triumphant end on the Western Front.... The disembark-ation at Havre and the speed with which the Expeditionary Force was sent to France and mustered on the Belgian frontier upset the whole of their calculations, and frustrated their plans.[18]

The volte-face in Lloyd George's views on this issue is not acknowledged.

III

The Western Front having settled into stalemate by the end of 1914, Lloyd George began to search for a solution. He devotes three chapters in the first volume to the discussions on strategy in the winter of 1914–15, entitled 'The Strategy of the War: Eastern vs Western Fronts', 'The War Council and the Balkans' and 'Allied Procrastination'. He argues here that if increasing Britain's productive capacity in order properly to equip a vastly expanding army had been difficult, 'the parallel task of ensuring that our resources of man-power and munitions should be used in the most effective manner was still harder'.[19] The generals displayed a lack of energy and imagination when confronted by the conditions on the Western Front at the end of 1914. They demanded more frontal assaults on the virtually impregnable German defences in the west. Politically, it remained 'business as usual' – there was a 'sense of leisureliness, if not of casualness' in the Government's activities, and more effective and energetic direction was sorely needed.[20]

In Lloyd George's view there were few grounds for the Government's complacency. While the Allies had scored some successes, on every front there lurked a situation ripe for disaster. Russia was lacking in arms and munitions, Serbia's position was 'precarious', and British preparations for a large-scale continental commitment were painfully slow. A large well-equipped British Army might not be able to take the field until the third year of the war. Moreover, Belgium and some of the richest and most productive areas of France remained in enemy hands.[21] In the West, the East and in Serbia all the major Powers' offensives had not brought the results expected. The carefully thought out war plans of all the belligerents had failed.[22] Any proposal to deviate from these plans, such as John French's suggestion that the BEF occupy Antwerp instead of assisting the French, had been turned down. The battles of 1914

> shattered every military dream and wrecked every military hope on both sides. . . . Every army had its failures. Every army had its successes. . . . But no one had any clear notion of what to attempt next. New plans must therefore be thought of for the 1915 campaign.[23]

With these factors in mind, he wrote to Asquith on the last day of 1914, requesting that as a matter of urgency a series of meetings of a War Council – or small committee of the Cabinet – be held, for to continue as they were would achieve nothing. He pointed to the shortcomings of the military in dealing with munitions production, and noted that 'no real effort has been made until this week to ascertain the Russian position' with respect to arms and munitions requirements.[24] Asquith agreed and the first meeting was scheduled for 7 January.

Lloyd George was not the only political or military leader who by the end of 1914 was questioning Allied strategy. Sir John French proposed turning the German flank by a combined naval and military operation to take Ostend and Zeebrugge. Churchill advocated action against Germany in the Baltic and Turkey in the Dardanelles, while Hankey in his 'Boxing-Day Memorandum' urged the occupation of Constantinople by a combined Anglo-Greek-Bulgarian force. Lloyd George for his part became convinced of the merits of attacking Austria through the Balkans and Turkey in Syria, and his memorandum 'The War. Suggestions as to the Military Position', circulated to the War Council, embodied his first substantial attempt to influence the strategic direction of the war.[25]

Lloyd George's memorandum, printed in full in the *War Memoirs*, argued that it was beyond the power of the Allies, at present at least, to achieve the overwhelming dominance in men and guns on the Western Front necessary to break the German defences. On the other hand, since it was impossible for the Allies, it was equally impossible for the Germans to break the Allied defences. Given this fact it would make more sense, he wrote, both militarily and politically, for Britain to deploy the new armies in a more promising theatre. Most of the British forces could be pulled out of France leaving the French on the defensive and well able to hold the Germans. Perhaps 400,000 British troops could be left in Britain in case of an emergency in France.

Experienced British troops, alongside the new armies, could be used in two independent operations against Germany's allies. Of the major operation he proposed, an attack on Austria-Hungary, he argued that it could have far-reaching effects. British forces would land at Salonika, or on the Dalmatian coast – he later suggested Ragusa – and, in conjunction with Romanian, Greek, Montenegrin and Serbian forces, launch an offensive into Austro-Hungarian territory. He envisaged a combined force of between 1.4 and 1.6 million troops, which would have local numerical superiority and have the effect of diverting substantial Austrian forces from the Eastern Front and lengthening, and thereby weakening, the Austrian lines. Given the military, political and economic weakness of Austria-Hungary, it would be difficult if not impossible to defend this new line without German assistance. Germany would then have to decide whether to respond to the Austrian appeals, thereby weakening their own fronts in the West and East, or abandon its ally, in which case Austria would quickly collapse. In this last event the Allies could then concentrate on Germany, which would be then fighting on three – weakened – fronts.[26]

A second operation of more limited scope, would be to eliminate the Turkish force then massing in Syria for an attack on Egypt. Once the Turks had commenced their attacks upon the Suez Canal, a British force of 100,000 should be sufficient to cut them off from their lines of communication and supply, and they would then be forced to 'either fight or surrender'.[27] The Turks would then be wiped out by the superior British force and the whole of Syria would fall into British hands. As a bonus, Turkish pressure on the Russians in the Caucasus would be relieved by this operation.[28]

Lloyd George argued that these operations 'would have the common purpose of *knocking the props under her* [Germany] and the further purpose of so compelling her to attenuate her line of defence to make it more easily penetrable'.[29] They would also have, if successful, the effect of achieving a definite victory, vital to maintain public morale and to attract neutrals to the Allied cause.[30] He concluded his memorandum by emphasizing the need for careful and thorough preparation; transport would have to be organised, intelligence gathered and the troops concentrated at convenient points.[31]

Was this a genuine proposal for action in the Balkans, or something less?[32] The evidence suggests that he was sincere and that he wanted concrete steps taken in preparation for an attack on Austria. Thus in the War Council of 13 January 1915, Lloyd George stated, 'If...General Joffre failed to achieve success [in planned offensive operations], we ought to try some entirely new plan, and we ought to start immediately to prepare for this. The question *should not merely be studied, but actual preparations should be made*, including the provision of any necessary railway material, horse boats,.&c.' This is urged by Lloyd George *twice* at the same meeting.[33] He saw real possibilities for a strategic breakthrough.

Lloyd George's hopes for success in the Balkans were based mainly on the assumption of Austrian weakness and vulnerability to Allied attack. He pointed to the multi-racial nature of the Austro-Hungarian Empire and the tensions and strains placed upon the unity of the Empire and its army by this factor. Fully three-fifths of the population resented Austrian rule. The Slavs, Romanians and Italians who made up such a large proportion of the population 'had been straining for freedom from the domination of a privileged racial caste, and their prospect of gaining it would be accelerated by the defeat of the German regime'.[34] Furthermore,

What made Austria specially vulnerable was that the provinces contiguous to her actual or contingent foes were populated by the races who by blood were nearly related to the enemies of the Empire. This proved to be a source of weakness to the Austrian armies during the whole course of the War...Whenever the Russians gained an appreciable advantage in their attacks, Slavonic regiments surrendered with ease and even with ill-concealed satisfaction...One Czech regiment marched through into predestined captivity in Russia with the band playing.[35]

Not only did the ethnic heterogeneity of the Austrian armies militate against its effectiveness on the field of battle, but their training, organisation, equipment and leadership did not compare with Germany's:

> Austria was often a source of weakness, and constantly a source of anxiety, to the German Supreme Headquarters, and more than once they had to detach troops which they could ill dispense from their own special tasks and their own frontiers, in order either to save Austria from collapse or to clear some impending menace from her frontiers.[36]

Austrian strength was a chimera; it was consistently overrated by French and British military authorities, and they continued their futile and costly attacks in France while neglecting a 'vulnerable front' that could have been breached with a third of the troops and material used in the West.[37]

It could be argued that Lloyd George's analysis of Austria's weakness was borne out by its record during the war, particularly on the Russian Front, where they constantly had to be rescued from disaster by their German allies. On the other hand, the Austro-Hungarian army maintained substantial forces in the field until the end of the war, whose strength and resilience were best demonstrated most clearly on the Italian Front, where it withstood repeated attacks on its positions by the Italians on impossibly difficult terrain until the last months of the war.[38] Politically, despite its heterogenous and restless ethnic mix and its severe economic problems, the Empire managed to remain intact until the end. Lloyd George, however, by emphasizing the Empire's instability and weakness, undermines one of his own key points in his 1 January memorandum. His Balkan strategy, which recognised Germany as the principal enemy, aimed to 'bring Germany down by the process of knocking the props under her'.[39] If Austria was truly as weak as Lloyd George suggests, and in constant need of support from its German ally, then Austria was hardly a 'prop' for Germany, and if it was it was rather a shaky and unsteady one. While avoiding collapse until the end, Austria, in a similar fashion to Italy in the Second World War, was a drain on Germany's resources and was constantly having to be rescued from defeats by its more powerful ally.

The success of Lloyd George's Balkan scheme also hinged upon the willingness and ability of the Balkan states to cooperate and rally to the Entente[40] and combine in an anti-German, anti-Austrian confederation. Hankey also reached the same conclusion, and his 'Boxing Day' memorandum summarised this view by pointing to the possible territorial gains that the members of a Balkan confederation might expect to gain from such an arrangement:

> If the whole of the Balkan states were to combine there should be no difficulty in securing a port on the Adriatic, with Bosnia and Herzogovina, and part of Albania, for Servia; Epirus, Southern Albania, and the islands, for Greece; and Thrace for Bulgaria.[41]

The idea of a Balkan confederation was not the product of Hankey's and Lloyd George's fertile minds alone. Grey and the Foreign Office had realised from the beginning of the war the advantages such a grouping would bring, but also the great difficulties there were in attempting to bring it about. In response to Greek Prime Minister Venizelos expressing strong support for such a confederation as early as 10 August 1914, Grey told the British post in Athens that 'His Majesty's Government are most strongly in favour of such a confederation' but the territorial adjustments would have to be worked out among themselves.[42] At the least, if a confederation was formed which included Romania, then Greece and Serbia should 'propose something that would be attractive to Bulgaria'.[43]

If Grey was one who was aware of the difficulties of uniting the Balkan states, A.J. Balfour, former Tory Prime Minister and a member of the War Council, was another. He wrote a carefully argued response to Hankey's memorandum which could apply equally, as David French has observed, to Lloyd George's arguments.[44] He did not deny that there were advantages to the Entente in having the Balkan states combine in an anti-German and anti-Austrian confederation, but pointed to the difficulties in carrying out such a policy:

> the questions involved are, I fear, so difficult that months of preliminary negotiations would be required to allay passions due to events in the past, and to arrange such a division of the spoils as would satisfy these jealous little states.[45]

Both Grey and Balfour doubtless had in mind the example of the Second Balkan War, when the alliance among the Balkan states which defeated Turkey disintegrated and they fought amongst themselves over the territorial spoils. And far from Germany being dependent upon its allies, on the contrary, Balfour knew that Germany was 'perfectly indifferent to the fate of her Allies, except in so far as her own fate is bound up with it'. Operations against Turkey – and, by implication, Austria – would *not* end the war. However successful they were, they 'must be regarded as *merely subsidiary*'.[46]

Writing twenty years later Liddell Hart took a more positive view of Lloyd George's Balkan proposals than Balfour. He was in broad agreement with the thrust of Lloyd George's argument, which is not too surprising as it is broadly in line with his own predilection for the 'indirect approach'. Even he, however, found some of Lloyd George's assumptions 'questionable'. He agreed with Balfour in his assessment of the difficulty of cajoling the Balkan states into the collaboration upon which the plan depended. Liddell Hart also pointed out that the memorandum discussed operations too frequently in terms of 'numbers of men', but, he argued, Lloyd George can hardly be faulted on this point as the military continued to calculate on this basis throughout the war.[47] Indeed, also important when assessing the military strength of the Balkan states were such factors as equipment, morale and the quality of command. (He could have added here that the Balkan states, even if they could have resolved their differences and acted in concert against the Central Powers, needed arms and ammunition which only the Entente could provide. Britain and France in 1915, however, had no capacity to equip either the Balkan states or indeed the Russians to the level required.) Further, Liddell Hart argued that Lloyd George's suggestion that Allied forces could land at either Salonika or the Dalmatian coast overestimated 'the existing capacity of communications', but he pointed out that later evidence suggested that communications and supply facilities in the areas could have been developed to a more appropriate level given more timely attention to the matter.[48]

Lloyd George's memorandum, along with Hankey's and Churchill's proposals, certainly initiated a long and often fierce debate on British and Allied strategy between the so-called 'Easterners' and 'Westerners'. It should be kept in mind, however, that it was a debate concerned with peripherals, not fundamentals. The crucial importance of the Western Front was recognised by all British policy-makers early in the war. This was, after all, where the bulk of British forces were deployed, continuously, from 1914, and there was never any suggestion, under Asquith or later under Lloyd George, that the BEF be withdrawn from France and sent to some other theatre. Even the so-called 'Easterners' – Lloyd George's strategic ideas notwithstanding – realised that the war would be won or lost for Britain in France.

Lloyd George, indeed, argues that the division of opinion which developed over strategy was not clear-cut in terms of either 'Easterners vs Westerners' or between 'amateur vs professionals'.[49] His proposals to open another front in the Balkans received, he claims, significant support from sections of the military in both Britain and France. Lord Kitchener was one who, Lloyd George argues, was fully aware of the impossibility of breaking through the German line in France and Flanders without incurring an unacceptably high level of casualties, and who was open to suggestions as to alternative theatres of operations. As Kitchener wrote, 'The feeling is gaining ground that, although it is essential to defend the line we hold [on the Western Front], troops over and above what are necessary for that service could be better employed elsewhere.' He asked French,

> What are the views of your staff? Russia is hard pressed in the Caucasus, and can only just hold her own in Poland. Fresh forces are necessary to change the deadlock; Italy and Roumania seem the most likely providers; therefore some action that would help bring these out seems attractive, though full of difficulties.[50]

This letter, however, hardly endorses Lloyd George's suggestion of a large commitment of British troops to the Balkans. Kitchener was sceptical as to the value of such adventures. His chief difficulty at this stage of the war was the lack of fully trained troops. After all, if only a small force was sent it would, in Kitchener's view, have been 'useless unless followed up by others...we should be laughed at' and of course most British forces were of necessity 'tied up in France'.[51]

Sir John French's views, as briefly referred to in the *Memoirs*, could also be interpreted to imply some support, or at least willingness to consider proposals for operations in other theatres. According to Lloyd George, at the War Council of 13 January 1915, he argued that a 'complete success against the Germans in the Western theatre of war, though possible, was not probable'. If it did not occur, then the Allies would indeed find it necessary and desirable to 'seek new spheres of activity – in Austria, for example'.[52] Initially Lloyd George's passage on French was much stronger. He asserted that 'Sir John French also favoured the proposal for an attack on the south-eastern flank of the enemy'.[53] Hankey warned that Lloyd George was overstating the case and succeeded in softening the passage. He reminded Lloyd George that at the time of this meeting French was pushing his own pet project for an advance on Zeebrugge on the Flanders coast. And French had written to Kitchener on 2 January criticising all of the eastern plans 'and ended up by expressing a strong preference for the employment of our armies in France'.[54] To be sure, French's support for the deployment in France of the new armies was primarily for *defensive* reasons, and he made it clear that he thought ultimate victory over Germany would be achieved *in the east*. In the final analysis, however, contrary to Lloyd George's assertion, Sir John's view was that 'not a man could be diverted from France to any other theatre of operations without the consent of the French, and this would never be attained'.[55]

Some French generals too, Lloyd George claims, were also attracted by operations in the 'east'. In particular Lloyd George refers to Generals Gallieni, Franchet d'Esperey and Castelnau – the latter on 'unimpeachable authority'.[56] General Gallieni, in particular, recognised that it was impossible for the Allies to break through on the Western Front: 'The German offensive on the Yser, made under excellent conditions and which nevertheless failed, proves that to us. Therefore we must find another way.'[57] General Joffre, however, at this time the real power in French strategic policy, remained confident of a breakthrough in the west and was determined to concentrate all available forces for that purpose.

In citing this support from sections of the British and French military, Lloyd George sought to refute accusations levelled against him during and after the war that he was a mere amateur dabbling in strategic and military matters; as he wrote:

> I have quoted sufficient military authority of unchallenged distinction to make it clear that my idea of an attack on the Central Powers through the Balkans was not the wild phantasy of an inexpert civilian mind, wandering recklessly into regions which he was not qualified to explore.[58]

Perhaps, but the authorities who counted at that time, Joffre and the British General Staff, were united in their view that all available forces should be concentrated in France and that operations in other theatres were secondary to the overriding aim of driving the Germans from French soil. As Sir William Robertson repeatedly told the Cabinet: 'Every fool knows that you cannot be too strong at the decisive point', a view which he and most of his colleagues propounded vigorously throughout the war.[59] Against this opposition, Lloyd George's proposals could but make little headway.

The case against an 'Eastern' or more accurately a 'peripheral' strategy was well put, however, many years later, by J.F.C. Fuller. Following Clausewitz, who stated that the aim of a war against an alliance should be 'the defeat of the principal partner', as this was 'the centre of gravity of the whole war', Fuller argued that in 1914 the

> allied aim was to defeat Germany, since her defeat would carry with it the collapse of her allies. In what locality could Germany be most profitably struck? The answer depended on the most practical allied line of operations, which...was governed by the location of the allied main bases. They were France and Great Britain, and in no other area than France could the ponderous mass armies of this period be fully deployed and supplied in the field. The main bases and the main theatre of war were fixed by geography and logistics, and no juggling with fronts could alter this.[60]

Fuller made the further point that the proponents of what he called the 'strategy of evasion' did not understand that merely finding another front where the enemy's defences were 'less formidable' than in France and Belgium would not solve the problem of 'bullet, spade and wire'; it was this 'which was the enemy on *every* front, and their geographical locations were purely incidental'.[61] This last point is clearly demonstrated by the nature of the war as it developed in the Dardanelles, in Italy and the Balkans. Operations in these theatres could not be described as a war of movement. In Europe it was only the Russian or Eastern Front that differed significantly in this respect from the common experience of armies during the First World War.

IV

The British Government did not accept Lloyd George's proposal for an assault on Austria-Hungary, but instead, persuaded by Churchill's vision of knocking Turkey out of the war, decided to launch a naval attack on Turkish positions on the Gallipoli peninsula with Constantinople as its objective.[62] As a purely naval operation, it must have seemed to Lloyd George that it did not necessarily mean that his Salonika plan would not go ahead; he commented in the War Council that he 'liked' the idea. He later, however, expressed some reservations. When the prospect of military action against Turkey first arose, he predicted that defeating the Turks would not be as simple as some expected.[63]

Lloyd George argues that by deciding for the Dardanelles and effectively rejecting the Balkan option until later in the year, the Allies missed an opportunity to end the war by 1916. But he fails to consider the caution of the Balkan governments, particularly Romania and Bulgaria, who were not about to join an alliance with the Entente Powers unless it was clear they were winning the war, and the course of events in 1915 gave no such assurance.

While Lloyd George would clearly have preferred to see his Balkan plans put into effect, he raised no fundamental objection to the Dardanelles operation. In the *War Memoirs*, however, he emphasises the obvious risks involved in the proposed operation; such action had been the object of study 'more than once' in previous years, and each time it had been 'condemned' as too much of a risk without the occupation of not only the Gallipoli peninsula but also the Asiatic shores of Turkey. The dangers were obvious:

> that of forcing by marine action a passage through narrow straits commanded on both sides by defensible heights. It was always apprehended that even if the Narrows could be forced in spite of mines and fortifications, they might be closed against the return of the Fleet as long as either of the two shores remained in the hands of the enemy.[64]

This difficulty, he adds, would not have been so serious if Grey had not, at the beginning of the war, rejected a Greek offer to occupy the Gallipoli peninsula. This was another of Grey's 'tiresome hesitancies' which helped to prolong the war, and condemned the operation in the Dardanelles to failure.[65]

Other factors added to the dangers of a Gallipoli venture. What began as a purely naval operation gradually required more and more troops; from a small force which would merely occupy the peninsula after the Navy had reduced the forts and other Turkish positions, to the realisation that a substantial number of troops would be required to launch an assault on the Turkish defences after it had become clear that the Navy had failed in its mission. As has been noted, Lloyd George is on record as 'liking' the naval plan. In the *Memoirs* he insists that more men were needed; enough to occupy Gallipoli and the Asiatic shores. But Kitchener could not spare them. Lloyd George claims he suspected at the time ('and I know now') that Kitchener's reluctance to provide more troops had little to do with their availability. Rather, Kitchener was apprehensive of denuding Britain itself of troops for fear of invasion. He also feared a Russian collapse, which would thereby release more German troops for the West. And Kitchener had little regard for the Territorial Army, and so was initially reluctant to release these troops for front-line service in any theatre.[66] These all served to limit the numbers of troops available in new operations.[67]

One may agree with Lloyd George's basic premise that the Dardanelles operation, attempted by the Navy alone, was doomed to failure. Even with double the number of troops which were actually committed to the theatre in the course of 1915, it is difficult to envisage them reaching their distant objectives, Constantinople, and the defeat and subsequent dismemberment of the Turkish Empire.[68] Suffice it to note that Lloyd George approved of the plan when it was first raised in the War Council, and in subsequent weeks raised no serious objections, while at the same time he continued urging contingency preparations for the Salonika operation. He also expressed, it is true, the hope that the Army 'would not be required or expected to pull the chestnuts out of the fire for the Navy'. If the Navy failed in the Dardanelles, the Allies should 'be immediately ready to try something else'.[69] As John Grigg has noted, Lloyd George was proved right and the Army was eventually required to do precisely what he had warned against.[70]

There are several points in this discussion of the Dardanelles operation which merit closer examination. First Grey's timid diplomacy. The Foreign Secretary had valid reasons for his decision to reject the Greek offer of 18 August 1914 to place 'all the naval and military forces of Greece at the disposal of the *entente*'.[71] In Grey's view acceptance would have provoked a hostile reaction from other regional powers and 'would prejudice any attempt to form a Balkan Bloc'.[72] If Greece came in on the Entente side, Turkey would quickly enter the war on Germany's. Also probable was the early entry of Bulgaria into the war alongside the Central Powers. The last factor was the effect on Russian participation; both Russia and Greece had ambitions concerning Constantinople, and an adverse Russian reaction to Greece's entry may have caused serious tensions to arise between the western powers and Petrograd.[73] Britain was not yet at war with Turkey or Bulgaria, and Grey was naturally concerned with maintaining goodwill between Britain and Russia.

Other points are equally dubious. For example, in the early months of the war, Kitchener was certainly apprehensive of a German invasion of Britain, and as Secretary of State for War was correct to take precautions against this eventuality. By the early months of 1915, however, as Hankey later reminded Lloyd George, this fear had abated: 'The sentence beginning, "It was due to incomprehensible fear" [of a German invasion] etc. is not quite accurate. By this time Lord K. had temporarily, at any rate, got over his fears of an invasion.'[74] A more plausible reason for retaining trained troops in Britain was in case of emergency in France, which Lloyd George himself suggested would be wise policy in his 1 January memorandum.

Lloyd George also points to Kitchener's fear of a Russian collapse as a reason for his reluctance to release troops for Balkan and Eastern Mediterranean adventures. Indeed, he writes that Kitchener's initial refusal to spare more than a brigade was primarily due to apprehension that the Germans would use such an opportunity to transfer troops to the Western Front.[75] It must be said, however, that Lloyd George too was fearful of Russia succumbing to German power, although the two men drew different conclusions from the possibility. On 26 February, Lloyd George feared Russian collapse to be imminent, indeed 'so imminent that we ought to lose no time in sending special missions to the Balkan states to try and induce them to come in before it was too late'.[76] Kitchener replied by objecting to the term 'collapse': 'The Russian position was difficult and dangerous, but "collapse" was too strong a word. In his opinion, the Russians had done very well. The Germans had been astonished at their powers of resistance.' Lloyd George, however, 'adhered to his view'.[77] At this point Lloyd George was convinced of Russia's imminent collapse, not Kitchener. A significant difference between the two, however, was that Kitchener thought that in such an eventuality Germany would transfer troops *to the West*, with consequent danger to Allied positions, while Lloyd George thought that Germany 'would [not] send their forces West, but would endeavour to smash Serbia and settle the Balkan question'.[78]

Once the British Government was committed to action in the Dardanelles and preparations were proceeding, Lloyd George, still convinced of the soundness of his Balkan strategy, continued to press for at least preparations to be made for Allied action in the Balkans, to save Serbia from disaster and to bring the Balkan powers into the war. Despite some sections of the French military being in favour of the Salonika option (as noted above) Joffre maintained his opposition to peripheral operations while France remained in danger.

Lloyd George visited Paris in early February 1915, ostensibly to confer with his French and Russian counterparts on financial questions – primarily on financial assistance to the Russians – as Frances Stevenson noted: 'by far the most important part of C.'s mission to France bore on the military question'.[79] In the *War Memoirs*, Lloyd George quotes in full his long letter to Grey written after his return. His diplomacy was successful in so far as he received apparent support for his Salonika proposal from a wide range of French political figures, and from Sir John French and his newly appointed Chief of Staff, William Robertson.[80]

The French had wider political objectives in their support for Salonika. As Lloyd George wrote:

The French were very anxious to be represented in the expeditionary force. Briand thinks it desirable from the point of view of a final settlement that France and England should establish a right to a voice in the settlement of the Balkans by having a force there. He does not want Russia to feel that she alone is the arbiter of the fate of the Balkan peoples.[81]

It was now a matter of persuading Joffre, as it was he, Lloyd George knew, who controlled French war policy. To this end Briand and Poincaré, the French President, thought that if an Allied Joint Note were addressed to Romania and Greece, asking whether they would throw in their lot with the Allies if two divisions were sent to Salonika, and if they agreed, then Joffre could hardly refuse the sending of the troops.[82] Lloyd George noted that Briand thought it 'preposterous' to think that if a mere 40,000 men from the west 'brought in 800,000 from the east, thus withdrawing pressure on the west, any General could possibly object to such a plan', and urged that such a Note be sent at once.[83]

While in France, Lloyd George also saw French and Robertson. At first, French was hostile to the Salonika plan, 'not in principle, but on the ground that he could not spare the troops'.[84] Robertson joined the discussion, and after Lloyd George explained his plans to him, he praised it, saying it was 'good strategy', and this influenced French towards a more favourable view of the proposal.[85] French ultimately agreed that if Romania and Greece joined the Allies in response to an Allied Joint Note undertaking to send two divisions to Salonika, he would at least make one division available.[86]

In the end, however, the Greek Prime Minister Venizelos, turned the Allied offer down. Without evidence of Allied power, he was unable to gain the support of the King or the General Staff; in this respect, circumstances told against the Allies, for the preliminary bombardment of the Dardanelles forts had been postponed from 11 to 19 February.[87] Venizelos was also reluctant to move without Romania, and that country too was not ready to enter the war (and would not do so until the following year). The Salonika plan then fell into abeyance until later in the year, and attention focused, from late February, on developments in the Dardanelles.

V

Lloyd George's thoughts on the strategic problems produced by the stalemate on the Western Front indicate that imagination, energy and impatience with dogma which were to reach full fruition during his Prime Ministership during and after the war. It is, however, perhaps fortunate that these ideas were not translated into practice, as they might well have produced more military disasters. And indeed, there was little hope of them being accepted by the military: Gallipoli, Salonika and the Middle East were, throughout the war, regarded by the generals and much of the political leadership as little more than sideshows. The real battle for Britain was inevitably on the Western Front.

His proposal for the BEF to be deployed in Antwerp at the outbreak of war was one of great risk: it laid the BEF and the Allies open to defeat in detail. In the Balkans, Lloyd George dismisses the difficulties of the terrain and the lack of transport facilities for large numbers of troops as details, as he does the Central Powers' advantage in mobility conferred by their operating on internal lines. It is instructive to examine the role of Allied troops in the Balkans during the war. From the first landing at Salonika at the end of 1915, almost until the end of the war, this expeditionary force almost seemed more occupied with Greek internal politics than with fighting the enemy. Under strength and incapacitated by sickness, it launched no significant attacks on the enemy until 1918. Likewise, the expeditionary force despatched to topple the Ottoman empire failed ignominiously in its task.

Lloyd George's first foray into strategy, the first big strategic 'if only', reveals him as an amateur, one of undoubted ability and imagination, but still an amateur who often ignored political, military and logistical realities. His failure to impose his vision upon the generals and more importantly the government did not mean that he gave up. On the contrary, this episode marks, as he saw it, the beginning of his struggle to reassert civilian control over the conduct and strategy of the war. For the next year, however, his attention was elsewhere. His energies in the year from June 1915 would be fully utilised in producing successfully the munitions of war which British troops in France so badly needed.

4
Munitions 1914–16

I

The establishment and development of the Ministry of Munitions by Lloyd George in 1915–16 was one of the Asquith Coalition's few success stories, and the chapters devoted to munitions remain (in contrast to other chapters of the *War Memoirs*) a valuable contribution to our historical understanding of a comparatively neglected topic.[1] War production was put on a sounder footing and rose dramatically from 1916. Lloyd George and his new ministry, he claims in the *War Memoirs*, laid the foundation in 1915–16 for the Allies' material superiority in 1917–18. His account of the work of the Ministry of Munitions in the *War Memoirs*, however, can be criticised on a number of fronts. His allegations of War Office inefficiency prior to his appointment in June 1915 are, for example, greatly exaggerated, and to a significant extent quantity came at the expense of quality in many areas.

This chapter focuses on, first, Lloyd George's criticisms of the efforts of Kitchener and the War Office up to June 1915, and then on three key munitions programmes under the Ministry of Munitions; shells, guns and machine-guns (to give a balanced picture of the ministry's achievements in these spheres, I go beyond the actual tenure of Lloyd George at the Ministry). The chapter concludes with a consideration of the first use of the tank. Although the first tank was deployed on the battlefield after Lloyd George left the Ministry of Munitions, its early development took place while Lloyd George was still Minister, and he is a severe critic – as was Churchill and others – of its first use on the Somme in September 1916. Just how reliable and plausible is Lloyd George in dealing with these issues?

II

Two events triggered the demise of the Liberal Government and the construction of the first coalition and with it the Ministry of Munitions. The first was the publication on 14 May of an article, inspired by the Commander-in-Chief of the BEF himself, alleging that the most recent British attack in France had failed due to a shortage of shells, in particular high explosive. If the German front was to be broken, Lt. Col. Charles à Court Repington, military correspondent of *The Times* argued, what was needed was: 'more high explosives, more heavy howitzers, and more men. This special form of warfare has no precedent in history. It is certain we can smash the German crust if we have the means. So the means we must have, and as quickly as possible.'[2] The trouble was, from the Government's point of view, was not just that a shell shortage had been revealed, but that both Asquith *and* Lloyd George had recently assured the public and the House of Commons that the army was *not* suffering from a shortage of shells. Repington's revelations were highly damaging.[3]

The Government, however, may well have survived for some time longer were it not that on 15 May Lord Fisher, the First Sea Lord, resigned, or, rather, abruptly and dramatically abandoned his office and let it be known that he had fled to Scotland, although in fact he had merely decamped to a central London hotel. His departure was the culmination of disagreements with Churchill over policy and strategy in the Dardanelles. No amount of persuasion or appeals to duty would induce him to return, except on his own terms, which would have left Fisher in 'complete control' of naval affairs.[4] Asquith commented that Fisher 'ought to be shot'.[5] In Lloyd George's view, Fisher's resignation was the 'match which, applied to the general discontent everywhere, blew up the complacency of statesmen' and destroyed the last Liberal Government.[6]

Providing the army with adequate munitions supplies and avoiding any more scandals over shell shortages was one of the most pressing questions facing the Prime Minister during the reconstruction of the ministry, and Asquith was soon persuaded of the desirability of removing responsibility for munitions production from the War Office and establishing a new department with Lloyd George as Minister. Munitions would a formidable challenge for Lloyd George. If mishandled, it could break his political career. As Northcliffe wrote, membership of this government would be burden enough, but Lloyd George had 'cheerfully accepted the weightiest burden of all'.[7] As it turned out, of course, taking on the Ministry of Munitions was not the undoing of Lloyd George, but rather, with a brief digression at the War Office, paved his path to the Prime Ministership.

Until the establishment of the Ministry of Munitions, that burden had been Kitchener's, and Lloyd George is highly critical in the *War Memoirs* of the way he and his Master-General of the Ordnance Von Donop had handled, or rather *mis*handled this responsibility. The War Office record since August 1914 was, in Lloyd George's view, a record of muddle, incompetence and failure. Before the outbreak of war, he argues, the War Office had failed to keep abreast of technological change, with the result that when war came all kinds of items – such as high explosive shells, heavy artillery and machine-guns – were in desperately short supply.

Compounding the failure to keep up with technological developments, according to Lloyd George, the War Office, after August 1914, refused to deviate from its pre-war practice of confining new contracts to the already established and limited number of firms with the expertise and experience in production of munitions. These firms, he alleges, together with the Royal Ordnance Factories, were considered by the War Office sufficient to meet the needs of the army in peace and war. Other firms which offered to help were rebuffed.[8] The result was a 'narrow bottleneck of overworked firms'. It should have been no surprise when the first shortages made themselves felt in October 1914.[9]

Here it is perhaps worthwhile noting that shortages of munitions in late 1914 and early 1915 were not unique to the British army. All of the belligerent armies suffered shortages at this time. The intensity and nature of the fighting on both Western and Eastern Fronts had confounded pre-war expectations.[10] Thus Kitchener cannot be seen as necessarily more incompetent than his continental counterparts. Indeed, Kitchener was a good deal more flexible and far-sighted than Lloyd George gives him credit for. It was Kitchener who first looked beyond the confines of Whitehall and began to bring into administration able men of business such as George Macaulay Booth (men of 'push and go'), a practice later greatly expanded by Lloyd George. Kitchener also quickly realised that this war would not be 'over by Christmas' and initiated the massive expansion of the army and laid plans to equip it. As early as October 1914, large munitions orders had already been placed with firms in the United States, and War Office orders at both home and abroad were of such magnitude that the army was to be dependent on these munitions long after the creation of the Ministry of Munitions. Thus, according to one account, by the end of December 1915, 16,460,501 shells had been delivered, almost 14 million of which had been ordered by the War Office and only 2.7 million by the new Ministry of Munitions.[11] Moreover restricting War Office orders to a small circle of firms made sense; after August 1914 War Office staff was greatly reduced by the exodus to France and, as Hew Strachan has argued, keeping management problems restricted to only a small group of firms made the Master-General of the Ordnance's task a more 'realistic' one.[12] And in any event, by May 1915, some 2,500 additional firms had subcontracted with the main armaments firms and were thus involved in some aspect of munitions production.[13]

As Lloyd George suggests, however, it was one thing to place orders, and quite another to ensure timely delivery. The deficiencies in the supply of munitions was more than an issue with which Lloyd George could 'hammer' Kitchener for purely political reasons.[14] There were problems and change was needed. The War Office was not vigorous enough in its attempts to secure sufficient labour and machinery to enable suppliers to deliver on time and it was reluctant to provide sufficient finance to enable expansion of existing plant. Nor did it seem inclined, despite Kitchener himself assuming that the war would last for years, to take that 'long view' of military needs at which Lloyd George and the Ministry of Munitions would become so adept, and which would under the new régime entail increasing the number of firms to which munitions contracts were given, and, in time, to the state itself constructing huge munitions factories and thereby directly assuming a major share of the burden of expanding munitions manufacture.[15] The task, by June 1915, had become, simply, too large and complex for one department of the War Office to handle, a consequence of the British decision to raise a mass continental army, indeed the largest raised in British history. As Duncan Crow has suggested:

> Perhaps inefficiency [of the War Office] is entirely the wrong word: it implied the ill-working of a machine. In this case the machine was working fairly well – but it was the wrong machine. It was one which had been constructed for another scale of purpose. What had to be done was to create a new machine.[16]

III

The task of constructing that 'new machine' fell to Lloyd George. The fall of the Liberal Government in May 1915 was at least partly triggered by the publicising of a munitions shortage on the Western Front. In consequence, the main task facing any newly appointed Minister of

Munitions was to ensure that there would be no more scandals on that score. In this, Lloyd George was to prove a success. After securing, with some difficulty, suitable accommodation and office furniture for himself and his staff, he plunged into a massive reorganisation of munitions production which saw numbers of guns and shells produced for the fronts increase dramatically over the following years.[17]

By June 1915, the character of the war on the Western Front had settled into a generally static trench warfare where attacks won little ground at great cost. Both sides were well and truly – and literally – dug in, and the kinds of weapons needed were different to that required by mobile warfare. In particular, more heavy guns and high explosive were called for. At this time the situation in respect of both was in the British case far from satisfactory. Deliveries of guns, despite significant War Office orders, were lagging. While just over 800 of the main field gun, the 18 pdrs, had been delivered, only very small numbers of the heavier calibres had been received by the army.[18]

Lloyd George's first opportunity to ascertain the requirements of the army was at a conference in Boulogne on 19–20 June. Present were Albert Thomas, French Under-Secretary for Munitions, with whom Lloyd George was soon to establish a good rapport, and other French and British representatives, including General John Du Cane, sent, at Lloyd George's request, as Sir John French's 'best artillery expert'. At this conference it rapidly became clear that previous orders for guns and ammunition were inadequate for the conditions of trench warfare, and that they would have to be radically modified in quality and quantity. For Lloyd George and Du Cane the conference 'revolutionised the whole of our ideas as to the scale and character of the requirements of our Army'.[19]

The French representatives argued that trench warfare required that armies should be supplied with as many heavy guns or howitzers as field guns, and that the heavy guns should be 6 in. or above in calibre, as the medium pieces were useless against German entrenchments. In addition, they also urged that the ammunition for these guns should be almost exclusively high explosive rather than shrapnel, and that Allied output needed to be raised to 1.75 million shells per week. The enormous task which these recommendations represented is indicated by the fact that at that time the British army had 1263 field guns and howitzers, but only 61 heavy pieces of 6 in. or above.[20] At the conclusion of the conference, Du Cane told Lloyd George that he would consult with Sir John French and a revised estimate of the army's requirements would soon be forwarded to London.[21]

This duly arrived.[22] It was based on a British army of 50 divisions (the War Office had, however, attached an estimate of the additional requirements for an army of 70 divisions) and after discussion formed the basis for the Ministry's Programme A. This provided for a total of 8881 guns, most of which were to be delivered by the end of March 1916.[23] In July, however, Programme A was quickly superseded by Programme B, which was based on an army of 70 divisions and substantially increased French's heavy-gun targets.[24] By August, Lloyd George had become convinced that even Programme B would not suffice. As he writes in the *War Memoirs*: 'I was convinced that for the success of our operations, an overwhelming mass of guns of the heaviest calibres was essential – an opinion confirmed by the success of our advance at Hooge, after a thorough preliminary bombardment with heavy guns, in early August.'[25] Military reverses for the Allies in August – particularly the Russian retreat and the failure of the Allied landings at Suvla Bay[26] – convinced Lloyd George that a greater effort was needed on Britain's part:

> After careful enquiry as to possible sources of supply in this country and abroad, I decided to put in hand a very greatly increased programme, which would provide guns on a scale ranging for some types up to 25 per cent above the War Office allowance, and this not for 70, but for 100 divisions.[27]

In historian R.J.Q. Adams' words, Lloyd George was planning to 'budget for surplus'; to 'produce greater quantities of munitions than the War Office sought, in anticipation of both the British Army and the War itself growing larger'.[28]

'Programme C' therefore provided for a total of over 10,600 guns and howitzers of all calibres for a 100 Division Army, an increase of 1035 over Programme B.[29] Most of the new orders – over 7100 guns, with a disproportionate increase in heavy guns – were to be delivered by September 1916. Lloyd George was even prepared to order more if it was demonstrated that such orders would lead contractors to expand plant capacity and increase output in the first half of 1916.[30]

This new programme, he writes in the *War Memoirs*, led to 'furious' protests from the War Office, although by early September the War Office itself had come to the conclusion that the figures specified in Programme B were inadequate.[31] But Lloyd George's proposed increases went far beyond what the War Office thought necessary or practicable. Kitchener considered that finding the extra personnel to man all these guns – 4980 officers and 119,198 other ranks by his calculation, over and above the additional men already envisaged – would be impossible. He estimated that over 600 of the heavy guns and howitzers to be ordered under Programme C were surplus to army requirements, and recommended that some or all of these be manufactured to the Russian calibre or pattern (to enable them to use Russian shells) and shipped to Russia.[32]

Lloyd George refused, however, to cancel any of his orders for heavy guns. In Cabinet, as he relates in *War Memoirs*, he also refused to allow any of the 'surplus' guns be manufactured to the Russian pattern, arguing that if surplus guns were to become available to be sent to the Russians it would be possible to send ammunition as well. Here, again, it should be emphasised, it is clear even from the *War Memoirs* account that Lloyd George's first priority was equipping the BEF in France with an abundance of guns and shells to enable it to carry out operations which, in the chapters in *War Memoirs* devoted to 1916–17, he would describe as futile, ill-conceived and sheer folly.[33] Indeed Lloyd George complains in the last volume of the *War Memoirs* (in the chapter devoted to Haig's diaries as published in Duff Cooper's biography of Haig) that there was not one expression of thanks for the service which Lloyd George rendered to Haig and the BEF in 'hustling the guns and ammunition with which his army was equipped'; the 'terrific bombardment which expended tens of millions of shells at Passchendaele was also made possible through the exertions of the organisation [that is the Ministry of Munitions] which had been set up' by none other than Lloyd George. His indignation at Haig's lack of gratitude sits uneasily, to say the least, with his bitter condemnation of these military operations.[34]

While it is difficult to compare precisely War Office estimates, Lloyd George's programme and actual deliveries, some general figures give some idea of the fulfillment of his plan and also the dramatic increase in gun production of all calibres, but the larger types in particular (Table 4.1).

This is apart from the guns supplied to Allied armies. In all, a total of 20,971 new guns were delivered during the war, of which only 3481 were delivered in 1914–15. Two things standout here. First, the rise in

Table 4.1   Artillery deliveries (July–September 1915, 1916, 1917)

	Light	Medium	Heavy	Very heavy	Total
1915	997	193	16	N/A	1206
1916	501	449	256	134	1304
1917	1187	285	370	234	2076

Source: History of the Ministry of Munitions, II, Part I, p. 44.

the absolute numbers, but second, and more importantly, the disproportionate rise in the numbers of heavy and very heavy guns. By 1918
the BEF could fairly accurately be described as a 'big gun' army.

IV

Lloyd George writes in the *War Memoirs* that upon assuming office as
Minister of Munitions increasing the supply of shells was his immediate
aim 'for it was the shell shortage which had chiefly impressed the
popular imagination and brought about the crisis which gave birth to
the Ministry'.[35] Sir John French estimated in June 1915 that the absolute
minimum requirement to enable the BEF to carry out effective offensive
operations was 17 rounds per gun per day for the 18 pdr, with a proportionate ration for other calibres. Over previous months, he wrote, the
rations had fallen far below the minimum (sometimes to 10 or below),
with a consequent diminution in offensive capability and a drop in
morale.[36]

Purely on the basis of the daily ration per gun on the Western Front
at various stages of the war, the achievement of the Ministry of Munitions
was significant. The daily ration of the main field gun, the 18 pdr, set at
17 in January 1915, increased to 25 in June 1916, 50 in September 1916
and 38.5 by September 1918. The ration for the 6-in. howitzer was set at
15 in January 1915, increased to 25 in June 1916 and 43.5 in September
1918; while for the 9.2-in. howitzer the figures were 12 in January 1915,
30 in September 1916 and 24.5 two years later (it should be noted here
that in 1918 the much larger number of guns and howitzers available
on the Western Front of all calibres was thought to compensate for the
slight dropping off of the number of shells provided for each piece).[37]

In June 1915, however, shell shortages were causing great concern.
Between August 1914 and the end of May 1915, the War Office had
placed orders with British and overseas firms for nearly 40 million
shells. Out of a total of nearly 6 million which were due by the end of
May 1915, only one third had been delivered. The shortfall was particularly acute in those types which were of greatest use in France. Only
12 per cent of high explosive 18-pdr shell had been delivered; 7000 out of
26,075 9.2-in. high explosive, while not a single 12-in. high explosive
shell had arrived.[38] Industrial capacity had clearly been outstripped by
demand. The problem was the limited industrial capacity of the existing
firms. As with the gun programme, it was felt by Lloyd George and the
new Ministry that large orders would encourage firms to expand
plant and machinery. In this field, the Government took a direct

hand and by the end of 1915, as Lloyd George writes in the *War Memoirs*, in addition to the Royal Factories at Woolwich, Waltham Abbey, Enfield Lock and Farnborough, the Ministry of Munitions had established 73 new national factories – 36 national shell factories, 13 national projectile factories (for heavier types of shell), and 13 national filling factories. In addition there were eight factories for manufacturing explosive, a factory for filling trench mortar bombs, and two gauge factories. By the end of the war the number of national factories totalled to 218.[39]

During the little over four years of war, more than 196 million shells of different natures were filled and completed in Britain, and another 21 million were completed in Canada and the United States for British forces.[40] Of these 217 million rounds, approximately 28 million were heavy (6 and 8 in.) and some 7.5 million very heavy (9.2 to 15 in.). Examination of the statistics which differentiates between sources of output reveal the vital role of the national factories in equipping the BEF. To take the heavy and very heavy categories, in 1916, of the former, out of over 4.2 million completed, over 3.9 million were completed in the national filling factories. In the same year, of over one and a half million very heavy shells, 1,321,000 were completed in national factories.[41] Without the early and energetic establishment of the national factories by the Ministry of Munitions under Lloyd George, it is hard to imagine where the shells, used with no little effect on the Somme, would have come from.

V

The rapid expansion of the gun and shell programmes was not achieved without some cost. As heavy as the barrage was on the Somme, that battle demonstrated that Britain had not overcome all its munitions problems. Expansion of industrial capacity led to poor quality control and design faults and problems. One estimate states that during the Battle of the Somme, some 25 per cent of all guns were out of action for various reasons, including design flaws and poor materials.[42] Edmonds, in the official history, commented on such faults as the 'poor quality of the firing tubes' in some of the heavy guns, and 'weak buffer-springs' in the 18 pdrs.[43] Apart from such faults, there was at the Somme a continuing shortage of guns, particularly those of a heavy nature, in the light of the tasks the artillery was called on to perform.[44] A near abundance of both guns and shells was only really achieved in 1917–18.

The significant achievement in shell production by Lloyd George and the Ministry of Munitions was also marred, to a certain extent, by a 'sacrifice of quality to quantity'.[45] As Kitchener acknowledged, this was also experienced by the French and other belligerents in the early months of the war after the hasty expansion of armaments industries: 'he [Von Donop] has enabled us to avoid the dangers to the troops, from which we know some of our Allies have suffered, arising from the use of material which has been hastily constructed and allowed to fall too far below the accepted standards'.[46] After the establishment of the Ministry, British output began to suffer similar problems. In 1915–16, due to the inexperience of firms, poor-quality steel and defective gauging, and partly 'to the difficulty of training inspectors rapidly enough to keep pace with the growing output of ammunition', the quality of the shells being manufactured was 'not very satisfactory'.[47] In the lead up to the Battle of the Somme when every effort was made to increase output, some shells were even being released without being inspected.[48] Moreover, there were serious problems in developing a reliable fuse, as Lloyd George himself explained to Edwin Montagu:

[the] 'Hadden and Von Donop Fuse which I inherited and was compelled by the terms of my office to manufacture, first of all burst prematurely; then to obviate that a delay action was introduced, and the shell would not burst at all. Du Cane and his men have now invented another fuse, but it will take time to manufacture it. Meanwhile I fear there are hundreds of thousands, maybe more, of rounds in France of the old Von Donop stuff. God Bless him![49]

The effects were felt during the Somme operations when up to one third of the shells fired by the British failed to explode.[50] This could have lethal consequences for attacking troops – enemy wire left uncut was a formidable obstacle. There were also periods when there was a high incidence of shells exploding prematurely. An officer of the 32nd Divisional artillery wrote in July 1916, for example, that '4.5 ammunition was not so good there were several prematures which damaged equipment.... About 20×18 pdr and 6×4.5 were out of action at one time or another... prematures in the case of 4×4.5 How'.[51] Indeed, 4.5-in. howitzer ammunition was notorious for its unreliability; as Edmonds records, they developed 'explosions in the bore and prematures 4 or 5 yards from the muzzle, and batteries formed of them were for a time known as "suicide clubs" '.[52] There were also shortages of shells at certain periods during the Somme – as Edmonds has noted, it was only by the 'constant husbanding of ammunition could the operations be kept going'.[53] Over time, however, most problems were solved. The supply and reliability of shells had improved greatly by 1917 (in particular, through the adoption of more reliable no. 106 fuse which became widely used by 1917).[54] By that year 'near-abundance' prevailed on the Western Front.[55]

VI

Another weapon where supply struggled to keep up with the demand from the British armies in the first months of the war was the machine-gun. This, according to Lloyd George, was the most 'lethal' weapon of the war.[56] He writes of the deep impression made upon him by photographs taken of dead Highlanders lying in swathes in front of a single German machine-gun on the battlefield of Loos; they convinced him of the extraordinary power of this weapon.[57] Indeed, the machine-gun demonstrated its effectiveness over and over again during the Great War, in both defence and attack. Lloyd George was wrong, however, in calling it the most lethal of the weapons deployed on the Western Front. That distinction goes unequivocally to the artillery; almost 60 per cent of British casualties were caused by that arm.[58]

Before 1914 the usefulness of the machine-gun was not at all clear to many in the military in Britain and elsewhere. In the British army, the machine-gun was characterised as a 'weapon of opportunity rather than an essential munition of war'.[59] The attitude of senior officers was certainly mixed, although it must be stated that among the European powers the British were alone in incorporating the machine-gun as 'part of standard formations by 1904, with a section of Maxim guns constituting an organic part of each battalion and operating together with the unit in the field'.[60] The British military leadership before the war were not as obscurantist and backward looking as Lloyd George contends.[61] Lloyd George's main complaint, however, is that even after the experience of the Russo-Japanese War[62] and the first months of the Great War, the British generals still considered the pre-war establishment of two per battalion as sufficient (albeit a minimum).

In the months after August 1914, however, the army's requirements were being continually revised upwards. By May 1915, General Headquarters (GHQ) asked for four light Lewis guns per cavalry and infantry unit in addition to the four Maxim or Vickers guns already required. In June, total requirements were understood to be 13,000 guns, based on an establishment of eight machine-guns per battalion, and this became the basis for the first Ministry of Munitions programme. Soon after, it was proposed that the requirement be raised to 16 guns per battalion, and this was adopted in January 1916.[63]

Thus Lloyd George's implication that he caused the machine-gun establishment to be raised from 2 to 64 guns per battalion is misleading. In one of the most celebrated passages of *War Memoirs*, Lloyd George describes his reaction to a restatement of the army's requirements by no less than the Secretary of State for War, Lord Kitchener himself; he considered two per battalion the minimum, four the maximum and 'anything more a luxury'. Lloyd George told Geddes to take 'Kitchener's maximum . . . ; square it; multiply that result by two, and when you are in sight of that, double it again for good luck'; result, 64 guns per battalion.[64] More plausibly in another version of this episode Lloyd George told Geddes that the army needed such 'luxuries' and instructed him to 'double Lord Kitchener's maximum for luck, to double it again for contingencies, and prepare to turn out machine-guns at the rate of *16 per battalion* raised'.[65] The published version, however, is the one which has stuck. While the end result of these calculations differ, the essence of Lloyd George's intentions remained the same; to brush aside War Office doubts and objections and massively increase the number of machine-guns available to the army.[66] As John Terraine pointed out, an establishment of 64 guns per battalion was established later in the war, but they were *Machine-gun Battalions*. The Machine-gun Corps was formed in October 1915:

> The heavy (Vickers) machine-guns were concentrated in its hands, and in due course one battalion was provided for each infantry division. These battalions actually had sixty-four guns. With the 13 battalion division of 1915–18, that works out at a proportion of just under five guns per infantry battalion. So the difference between Lord Kitchener's dull lack of vision and Lloyd George's war-winning perspicacity turns out to be slightly less than one gun per battalion.[67]

The advent of the Ministry of Munitions, however, did transform the situation regarding the manufacture and supply of machine-guns. Before June 1915 orders placed by the War Office remained comparatively modest. Only four new contracts for the heavy Vickers machine-gun, for example, had been placed for a total of 1792 guns. Due to be delivered by June 1915, there was by that date a shortfall of 770.[68] And of a total of 1500 light Lewis guns ordered, only 621 had been delivered by July.[69] On 1 June 1915 the total of all types of machine-gun in service with the British army was 1330, fully 60 per cent below establishment.[70] Clearly something had to be done to expedite delivery of existing orders at the very least.

In the words of the *History of the Ministry of Munitions*, as soon as the Ministry was established 'a vigorous and extended programme for securing the numbers of guns required was undertaken'.[71] Lloyd George and Geddes were both aware of the need for a 'long view' in machine-gun contracts, and this was embodied by the first Ministry contract for 12,000 Vickers guns in July 1915, and another for 6000 guns with the Colt Company in the United States. Financial assistance was extended to Vickers to extend their plants, and by the end of the war the productive capacity of the two Vickers factories at Crayford and Erith reached nearly 5000 guns per month.[72]

Production of the light Lewis gun was also expanded greatly. By the beginning of June 1915 the War Office and Admiralty had placed contracts for 2000 guns with the Birmingham Small Arms Company. Upon the formation of the Ministry of Munitions it was proposed that a further 4000 be ordered, but the firm was planning extensions for rifle output, and a decision needed to be made as to whether rifles or machine-guns should receive priority. Lloyd George decided on machine-guns. Capital was advanced to the firm for extensions, and another contract was placed for 10,000 guns and these were delivered by the end of May 1916. By the end of the war the firm was producing an average of 1600 per week.[73]

The overall increase in the production of machine-guns was dramatic. Production of the Vickers gun rose from 2405 in 1915 to 7429 in 1916, 21,782 in 1917 and 39,473 in the final year of the war. The respective figures for the Lewis gun are 3650, 21,615, 45,528 and 62,303. In all, over 240,000 machine-guns were delivered to the forces during the war, with 26,900 of these being supplied to the Allies.[74] Not only the infantry were abundantly equipped, but also tanks and aircraft of the Royal Air Force. Production was set to expand even further in 1919. Lloyd George writes that he did not think 'we ever had too many machine-guns up to the end of the War'.[75] Whatever the details of the precise numbers required and provided to each battalion, the machine-gun programme begun under Lloyd George's auspices certainly provided enough guns to satisfy the army's needs.[76]

VII

The Great War saw the deployment of the machine-gun on all sides, on a huge scale, and to great effect. It also saw the invention and first deployment of a weapon of great potential which according to Lloyd George and others could have been used to much greater effect than it was: the tank. This was one of the most significant military innovations of the First World War. Not so much because of what it achieved in 1916–18, but for its later role in military operations in 1939–45 and beyond. The Ministry of Munitions with Lloyd George at its head played a not inconsiderable part in its early development, although he concedes that his involvement came relatively late. In the *War Memoirs*, Lloyd George's focus is not, as when he is discussing other categories of weapons, on the machine's origins, invention or production history, but rather the use to which it was put in the field by the British military command after Lloyd George had left the Ministry of Munitions.[77]

In Lloyd George's view, the tank was the one outstanding and dramatic 'mechanical innovation of the war'; the 'ultimate British reply to the machine-guns and heavily fortified trench systems of the German Army, and there is no doubt whatever that it played a very important part in helping the Allies to victory'. If it had been used more intelligently on the battlefield, he argues, it would have played an even greater part in the Allied victory. Nonetheless, he concludes, it saved many lives, and was a morale booster and spread 'terror and fear' in enemy ranks.[78]

Tanks were first deployed on the Western Front during the Somme campaign in September 1916. Haig placed considerable faith in the new invention, and had wanted 150 tanks for use by the end of July.[79] Only one third of this number, however, were available in France by mid-September, by which time the battle had been in progress for two and a half months. Of the 49 tanks available on 15 September for what became known as the Battle of Flers-Courcelette, many did not reach the starting line, and numbers were soon further reduced by mechanical failure, so that perhaps 20 took an effective part in the attack.[80]

Winston Churchill in *The World Crisis* perhaps expresses rather better than Lloyd George the nub of their objections to Haig's decision to deploy the tanks on the Somme:

The first twenty tanks, in spite of my protests and the far more potent objections of Mr Asquith and Mr Lloyd George, were improvidently exposed to the enemy at the Battle of the Somme. The immense advantage of novelty and surprise was thus squandered while the number of tanks was small, while their conditions experimental and their crews almost untrained. This priceless conception, containing if used in its integrity and on a sufficient scale, the certainty of a great and brilliant victory, was revealed to the Germans for the mere petty purpose of taking a few ruined villages.[81]

E.D. Swinton also criticised Haig, arguing that he 'threw away a surprise', sacrificing the prospect of a great 'coup' in the future for small immediate gain. While Swinton concedes that the only really conclusive test of a new weapon is its 'actual use', he argues that most faults in the tank could have been eliminated through more rigorous testing.[82] The official history also questioned the decision to use them on the Somme in such small numbers.[83] Lloyd George writes in the *War Memoirs*:

> the decision of the army chiefs to launch the first handful of these machines on a comparatively local operation in September 1916, instead of waiting until a much larger number were available to carry out a great drive, has always appeared to me to have been a foolish blunder. It was contrary to the views of those who had first realised the need for such a weapon, had conceived it, fought for its adoption, designed it, produced it, and carried out the training of those who were to man it in the field. We made the same error as the Germans committed in April 1915, when by their initial use of poison gas on a small sector alone, they gave away the secret of a new and deadly form of attack which, had it been used for the first time on a grand scale, might have produced results of decisive character.[84]

The last point can be quickly disposed of. The British, if it was an error to deploy the tanks in small numbers on the Somme in 1916, certainly did not pay the same penalty as the Germans when they introduced gas on to the battlefield. The Allies quickly developed their own gas warfare capability; the Germans, however, failed to realise the potential of the tank and produced only a handful of an extremely cumbersome and ineffective machines by the end of the war.[85]

How should the tanks have been used? For Lloyd George, the tanks were not correctly used until the end of 1917. The mass use of tanks at the Battle of Cambrai:

> will, I think, go down in history as one of the epoch-making events of the War, marking the beginning of a new era in mechanical warfare. Nevertheless, even after the remarkable success of the machines, there was a slowness to realise and a reluctance to admit their potentialities, alike as savers of life and begetters of victory.[86]

Churchill put the objections as to the early misuse of the tank more fully and eloquently. He was in no doubt:

> Accusing as I do all the great [Allied] offensives of 1915, 1916 and 1917, as needless and wrongly conceived operations of infinite cost, I am bound to reply to the question, What else could have been done? And I answer it pointing to the Battle of Cambrai, '*This* could have been done'. This in many variants, this in larger and better forms ought to have been done, and would have been done if only the Generals had not been content to fight machine-gun bullets with the breasts of gallant men and think that that was waging war.[87]

What then occurred at Cambrai in late 1917 to so arouse Lloyd George's and Churchill's recriminations?

By the time that the Flanders offensive ground to a halt in early November 1917, Haig was badly in need of a victory.[88] With the battle in the north at an end, he now had the troops to attempt to achieve one further south on ground more favourable for the tanks. The commander of the Tank Corps, Brigadier-General Hugh Elles, eager for chance to employ the tanks *en masse*, recommended an attack in the Cambrai area, in the Somme sector south of Arras.[89] Haig was certainly not one of those who was slow to realise the potential of the tank and he agreed to the deployment of an unprecedented number of tanks for this operation. There were, however, to be *two* striking features of the Cambrai offensive which contributed to its initial success. The first was indeed the use of tanks. Fully 476 were available, 378 of which were 'fighting' tanks and the remainder carried supplies. The second distinctive feature of the offensive, however, was the change in artillery tactics. The Battle of Cambrai, indeed, is more notable for the new artillery methods used (although this aspect of the operation is not mentioned by Lloyd George). The artillery, thanks to the effectiveness of such newly developed techniques as flash-spotting and sound-ranging, was able to bombard enemy positions without previous registration. No week-long preliminary bombardment of enemy positions would warn the enemy that an attack was in the offing. This meant of course that the enemy wire would be intact at zero hour, and the principal task therefore for the tanks was to crush this obstacle. Coupled with an over-whelming superiority in British artillery over German, it meant that the latter on 20 November were confronted with not one but two major – and unpleasant – surprises.[90]

If Cambrai demonstrated the tanks' potential, it also underlined its continuing vulnerability to enemy artillery and its unreliability. Fully 179 were out of action by the end of the first day of the offensive. By the end of 48 hours it was fairly clear that the attack could not be sustained. And the significant gains that had been made by the Third Army in the first phase of the battle (to 30 November) – up to four miles in some areas – were almost equalled by German forces when they counterattacked on 30 November without the aid of tanks. The Battle of Cambrai, while certainly a striking demonstration of the capabilities of the new arm, did not reveal it to be the 'begetter of victory' that Lloyd George and others – notably Churchill – suggested.

This is underlined even more clearly when one considers the campaigns of 1918. On only one occasion during the course of that year was a comparable number of tanks – as had been used at Cambrai – available for an operation in a sector of the British front. On 8 August 1918 over 400 tanks (along with 11 infantry divisions, three cavalry divisions and some 2000 guns) were available to the Fourth Army commander General Rawlinson to attack German positions east of Amiens. On the first day the enemy had been driven back seven miles on a front of 11 miles; German losses were 27,000 compared with Allied losses of 9000. This was indeed a black day for the German army. The tanks' contribution to this victory was important. But on the second day only 155 tanks were available, and on subsequent days this number diminished even further. This battle, like Cambrai before it, while it revealed the potential of the tank in offensive operations, also confirmed its unreliability and vulnerability to enemy shellfire. For the rest of 1918, tank numbers on the Western Front remained small, rarely reaching over 100 concentrated for an operation, and there were four occasions where they numbered over 50. Clearly, an explanation of the Allied victories during the '100 days' cannot rest on the tank alone.[91]

There were, in fact, good arguments for GHQ's decision to use the tank before large numbers were available. Any commander would naturally wish to use any new and promising weapon in his arsenal in an upcoming attack, and Haig was no exception. Moreover, as one officer stated, the Battle of Flers was a 'valuable try-out' and he regarded as 'appalling' the idea of attacking with 300–400 slow, unreliable Mark 1 tanks completely untested in battle. It was also felt important at this early stage in the development of the tank that the success of the operation should not be dependent upon the success of the new weapon, which were after all an unknown quantity.[92] Lessons were learnt during this trial in construction and design. One result of the experience on the Somme was that work began on the design for a smaller, faster tank, eventually known as the 'Whippet'.[93]

What of the secrecy and surprise value of the tank? The secret could hardly have been kept indefinitely while the numbers were built up to the several hundred demanded by some.[94] A trial on the scale of Flers enabled crews to gain valuable experience and they were then able to train others for the ever larger numbers of tanks which would become available over the next year. The tanks limited success, moreover, led the Germans into thinking they were of little value. Certainly they employed few countermeasures to the tank, and at the Battle of Cambrai in 1917 the force of nearly 400 tanks met with 'no opposition in the form of anti-tank defences' and certainly the Germans did not put any special effort into building their own tank. *Their* dramatic – but shortlived – 'breakthrough' in March, 1918, moreover, owed nothing to the tank.[95]

VIII

Lloyd George's tenure at the Ministry of Munitions was a success although not entirely without blemish. The work of Lloyd George and his new Ministry played a pivotal role in clearing bottlenecks and organising the industrial expansion necessary to supply the largest army ever put into the field by Great Britain. Most historians have recognised his achievement. The *War Memoirs* chapters dealing with the Ministry of Munitions are perhaps the most convincing in the entire six volumes, because while they are again presenting his case, they are based on statistics which have not been seriously disputed. There were shortcomings – the vast number of British-made unexploded shells still lying in north-eastern France almost ninety years after the end of the war is testament enough to that – but such problems as poor quality control were inevitable in such a large and rapidly executed expansion of the munitions industry. Lloyd George, in short, had reason to be proud of his achievement at Munitions, for he and the new Ministry laid the foundations for the marked Allied material superiority which was utilised to such telling effect in the final months of 1918. Politically, his achievements at the Ministry of Munitions laid the foundation for his elevation to the Prime Ministership.

5
'To a Knock-Out': War Office and Political Crisis 1916

By the time of Kitchener's death in June 1916, Lloyd George had completed his task at the Ministry of Munitions. The new ministry was well established, he had successfully wrested control of the munitions industry from the military, and British forces abroad were beginning to be adequately provided with shells, guns and other requirements. A move to the War Office was ostensibly a promotion, but the reduced powers of the office of Secretary of State meant that Lloyd George did not gain any significant influence over British strategy or military operations. His achievements were modest and his tenure frustrating. In any event he was Secretary of State for a mere five months, until political developments brought him to the Prime Ministership and thus greater power over and responsibility for the national war effort. How Lloyd George used Prime Ministerial power and how this is presented in the *War Memoirs* is the subject of subsequent chapters.

II

Secretary of State for War Lord Kitchener was on board cruiser *HMS Hampshire en route* to Russia when on 5 June 1916 it hit a German mine and sank. Despite losing much of his power and responsibilities over the previous year, his loss was keenly felt by the public, if not by his colleagues in the Cabinet. It was soon apparent that Lloyd George was favourite to replace him. He was not, however, particularly eager to take the post. He was aware of the limitations which had been placed on the Secretary's powers when Robertson was appointed CIGS in December 1915. By Order-in-Council the CIGS had been made chief military adviser to the government and was charged with issuing all government orders in regard to military operations. Negotiations between Kitchener and Robertson changed little and the Secretary of State became little more than a figurehead.[1] This made the post much less attractive than it might have been; as Lloyd George writes in the *War Memoirs*:

> I had no liking for the prospect of finding myself a mere ornamental figurehead in Whitehall. It is a part I would play grudgingly and gracelessly. Had the Secretaryship of State been a live office where the Minister exercised the supreme control subject to the Prime Minister and Cabinet, I would have welcomed the promotion.[2]

After an exchange of letters with CIGS Sir William Robertson, however, which clarified some points, he was finally persuaded and his appointment was announced on 6 July. He accepted, he writes, with 'considerable misgivings, partly on the ground of general War policy and partly because I disliked working in fetters'.[3]

Of Lloyd George's tenure at the War Office, Robertson's view was predictably critical. He wrote in his memoirs:

> Of the results of Mr Lloyd George's six months reign at the War Office there is nothing of much interest to record, for he was connected with no measure having any special influence on the course of the war.... He preferred his own strategical ideas to those of the General Staff, and of administrative work...he left as much as possible to be done by the Under-Secretary of State, Lord Derby. He was, in fact, so much occupied with political activities, especially during the two or three weeks which preceded Mr Asquith's resignation, as to devote considerably less than undivided attention to the affairs of the Army.[4]

This does Lloyd George something of an injustice, but perhaps Robertson may be excused. Their relationship from July 1916 was not exactly a happy one, and Lloyd George was after all responsible for his removal from office in February 1918.[5]

Lloyd George himself saw his two main achievements while at the War Office as the reorganisation of military transport in France and the clearing up of the 'muddle' in Mesopotamia.[6] Of the latter I will say little. The relevant chapter in the *War Memoirs* catalogues in some detail the logistical 'mess and muddle' engineered by the military administration in that theatre. Indeed, it is presented as a 'perfect example' of what the military was capable of 'if entirely freed from civilian "interference"'.[7]

By the time Lloyd George became Prime Minister, operations and logistics in Mesopotamia were certainly on a sounder footing, although the improvements owed at least as much, probably more, to Robertson and the General Staff as to Lloyd George.[8]

Lloyd George could certainly claim greater credit for the improvements implemented in military transport in France from the latter half of 1916. To emphasis again the incompetence of the military, in the chapter on transport he would show how the generals were 'unable to cope with the vast problem of Movement…and how here again disaster was narrowly averted by the aid of a *civilian* expert'.[9] That civilian was Sir Eric Geddes, an expert in railway construction and organisation and fresh from his achievements at the Ministry of Munitions.

While there had been huge increases in munitions production by June 1916 thanks to people like Geddes, reports continued of shortages in France. These were caused by congestion and bottlenecks in road and rail transport between the Channel ports and the front. Soon after Lloyd George was appointed Secretary of State for War, he persuaded Haig to receive Geddes and allow him to see the existing transport arrangements. As Lloyd George writes, Geddes was received with perfect courtesy. When, after two days, Haig asked him if he had seen everything, Geddes replied that 'he had seen enough to think about, but did not know what to think yet'. After a few more days, he told Haig that he had seen 'nothing which the ordinary distinguished tourist would not have been shown'; what he needed was a month.[10]

Like much of the transport chapter, the basis of this account was information provided by Geddes at a series of interviews with Sylvester in late 1932. Part of this material relating to this passage is of particular interest for the light thrown on Lloyd George's treatment of Haig in the *War Memoirs*. In one interview, Geddes told Sylvester that

> Haig was most courteous to Geddes, but the Staff showed him nothing. On the last night, Haig said to him: 'Have you seen everything?' G[eddes] replied: 'I have been most courteously treated'. 'Have you seen the transport?' 'I haven't been intended to see that. If you really would like a report, I must stay here a month. Give me a billet, and I'll do it'.[11]

Another version of this conversation was contained in Geddes' 'Family Tree' prepared earlier by Geddes for reasons quite unrelated to Lloyd George's *War Memoirs*, and which Sylvester described as a 'very secret document of a personal character'.[12] Geddes allowed Sylvester to take extracts from the 'Family Tree' and in the relevant extract relating to Geddes' conversation with Haig, there is no reference to the Staff showing him 'nothing'. Sylvester sought clarification. It appeared that a separate conversation between Lloyd George and Geddes had left the former under the impression that Geddes had told Haig that 'they' (the Staff) had shown him 'nothing'. This 'would suit his [Lloyd George's] purpose so far as his book is concerned'.[13] Geddes, however, confirmed that after two days he had told Haig that he had seen 'enough to think about' and that after a week he had told Haig 'that he had been shown nothing which the ordinary distinguished tourist would not have been shown', which is exactly as it appears in the *War Memoirs*.[14] Clearly, it would have fitted Lloyd George's emerging picture of Haig and his Staff if after having promised Geddes that he would see everything, they had showed him nothing.

Geddes did return to France, however, and the programme he prepared was welcomed by Haig, and Geddes in the end held the two positions of Director-General of Military Railways at the War Office and Director-General of Transportation in France. The programme over nine months hugely expanded both light and standard railways and built many new roads and repaired old ones. The bottlenecks and congestion, by the time Geddes returned to London, had been greatly reduced.[15] Lloyd George cannot deny that Haig welcomed Geddes' assistance, and indeed he deserves much of the credit – there was opposition to Geddes' appointment at both GHQ and on the Army Council.[16] But as John Grigg points out, without Lloyd George Geddes 'would not have been in France at all'.[17]

While Geddes was reorganising and transforming military transport in France, the most costly battle in British military history was underway on the Western Front, which probably persuaded Haig that Geddes' services would indeed be of some use. The Battle of the Somme was launched on 1 July; on that first day some 57,000 British servicemen became casualties and over 19,000 were killed. The battle continued for several months. Lloyd George's appointment as Secretary of State was announced a few days after the launch of the offensive. However much he might have deplored Haig's seemingly barren and costly strategy, he, as Secretary of State, had little power to influence events.

His comments on the Battle of the Somme are of interest, particularly in the light of his previous ministerial incarnation at the Ministry of Munitions. According to Lloyd George he was convinced of the plan's futility well before it was implemented.[18] The Somme ranked with Verdun as 'one of the two bloodiest battles ever fought on this earth *up to that date'* (thus neatly leaving provision for his inclusion of Third Ypres or Passchendaele in that select group in a later volume).[19] Casualties on both sides amounted to over a million. He dismisses the argument that the Somme was responsible for the German failure at Verdun. The Germans there, he argues, were already at the end of their tether.[20] And the Somme certainly did not save Russia (if it was ever meant to): 'One-third of the Somme guns and ammunition transferred in time to the banks of another river, the Dnieper, would have won a great victory for Russia and deferred the Revolution until after the War.'[21]

Indeed, the Allied attack on the Somme was so futile and such a failure and had so little effect on the Germans that the latter, Lloyd George notes, were well able to mount an all-out assault on Romania and effectively drive it from the war while the battle in France was continuing.[22] The generals, realising at the end the failure of their strategy, claimed that German losses on the British front alone were a million men. In reality, Lloyd George claims, the British lost 50 per cent more men than the Germans, and the French also lost more on their front.[23] The Somme in short was 'gigantic, grim, futile and bloody' – a 'futile massacre'.[24]

This is of course strong criticism and foreshadows the even stronger criticism he would level at Haig's strategy and conduct of operations in late 1917. However much we may agree with Lloyd George that the Battle of the Somme was badly conducted, horrendous in its casualties and minimal in its gains, two correctives need to be applied to Lloyd George's account. First the matter of casualties. As I have noted, Lloyd George claims that the British losses were 50 per cent more than the Germans, while the French also lost more on their front. Liddell Hart pointed out to Lloyd George that he exaggerated British casualties; and later best estimates agree with him. Allied casualties combined were greater than the German, and the British indeed lost more men than the Germans, but the gap was not nearly as large as Lloyd George suggests. The British, according to some calculations, lost over 400,000 – perhaps 450,000 and the French about 200,000, while the Germans suffered significantly less.[25]

Second, Lloyd George cannot resist citing some German sources which reveal the devastating effect of British fire-power during the Battle of the Somme. Thus the history of the 27th (Württemberg) division, he writes, stated: 'What we experienced surpassed all previous conception. The enemy's fire never ceased for an hour.... *Our artillery was powerless against it*';[26] the Somme (from another account) 'was the muddy grave of the German field army, and of the faith in the infallibility of the German leadership, dug by British industry and its shells'; and 'the immense material superiority of the enemy did not fail to have its psychological effect on the German combatants. The enemy commanders may put this down to the credit side of their account as the profit of their attrition procedure.'[27] This evidence, according to Lloyd George, 'demonstrates beyond challenge the importance of the success achieved by the Ministry of Munitions in equipping our forces for battle'.[28]

So it does, but it also contradicts his verdict elsewhere in the *War Memoirs* on the Battle of the Somme as a 'futile massacre' mainly of British troops. Such evidence goes at least some way to demonstrate that Haig's strategy *was working*, at least to the extent that it was inflicting considerable damage on the enemy. Which brings us to one of the paradoxes of Lloyd George's war record and his treatment of it in the *War Memoirs*. He had spent a year as Minister of Munitions presiding over the enormous expansion of Britain's munitions producing capacity, and the end products were guns and shells that were mainly destined not for Russia, or Salonika, or anywhere else but the British army in France. With his translation to the War Office, he presided over a military machine which from 1 July 1916 was making full use of those guns and shells. Yet Lloyd George in the *War Memoirs* argues that all such large-scale offensives on the Western Front were futile, wasteful and foolish. There is no attempt to address this contradiction in the *War Memoirs*.

III

In the second half of 1916, Lloyd George writes that a 'succession of sporadic and untraceable attempts in certain quarters to bring about an inconclusive peace' were made. The most important of these, from the British point of view, was from the United States. Lloyd George was convinced, however, that a negotiated peace at this stage of the war could only work in Germany's favour. For Germany, he writes – incorrectly – had reached the furthest extent of its conquests and Britain was only beginning to reap the fruits of mass mobilisation.[29] It would be, Lloyd George argues, a 'disaster if peace were made before it had been demonstrated clearly that no military machine…could prevail in the end against the aroused conscience of civilisation'.[30]

There were those inside the Cabinet, however, according to Lloyd George, who would have welcomed an attempt at mediation by the United States. Grey, Lord Lansdowne, Reginald McKenna and Walter Runciman all harboured grave doubts as to the military position of the Allies and 'the outlook for our shipping, our food supplies, and financial reserves'. Some were increasingly of the view that Britain would not be able to continue the war beyond the end of 1916.[31]

At the end of September Lloyd George agreed, at Lord Northcliffe's request, to be interviewed by the American correspondent Roy W. Howard. Northcliffe informed Lloyd George that Howard had told him 'certain disquieting things' – that Germany was about to propose to Washington that the US Government offer mediation and that Wilson, with an election pending, would be under 'strong temptation' to agree in order to secure the German–American vote, which might 'turn the scale'.[32] Howard, aware of this, asked for a 'clear statement of the British position'. This statement became the famous 'knock-out blow' interview.[33]

The interview, headed 'Never Again. Battle-Cry of the Allies. No Time for Peace Talk, Mr Ll. George's Warning to Neutrals' was a blunt attack on those 'misguided sympathisers and humanitarians' who were 'squealing' for an end to the war.[34] He warned that:

> The whole world – including neutrals of the highest purposes and humanitarians with the best of motives – must know that there can be no outside interference at this stage. Britain asked no intervention when she was unprepared to fight. She will tolerate none now that she is prepared until the Prussian military despotism is broken beyond repair.

The British soldier, he argued, was fighting for the purest of motives, to see 'fair play to a small nation trampled upon by a bully. He is fighting for fair play. He has fought as a good sportsman.' In the early months of the war he had taken a 'hammering'. But now that he had the tools and numbers to fight back effectively, there would be no premature peace. The war would be fought to a 'knock-out'. Britain was prepared to fight however long it took to defeat Prussian militarism and despotism – there was 'neither clock nor calendar in the British Army to-day'.

Regarding Britain's allies, Lloyd George asserted that the world had 'not yet begun to appreciate the magnificence, the nobility, the wonder of France'. While for the British it was 'the sporting spirit' which 'animated' the army, for the French it was defence of the *patrie* – 'that fiercely burning patriotism that will sustain the Army to the end regardless of when that end may come'. And Lloyd George assured Howard that Russia would 'go through to the death'. Russia 'has been slow to arouse, but she will be equally slow to quiet'. There were, in short, 'no quitters' among the Allies. While these sentiments differed little from official Cabinet policy, the language was blunter and more forceful.

Howard noted that Lloyd George 'looks and acts more like an American businessman than any other Englishman [*sic*] in public life' and spoke 'real United States' – Lloyd George clearly calculated that this would appeal to his principal target audience, the American public.[35]

The interview did not appeal, however, to some of Lloyd George's Government colleagues. Grey, who on the whole, as he wrote to Lloyd George, assented in and admired most of what was said, deplored the warning to Wilson and was fearful that it would shut off the possibility of American mediation for good.[36] The Chancellor of the Exchequer Reginald McKenna thought the warning to the Americans 'sheer lunacy'; Lloyd George, he told C.P. Scott,

> thought he could say what he liked and nothing would happen because the war profits reaped in the US were so great. But you could never be sure and you might easily go too far. 'I need not tell you', he added, 'that for my department his action is most injurious. I am in the position now of borrowing from America two million pounds a day.'[37]

Britain was indeed in a precarious financial position in the United States, particularly so when, after being re-elected in November, Wilson advised the Federal Reserve Board to strengthen a proposed warning to the banks 'against investing too heavily in short-term securities'.[38] As Britain was planning in November 1916 to finance its overdraft at J.P. Morgan's through the marketing of short term, unsecured Treasury bills, this had the potential to hit Britain hard and was clearly a way of bringing pressure to bear in advance of a formal peace initiative (which would come in December).[39] Some historians have attributed Wilson's intervention to anger at Lloyd George's 'interview' with Roy Howard while others have dismissed this episode as of little importance.[40] It is undeniable, however, that for some months there was a great deal of uncertainty in British finances from November 1916, and it was really relieved only when the United States entered the war the following April.

Lloyd George, in his defence, points to a communication from Spring-Rice in Washington regarding the good effect it had in the United States.[41] Wilson, contrary to Grey's fears, was quite undeterred in his quest for peace and shortly Lloyd George's newly established War Cabinet would find itself considering how to best respond to a formal proposal from the American President.[42] Lloyd George could also point to the good effect the interview had had on the French; according to Le Roy-Lewis, British military attaché in Paris, a good many of the people he had talked to, both 'political and journalistic', expressed the view that such a statement of Allied resolve was 'badly needed'.[43] George Buchanan in Petrograd warned, however, that the interview was being used in Russia by German agents in Russia arguing that it was Britain that was forcing Russia to continue an unnecessary war, and was therefore responsible for the misery and poverty of the poorer classes.[44]

While the impact of the interview was mixed, the real significance of the 'knock-out blow' episode is that Lloyd George gave voice to what was undoubtedly the prevailing mood in the country. He expressed in clear and unmistakable terms the public determination to win the war 'and not merely to end it'. By speaking out so forcefully, his stature as the most aggressive and determined member of the Government was enhanced, as was also his role as a 'natural leader' of the country.[45] What, finally, is worthy of note is that however Lloyd George might deplore the costly 'futility' of offensives on the Western Front, where else would a 'knock-out blow' come but on the Western Front? In the famous interview, Lloyd George is revealed as just as much a 'Westerner' as Robertson or Haig.

IV

In the *War Memoirs* Lloyd George describes the Asquith Cabinet as it was by November 1916 as the 'Cabinet of Indecision'. Much of the responsibility in Lloyd George's view lay with the Prime Minister himself. A Prime Minister in wartime, he writes, must have 'courage, composure, and judgement'. These qualities, he concedes, Asquith possessed to a 'superlative degree'. But a wartime Prime Minister also needed 'vision, imagination and initiative...untiring assiduity, must exercise constant oversight and supervision of every sphere of war activity...driving force to energise this activity, must be in continuous consultation with experts, official and unofficial...[and] a flair for conducting a great fight'. Asquith was clearly deficient in these qualities, and moreover by late 1916 was tired, 'overwhelmed, distracted, and enfeebled' by the weight, range and complexity of his tasks.[46]

Prime Minister since 1908, Asquith by 1916 was 64 years of age. While as late as May 1915 his political skills were clearly demonstrated in his deft handling of the reconstruction of the Government, by the middle of 1916 his grip was weakening. The Earl of Crawford and Balcarres, appointed to the Cabinet in July 1916 as President of the Board of Agriculture, recorded his impression of the Cabinet and Asquith:

Went to Downing Street for my first Cabinet. It is a huge gathering, so big that it is hopeless for more than one or two to express opinions on each detail – great danger of side conversation and localised discussions. Asquith somnolent – hands shaky and cheeks pendulous. He exercised little control over debate, seemed rather bored, but good-humoured throughout. After a complicated discussion on Franchise he exclaimed, 'Well, this is the worst mess I've ever been in' – 'and you have been in a good many, haven't you', said Bonar Law and we all laughed (outwardly).[47]

Discussions went on too long, decisions were postponed, and by November the conviction was growing that there had to be some change in the war direction. Asquith's 'wait and see' approach was not appropriate in wartime. According to Lloyd George's account, the catalyst for translating his general dissatisfaction into action was an inter-Allied conference in Paris in November.[48]

In that month, after receiving a review of the military situation from Robertson which 'did not present a cheerful outlook', Lloyd George proposed to the War Committee that two Allied conferences be held. The first should be in Paris with representatives from Britain, France and Italy. The main object of this meeting should be to insist that the Western Allies confer with the Russians with a view to achieving greater inter-Allied coordination and cooperation. The War Committee agreed, stipulating that the Paris meeting should be held prior to the military conference in Chantilly scheduled for 15 November. In the event the two conferences were held simultaneously. It was also agreed that if the conference arrived at important conclusions, a conference in Russia – the first during the war at the ministerial level – would go ahead.[49]

For the Paris meeting Lloyd George prepared a memorandum which he intended Asquith to read to the full conference, and which embodied his views on the progress of the war and the steps which in his view the Allies needed to take to achieve success.[50] This paper, 'full of recrimination about the past and baleful remarks about the present', emphasised the importance of the Eastern Front and had as its central recommendation that political and military leaders of the Western Allies should confer with their counterparts in Russia with the object of determining 'what it is possible to do on the Eastern Front, and what is the nature and importance of the help which the west ought to give to the east'.[51] Far from reading the whole paper to the conference, however, Asquith first revised and abridged the document, taking, as Lloyd George writes, all the 'sting' out of it, and then read it hurriedly to the French representatives before the conference began in a 'hole-in-the-corner, informal, unrecorded conversation'.[52]

After this disappointing start, the first session of the conference went relatively well from Lloyd George's perspective. Ministers agreed in principle to a meeting in Russia and on the importance of operations in the Balkans, although the proposed increase of the Allied army in Salonika to 23 divisions Lloyd George thought quite inadequate. The conference also reaffirmed that Allied Governments rather than the staffs had the primary responsibility for policy and grand strategy. But on the second day the politicians were joined by the generals who had been meeting at Chantilly. They had agreed that offensives on all fronts should be continued as far as possible in the winter, and fully renewed in February 1917, and that Allied forces in Salonika be increased with a view to securing the early defeat of Bulgaria.[53] The politicians, fresh from asserting their right to decide on strategy, meekly adopted the generals' decisions 'lock, stock and barrel'.[54] It was clear to Lloyd George (so he writes) that the acceptance of the generals' conclusions meant that nothing more would be done 'except to repeat the old fatuous tactics of hammering away with human flesh and sinews at the strongest fortresses of the enemy' (the Western Front); the conference had turned into a 'complete farce'.[55]

Did Lloyd George feel this way at the time? After all, there did seem to be a new emphasis on increasing Allied forces in the Balkans and upon the defeat of Bulgaria which might have been expected to have pleased him. And indeed according to Frances Stevenson, Lloyd George thought the conference was 'very satisfactory' in the decisions taken, that is more troops for the Balkans and more help for Russia. She commented that as it was the Russian Chief of Staff's policy that the 'war will be won in the Balkans', the decisions taken reflected the conference's acceptance of the policy: 'Sir W. Robertson has therefore been beaten in his strategy.' But Lloyd George still harboured doubts as to whether the decisions would actually be carried out. Too many decisions had been taken in the past with nothing or little being done about them. The Allies were too late to save Serbia, and now he felt – correctly – that it was too late to save Romania: 'He feels that we have lost our chance, and he is very, very depressed at the outlook. He says he would like to resign & be made instead President of the War Committee.'[56] And above all there seems no reason to doubt that he was aware that the British and French generals remained committed to winning the war on the Western Front.

It was in Paris, according to the *Memoirs*, when, after the conference had ended, and when the implications of the conference resolutions were sinking in, that he and Hankey went for a walk. It was then, Lloyd George relates, that Hankey first proposed that Lloyd George should push for the setting up of a small war committee for the day to day running of the war, 'independent of the Cabinet'. Asquith was tired and could not manage chairing such a committee on a daily basis. Both Hankey and Lloyd George, however, agreed that Asquith should remain Prime Minister.

> It was decided, therefore, [Lloyd George writes] that on my return to England I should place the proposition before the Prime Minister; but that before I did so it would be best to sound Bonar Law, whose good will and approval it was essential to secure. I wired from Paris to Lord Beaverbrook, [then Max Aitken] asking him to arrange a meeting between Bonar Law and myself the following day.[57]

This is, as John Grigg has noted, exaggerating the impact of the conference.[58] Apart from the resolutions of the conference not being quite as bad as indicated in the *War Memoirs*, according to Beaverbrook Lloyd George was proposing a 'real' War Council of three members well before Paris.[59] It is clear that the idea of a small 'War Council' or committee to run the war was not new.[60] Sir Edward Carson in particular had been pressing for a small *executive* war committee, that is a committee which would in fact be the Cabinet, since late 1915.[61] Even Asquith's War Committee had been established initially with a membership of only three, but by December 1916 it had grown to nine members, with other ministers and officials in frequent attendance (although of course this body was still, in effect, a sub-committee of the Cabinet and not an executive body).[62]

According to Lloyd George's account, after the Paris conference he felt in his 'bones' that 'unless some new energy and inspiration were injected into the War direction', Britain would be facing disaster. He consequently came to the conclusion that he 'must act without delay'. To achieve anything, he realised, he must obtain the support, first, of Sir Edward Carson, the unofficial leader of the opposition in the House of Commons, who had long been convinced of the need for a restructure of the Government and by now wanted Asquith out. Second, and even more importantly, Bonar Law had to be won over. He was more cautious – he wanted Asquith to remain Prime Minister – and was more suspicious of Lloyd George's motives. But he too was persuaded that a change was needed, and that Asquith needed to be removed from the direction of the war. After negotiations, Lloyd George prepared a memorandum for Asquith outlining his proposed model.

The sequence of events which followed has been told and retold many times.[63] Briefly, Asquith, at first conditionally agreeing to Lloyd George's proposed scheme, quickly changed his mind after consulting with some of his Liberal colleagues and also after *The Times* portrayed it as a defeat for the Prime Minister.[64] Lloyd George promptly resigned. The Unionists, although wary of Lloyd George, became convinced that a reconstruction was necessary, and proffered their resignations. Asquith, according to some interpretations sure that Lloyd George could not form a Government, then resigned. After a conference of the party leaders at Buckingham Palace, shortly after which Asquith served notice that he would not serve under anyone else, the King commissioned Bonar Law to form a Government, but he soon abandoned the attempt. Lloyd George was then asked, and 'kissed hands' on 7 December.[65]

Lloyd George states that he entered into the negotiations with every intention of retaining Asquith as Prime Minister.[66] Edwin Montagu wrote on 6 December after breakfasting with Lloyd George that he was

> still firm in his assertion that the very best possible arrangement was that he and the Prime Minister should work together. He is at a complete loss to understand why the Prime Minister, after he had agreed to a scheme which he himself proposed to George on Monday afternoon...should on Monday night have gone completely around.... He told us that if the King sent for him he would say that the arrangement that he thought best for the country was a reconstructed Government under the Prime Minister.[67]

Chamberlain too recorded Lloyd George's readiness to serve under Bonar Law.[68] But was such an arrangement workable or practical? The proposed schemes which envisaged Lloyd George becoming Chair of the War Committee and either Asquith or Bonar Law occupying 10 Downing Street, contained a serious flaw, which all three protagonists – including Lloyd George – must have recognised. In a nation committed to a major war, if not a 'total' war, it is obvious that the most important, the most crucial component of Government policy had to be relating to the conduct of war. The war effort, by the third year of hostilities, was touching upon practically every area of government policy. Thus in a government structure which includes a Minister chairing the War Committee charged with full powers in regard to the conduct of the war, and a Prime Minister responsible for everything else, what is the use of the latter? Such a Prime Minister shorn of powers relating to the war effort would be reduced practically to a figurehead role, and if not shorn of those powers there would be a constant tension and instability between the two power centres resulting in an inevitable clash, with the loss of one or the other (and his followers) to the ministry. In the former scenario, was not the monarch a perfectly good figurehead? And in the latter, was it not better to avoid that instability and translate the more dynamic and inspiring of the two figures to the symbolic and substantive leadership role; that is, the form and substance of power would reside in the same person?

Bonar Law certainly thought so. After it was clear that Asquith could not continue, Lloyd George emerged on 7 December as Prime Minister for two main reasons. First, Asquith's refusal to serve under anyone else, which meant that Bonar Law would find it extremely difficult to attract enough Liberal not to mention Labour support if he were to attempt to form an administration,[69] and second, because of Bonar Law's realisation that Lloyd George, in the absence of Asquith as Prime Minister, was the best man for the post in wartime. Certainly he was clearly the best man to have control of Britain's war effort, and Bonar Law was convinced it was desirable to have the two go together.

V

Lloyd George's first task was to construct a Government. This would not be easy. All senior Liberals refused to serve under Lloyd George. Thus he would have to draw most of the personnel for the new Government from Unionist and Labour ranks, supplemented by several 'men of push and go' from the world of business and industry, and, in time the press.

Years after the events, Hankey commented on Lloyd George's treatment of this in *War Memoirs* drafts. He contrasted the slowness of Asquith in May 1915 to the speed with which Lloyd George carried out the formation of his administration in 1916. He commented that Lloyd George did not take 'enough credit for the extraordinary celerity with which you formed the War Cabinet and got to work'. The King, Hankey wrote, commissioned Lloyd George to form a Government no later than Friday 8 December and the first meeting of the War Cabinet was held the next day, and during the following week it met every day at least once, on one occasion three times.[70] Lloyd George agreed and writes in the *Memoirs* that he well remembered the

leisurely and even dawdling way in which the first Coalition had been pieced together and the precious days wasted in discussion over appointments to Ministerial posts, whilst important decisions . . . had to await the weighing and balancing of personal 'claims' rather that merits. . . . I was called to the Premiership on the 7th December, and on the 9th the War Cabinet had been constituted and actually met to transact business.[71]

Lloyd George ensured majority Labour support for the new Government by the offer of a seat in the War Cabinet, the creation of Ministries of Labour and Pensions, two further Undersecretaryships and a Labour representative in the Whip's office. Lloyd George also pledged not to introduce industrial conscription. He won Tory support by promising to retain Haig and Robertson in their positions and to exclude Churchill from the new Ministry, and with the inclusion of Bonar Law, Lord Curzon, Austen Chamberlain, Lord Robert Cecil, Walter Long, Sir Edward Carson and Lord Derby in senior positions. Lloyd George could also reckon on the support in the House of a good proportion of the Liberal backbenchers.

Where difficulties lay was with the Liberal ex-Ministers. Lloyd George believed at the time – and when writing the *War Memoirs* – that the Liberal ex-ministers had formally pledged not to take office in a Lloyd George administration. As he writes, when he

came to consider what the Liberal quota of the Ministry was to be, I was confronted with a resolution carried by all the Liberal Ministers at a meeting to which I was not summoned, binding each and all not to serve under me. This decision was responsible for the disastrous split in the Liberal Party which diminished its influence, paralysed its energies, and distracted its purpose for all the years that have ensued since 1916. Even to this day it poisons relations between men whose cordial co-operation is essential to the well-being of Liberalism.[72]

It is quite true that all the senior Liberal ex-ministers remained loyal to Asquith and stayed out. But it is highly doubtful that there was a collective resolution or pledge to refuse office. Montagu assured Lloyd George that there was so such resolution, while Samuel wrote later

There was no such resolution passed at any meeting at which I was present, nor did I ever hear of one being passed in my absence. If there had been I should certainly have remembered it, and should have included it in the records of our meetings which I made at the time. And it would not have been possible for Asquith to have said to me on December 8 that each of his former colleagues, if invited to join the Lloyd George Government, must arrive at his own decision.[73]

Whatever the truth on this point it is certain that Lloyd George welcomed the opportunity to be rid of many of them, particularly those such as McKenna, Grey and Runciman. They were quite dispensable. There were figures, however, below the top rank with whom he was prepared to work.

Churchill was a special case. He had by December 1916 been out of office for just over a year. He certainly wanted to return and Lloyd George also wanted to give him a place. But as noted earlier, one of the specific conditions for Unionist cooperation was the exclusion of Churchill from the Government. In discussions on the issue, Lloyd George writes, the Unionists dwelt on Churchill's shortcomings and mistakes. They recognised his courage and energy, but they asked why he had fewer followers than any other prominent politician in the country. There was, of course, his 'ratting' on the Unionists in 1904. But was this the real reason? No. Their explanation was that

> His mind was a powerful machine, but there lay hidden in its material or its make-up some obscure defect which prevented it from always running true. They could not tell what it was. When the mechanism went wrong, its very power made the action disastrous... He had...revealed some tragic flaw in the metal.[74]

Hankey attempted to persuade Lloyd George to modify this passage, regarding it as 'frightfully damaging'. He explained his concerns:

> Although Churchill is my friend I am not pleading for him on that ground. At the present time he is rather down on his luck and this passage will hit him dreadfully. It will always be quoted against him if he is ever in, or aspires to get into, office again. I would suggest your re-examining and perhaps re-writing your sketch of Churchill, and the omission of this particular passage.[75]

Lloyd George retained the passage, but softened it somewhat, making it clear that he was referring to the views of Churchill's Unionist critics by adding 'Here was *their* explanation... *They* could not tell... in *their* opinion...'.[76] Lloyd George then writes that he was forced to wait some months before he dared offer Churchill a post in the Government. Even then the ministerial crisis rocked the foundations of the coalition.[77]

Lloyd George's decision to offer Churchill Munitions in July 1917 was, he writes, vindicated by his subsequent achievements.[78]

The one senior Liberal offered a post by Lloyd George was Herbert Samuel. The former Home Secretary:

> had taken no part in any of the intrigues that went on. He [had] always done his own snaring. He was a competent and industrious administrator, and I was persuaded that he could preside with neat efficiency over one of the Offices which owing to the War did not demand exceptional gifts of an original kind.... During the War he had done nothing in particular, but he had done it very well.[79]

After several more comments in this vein, Lloyd George relates that Samuel declined the offer (of a return to the Home Office). Samuel did not have any confidence in the endurance of the new Government. Lloyd George writes that when he told Samuel that he should not be surprised if the Government lasted five years, the only reply was an 'incredulous chuckle'.[80]

Samuel, however, recounts a different story. To be sure, he did not think the Government would last. But he also held the view that there should be men of experience available to form an alternative government 'if things went wrong', and also that he did not care for the way the change of government had come about. In particular the press campaign against Asquith had been intolerable.[81] He also felt uneasy with the new War Cabinet system – ministers not in the War Cabinet would have no share in framing decisions while at the same time sharing in the responsibility for those decisions, and the proposed membership of the War Cabinet did not inspire him with confidence.[82]

Lloyd George's account is so slighting that one can sympathise with Samuel when he wrote that it 'makes one wonder why he should have wished me to join his own Administration'.[83] Lloyd George's clear dislike of Samuel dated from before the war, and was often coloured with vaguely antisemitic rhetorical 'flourishes'.[84] By the 1930s, however, there was even more reason to dislike Samuel (and most other senior Liberals). It was Samuel who took over the Liberal leadership from a stricken Lloyd George in 1931 and led the party into a general election – allied with a protectionist Tory party – which Lloyd George thought was quite unnecessary and, indeed, the 'most unpatriotic into which this country has ever been plunged', and remained in the National Government as Home Secretary and leader of the main grouping of Liberals until his resignation in September 1932.[85] In contrast, the

Lloyd George 'family group' of Liberals – Lloyd George himself, daughter Megan, son Gwilym and Goronwy Owen[86] – remained outside the Government, isolated and powerless, until their eventual reunion with the rest of the Liberal party in the mid-1930s (*after* Samuel was defeated in the 1935 election and was given a peerage).[87] According to Rowland, Lloyd George never forgave Samuel 'for what he regarded as treachery of the vilest nature', and indeed he could refer to Samuel as late as 1939 as the 'politician he hated most'.[88] Samuel, therefore, was never likely to receive sympathetic treatment in the *War Memoirs*.

Edwin Montagu, appointed by Asquith to replace Lloyd George at the Ministry of Munitions, was another Liberal whom Lloyd George thought, despite his closeness to Asquith, might be tempted by an offer of a ministry. As Lloyd George puts it in the *War Memoirs*:

> Another Liberal Minister whose gifts of resource and imagination would have been of service in the prosecution of the War was Mr Edwin Montagu. Having regard to the close friendship which existed between him and Mr Asquith, he hesitated to join my Government just then. Later on he came in.[89]

His opinion of Montagu, however, was anything but consistent. In November 1916, Scott recorded that neither Lloyd George nor Christopher Addison spoke very 'respectfully' of Montagu:

> He [Montagu] was 'rattled', 'anything rattled him', he was nervous in grappling with labour difficulties, sought cover as was the manner of his race [Montague, too, was Jewish] grew hollow cheeked under the strain. All the same [Scott concluded] he may very well be handling labour more prudently than George did.[90]

Unlike with Samuel, however, there was certainly no axe to grind with Montagu stemming from events in 1931, or even the 1920s – Montagu had died prematurely in 1924, and indeed after a 'decent interval' he had joined the Lloyd George coalition as Secretary of State for India in July 1917.

In December 1916, however, Montagu was in an agony of indecision. He told Asquith on 5 December (when the outcome of the crisis was still uncertain) that he was in anguish, for he did not want Asquith to be deposed yet at the same time he could not imagine that any government could prosecute the war successfully without Lloyd George playing a prominent part. A combination of Asquith and Lloyd George was what intelligent opinion wanted, and it was what Montagu himself wanted.[91] He was, however, more in sympathy with the new Government than with Asquith and his followers. He believed in Lloyd George, and the one thing, he wrote, which kept him out was his affection for Asquith and the feeling that he would have deserted him. It appears he was offered various posts (through Bonar Law rather than Lloyd George), all of which he turned down.[92] Montagu himself insisted that he had not received an offer to join the Government: 'I know that this is because George did not want a refusal, and that if at any time I had sent him a message to say I would come in, I should have been invited to join.'[93] He gathered, however, that as Bonar Law had taken the Exchequer, he would, in the event he was willing to join the Government, go to the India Office. He would not have consented to do this, he wrote, as it had little to do with the war effort, although seven months later this was precisely the office he accepted.[94]

On other Liberals Lloyd George was predictably critical. Reginald McKenna was 'plainly impossible'; he was an arch intriguer who played a key role in the break-up of the Asquith coalition and who had moreover 'defeatist propensities'. Walter Runciman had always failed in the offices he had held. His most 'conspicuous attribute' was a 'glib inefficacy' which, he continues, 'can explain and expound with forcible and relevant fluency what he is after and why he has never got it'. As for Grey, further to criticisms already made, he noted that he was paralysed by the responsibility of action in war, and he could not 'think of any suggestion of his that contributed in the least to the effective prosecution of the war'. As with the case of Samuel, these comments were prompted not only by wartime events, but also (in most cases) postwar politics when the Liberal Party was divided more than once and these senior Asquithians – notably Grey and Runciman – remained opposed to Lloyd George.

The fact that most of the Liberals remained outside the Government was in fact a boon in that it allowed Lloyd George to bring in outsiders – industrialists and business men like Sir Eric Geddes (who would later be appointed First Lord of the Admiralty), others like academic H.A.L. Fisher, Vice Chancellor of Sheffield University, as Minister for Education, Sir Joseph Maclay, the Glasgow shipowner, as Shipping Director, and Neville Chamberlain, son of Joseph Chamberlain and Lord Mayor of Birmingham, as Director of National Service. Most were successes, except for the last named, whose appointment is one of the very few mistakes to which Lloyd George admits – 'it was', he writes, 'not one of my successful selections'.[95]

The War Cabinet which met on the morning of the 9 December was radically different to the Cabinet which preceded it, and indeed quite different to the model proposed by Lloyd George in his letters to Asquith, which of course envisaged that Asquith would remain as Prime Minister. Under Asquith's Prime Ministership, the Cabinet consisted of over twenty members, and the committees which were formed – the War Council, the Dardanelles Committee and the War Committee – to deal with the conduct of the war were subordinate to the Cabinet. Thus the latter body could frustrate the decisions of the War Committee. This would not happen under the new regime. And in contrast to Lloyd George's original plan which envisaged the Prime Minister playing only a supervisory role in relation to a small war committee which would exercise the real power over the conduct of the war, in the new system under Lloyd George as Prime Minister the 'forms of power and its substance' would go together.[96] The War Cabinet consisted of just five – Lloyd George, Bonar Law, Curzon, Milner and Arthur Henderson, and took the place of the Cabinet. Bonar Law as Chancellor of the Exchequer was the only member with portfolio responsibilities, thus the War Cabinet was free to concentrate on the running of the war. Ministers outside the War Cabinet and military leaders would be called only when needed (although in the event Balfour as Foreign Secretary attended more often than not). In addition the War Cabinet would now work to an agenda paper; discussions would be based on memoranda prepared by the Minister concerned and circulated; and decisions would be recorded by the Cabinet Secretariat presided over by the efficient Hankey and circulated to all concerned, including the King. Gone was the necessity of the Prime Minister writing a letter to the monarch after each Cabinet meeting, summarising its conclusions. Gone too would be any doubt – in theory at least – as to what decision had been reached by the War Cabinet on a particular issue.[97] These measures were part of the reason that the Lloyd George War Cabinet, serviced by its efficient Secretariat, would prove to be a more industrious and dynamic body than its predecessor.[98]

VI

Thus, according to the *War Memoirs*, the change of government in 1916 brought a more business-like, and more importantly a more *war*-like team to power, a team that arrested the drift and brought more focus and drive to the direction of the war (in some senses at least). Lloyd George's account of the events of December 1916, however, is in some important aspects clearly influenced by postwar politics just as much as the events of the war years, and should be treated with some caution.

The events of December 1916 had momentous implications for British politics. It produced, most seriously, a split in the Liberal Party which soon assisted Labour to replace the Liberals as the second party in the state. The 'Coupon Election' of December 1918 entrenched Lloyd George's coalition government with a massive majority over the opposition, composed of Labour and the remnants of Asquith's Liberals. But the fragility of Lloyd George's position was revealed in October 1922 when the Unionists voted to withdraw from the coalition at the famous meeting at the Carlton Club. Neither Lloyd George nor the Liberals held office again.

The effect of the change of regime on the direction of the war, given Lloyd George's views on strategy as presented in the *War Memoirs*, might have been expected to produce a change of emphasis away from the Western Front to the peripheries. Yet it did no such thing. In the coming year, at first Lloyd George tried to promote the idea of a big offensive in Italy. Unsuccessful, he then began demanding that the British army cooperate in a major French-led offensive on the Western Front. The costly failure of this, the Nivelle offensive and then subsequently the Third Battle of Ypres would be the most difficult for Lloyd George to explain away in the *War Memoirs*.

6
The Nivelle Offensive 1917

I

Kingsley Martin wrote of the third volume of the *War Memoirs* that in 'dealing with the ghastly Nivelle offensive one feels that Mr Lloyd George's account may have been unconsciously influenced by the fact that he himself was an enthusiastic supporter of General Nivelle'.[1] There are few passages in the *War Memoirs* in which this is more apparent than in that which deals with the Calais conference of February 1917 where, to Robertson's horror, he attempted to subordinate Douglas Haig and the BEF to General Nivelle. One must doubt, however, that it *unconsciously* influenced Lloyd George when he was writing this particular section. He had, after all, ample material to provide a full and frank account, but he deliberately omitted the salient facts of this unfortunate episode which reflected little credit upon himself.

The failure of Nivelle's spring offensive, which Lloyd George backed so enthusiastically, had far-reaching political and military consequences. It marked the turning point in the military balance of power between the two major Western Allies. The attack's failure and the subsequent outbreak of severe unrest, even mutiny in the French army, led to British forces assuming the main burden of offensive operations in the west for the next year. Douglas Haig as Commander-in-Chief of the BEF, therefore (subject to the policy of the British War Cabinet), would, at least until the Americans arrived in force and the French fully recovered, be the deciding voice in determining strategy in the west.

The Nivelle episode also had certain political consequences for Lloyd George. He had supported Nivelle with none of the reservations he habitually displayed towards Haig's conduct of operations, to the extent of employing what could be described as devious methods to place Haig and the BEF under Nivelle's command. This intrigue strained relations between Lloyd George and the British military leadership, and when it was clear that the offensive had failed and Nivelle became thoroughly discredited (and then replaced by the more cautious Pétain), Lloyd George's position when it came to negotiating future strategy was inevitably weakened.

Both the shift in military power and Lloyd George's weakened position (although the latter can certainly be exaggerated) became vitally important when it came to considering Allied strategy for the remainder of 1917. Both developments led directly to the Third Battle of Ypres or Passchendaele (or, as Lloyd George derisively describes it, the 'Campaign of the Mud'). For it was clear that, if Haig was given the choice, Flanders would be his preferred area of operations, and with the political leadership unable or unwilling to impose an alternative, an offensive in Flanders of some kind became inevitable (although the battle that Third Ypres became was not). There is, however, even in the light of these developments, no admission of error or lapse of judgement in the *War Memoirs*. On the contrary, Lloyd George justifies his conduct as being in the interests of the higher goals of Allied unity – more specifically, unity of command – and a more efficient prosecution of the war, and his criticisms of the British generals, particularly Haig and Robertson, are no less robust than elsewhere in the *War Memoirs*.

II

The irony of the Nivelle affair is striking. Lloyd George, hitherto the most prominent opponent in the British Government of great land offensives on the Western Front, within weeks of becoming Prime Minister fully endorsed such an operation. General Nivelle, to be sure, assured Lloyd George that it would not be allowed to degenerate into another Battle of the Somme. If decisive results were not achieved within 48 hours, he promised, it would be terminated. Moreover, Nivelle's plan had the advantage that the main attack would be carried out by French troops. Lloyd George's support for Nivelle, however, was still significantly at odds with his previous attitude. How did this come to pass?

On 8 December 1916 Hankey, secretary to the new War Cabinet, presented Lloyd George with a memorandum on the military position. Hankey more or less shared Lloyd George's strategic views, and although he argued in his paper than there should be a renewal of offensive operations in the west once the weather permitted (the 'Power which takes the offensive loses less that the Power which takes the defensive' he argued, curiously, given the horrendous casualties suffered by the BEF during the Somme offensive)[2] he was apprehensive of an Austrian offensive in Italy. To counter his threat, he argued that British and French guns should be transferred to the Italian Front while the Western Front was relatively quiet. This would not only aid the Italians in their defence against any enemy attack, but would also offer them the opportunity to launch effective operations themselves, the Austrian naval base at Pola being a particularly attractive prize.[3]

Hankey's proposal was entirely in keeping with Lloyd George's thinking, and he made it the centrepiece of a memorandum prepared for an inter-Allied conference to be held in Rome on 5–7 January. This was his first opportunity as Prime Minister to attempt, as he states in the *War Memoirs*, a 'fundamental reconstruction of Allied strategy on all fronts'. He proposed that an attack be launched against Austrian forces by an Italian army reinforced by Allied artillery from France. While not even Lloyd George was prepared to envisage no action in the west, the main offensive operation in 1917, he wrote, should be in the Italian theatre, for it was there, as he argues in the *War Memoirs*,

> You could reach the enemy's vitals...I laid great stress on the fact that the Austrians were the weakest enemy, and I suggested we ought to strike at the weakest and not the strongest point on the enemy front. Germany, I pointed out, was formidable so long as she could command an unbroken Austria, but if Austria were beaten Germany would be beaten too.[4]

The multinational Austrian army was weakening, he argues, and suffering from low morale; many of its troops felt no great loyalty to the Habsburgs or their cause. The Italians, on the other hand, had already made considerable advances against troops such as the Croats and Czechs whose hearts were not in the struggle. Artillery reinforcements would tip the balance in favour of the Italians and would also facilitate surprise, something almost impossible on the Western Front.

If successful, Lloyd George argued, the rewards would be considerable. Faced with defeat on the Italian Front, Austria would be forced to transfer troops from the Eastern Front, and their German allies would thus have to extend their lines in the east to compensate, and possibly transfer troops from France.[5] In the latter event, of course, prospects would brighten for any Allied offensive on the Western Front. A success in Italy might even provide enough of a shock to knock Austria out of the war, leaving Germany isolated.

Such speculations, however, were qualified by two and as it turned out rather important conditions for the loan of artillery to the Italians. They are two good indications that even for Lloyd George Britain's main military commitment remained in France. The first condition was that such guns that would be loaned to the Italian army would be sent to Italy for a definite period of time and returned to France after the conclusion of operations.[6] Second, and significantly, there was no mention of any transfer of Allied troops from France to Italy. They would remain in France. At the conference it soon became clear that these conditions meant that the Italian command quickly lost any enthusiasm they may have had for a major offensive against Austria. General Cadorna, the Italian Commander-in-Chief, asked:

> for how long the material would be at his disposal? This was really an essential point. He gathered...that the material would have to be returned by 6 May....to be useful for offensive operations the material must be back some eight or ten days before the offensive began. Then an allowance had to be made for the time necessary for the transport to and from France. Time also had to be allowed for loading and unloading off the railways. Then there were the different methods of the various nations to be considered in regard to technical matters, such as fire control, the use of metres instead of yards... After you had made allowance for all these things, he asked how much time remained?[7]

Lloyd George wrote later of the Italians: 'I may possibly have been over enthusiastic in regard to a subject which I certainly regarded as being of transcendental importance, but one aspect of the discussion which astonished me was the comparative lack of enthusiasm shown by our Italian Allies especially.'[8] There is little mystery, however, to the Italians' reluctance to support Lloyd George's plan. Apart from technical problems, the Italians were justifiably nervous about launching a major offensive against Austria without any troop reinforcements from the Western Allies and with no major operations underway in France. Such an offensive launched under such conditions was certain to attract substantial German assistance for the Austrians.[9] This crucial factor, however, does not enter into Lloyd George's calculations.

At the Rome conference, Italian fears and objections coupled with the British and French generals' strong preference for continued offensive operations in France proved too strong an obstacle for Lloyd George to overcome. After much discussion it was agreed to refer the whole question to the staffs for further study, thus effectively ensuring it would be shelved. Lloyd George's failure to effect a change in Allied strategy was complete; his lack of realism in proposing such a change is evident. The British General Staff and the French were, inevitably, opposed to the transfer of resources and effort from France to Italy; most importantly the Italians, upon whose agreement Lloyd George was utterly dependent for the acceptance and implementation of his proposals, were understandably reluctant to bring the combined might of the German and Austrian armies down upon their heads. For the British, then, the result of the conference was that the only alternative was another offensive in France.

Lloyd George's proposals also suffered from the same muddled thinking as had his proposals of January 1915, when he proposed an Allied attack on Austria from Greece with the participation of the armed forces of a Balkan confederation, and he memorably described the Austro-Hungarian Empire as Germany's 'prop'. With this prop knocked away, he fondly believed, Germany would come crashing down to defeat. This was even more mistaken in 1917 than it was in 1915. Germany was Austria's 'prop', if the analogy applied at all. The fall of Austria would, at this stage of the war, have done little to hasten Germany's early fall.

While the Rome conference achieved some progress in certain areas such as the troublesome Greek situation, the agreement to open an overland route to the Allied armies in Salonika, and to convene a shipping conference in the near future, nothing could hide the fact that the major purpose of the conference for Lloyd George – a 'real and not a sham co-ordination of strategy' with the object of inflicting a major defeat on Germany's principal ally, was not achieved. It seemed it was to be business as usual for the generals; the 'military staffs were left in possession of the field', as Lloyd George writes.[10] Events, however, were to turn out quite differently, and the generals' apparent victory would not remain unchallenged.

III

The operation which was to be carried out on the Western Front in April 1917 was not to be that agreed to by Allied generals at Chantilly the previous November and confirmed by political leaders in Paris. It will be recalled that the Chantilly conference envisaged the resumption of the offensive on the Somme as soon as the weather permitted (rather earlier than April) and that this would be synchronised with offensives on other fronts. On 12 December, however, General Joffre was replaced as French Commander-in-Chief (in the north and north-east at least) by

General Robert Nivelle. Due to his recent successful operations which resulted in the recapture of Fort Doaumont, he was held in great admiration by the French public and Government.[11] He was convinced by his successes at Verdun that if his methods were implemented on a larger scale he could break the deadlock on the Western Front. He emphasised overwhelming artillery bombardment, a creeping barrage and complete surprise; operations must be 'short, sharp and decisive'.[12]

Nivelle travelled to London in January to explain his plan to the British Government. He proposed that the initial attack be launched by British forces out of Arras, primarily to draw in and exhaust German reserves. Once this operation had achieved its goal, French forces would deliver the main attack on the Aisne front. He expected a breakthrough of the German line to take between 24 and 48 hours. If, at the end of 48 hours, the line had broken, it would be rapidly exploited by all available forces including cavalry. If it had not, then the attack would be terminated.[13] His plan had the attraction that in the event of failure, there would be ample time to mount operations elsewhere. For Lloyd George, this meant, preferably, Italy; for Haig, as we shall see, it meant Flanders.

The London conference was Lloyd George's first substantial encounter with Nivelle. He was clearly impressed. He writes in the *War Memoirs* that Nivelle had a 'brilliant record' at Verdun; he had an 'intellectual quality' which led Lloyd George to expect a 'fresh survey' by Nivelle's 'fresh mind unhampered by commitments or traditions, of the possibilities of the vast battlefield of the War'.[14] Little was known of his 'endowments as a strategist on a vaster field of operations', and, in the event, Lloyd George was to be bitterly disappointed by Nivelle's performance as French commander. Despite this, however, Lloyd George could still, in the *War Memoirs*, record as 'unfortunate' that Nivelle was not put in charge of the whole French war effort, as Joffre had been.[15] As he told Frances Stevenson at the time, 'Nivelle has proved himself to be a Man at Verdun; & when you get a Man against one who has not proved himself, why, you back the Man!'.[16] It certainly helped Nivelle's case that he was able to explain his plan in fluent English.[17]

Whether or not Nivelle 'captivated' Lloyd George (which he strenuously denies in the *War Memoirs*), the Frenchman certainly seemed to offer a plan rather more hopeful than a return to the Somme slaughter, and certainly more achievable than a great Italian offensive against Austria.[18] It seemed to Lloyd George that the only other alternative to Nivelle was to do nothing but for each army to sit in its trenches waiting for something to happen. Nivelle was offering new hope to a war-weary France, which otherwise, some feared, might be tempted towards a compromise peace. Soon Lloyd George became so convinced of the potential of the Nivelle plan that he determined to place Haig and the BEF under his command, whether Haig agreed or not.

IV

One prominent theme of the *War Memoirs* is the need for greater unity among the Allies. Lloyd George, according to his account, consistently argued for greater cooperation and sharing of resources, and that the separate fronts be regarded as one. The corollary of this view was the need for unity of command of Allied forces. If the British and French armies, Lloyd George argues in the *War Memoirs*, had

> been as completely under the control of one Generalissimo as they became after the Beauvais decision in April 1918 [when the Allied forces in France came under the direction of General Foch] the Nivelle strategy, while it might not and probably would not have achieved a decision, would have secured a notable success.[19]

During the Great War, Germany was clearly dominant among the Central Powers. In 1939–45 the Western Allies, profiting from the experiences of 1914–18, instituted an effective system of supreme command for major operations. It took until April 1918 and the crisis stemming from the success of the German offensive in France for a workable model of a unified command to be achieved on the Western Front. The Calais conference of February 1917 is presented by Lloyd George as the first attempt to achieve unity of command; but it should be seen rather for what it was, a bold and clumsy attempt to subordinate Haig to Nivelle. The arrangements worked out at the Calais conference failed dismally and discredited the idea of 'unity of command' for some time afterwards.

The Calais conference was held for two main reasons. The first was to clear up the transport problems in France which were becoming more acute as the offensive drew nearer. Suspicions held by Lloyd George that Haig was using this issue to delay the offensive appear to be unfounded. The seriousness of the situation was confirmed by none other than Sir Eric Geddes, controller of military railways in France and Lloyd George's own appointee.[20]

The second and more important issue which Lloyd George wanted settled in Calais was the potentially explosive one of, in Lloyd George's words: the 'supreme responsibility and direction for the plan of action, and for carrying it during the course of battle'.[21] Now the *War Memoirs* leave the clear impression that the conference was called solely to deal with the transport question. The index entry reads: 'Calais Conference (of February 1917) on Army Transport, 1501 et seq.; terms of agreement 1504–5'.[22] The text devoted to the conference in volume III is mainly concerned with transport and criticism of Haig for creating this problem. And Lloyd George explicitly states that the conference of 'Ministers and Generals had to be summoned to adjust the differences which had arisen' on the transport question.[23] In reality by the time of the conference there was little need for a conference to discuss transport.[24] The real issue to be discussed in Calais was the question of command. And for Lloyd George and the French, at least, this question had been settled before the conference began, although Robertson and the man to be most affected by their decision, Haig, did not know it.

On 15 February Lloyd George and Hankey met with the French *Grand Quartier Général* (*GQG*) representative to the War Office, Bertier de Sauvigny. The Frenchman was told in clear terms that for Nivelle to have the best chance for success in the coming offensive he must have control of not only the French army but also the British. The

> prestige which Field Marshal Haig enjoys with the public and the British Army will make it impossible to subordinate him purely and simply to the French Command, but if the War Cabinet realises that this measure is indispensable they will not hesitate to give Field Marshal Haig secret instructions to this effect, and, if need be, to replace him ... It is essential that the two War Cabinets should be in agreement on this principle. A conference should be held as soon as possible, for although the date by which the British Armies will be ready has been retarded by a fortnight owing to the congestion of the French railways, it is nevertheless so near that we must take a decision as soon as possible.[25]

No account of this important meeting appears in the *War Memoirs*. Bertier wrote at once to Generals Lyautey and Nivelle, and the latter proceeded to formulate the terms of his *projet d'organisation* for the Allied armies in France. Thus when Nivelle was asked at the Calais conference for his proposals regarding command arrangements, as an anonymous marginal note on a draft of Lloyd George's Nivelle chapter put it, he had a 'cut and dried scheme up his sleeve' and Lloyd George was aware, at least in broad outline, of what was coming.[26]

Nine days after the meeting with Bertier, Lloyd George received his authorisation from the War Cabinet to pursue unity of command, or, to be more precise, to seek:

> A full explanation of their [the generals] plans for the campaign of 1917; to use his best endeavours to ascertain any points on which there might be a difference of opinion between the two Commanders-in-Chief; in concert with M. Briand to decide any such differences of opinion on their merits; [and most crucially] to aim more especially at the adoption of such measures as might appear best calculated, as the result of the discussion at the conference, to ensure unity of command both in the preparatory stages of and during the operations.[27]

The significance of this meeting, from which both the Secretary of State for War Lord Derby and Robertson were absent, is that it on the one hand allowed Lloyd George to claim – with some exaggeration – the War Cabinet's full authority to enter into arrangements regarding the question of command which in his judgement would best promote the success of the offensive. On the other hand, Robertson and Derby, due to their absence from the War Cabinet that day, could with justice argue that they were ignorant of the whole affair until it was raised in Calais; their absence also lent plausibility to their accusations of deception against Lloyd George. As Robertson wrote, he had not the opportunity to give advice on the issue as 'I was not present at the meeting having previously been told by the Secretariat of the War Cabinet not to attend unless I had anything special to bring forward'. The first intimation he received that any change in the Allied command was being contemplated was, he claimed, at nine o'clock on the evening of the 26 February in Calais, that is the first day of the conference. What is clear in all this is that Derby, as the Government Minister responsible for the BEF, and Robertson, as the chief military adviser to the Government, should have been consulted on such an important issue, and that Lloyd George deliberately kept his two most potentially troublesome colleagues away from this crucial meeting of the War Cabinet.[28]

The French and British political and military leaders gathered in Calais on 26 February 1917. Lloyd George, Robertson, Haig, Eric Geddes (in his capacity as Director-General of Military Railways) and Hankey represented the British Government, while Premier Aristide Briand, Minister of War General Lyautey, General Nivelle and a number of transport officials represented the French. Hankey acted as secretary.

Lloyd George in the *War Memoirs* notes that much of the discussion was devoted to transport; a very different impression, however, is given by the official record and other accounts, including draft chapters for the *War Memoirs* in the Lloyd George papers.[29] Robertson recalled that the 'proceedings in regard to transportation occupied a very short time. They seemed to have no attraction for either M. Briand or Mr Lloyd George'; while Hankey noted, 'Dull conference on railway matters to start with. This was followed at 5 pm by a conference that was by no means dull.'[30] The reality was that after an inconclusive discussion of the transport issue, ministers decided that such matters were best left to the experts meeting separately. After a short break in proceedings, the second session began, according to the official record, at 5.30 pm. The real business of the conference then got under way. In the *War Memoirs*, this is summarised in one paragraph:

> There were fresh difficulties in adjusting questions as to the supreme responsibility and direction for the plan of action, and for carrying it out during the course of battle. Sir Douglas Haig was given the supreme command of the combined British and French troops in the arduous offensive at Passchendaele [in totally different circumstances, see p. 136]. But he and Robertson demurred at the idea of a united command in the spring offensive. In all, three conferences had to be held, two in London and one in Calais, before an agreement was reached.[31]

This is Lloyd George's account of the Calais conference as it related to the important question of command. Fortunately, there is not only the official record, but also other detailed accounts which provide a more complete picture of what transpired.

After the resumption of proceedings, Lloyd George asked Nivelle to speak frankly on what preparations were needed to ensure complete success. Were any 'alterations' necessary in the 'present arrangements'? What Lloyd George had in mind with his somewhat cryptic language (as recorded in the minutes) was clear, for he had commented earlier that the enemy were as 'one army under a single command. The nearer the Allies could approach to one army the better.' This was meant to be the cue for Nivelle to produce his plan for a single, *French* command. Nivelle, however, limited himself to arguing that the 'limits of the special powers of the man who was responsible should not be restricted either in time or scope [and that] the whole of the preparations and the execution of the projected operations ought to be in the same hands without any limits as regards time'.[32] On Hankey, at least, he made a poor impression. He recorded that Nivelle 'got red in the face, talked generalities, and beat about the bush, Briand and Lyautey failing to help him out at all'.[33] Nivelle, clearly, was unable or unwilling to present concrete proposals, so Lloyd George asked him to 'put down on paper the rules which he considered ought to guide the two Generals', and with that the conference adjourned.[34]

Shortly afterwards, at approximately 8 pm, Nivelle's *projet d'organisation* was in Lloyd George's hands. Nivelle had more than met Lloyd George's wishes. He proposed that the French Commander-in-Chief have authority over the British forces on the Western Front 'in all that concerns the conduct of operations'. In particular, this authority would cover: 'The planning and execution of offensive and defensive actions; the dispositions of the forces by Armies and Groups of Armies; the boundaries between these higher formations; [and] the allotment of material and resources of all natures to the Armies.'[35] This was not all. A British Chief of Staff would be attached to GQG who would be the chief liaison between the French command and the British War Cabinet; he would also transmit Nivelle's orders to Haig. As for the latter, in effect his authority would be limited to questions of personnel and discipline, and even this was to be shared with his Army commanders.[36] The BEF, in short, was to be almost indistinguishable from any other French army or army group under Nivelle's command.

Robertson's and Haig's reaction to this document may be imagined. Robertson was furious and both were ready to resign if Lloyd George insisted upon its adoption.[37] Even Hankey wrote – accurately – that the plan reduced Haig to a 'cipher' and that it 'fairly took my breath away'.[38] Lloyd George overrode their protests by revealing that he had the War Cabinet's authority to secure unity of command – thereby admitting that he had 'known all along what was coming, and had been holding out on his military associates' – and he intimated that while details of the plan were open to amendment, the principle of French command of the BEF was not negotiable.[39] But even Lloyd George agreed that Nivelle had gone too far.[40] After much negotiation, Hankey managed to formulate a compromise. This stipulated that Haig was to 'conform his preparations' and his 'plans of operations' to those of Nivelle; Haig was to have the right, if he felt the safety of his army was threatened, to depart from Nivelle's instructions and appeal to London; moreover, the arrangement was to be implemented for the duration of the upcoming offensive only. This draft was accepted by the conference, with one minor amendment proposed by Briand reserving to the two governments the right to decide when operations were to be terminated.[41] Even this document, however, remained highly unsatisfactory to both Robertson and Haig. As the former wrote to Haig: 'We ought not to have *signed* the document.'[42]

Robertson argued in his memorandum detailing his objections that he was not consulted; in fact he was asked not to attend the relevant meeting of the War Cabinet. In his memoirs he wrote: 'Nothing could be of greater military importance than the change of command proposed, and I could not understand why the War Cabinet – or Mr Lloyd George, whichever it was – should have deliberately kept me in ignorance of their intentions and of their communications with the French Government.'[43] The reason, of course, why Lloyd George kept Robertson in the dark was that he knew that Robertson would create difficulties and raise objections and appeal to the other members of the War Cabinet against any plan to place Haig under Nivelle. Not that this excuses Lloyd George's conduct.

But Robertson's objections also focused on the substance of the agreement. He argued that effective cooperation with the French was already in place, in fact had been since December 1915. Kitchener's instructions to Haig at that time stated that while Haig was to 'support and cooperate' with the French, and the closest cooperation as a united army should be his policy, his command remained an independent one, and in no way did he come under the orders of a foreign general. This had worked well under the Joffre régime and would have continued to do so; there was therefore no need for any new agreement concerning the command of the Allied armies in France. It was, moreover, unwise to 'entrust the command of our armies to a foreign general', especially one who was junior in rank to Haig and less experienced in high command. He also argued that officers and men always preferred to fight under their own commanders, and that the Dominion governments might resent their forces being placed under a foreigner. Robertson's trump card was that 'no British soldier could constitutionally be placed under the orders of anyone not holding His Majesty's Commission'.[44]

Such objections from a soldier with Robertson's background and experience could not be dismissed lightly. Lloyd George's War Cabinet colleagues were indeed far from sharing Lloyd George's blind trust in Nivelle and were receptive to Robertson's arguments.[45] Even Lloyd George probably realised he had overreached himself. In the *War Memoirs* he dismisses Robertson's objections, arguing that they simply meant more delay in launching the offensive,[46] but at the time he was forced to bow to pressure and agree to another conference to further define the roles of Nivelle and Haig, and forced to agree to a message indicating the War Cabinet's full confidence in Haig.[47] This became even more necessary after Haig and his supporters complained of Nivelle's 'brusque' and peremptory tone in his 'directives' to Haig, and Nivelle became convinced that Haig was deliberately dragging his feet in his preparations for the attack.[48]

The London conference of 12–13 March seemed to settle matters and smooth ruffled feathers. As Lloyd George writes in the *War Memoirs*, after 'a good deal of palavering, the trouble was once more arranged. Clumsy despatches had been reproved and sore heads poulticed.'[49] Nivelle's authority was further 'defined and restricted', and Lloyd George himself informed the conference that Haig enjoyed the full confidence of the British Government and that he was regarded with much 'admiration' by the British public.[50] In fact Nivelle's authority was in the end so restricted that in practice Haig retained his independent command and the projected attack on Vimy Ridge was planned and implemented quite separately from the main French operation.[51]

Unity of command was a worthwhile goal. A divided command in the conditions of coalition warfare could be fatal. The Nivelle proposals were, however, fundamentally flawed. They left Nivelle in command of the French army, in addition to overall control of the Allied armies on the Western Front. John Buchan identified the problem accurately: 'It was not a unified command; it was the placing of one army in subordination to another, and yet not in complete subordination, for Haig could not rid himself of his responsibility to his own Government, and the British War Cabinet reserved the right to interfere.'[52] Statesmen in 1918, however, and later in another war, in 1942–45, devised a more efficient and workable system whereby supreme commanders were placed above national commanders and were answerable to both governments. In both instances, there was not in appearance or in substance the subordination of one army to another.

The Calais conference played an important part in poisoning relations between Lloyd George and the British military leadership. Robertson wrote that he thought Lloyd George an 'awful liar' and he could not 'believe that a man such as he can for long remain head of any Government. Surely some honesty & truth are required.'[53] Haig wrote even before the Calais conference that he had 'no great opinion of LG *as a man or a leader*'; he would later describe him as 'most unreliable' and a 'cur'.[54] Neville Lytton, head of the Allied 'press camp' at GHQ, many years later summarised what many senior military figures felt about Lloyd George: 'Lloyd George himself has never known how to behave to soldiers and sailors for the simple reason that loyalty, fidelity & discipline are virtues quite unknown to him.'[55]

These views on Lloyd George's character can only have been reinforced by the contents of the third volume of the *War Memoirs*. Lloyd George begins by promising to tell the story without fear nor favour to anyone, for it was 'time the whole of the facts about both the Nivelle and Passchendaele affairs should be stated without variation or varnish to suit anybody'.[56] Some twenty pages later, however, he qualifies this by adding:

> I do not propose to give a detailed account of the difficult negotiations that led up to the final arrangements for the Nivelle offensive. That would occupy too much space. I have perused with arduous care the mass of correspondence, memoranda and minutes which constitute the full record of what took place before the operations of April, 1917, commenced, and I propose to summarise them so as to give a fair and impartial impression of what happened.[57]

Lloyd George summarises the events of the Calais conference to the point of obliteration. This becomes particularly clear when drafts in the Lloyd George papers are examined.

As I have already noted, the published account of the Calais conference amounts to very little; approximately one and a half pages on the transport issue, a bare half page on the command arrangements, a reprinting of the final text of the Calais agreement and then a fuller discussion of Haig's and Robertson's objections stemming from the adoption of the agreement. This is inadequate considering the importance of the conference in the relations between Lloyd George and the generals, its significance as Lloyd George's first attempt at securing 'unity of command', and indeed considering the effect of Nivelle's failure on Lloyd George's own position and on the subsequent course of operations on the Western Front.

Drafts provide a much fuller and more balanced account which is less gratuitously critical of Robertson and Haig. In particular that draft labelled 'Bible' provides a detailed account of the events leading up to the Nivelle offensive, including the Calais conference. Even this makes no reference to the contacts between Lloyd George and the French which led to Nivelle's *projet d'organisation*. There are, however, marginal notes which provide clear evidence that it was known that giving an account of the Calais conference in the *War Memoirs* was going to be awkward. Thus alongside a passage describing the War Cabinet meeting of 24 February (from which Robertson and Derby were excluded) and the Haig–Nivelle exchanges prior to Calais, there is a note headed 'IS THIS TRUE?':

> Both Civrieux in *L'Offensive de 1917* p. 40 and Rousset in *La Bataille de L'Aisne* p. 21 say that Mr LG had a talk on 14 or 15 February with the French Asst Military Attache, Bertier de Sauvigny and Col Hankey, in which he said that the War Committee would give secret orders to Haig to subordinate himself to Nivelle and would remove him if necessary if he did not comply. Hankey does not remember. IF NOT IT SHOULD BE CONTRADICTED.[58]

We now know, of course, that this is exactly what happened. It could not be contradicted. Then, just prior to the discussion of the Calais conference, another marginal note appears:

> NB There is no record of whether it was settled categorically at the War Cabinet to put Haig under Nivelle. This section needs very careful revision by Mr LG himself as to the decision to subordinate Haig to Nivelle which was the action of the Govt acting within its power. The record says nothing.[59]

Then, at the point when Nivelle is requested to put forward his proposals regarding command arrangements is scrawled in the margin: 'This is as recorded [in the official record of the conference] but it is suggested that Nivelle had a cut and dried scheme up his sleeve worked out with the knowledge of the British Government.'[60]

One can only assume, then, that the omission of this material from the *War Memoirs* was a deliberate decision by Lloyd George (as has already been noted he took great pride in the fact that he wrote his memoirs himself) in the interests of presenting his record in a more favourable light. It would have been, after all, damaging for a former Prime Minister to admit to seeking, in secret collusion with the French Government, the subordination of the Commander-in-Chief of the BEF, a Field Marshal in command of the largest army in British history, to a French general, junior in rank and inexperienced in high command, especially in the light of Nivelle's subsequent failure. Lloyd George, perhaps wisely, did not try, but consequently his account contributes little to our understanding of this crucial episode.

V

The British operation out of Arras, designed to be a preliminary to the French attack and to draw in the German reserves, was initially a brilliant success, at least by Western Front standards. On the British left, Vimy Ridge was quickly captured, and in the centre British troops advanced to a depth of three and a half miles. Only on the British right were the gains disappointing, and operations here soon degenerated into the familiar bloody assaults against strongly defended positions.[61] The French operation, begun on 16 April, captured ground and significant numbers of enemy guns, and did not do much worse than many other previous offensives on the Western Front. Yet the occupied ground and captured guns did not remotely match the expectations aroused by Nivelle's confident predictions of a breakthrough or rupture of the enemy lines. And despite his assurances that the offensive would be terminated if by the end of the first 48 hours this goal had not been achieved, and regardless of the politicians' resolution at Calais that they, rather than the generals, would call a halt to the offensive if he was not successful, operations continued, with diminishing returns and at horrendous cost in lives until early May. By this time, at last, the French Government had had enough, called a halt to the proceedings and replaced Nivelle with Pétain.

The Nivelle offensive, on its own, had little to distinguish it from other failed Western Front offensives. It was rather the *consequences* of its failure to the French army, and consequently to the conduct of operations on the Western Front for the remainder of the war, for which it has largely been remembered. The intense disappointment caused by the disparity between Nivelle's assurances and the reality on the ground led quickly to widespread unrest and mutiny in the French army. For many months after May 1917, the French were simply unable to mount serious offensive operations on the Western Front. Lloyd George, his policy of support for Nivelle in tatters, was then faced with Haig's long-held determination to commence operations in Flanders. Lloyd George's response to this will be examined in the next chapter. What concerns us here is his explanation in the *War Memoirs* for Nivelle's failure.

Perhaps the first point made by Lloyd George worthy of note is that the Nivelle offensive was not the unmitigated disaster that critics have suggested. He relates that a delegation from the French parliament viewed the battle and that some of its 'horrors' were witnessed by them and 'excited them to a wail of exaggeration as to the numbers of the fallen'.[62] On the contrary, he argues, quoting approvingly part of the report issued after the events by a French commission of inquiry, the losses were not unusually high:

> they did not exceed those which had occurred in previous great battles. The battle of April 1917, may be compared to the battle in Champagne in September 1915.... the losses in Champagne in September 1915 on a front of 40 kilometres were 125,000. Those on the Aisne during a similar period on a front of 80 kilometres did not exceed 117,000 men.[63]

As to the gains of the offensive, Lloyd George again happily quotes the inquiry report which stated that while the offensive was 'far from obtaining the results hoped for', it was, nonetheless, 'a real success for our armies'. How so? Preparations for the offensive, the commission argued, had forced the Germans to evacuate 2000 square kilometres of occupied territory when they withdrew to the Hindenburg Line. The attack itself had resulted in the capture of 55,000 prisoners, 800 guns and 1000 *mitrailleuses*. And by drawing off German reserves, it had also 'cleared the Italian Front in the Trentino, got rid of all danger from the Russian Front and gave the initiative in the operations into our hands'.[64]

Indeed, even among the British political elite and while the war continued, the conviction that Nivelle had not failed, and that he was removed more for political reasons than failure on the battlefield was not unknown. Former Liberal Chief Whip Lord Murray of Elibank wrote to Lloyd George in 1918 that the Nivelle offensive was stopped by French 'political interference and amateur strategy just when it was on the point of producing a great success'. Murray's discussions with Nivelle in Algeria (where he had been posted after his dismissal as Commander-in-Chief) and the findings of the French Committee of Inquiry led Murray to suggest that:

> If it had been allowed to go on, your policy would have brought the war to an end in 1917. Nivelle fell as Joffre had fallen, because Pétain intrigued against them so as to get the supreme command for himself. The finding of the French Court of Inquiry... completely exonerated Nivelle from the criticisms which were made against him in some quarters.... It was Nivelle's plan last year that enabled the French to clear 2,000 square kilometres of ground, to take 800 guns, 1000 machine guns and 55,000 prisoners... We were nearer winning the war under Nivelle that we have ever been, and he is, as Lord French said in a private letter the other day, which I have seen, 'one of the greatest soldiers that France has ever possessed'.

Murray urged Lloyd George to use his influence with Clemenceau to bring Nivelle back from exile.[65] It is fair to assume, however, that Murray wrote in ignorance of the full consequences of Nivelle's offensive, of the unrest and mutiny which followed in the wake of his failure to break the German line as he so confidently predicted he would.

Even given the offensive's 'successes', however, Lloyd George acknowledges in the *War Memoirs* the inescapable fact that after the Nivelle offensive, through sheer exhaustion and intense disappointment at the lack of results (given Nivelle's assurances), the French army was shaken by widespread disaffection and even mutiny, and ceased 'for a whole year to be an effective fighting machine'. Where did blame lie for this terrible outcome?[66]

The key element of Nivelle's plan, argues Lloyd George, and the fundamental difference between it and the Chantilly plan, was surprise. The 'principal feature' of Nivelle's attack was 'that it would mystify the enemy as to the place of the main attack, and thus take the Germans completely by surprise. It was a brilliant strategic conception.'[67] Why, then, did it fail? Because surprise, 'which was the essential condition of its success, totally disappeared'.[68]

The reasons for this were many. There were the repeated delays in launching the offensive. Nivelle had originally planned to be ready by the middle of February. At that time, Lloyd George argues, there would have been a good chance for a significant success. There were in all only eight German divisions in and behind the lines in the relevant sector, as opposed to the forty which were deployed in mid-April when operations finally began. The delay, Lloyd George charges, 'transformed the whole character of the operation'.[69]

One important factor in producing this delay was, of course, the question of command. The attempt to secure 'unity of command' was resisted 'so vigorously by Robertson and Haig that the delays caused by the time spent in allaying suspicions and adjusting differences destroyed the effectiveness of the plan'.[70] Haig's reluctance to take over more of the French line and his demand for more trains meant yet more delay.[71] Lloyd George, predictably, fails to acknowledge his own key role in fostering suspicions and differences between the French and British generals, and, even more so, between the British generals and their political masters. His attempt to force Haig to accept his subordination to Nivelle at Calais and after did more than any other action to poison the atmosphere between the British and French headquarters, and between GHQ and the War Office, on the one hand, and Downing Street on the other.

The two-month gap between the time the offensive was supposed to and when it did in fact begin also saw a major development, this time on the battlefield, which affected Nivelle's chances for success. The Germans decided to shorten their line and withdraw from the vulnerable salient between Arras and Soissons to the strongly fortified positions of the Hindenburg Line. Since the evacuated area was precisely that which Nivelle intended to attack, the development seemed to some to call into question the whole basis of Nivelle's plan. In addition, the Germans achieved complete surprise – Allied intelligence entirely failed to predict it.[72] For Lloyd George, whether Nivelle should have abandoned his plans was a question he professes himself unable to answer (one wonders whether he would have been so reticent if the general in question had been Haig rather than Nivelle), but he does suggest that it affected the Nivelle plan rather less than it would have the discarded Chantilly plan. What for Lloyd George was clear, however, was that the withdrawal gave the Germans three advantages. First, their new position on the Hindenburg Line was immensely stronger. Second, the Germans were now able to add several much needed divisions to their reserve. And lastly, it seriously, even fatally dislocated Allied plans.[73] Of course, if the dislocation was so serious, then surely it is perfectly clear that Nivelle *should* have changed his plans. Lloyd George fails to note this important contradiction in his account.

Indeed, it was the perception of several of Nivelle's subordinate army commanders that the withdrawal entirely removed the basis for his planned offensive. Together with the advent of Painlevé as Minister for War, who did not support Nivelle, this led to several high-level conferences which subjected Nivelle and his plans to considerable criticism. Nivelle's offer of resignation was rejected by the Government, however, and preparations proceeded.

The longer the delays, the more, inevitably, the enemy would discover regarding the Allies offensive plans, and the more he knew, the better prepared his defences would be. The Germans were assisted by the lax security surrounding the preparations. Nivelle's plans were widely discussed in political circles in London and Paris, and this lack of discretion was made worse, according to Lloyd George, by two separate incidents where highly secret documents fell into the hands of the Germans. The first occurred in mid-February, when a local German attack led to the capture of an 'order of the 2nd French Infantry Division, dated 29 January, clearly pointing to a great French offensive on the Aisne for April'.[74] The second incident was the capture of a French NCO on 4 April, who was in the possession of a document which gave the order of battle 'of the troops north of the Aisne and various corps object-ives'.[75] For Lloyd George, as this was the first time this had happened on either side, it was difficult to believe that these events were 'fortuitous'; due to the internecine conflict inside the French High Command over Nivelle and his plans, the 'facility with which the most revealing of these secret papers found their way across the line gives rise to a feeling of suspicion which it is difficult altogether to suppress'.[76] It hardly needs to be said that there is not a shred of evidence for such an accus-ation. It was indeed part of Nivelle's 'method' that plans for the upcoming offensive be disseminated to a much wider circle than normal within the relevant formations to instill greater confidence in those plans. In any event, according to Lloyd George, Nivelle's 'surprise had developed into the most elaborate and best advertised attack in the War'.

The key point in all of this, and what made the consequences of Nivelle's offensive such a disaster, is the disappointment caused by the stark contrast between the expectations aroused by Nivelle's appoint-ment and his assurances and the actual course of events on the ground. Not only did he utterly fail to reach even his initial objectives, but when this failure became clear to all but his most blind supporters (a rapidly dwindling band) the offensive continued at mounting cost, like other offensives before it. This was the point when the 'French army entered a state of collective disobedience' and practically ceased to exist as an offensive force.[77] This was Nivelle's great failure, and any number of references to the number of guns captured, or the delays caused by Haig's and Robertson's mischievous and damaging objections to 'unity of command' or difficulties in taking over more of the French line can not for long obscure this.

VI

Lloyd George's role in the Nivelle affair was important, even crucial. It was he, with all his authority as Prime Minister, who threw his unquali-fied support behind a French commander untested in high command in the face of doubts expressed by his own expert military advisers, other French generals and even, eventually, the French Government. It was Lloyd George who was the driving force behind the subordination of Haig to Nivelle, which had a lasting effect on the generals' attitude towards Lloyd George. The crucial role played by Lloyd George in these events would normally lead to a reasonable expectation that in the event of failure he would, in the *War Memoirs* at least, have accepted his share of the blame – he would certainly have claimed the credit if the result had been different. But it was not in Lloyd George's nature to admit to so massive a miscalculation. In his version he behaved correctly in the pursuit of unity of command and military success. He was, however, as Frances Stevenson noted in her diary, 'let down' by Nivelle and others.[78] To maintain this version, Lloyd George in the *War Memoirs* had to distort the facts and omit much important material, practices which he continued in his controversial treatment of the campaign which occupied most of the second half of 1917, Passchendaele.

7
'The Campaign of the Mud': Third Ypres 1917

I

Lloyd George's chapters on the Third Battle of Ypres[1] or Passchendaele are the centrepiece of his indictment of the British generals of the Great War, in particular Haig and Robertson.[2] Passchendaele for Lloyd George was one of the greatest follies of the war, and the importance he placed on these chapters may be gauged by the fact that they were published for greater impact as a separate pamphlet. They contain the most bitter and passionate denunciation of Haig and his strategy to be found in the *War Memoirs*.

Some critics and historians have taken the view that Lloyd George was unnecessarily vehement in these attacks on Haig. Hankey, normally supportive and complimentary of the *War Memoirs*, thought so and urged a thorough overhaul before publication.[3] David French has described the Passchendaele chapters as unrivalled as a piece of 'sustained invective' but not to be taken seriously as 'history'.[4] Thomas Jones wrote of them as the 'vitriolic outpourings of a prosecuting counsel in a criminal court, outpourings in which the most scornful, blistering epithets are hurled at the two defendants, Haig and Robertson'; while Robin Prior and Trevor Wilson tell of Lloyd George damning Haig 'up hill and down dale'.[5] It is these chapters which arguably have stuck most enduringly in the public mind, contributing in no small measure to the shaping of the public perception of Passchendaele (along with the Somme, though Lloyd George does not deal with the latter in any detail) as *the* worst battle of the Great War and distinguished chiefly by its mud, squalor, futility and Haig's mismanagement.

This chapter subjects Lloyd George's account to close scrutiny. I focus, in particular, on the origins of the offensive, the strategic debate as played out primarily in the War Policy Committee, to a lesser extent the War Cabinet, and then later in the 'battle of the memoirs' (and indeed historians), the charges of deception levelled at Haig and Robertson, the battle itself and its consequences. As I hope will become clear, the 'truth' about Passchendaele is much more complex than Lloyd George's biased, distorted and defensive account would have us believe.

II

Haig's desire to launch an offensive in Flanders with the object of clearing the Belgian coast, thereby eliminating the supposed threat to Allied shipping posed by German submarine bases in Belgian ports, has been noted in the previous chapter. In March 1917 Nivelle only secured Haig's cooperation by assuring him that, one way or another, the German threat from Flanders would be eliminated: a successful spring offensive would solve the problem anyway, and if it was unsuccessful, then there would be plenty of time to mount operations further north.[6] Haig thus agreed to Nivelle's plans with this understanding (although at least according to Lloyd George, Haig had no great confidence in Nivelle and continued his preparations in Flanders).

Here we come to the first of Lloyd George's allegations against Haig and Robertson. That, even while plans were being drawn up and preparations made for a great battle in Flanders, the two generals kept the War Cabinet in ignorance; it was only when the War Policy Committee convened in June 1917, he argues, and summoned Haig to present his plans for the campaign that the politicians were made aware of Haig's intentions. In short, without the War Cabinet's permission or knowledge preparations were underway for an attack in Flanders even while agreement was reached at Chantilly in November 1916, and then later with Nivelle, for major operations to be launched elsewhere on the Western Front.[7]

This, however, was not unusual, as Hankey pointed out to Lloyd George. He argued that based on precedent, there was some justification for Haig not formally submitting his plans until June. He did not think, for example, that the plans for Neuve Chappelle, Loos, the Somme or the Gallipoli landing were submitted well in advance. Indeed, Hankey went so far as to comment that he thought it one of the more 'admirable' features of Lloyd George's administration that it required plans to be formally submitted, for:

The supreme authority, which is responsible to Parliament and the public at home for the conduct of the War, has, in my opinion, an essential duty to make itself acquainted with the plans of all major operations ... Otherwise how is it to know what drain is to be made on the resources of the nation as a whole which it alone controls? There is no higher tribute that I could pay to your direction of the War than that you did insist on this. But, as I say above, Haig and Robertson had the bad precedent set by your predecessor under Lord Kitchener's influence and before we had really learned how to manage the central control.[8]

Lloyd George's charge, however, that the War Cabinet had no knowledge of Haig's projected operations in Flanders until June 1917 cannot be sustained. True, a formal plan was not submitted for the Government's consideration until June, but proposals for the recapture of the Belgian coast dated back to December 1914.[9] As the War Policy Committee report was to note, the Admiralty in particular had 'always insisted very strongly on the importance of clearing the enemy out of Ostend and Zeebrugge', and it supported in the War Council in January 1915 Sir John French's proposal for an operation with this purpose.[10] This and subsequent proposals had all been turned down as impractical. By November 1916, however, Asquith was sufficiently concerned by increasing German submarine successes against Allied shipping to write to Robertson (albeit in an unsigned letter) that the War Committee placed the utmost importance on an operation to clear the Belgian coast and asked him to report back to the War Committee (Hankey remembered that Asquith's letter to Robertson was prepared by him under 'personal direction from the Prime Minister'; he even had 'a note in my diary that I had to do it at a time when I was frightfully pressed').[11] At the Chantilly conference in November it was agreed that initial operations for 1917 would entail offensives on the Somme and Aisne sectors, after which the focus would switch to British operations in Flanders (again, according to Lloyd George, this was without the knowledge of the War Cabinet).[12] Robertson then wrote to Joffre indicating that the British Government wanted operations in Flanders designed to liberate these two ports included in the 'general plans of operation for next year'.[13] Robertson, according to Lloyd George, aware of impending political change, wanted to commit the incoming Cabinet to a Flanders operation.[14] But it is clear that Robertson was only acting on the instructions of the War Committee, of which Lloyd George himself, as Secretary of State for War, was a member.[15] Soon after the Chantilly conference confirmed the renewal of the offensive on the Somme in the coming year, Haig discussed the Belgian ports' problem with Robertson and Admirals Jackson, Oliver and Bacon in London, and they decided that a large-scale offensive to liberate Ostend and Zeebrugge was feasible and desirable.[16] And shortly after Haig secured the agreement of the French.[17]

Nivelle, however, insisted that any operations in Flanders would take second place behind the projected French offensive in the Aisne sector. As discussed in the previous chapter, Nivelle recast the Chantilly plans for 1917 and transferred the main role in the spring offensive to the French. Haig was persuaded to defer his Flanders operations by Nivelle's assurances that in the event his offensive failed Haig would still have time enough to attack in Flanders in fine weather. Haig remained convinced that it was

> essential that the Belgian coast be cleared this summer. I hope and believe that we shall be able to effect much more than that ... But it must be distinctly understood between us [he told Nivelle] that if I am not satisfied that this larger plan, as events develop, promises the degree of success necessary to clear the Belgian coast, then I not only cannot continue the battle but I will look to you to fulfill the undertaking you have given me verbally to relieve on the defensive front the troops I require for my northern offensive.[18]

Accordingly, the London Convention signed by Haig and Nivelle at Downing Street nine days later contained the proviso that:

> In case these operations [that is the British operation from Arras and the Nivelle offensive on the Aisne] do not achieve the success which is expected ... the battle will be broken off by agreement, in order to allow the British Armies to engage in other operations on a front further north, in co-operation with the Belgian Army and with the French Nieuport Group.[19]

The next day, according to Haig's diary, Lloyd George *himself* explained to the War Cabinet that the BEF 'must also agree to the date [for the offensive] which the French wished. ... by attacking early, the British would be able, if the attack by the French failed, to launch another attack later in the year at *some point further north*'.[20]

Two months later this was spelt out to the War Cabinet after a conference designed to clarify the terms of the Calais agreement. Haig explained the plan agreed by himself and Nivelle, and emphasised that the Allies must be ready to prepare for attacks elsewhere if Nivelle's operation failed. The BEF should:

1.   …continue making all preparations (as arranged) for attacks by 1st and 3rd Armies, keeping adequate reserves available either to support my 2nd Army (Ypres) or to exploit the success of our attacks near Arras.
2.   *If successful*, at Arras, exploit with all Reserves and the Cavalry.
3.   *If not successful*, prepare to launch attacks near Ypres to clear the Belgian Coast. All Cavalry will be required probably if this attack is successful.
The attack on Messines Ridge might be made in May, if desirable.[21]

The War Cabinet thus gave Haig its seal of approval to prepare for a Flanders offensive if Nivelle failed.[22] Present at this War Cabinet meeting were Lloyd George, Milner, Curzon, Henderson, Balfour, Derby, Robertson and Hankey. Those present could have been in no doubt of Haig's intentions.

To sum up therefore, the reasons why preparations and planning for an offensive in Flanders continued in the early months of 1917 were that, first, the Government in late 1916 had made it plain that it placed great importance on the clearance of the Belgian coast, and Robertson and Haig had acted accordingly. Second, in plans adopted at Chantilly, and, later under Nivelle, there was, arguably (depending on how much faith the British had in Nivelle's proposals) a more than reasonable chance of implementing a major operation in Flanders. Haig would have been irresponsible if he had not continued planning and preparation, although not to the extent, of course, of placing other operations in jeopardy. Why were these plans not laid before the War Cabinet? Here we may recall Hankey's advice of relevant previous practice of both Sir John French and Haig. But the War Cabinet, while quite aware that Haig preferred Flanders than Arras and the Aisne, was of course preoccupied with the details of the Nivelle offensive from January to April. It is not at all surprising that the Commander-in-Chief did not submit a finished plan (and it was not in its fully developed form until May in the wake of the failure of the Nivelle offensive) to the War Cabinet and that there was no detailed discussion of the plan at the War Cabinet level until June. In the *War Memoirs* on this issue, Lloyd George's intention is clear; it was to shift the responsibility for Third Ypres from the War Cabinet to the generals. In doing so, however, as John Terraine argues, he exposes that body – and himself – to charges of incompetence. If the Prime Minister and his War Cabinet knew nothing of the proposed attack until June, he was failing in his duties; if he and his colleagues knew, then the responsibility was theirs – above all, Lloyd George's.[23]

On 1 May, Lloyd George and his War Cabinet colleagues had to decide whether to continue to support Nivelle's offensive then still underway or try something else. It was clear that Nivelle had failed, and that as a result French policy was changing. Haig, in a letter read out to the meeting, concluded that whoever was in actual charge of the French army, Nivelle or the recently appointed Chief of Staff General Pétain, French policy was now 'defensive in character'.[24] General Smuts, the only military member of the War Cabinet, in a memorandum composed after his return from a visit to the front, was strongly for the continuation of the offensive, and if France declined to pursue an offensive policy, was strongly in favour of moving operations north: in an

endeavour to recover the northern coast of Belgium and drive the enemy from Zeebrugge and Ostend....something will have to be done to continue our offensive, and I see more advantages in an offensive intended to recover the Belgian coast and deprive the enemy of two advanced submarine bases, than in the present offensive.[25]

This advice would count for much in the decision of the War Cabinet; Smuts' views would also be important in Lloyd George's justification for permitting the Ypres offensive proceed.[26] The War Cabinet decided that the British delegation to the Allied meeting scheduled for 4 May in Paris, to be led by Lloyd George, would indeed urge the French to continue with offensive operations. If, however, it became clear that the French were inclined to adopt a defensive policy – carrying out limited attacks but conserving as far as possible the lives of its soldiers – then Britain should insist on regaining its freedom of action and demand that the French re-occupy those trenches so recently taken over by the BEF.[27]

Accordingly, when Allied leaders gathered in Paris on 4 May, Lloyd George pleased the generals by urging that offensive operations continue and that the generals must be free to decide on how and when to strike.[28] The 'time and place of the attacks, and the methods to be adopted, must be left to the military authorities responsible'; moreover:

the generals should keep their plans of execution to themselves, as when plans were communicated on paper to Ministers it was rare that the Ministers were the only people to know them. He added that he did not want to know the present plan of attack, nor the number of guns or divisions to be engaged; for it was essential to keep such details secret.[29]

The Allies must, he argued, go on hitting and hitting until the Germans 'crack', and he emphasised that he expected the French to fight vigorously. Lloyd George was here attempting to instil some more fight and spirit into the French, who were now inclined to limit operations on the Western Front.[30] Of course, the French had good reason for this. The French army had suffered appalling casualties since the outbreak of war; the army and nation were exhausted and demoralised, and the profound disappointment caused by the failure of the latest offensive would quickly lead to mutiny in the coming weeks, though the British War Cabinet would never be informed of the full extent of this.[31] Lloyd George, in the wake of the Nivelle fiasco, had little option other than to support the generals and renewed attacks on the Western Front.

The *War Memoirs* fail conspicuously to address the inconsistency between Lloyd George's performance at the Paris conference and his attacks on Haig for launching an offensive in Flanders. From one who only six months before had been urging the politicians to seize control of strategy from the generals, the transformation was startling. In the final analysis, as David French has concluded, Lloyd George 'only had himself to blame [for Passchendaele], for he accepted [indeed actively promoted] the conference's conclusion that the politicians should leave it to their military advisers to determine how and when these offensives were to be mounted'.[32] Lloyd George was, in effect, abdicating all responsibility for the forthcoming operations (although, as we have seen, he and the War Cabinet were aware of Haig's intentions). Having let his generals 'off the leash', it was dishonest to later reproach them for taking him at his word.

III

Haig's plans for the Flanders offensive were presented to and considered at the meetings of a War Policy Committee of the War Cabinet convened in June 1917. It will be useful at this point to pause in our consideration of Lloyd George's account and establish in broad outline just what Haig was intending to accomplish in Flanders.

The operation would consist of two distinct phases. The first would be an attack, by Plumer's Second Army, on the Messines Ridge south of Ypres, 'possession of which will be of considerable value subsequently whether for offensive or defensive purposes', as Haig put it.[33] If the Germans retained control of this high ground, they 'could watch every detail of any preparations the British might make for an offensive eastwards between Ypres and the Belgian coast'.[34] Its capture was therefore deemed essential.

There would then be an interval of several weeks before the second, decisive phase began, which Haig stated would only be launched if the 'situation is sufficiently favourable when the time for it [came]'.[35] The initial objective was the high ground surrounding the Ypres salient, the Pilckem, Passchendaele and Klerken ridges. The attack would then proceed north-east to Roulers and Thourout, and then swing north towards the coast. Success in this stage would trigger two further operations. Forces around Nieuport would attack German positions at Middlekirk, while a specially trained amphibious force would attack from the sea behind enemy lines. These operations would converge on the coastal area between Ostend and Zeebrugge; these strategic ports would be liberated and German forces driven out of Belgium.[36]

Haig's plan was ambitious. In the words of Prior and Wilson, Haig was clearly aiming for a 'great strategic victory'.[37] Mindful of the politicians' anxiety regarding great offensives and high casualties, however, Haig's language was cautious. It was to be a process of 'wearing out' the enemy rather than an attempt at breakthrough, and, he wrote, it could be stopped at any stage if was not going well:

> My plans and preparations are being made to advance by stages so arranged that, while each stage will give a definite and useful result, it will be possible for me to discontinue the advance if and when it appears that the means at my disposal are insufficient to justify a further effort.[38]

In reality, the plan envisaged an advance of greater magnitude than had been achieved by either side since the Western Front stabilised in late 1914. Lloyd George notes that it envisaged not just the capture of Passchendaele, which in the event would be the point of furthest advance before the offensive was terminated in November, but also of Bruges and even greater developments; references to 'masses of cavalry' implied, he argues, a 'beaten foe in full and disordered retreat. Where would that retreat end?'[39]

In his memoranda at the time, Haig's ambitions are certainly clear. On 12 June he wrote that further defeats for the Germans 'may have unexpectedly great results, which may come with unexpected suddenness'. Concentration of all resources in the west would make 'final victory more assured and which may even bring it within reach this year', and with 'sufficient force', provided Germany did not transfer large numbers of troops from Russia to the West (and, he argued, a success in the West would encourage greater Russian efforts in the East thereby keeping German troops from being thus transferred), it was 'probable that the Belgian coast could be cleared this summer. The defeats inflicted on the German troops entailed in doing so might quite possibly lead to their collapse.'[40]

Five days later in a further memorandum Haig argued that even a partial success would be useful, but it is obvious that he hoped for significant, even decisive results. A limited advance along the Belgian coast would render Ostend 'useless' to the German navy; but an advance to within artillery range of the Roulers-Thourout railway would severely disrupt and restrict the enemy's communications; while further advance in the direction of Bruges 'would most probably induce the evacuation of Zeebrugge and the whole coast line'. With the British front extended to the Dutch frontier the Dutch might even decide to join the Allies, which would enable the British to 'turn Antwerp and the German lines in Belgium completely, and to sever the German Lines of Communication through Liege'. Germany would then, he argued, have the unenviable choice between 'accepting terms', carrying out a potentially 'disastrous' retreat, or attempt to 'forestall the danger by violating Dutch territory'. Where indeed might the German retreat end?[41]

Haig's optimism was fuelled by the success of Plumer's Second Army in its attack on the Messines-Wytschaete Ridge. Assisted by the explosion of 19 mines (another two failed to explode) of almost a million pounds of explosive, and a massive artillery bombardment from a unprecedented number of guns on a relatively narrow front, British troops quickly gained their objectives with relatively few casualties. John Terraine argues that Lloyd George 'had not been impressed, even by the lustre of Messines'; the *War Memoirs*, however, tell a different story.[42] Here Lloyd George in particular praises Plumer's Chief of Staff Charles Harington for his meticulous staff work; 'nothing was left to chance' all the 'real' objectives were taken, and only light casualties incurred. Had Harington been at GHQ during Third Ypres, the latter 'would never have become one of the blackest horrors of history'.[43]

What did the success of Messines mean for the prospects of the main offensive to begin seven weeks later? While it was certainly an 'encouraging prelude',[44] the two operations were profoundly different in character, and it is reasonable to suggest that in one respect at least Messines was a 'one-off'. Much of the success on the first day (when all of Plumer's original objectives were taken) was due to the surprise and devastation caused by the detonation of the mines. This could not be repeated. Moreover, once the mines had exploded, the British had an unprecedented intensity in artillery fire-power at their disposal, and lessons learnt from previous operations meant that it was used more scientifically and effectively than ever before. But possibly the most important factor leading to success was that from the start Messines was a limited operation. Plumer's original goal was an advance of just 1500 yards. Haig later increased this to 3,000–4,000 yards to be achieved on the first day, and most casualties were incurred in subsequent days in advancing the additional distance. In the main operation, however, Haig was envisaging extending the British line to the *Dutch border*, clearing the Belgian coast and perhaps even forcing Germany *to accept terms*. These were two very different operations, and success in the first did nothing to guarantee success in the second.[45]

IV

The War Policy Committee was established on 8 June 1917 with Lloyd George in the chair, Curzon, Milner and General Smuts as members, Hankey as secretary and Bonar Law usually attending. It was charged by the War Cabinet with investigating the 'facts of the Naval, Military and Political situations' and held its first session on 11 June.[46] Early meetings were devoted to discussion of the broad strategic situation, particularly in regard to problems in shipping, the effect of American participation in the war, the possibility of renewed offensive operations on the Italian Front, and, most importantly for the prospects of Haig's proposed offensive, the state of the French army.

It was not until 19 June that Haig, buoyed no doubt by the triumph at Messines, made his first appearance before the committee and its real business began. Equipped with a large raised map Haig explained in detail his plan for the attack. Lloyd George recalls that at the climax of his presentation Haig

> spread on a table or desk a large map and made a dramatic use of both his hands to demonstrate how he proposed to sweep up the enemy – first the right hand brushing along the surface irresistibly, and then came the left, his outer finger touching the German frontier with the nail across.[47]

The War Policy Committee, Lloyd George writes, was then

> taken up into the aerial tower built during the last six months or more by the industry and imagination of GHQ to view this thrilling prospect. It is not surprising that some of us were so captivated by

the splendour of the landscape opened out to our vision that their critical faculties were overwhelmed. Mr Bonar Law, Lord Milner and I still remained sceptical.[48]

In an effort to overcome this scepticism, Haig and Robertson were moderate and cautious in their language, and it is this which strikes the reader of the minutes of the committee, rather than any Nivelle-like vision of breakthrough and victory.[49] Here Lloyd George was justified in arguing that Haig and Robertson were not in fact being entirely straightforward with the Committee. Haig sought to portray his plan as a process of wearing down the enemy through deliberate phases. He assured the Committee that while the plan promised success, no 'operation of war was a certainty. He pointed out that it was *only the beginning* of a very great strategical operation',[50] and that he had 'no intentions of entering into a tremendous offensive involving heavy losses. His plan was aggressive without committing us too far.'[51] Robertson loyally supported Haig, assuring the Committee that the operation would be conducted methodically and the situation would be carefully considered 'before making each fresh bound'.[52] It was argued, in short, that this would not be another costly attempt to break the enemy's front. It would not be another Somme. Lloyd George notes that such assurances 'had a considerable influence on the Committee'.[53] As we have seen, however, Haig was indeed envisaging a 'tremendous offensive' which was intended to bring great strategic results.

A great offensive in Flanders was not the only option open to the Committee. As Lloyd George reminded its members, there were alternatives. The first was to adopt what he called 'Pétain tactics':

a punch here and there and a process of wearing down the enemy. We had lots of ammunition and could punish the enemy heavily. Having in view the privations of the Germans, the prospect of a big reinforcement from America and of a regeneration of the Russian Army, the enemy, feeling that time was against him, might be considerably damaged by such a course.[54]

Indeed, he might have referred at this point to two, recent and successful operations which had demonstrated what could be achieved by these methods. Vimy Ridge and Messines had shown that careful preparation, thorough planning, superiority in artillery and surprise could result in solid gains. But Lloyd George passed quickly over this option. The man who just under a year before had called for the war to be fought to a 'knock-out' was not likely to be attracted to a strategy which, while economical with lives, appeared to result in only modest gains and did not promise a decisive victory; they would not, he thought, end the war.[55] Waiting for the Americans did not appeal; and moreover, there would be no 'regeneration' of the Russian army.[56]

Lloyd George's preferred option was a great offensive against Austria on the Italian Front. Here we are on familiar territory, for he had argued for just such an operation at the Rome conference in January, only to have it rejected in favour of the disastrous Nivelle offensive. His arguments in favour were not surprisingly much the same as on that earlier occasion. Austria was the weak link in the enemy alliance; its soldiers demoralised, its economy crumbling and its government eager for peace.[57] If Italy, with Allied assistance mainly in the form of artillery and ammunition, could capture the Trentino and Trieste, all the indications were that the Imperial Government would sue for peace. This would be the first step towards isolating Germany. Moreover, he told the Committee,

> What does it matter whether we fight Germans in the north of France or in Italy? The only difference would be that if we fought them in France we should be doing it at the expense of our own troops, whereas in Italy we can use the enormous reserves of the Italians.[58]

Italian troops would be fighting and dying, not British.[59]

This, then, was the choice. Between an ambitious offensive in Flanders designed to clear the Belgian coast and, according to Haig, quite possibly lead to Germany being forced to accept 'terms', or an offensive carried out by Italian troops but reinforced by British artillery and shells with the object of knocking Austria out of the war. The former carried much greater risk, as it meant British casualties and after the Somme and Arras it was increasingly coming home to politicians that manpower was not inexhaustable. The latter option was clearly less costly – for the British – but was of course dependent upon the Italians' willingness to risk German retaliation, in the absence of any major operation distracting the Germans on the Western Front (or on the Eastern Front for that matter: the last Russian offensive of the war – the 'Kerensky offensive' – would quickly grind to a halt). The Central Powers' 'weak' point, that is Austria, had, in other words, the potential to turn into a decidedly 'strong' point with German help.

Haig and Robertson, predictably, opposed Lloyd George's proposal vigorously. They disagreed with Lloyd George's estimate of Austrian morale, warned that Germany would support Austria, and pointed out that the Central Powers enjoyed the advantages of interior lines. More-over, they argued that it had always been 'accepted as the most effective form of war to attack and destroy the enemy's strongest forces as soon as possible if there is a reasonable prospect of success'. In their view, there were 'small prospects of success against Austria [which would be] supported in all probability by German troops'. On the other hand, there was 'a reasonable chance of success in Belgium, which may have greater results than even a bigger success against Austria, and which at least may be expected to open the way for greater results subsequently'.[60]

Additional arguments in favour of proceeding with the Flanders plan were provided by the Admiralty. Jellicoe, First Sea Lord, wrote that if the Germans remained in possession of Ostend and Zeebrugge the British position at the eastern end of the Channel 'would [become] almost untenable'. Together with Bruges, the two ports provided harbours which could accommodate large numbers of destroyers which could 'with great ease raid the Straits of Dover so effectually as to make almost a clean sweep of our forces'. Unless the Allies were able to clear the Belgian coast by next winter, Britain would have to 'increase very largely' the Dover force, at the expense of the Grand Fleet or from those naval forces engaged in anti-submarine work. Occupation of the Belgian coast also greatly assisted the Germans in their air raids on British targets. Turning the Germans out of northern Belgium was an 'absolute necessity' and every day's delay increased the danger.[61]

When called before the Committee Jellicoe was even more alarmist. He dropped a 'bombshell' by insisting that:

> if we did not clear the Germans out of Zeebrugge before this winter we should have great difficulty in ever getting them out of it. The reason he gave for this was that he felt it to be improbable that we could go on with the war next year for lack of shipping.[62]

According to Lloyd George, he at once challenged Jellicoe's 'startling and reckless declaration' indignantly.[63] Haig noted that a 'full enquiry is to be held as to the real facts on which the opinion of the naval authorities is based. No one present shared Jellicoe's views, and all seemed satisfied that the food reserves in Great Britain are adequate.'[64] In truth, this was not the first time that Jellicoe had expressed such pessimistic views; on 26 April, for example, Robertson wrote to Haig commenting on the situation at sea: 'Jellicoe almost daily pronounces it to be hopeless.'[65] Despite some historians' assertion that Jellicoe's state-ment marked a turning point in the Committee's deliberations, there is little evidence that it had any significant influence on the decision-making process.[66] And, of course, Jellicoe was patently wrong. Even if the ports were captured, U-boats and destroyers could be moved to other bases, and in any event they remained in German hands until the end of the war.[67]

On 21 June at the tenth meeting of the War Policy Committee, Lloyd George attempted a summing up of his case against Haig and Robertson.[68] In the *War Memoirs* he notes that some of his colleagues on the Committee thought that Haig's plan had a reasonable chance of success, that it was worth trying. In this respect, he argues, the assurances from Haig and Robertson that the offensive would be abandoned if it became apparent that it was not likely to succeed carried great weight. Lloyd George himself, however, together with, as he claims, the majority of the Committee members, were opposed to the offensive – he writes in the *War Memoirs* that he remained convinced that Haig was 'plunging into a perilous hazard' – but did not think they could impose a veto 'without a test being made of the possibilities of such an attack'.[69]

Accordingly, at the outset of his summation, Lloyd George in effect handed the decision over to the generals:

His view was that the responsibility for advising in regard to military operations must remain with the military advisers... he considered it would be too gross a responsibility for the War Policy Committee to take the strategy of the War out of the hands of their military advisers. This made it the more important that the military advisers of the Government should carefully weigh his misgivings in regard to the advice they had tendered. If after hearing his views, and after taking the time to consider them they still adhered to their previous opinion, then the responsibility for their advice must rest with them.[70]

Then followed his arguments against a major effort in Flanders which, indeed, add up to such a powerful case that the decision to let Haig proceed is quite reprehensible.

His most telling argument which ought to have been enough to damn the enterprise concerned the prospects of success. Haig and Robertson had maintained that the most effective way of prosecuting the war was to engage the enemy's strongest forces as long as there was a 'reasonable prospect of success'. Lloyd George noted in his summing up that he had 'never known an offensive to be undertaken without sure predictions of success', and asked why should a greater success be anticipated in Flanders than in the Battle of the Somme where an advance of only five or six miles was accomplished, and that at enormous cost. At that time, he recalled, the Government's 'military advisers were just as sanguine as they were now'.[71] Haig and Robertson were contemplating an advance in Flanders of 12–15 miles before the clearing of the coast could begin. This was, as noted earlier, a greater advance than either side had achieved throughout the war. Lloyd George argued, reasonably, that to achieve a success on such a scale, one of the following conditions was necessary:

1. An overwhelming force of men and guns
2. That the enemy should be attacked so strongly elsewhere that his reserves would be drawn off
3. That the enemy's *moral[e]* should be so broken that he could no longer put up a fight.[72]

He concluded that none of these conditions obtained at that time. The Allies did possess a slight superiority in numbers of troops, and a larger superiority in guns, though not overwhelming.[73] The French, racked by unrest and mutiny, were in no position to mount a large-scale attack elsewhere on the Western Front.[74] And despite Haig's intelligence reports indicating that German morale was about to crack, it held by and large until the end of the war. The essential point is, however, that nothing Haig and Robertson said in the Committee shook Lloyd George's view that the necessary conditions for a successful offensive did not exist. Thus on 6 July, well after Haig had returned to France having been authorised to continue his preparations, Lloyd George told his colleagues it would be better if two of them pressed the Flanders offensive on the French as *he did not believe in the plan*, and they would put it with greater force'.[75] His continuing aversion to a Flanders operation is also reflected in the restrictions the Government placed upon Haig. Lloyd George, despite his conviction that the offensive would fail, still refused to impose a veto and laid the responsibility for deciding strategy on the military.

The final report of the War Policy Committee sanctioned Haig's offensive, but with rather severe qualifications. This was, on paper at least, no open-ended authorisation for Haig to proceed as he thought fit. The Committee stated that the offensive should

> On no account be allowed to drift into protracted, costly, and indecisive operations as occurred in the offensive on the Somme in 1916, as the

effect of this might be disastrous on public opinion.... The Committee, therefore, attach the utmost importance to a frequent review of the results of the operations undertaken in Flanders from the point of view of the objectives actually achieved and likely to be achieved, and the comparative losses of the enemy and ourselves. If a degree of success commensurate with the losses is not achieved the offensive should be dropped.[76]

In the latter case, it was recommended that measures be taken to effect a rapid transfer of heavy guns to the Italian Front for an offensive against Austria.

The conditions placed upon Haig present two problems. The first is that the wording is somewhat vague and it is unclear who was to determine the appropriate success/loss ratio. The second is that it was not meant to be Haig. If it was to be the War Cabinet, this presupposes a close scrutiny of developments in Flanders, and accurate information. In the event, the political will was lacking for the former, and according to Lloyd George at least, the latter was largely kept from the War Cabinet.

<h1 style="text-align:center">V</h1>

One of the main factors, Lloyd George argues, in the War Policy Committee's decision to allow the Flanders offensive to proceed, was the deliberate withholding of information from the Committee by Haig and Robertson, information that most probably would have led to a quite different decision by the War Policy Committee. His motive for arguing thus is soon apparent: to further cement the proposition that the responsibility for what Lloyd George considered the 'biggest disaster of the war' lay squarely with the generals.[77] Thus, for example, Lloyd George accuses Haig and Robertson of concealing the true extent of the French mutinies and persuading the War Policy Committee that French support for the Flanders operation would be substantial. They also concealed from the Committee that the leading French generals were against the Flanders offensive; and misled the Committee as to the state of the ground and likely weather conditions. Lloyd George also alleges that the two army commanders Gough and Plumer were against the offensive and had appealed to Haig to call a halt.

We have already touched upon the French attitude to Haig's proposed offensive. In early May, it will be recalled, Lloyd George and his colleagues – including Robertson – had argued in Paris that the French should continue their offensive operations with all the means at their disposal, for the British could not hope to achieve a decisive result on their own. But the mutinies threw French support into doubt. In the War Policy Committee there were revelations of unrest and mutinies in the French army, although the true scale was not revealed. Rather than only the two regiments in which the Committee was informed mutinies had occurred, in late May and early June some 40,000 men were involved in nearly 50 divisions, or nearly half the French army. In putting down the disturbances, the French military authorities sentenced over 600 men to death, and in 75 cases the sentence was carried out.[78] The unrest was on a large scale. Does the fact that the War Policy Committee heard little of this indicate deliberate deception on the part of the British generals? Partly. The French themselves went to great lengths to keep the affair secret. It does appear, however, that some later reports, which revealed something of the true scale of the mutinies, were withheld from the Committee, so to that extent Lloyd George's accusation is warranted.[79] What perhaps impressed the Committee more than the limited information available regarding the French army were the reports describing the general demoralisation among the civilian population in France, and the political dangers this held.[80]

The mutinies – even the little information that was disclosed to the Committee – and the advent of a new leadership in the person of Pétain who stood for a more defensive policy on the Western Front, had seemed to Lloyd George to preclude the possibility of a really serious French attack to support the British offensive in Flanders. Haig and Robertson, however, both argued that the French would use all their available forces in support of Haig; Robertson later informed the Committee that the French would launch an attack with 18 to 20 divisions.[81] In the event, however, the French contribution would be limited to the deployment of the First Army under General Anthoine on Gough's left (under British command for the duration of the offensive), and the generals' assurances regarding the French effort had little effect on the Committee's report:

> That we cannot rely upon the French Army to take the offensive on a scale calculated to draw the German reserves to the French front in a strength commensurate with the numerical strength of the French army. The British army, if it takes the offensive, must, therefore, expect to encounter the bulk of the German reserves.[82]

It would appear, then, that the charge that Haig and Robertson misled the Committee regarding the scale of French support has no foundation. Moreover, by this stage Haig was satisfied that large-scale French cooperation was not essential to his plan. Haig was confident that the British could inflict a great defeat upon the Germans, even win the war, without French help. As he wrote to Robertson on 28 May, there was 'little doubt . . . that victory on the Western Front means victory everywhere and a lasting peace. And I have no further doubt that the British Army in France is capable of doing it, given adequate *drafts and guns*.'[83]

Haig's confidence in the BEF was fortunate (although not of course for the hundreds of thousands of men who were killed, wounded or went missing during the offensive), for there is some evidence that the French wanted little to do with such an ambitious operation. Far from pleading with Haig to undertake Third Ypres as a means of saving the French Army from collapse, leading French generals thought it was bound to fail. Thus General Sir Henry Wilson wrote in his diary on 20 May of a conversation with Pétain: 'He told me that, in his opinion, Haig's attack towards Ostend was certain to fail, and that his effort to disengage Ostend and Zeebrugge was a hopeless one.'[84] Foch was even more outspoken. He 'wanted to know who it was who wanted Haig to go on "a duck's march through the inundations to Ostend and Zeebrugge". He thinks the whole thing futile, fantastic and dangerous...Foch is entirely opposed to this enterprise, Jellicoe notwithstanding.'[85] These views were not divulged to the War Policy Committee.

Other charges made by Lloyd George against Haig and Robertson are unrelated to the role the French would play in the offensive. One of the more enduring argues that it was not disclosed to the War Policy Committee that the chosen battlefield was a reclaimed 'swamp', and that a bombardment on the scale proposed was certain to destroy its elaborate drainage systems and transform it into a sea of mud. Rain would make this so much worse. And rain would come. A GHQ investigation of the meteorological records for the area, Lloyd George claims, revealed that the 'weather broke early in August with the regularity of the Indian monsoon'.[86] Lloyd George includes a table of statistics showing alarmingly high rainfall in Flanders for 1914–17 in July, August and September.[87] To Lloyd George, the statistics showed 'what a reckless gamble it was to risk the life of the British Army on the chance of a rainless autumn on the Flemish coast'.[88]

The Flanders battleground, however, was not a 'reclaimed swamp'. The soil was not, to be sure, ideal for a major campaign in which artillery was dominant.[89] But if the weather had been reasonably dry, as Haig, based on weather records for previous years, could reasonably look forward to, then conditions would not have been quite so bad. It is clear that the advice given to Haig was not that the rainfall in July–October was regularly high, that it broke with the regularity of an 'Indian monsoon', and that he decided to proceed even though fully aware that heavy rainfall was likely to turn the battleground into an impassable swamp.[90] The head of GHQ's meteorological section was a noted London meteorologist, Ernest Gold, who by 1918 had risen to the rank of Lieutenant-Colonel. In 1958 Gold wrote a letter to the *Spectator* which should have settled the issue once and for all. He stated that the rainfall for August 1917 'was more than double the average; it was over five times the amount for the same period in 1915 and 1916'. He goes on to describe intelligence chief John Charteris' statement that the weather broke in early August with the regularity of an Indian monsoon as 'so contrary to recorded facts that, to a meteorologist, it seems too ridiculous to need formal refutation'.[91] Gold's claims have been supported by recent research which indicate that it could have been reasonably expected that the autumn months in Flanders *would be relatively dry*. Analysis of weather records for the years 1897–1916 revealed that the distinct trend was towards *dry* autumns. Similarly, it was found that in the 30 years to 1916, more Septembers and Octobers were anticyclonic (which suggests 'quiet and settled' weather) rather than cyclonic; that there were as many anticyclonic as cyclonic Augusts; and that based on analysis of the previous 30 years '*there is no reason* to suggest that the weather broke early in the month [i.e. August] with any regularity'. During the summers preceding 1917, 'August days were *more often dry* than wet'.[92] There is, then, no basis whatever for Lloyd George's charge that Haig concealed the state of the ground and the likely effect of the expected bad weather on the battleground. Haig, based on the reports from his meteorologist, could reasonably look forward to dry, settled conditions. That the rainfall in August and October was so heavy, turning the ground into a quagmire in which men drowned, was unlucky. Whether, by mid or late October, after heavy rains Haig should have terminated operations is a good question (to which I shall return). But there should be no controversy about his decision to launch the offensive in regard to the question of the weather.[93]

We have seen, then, that there are elements of truth in some of Lloyd George's allegations against Haig and Robertson. There was something of a cover-up of the extent of the French mutinies, and there is evidence that the French military leadership was less than enthusiastic regarding the prospects for an offensive in Flanders. Moreover there was no discussion of the suitability of the terrain in Flanders for a large-scale offensive. This last point, coupled with the advent of heavy rain throughout August, October and November, would become the worst difficulty faced by the BEF in achieving their objectives. Charteris wrote accurately as early as 4 August that the weather had destroyed any prospect for success.[94]

VI

Lloyd George sums up the 'achievements' of the Third Battle of Ypres by listing what Haig had *not* achieved:

> We had not cleared the Flemish coast. We had not broken through the enemy's defences into open country. The cavalry charge had not come off. Not a single cavalry horse had wetted his hooves in the slush.... The Passchendaele-Staden Ridge was only the first stage [of the projected advance]...the ridge...was 18 miles in length. After over four months terrible fighting, resulting in casualties which reached nearly 400,000... we had only captured five miles of the ridge...

Compared with the Nivelle offensive 'we took fewer prisoners, we captured fewer guns (about one-fourth)...and that with nearly three times the casualties we sustained in that operation, which was always alluded to by the Staff as a "failure" '.[95]

Indeed, by almost any criteria, the series of operations which ended on 10 November and has gone down in history as the Third Battle of Ypres must be considered to have failed.[96] The Belgian coast remained out of reach; indeed, the British advance at the furthest point was a mere 10,000 yards and such ground that had been captured, Haig realised, would be extremely difficult to defend in the face of a German attack.[97]

The principle reason for the catastrophe, Lloyd George argues, was Haig himself. First, of course, there was his obsession with Flanders, his disregard of the unsuitable ground and ominous weather reports, and his hugely ambitious plan. But once the offensive was under way, he remained ignorant of the conditions of the battlefield;[98] he placed too much trust in the optimistic reports of his staff – in particular Charteris, the intelligence chief, and Kiggell, Chief of the General Staff;[99] he was unwilling to admit that his plans were unrealistic and that he was asking too much of his men;[100] and he refused to listen to his army commanders, Plumer and Gough, when they advised that there was no hope of his goals being reached and that he should call a halt to the offensive.[101] Haig 'completely lost his balance'; far from calling a halt, he continued to contemplate the use of 'tanks and even cavalry' in the totally inappropriate conditions of the Flanders battlefield where persistent rain turned the battlefield into a quagmire.[102]

It is clear, however, that Haig was well aware of the state of the ground. In his diary, for example, he noted on 1 August: 'A terrible day of rain. The ground is like a bog in this low-lying country.'[103] And on 13 October, he noted of a meeting with his Army commanders that they all 'agreed that mud and the bad weather prevented troops from getting on yesterday', and he was told that the ground was so soft in places that 'light engines on the 60 cm. railways [were] sunk half-way up the boilers in the mud. The track has completely disappeared.'[104] Of the August operations he wrote:

> For four days, the rain continued without cessation, and for several days afterwards the weather remained stormy and unsettled. The low-lying, clayey soil, torn by shells and sodden by rain, turned to a succession of vast muddy pools. The valleys of the choked and over-flowing streams were speedily transformed into long stretches of bog, impassable except by a few well-defined tracks, which became marks for the enemy's artillery. To leave these tracks was to risk death by drowning, and in the course of the subsequent fighting on several occasions both men and pack animals were lost in this way. In these conditions operations of any magnitude became impossible, and the resumption of our offensive was necessarily postponed until a period of fine weather should allow the ground to recover... *the month closed as the wettest August that had been known for many years.*[105]

It was to become even worse in October and November. Of course, the fact that Haig knew of the terrible battlefield conditions in such detail makes it all the more reprehensible that it was decided in October and November to continue the offensive.

While Haig was well aware of the conditions on the battlefield, his knowledge of conditions on the 'other side of the hill' was not of the same quality. Brigadier-General John Charteris was notorious for supplying Haig with relentlessly optimistic reports on the state of German morale, their lack of reserves and the deterioration of conditions inside Germany.[106] This intelligence was a major factor in his advice to the War Policy Committee (although the Committee was not entirely convinced of the accuracy of such intelligence[107]) and in his determination to continue with the offensive in October and November.[108] But the crucial point here is that Charteris was only telling Haig what in fact he wanted to hear. On occasions Haig's optimism and confidence that the German army was on the verge of breaking went beyond even Charteris' reports.[109] Haig did not need Charteris to be unrealistically optimistic. The reality, however, was that despite the suffering caused by the awful conditions the German army was no nearer breaking point than the British, easily demonstrated by its stout resistance to British attacks and the mounting of local counter-attacks which meant that the British achieved but a fraction of their objectives.[110]

What of the allegations that Haig's two Army commanders, Generals Gough and Plumer, advised him to call a halt to the campaign? This charge has little foundation. Both Gough and Plumer supported Haig throughout the entire campaign. Harington, Plumer's wartime Chief of Staff, was incensed at Lloyd George's accusation that Plumer was opposed to the offensive. It was 'inconceivable' that Plumer's attitude was anything but 'utter loyalty' and that he was determined to 'carry out his Chief's orders to capture Passchendaele'; even after the victory at Broodseinde, 'he never gave a thought to stopping and turning back'.[111] In a private letter Harington was unequivocal:

I am not going to let LG get away with his statement that my Chief opposed Haig over Passchendaele. It is a d——d lie & must not be allowed to stand. I am only surprised that Gough has allowed himself to be used as Chief witness against his old Chief. I'm not going to have my old Chief used as a 2nd witness. Plumer had only one object & that was to get Passchendaele in accordance with Haig's orders.[112]

Harington wrote that his job in writing Plumer's biography 'begins and ends with clearing Plumer from LG's assertions that he disagreed with Haig over Passchendaele as he certainly did not'.[113] Charles á Court Repington as late as the middle of October 1917 found Plumer 'heart and soul' for the Flanders offensive;[114] while just prior to the Poelcappelle battle Harington told war correspondents that he fully supported continuing operations and that soon the cavalry would get through. As Prior and Wilson note, it is 'difficult to believe' that Harington spoke in this vein 'without authorization from Plumer'.[115]

As for Gough, in his memoirs he wrote that by 16 August after almost two weeks of heavy rain he told Haig that 'tactical success was no longer possible' and advised him to close the offensive down.[116] But according to Lord Esher, who saw him on 19 August, he fully supported Haig in continuing the offensive:

> Gough, whom I had a long talk with this afternoon ... is of the same opinion [as Haig] as regards the certainty of capturing all our objectives, but puts the final date next spring. He thinks the delay due to bad weather has upset the timetable too far to enable the complete objectives to be won this autumn.[117]

It is reasonable to assume that Gough, in claiming he advised closing Third Ypres down, was above all concerned with his reputation, which had taken such a battering after he was sacked as commander of the Fifth Army in March 1918. It would perhaps go some way towards a rehabilitation if it became public that he had recommended the termination of Haig's most notorious offensive. Moreover, his sacking inevitably affected his view of Haig. Thus in discussing the developments immediately before the German attack of March 1918, when it was arranged that the BEF (that is, Gough's Fifth Army) take over more of the line from the French, Gough noted Haig's disapproval and insistence that he would 'not be responsible for securing the extended front against all attack'. Whether, Gough continued:

> Haig's maintenance of this attitude in face of the almost annihilation of a British Army which had served him well in many battles can be called 'a fit of sulks' is a question, or whether the abandonment of the Fifth Army in face of the rather miserable efforts of the French to support it and deal adequately with the grave military situation created by the magnitude of the German blow, can be described as the best generalship at the moment, is also open to some criticism.[118]

Given then, his critical view of Haig and his concern to restore his reputation after March 1918, it is perhaps no surprise that he would seek to minimise his responsibility for Third Ypres.

That both Army commanders were against the Flanders offensive, or at least its continuance in October, seemed to be confirmed when Edmonds published the Third Ypres volume of the official history. He referred to a conference held on 7 October at which both Gough and Plumer told Haig that although they were willing to continue with the offensive, they would welcome a halt. Haig hoped, however, that at the least British forces would manage to drive the enemy from the Passchendaele–Westroosbeke sector of the main ridge.[119] Strong doubt has since been thrown on this meeting. It is argued that the meeting never took place; there is no contemporary documentation, no reference in Haig's diary, nor in Gough's or Charteris' memoirs.[120] It would appear, then, that in the absence of any conclusive evidence that this meeting took place and that Plumer and Gough said what they were supposed to have said, that it is probable that both Army commanders supported Haig to the end, and that Lloyd George's assertions serve merely to reinforce his case against Haig.

Haig and GHQ also deceived the public and the Government regarding the progress of the offensive. The public at home, Lloyd George argues, both 'official and unofficial, were dosed day by day with tendentious statements about victories won, and progress made towards more assured and even greater triumphs. Enemy depression became as deep and his morale as quaky as the bogs of Passchendaele.'[121] Reports on the progress of the battle issued by GHQ described victories which were in fact virtual defeats; British casualties were understated, while German losses became 'pyramidal'. This was GHQ's 'propaganda to the Press'. The public was misled as was the Government: GHQ 'could not capture Passchendaele Ridge, but it was determined to storm Fleet Street, and here strategy and tactics were superb'.[122]

It quite simply beggars belief, however, that no matter how much the press was trumpeting insignificant advances as great victories, the Prime Minister and his War Cabinet colleagues were not able to ascertain the true progress of the offensive. The War Cabinet had at its disposal sources of information not available to the general public. It will be remembered that Lloyd George and his colleagues were under an obligation, under the terms of the decision taken by the War Policy Committee, to monitor the progress of the attack (this will be returned to later). This was not done. Clearly, throughout most of this period, Lloyd George's mind was preoccupied with other things.

VII

It is sometimes argued that Passchendaele began as an attempt at strategic breakthrough, but when it became clear that this was not possible, a strategy of 'wearing down the enemy' or attrition, was adopted, making a virtue out of a necessity. Here is how Lloyd George puts it:

When it was realised some time in September that a break-through was impracticable and that the clearing of the Flemish coast this year was out of the question, GHQ substituted the policy of 'wearing down the enemy' as the primary purpose of their strategy. How did that thrive? We lost 400,000 men in our direct and subsidiary attacks. The enemy did not lose on the whole British Front during that period 250,000 men. Our losses were nearly five to every three of the Germans. In their Verdun offensive, the Germans had the excuse that they were slaying five Frenchmen for every three they lost. We could not claim that measure of justification for our persistence in the Passchendaele folly.[123]

Even in terms of attrition, then, the Flanders offensive was a failure. The fighting strength of the enemy was indeed greatly reduced, but that of the British army was reduced even further. Haig could not even use the terrible arithmetic of attrition in his favour. Is Lloyd George's charge justified?

The casualty figures for the Third Battle of Ypres have long been the matter of dispute. Most agree that the British losses were considerably less than those suffered at the Battle of the Somme the previous year. On the first day of the Somme, for example, the BEF suffered almost 58,000 casualties, of whom over 21,000 were killed.[124] In contrast, British casualties in Flanders from 31 July to 2 August were about 30,000.[125]

Casualty figures for the campaign in Flanders for both British and German forces, however, have generated much controversy. Brian Bond has argued that arriving at 'definitive' comparative figures for Third Ypres is complicated by three factors. First, the casualty records are incomplete, particularly for the German side; second, records from both sides relate to different periods and different sectors of the front. And third, it is alleged that the Germans did not include the figures for the lightly wounded, who would return to the front relatively quickly, whereas the British did.[126] This last point, indeed, has become most controversial. Edmonds had, in the volume of the official history on the Battle of the Somme, argued that because they did not include the lightly wounded in their statistics, it was necessary to add 30 per cent to the German casualty figures.[127] In the volume dealing with Flanders in 1917, he applied the same principle and arrived at totals of 244,897 British casualties and speculated that 'there seems every probability that the Germans lost about 400,000'.[128] This, it will be noted, almost exactly reverses the figures claimed by Lloyd George.

Edmonds' methodology, however, has come under serious attack.[129] Liddell Hart, for example, has claimed that Edmonds falsified the figures in order to 'make German losses appear larger than the British'.[130] Liddell Hart's figures differ dramatically from both Lloyd George and Edmonds.

He used as the basis for his calculations War Office figures for dead and missing (apart from those taken prisoner). Thus the British total for the whole front for July–December was given as approximately 94,000, with another 28,000 reported as having died of wounds, giving a total of 122,000. The German dead and missing for the same period were given as 64,000; died of wounds, on the same ratio as the British, gave a total of 83,000. Including those taken prisoner the totals came to 136,000 British and 120,000 German. Then, on the basis of German casualty lists Liddell Hart arrived at an average ratio of 1 dead to 2.35 wounded and on British lists 1 to 2.27 for the British. Taking this into account, he arrives at total casualties of 217,000 German and 278,000 British. But the War Office figures indicated that the ratio for Third Ypres was more like 1 to 2.76, and this resulted in a British total of 315,000. Deducting casualties incurred in quiet sectors and during the Cambrai operation, Liddell Hart concludes that British losses were about 300,000 and German just under 200,000.[131]

Two important articles by M.J. Williams also attacked Edmonds' calculations. Williams described Edmonds' methodology as 'unscholarly and unreliable' and his final figures for the Battle of the Somme unjustified.[132] This, of course, also casts doubt on his figures for Third Ypres. General Robertson, who was in a better position to know the figures than most, estimated 260,000 British casualties at Third Ypres.[133] Later studies of Third Ypres are invariably more cautious than Edmonds or Lloyd George. Thus Prior and Wilson conclude that British losses were about 275,000, while the German just under 200,000.[134] Heinz Hagenlücke estimates that Third Ypres cost the Germans about 217,000 casualties; the British 'were much higher', while Frank Vandiver argues that British losses were about 275,000 and German losses almost equal.[135] It is clear that there is still no consensus.

What can be reasonably concluded, then, regarding the losses of the British and German armies at Third Ypres? First, we can safely assume that Lloyd George's figures are seriously exaggerated in one direction, and Edmonds' in another. Both had a clear interest in suggesting numbers which supported their respective cases. Lloyd George was concerned with above all blackening Haig's reputation by emphasising the heavy losses suffered by the British army under his command – not only were the losses terrible, but accurate figures were not divulged to the Government. Edmonds' goal was to present the balance of attrition clearly in Britain's favour and thereby vindicate Haig's command and the record of the British army. In reality, both armies were grievously weakened. In the short term, the Germans appear, according to the most plausible estimates, to have emerged from the battle less weakened than the BEF. In the long term, however, Germany could less afford such losses. On the Allied side, in 1918 American troops would be pouring into France thereby replenishing Allied manpower on a large scale, although until April this would be a slow process. As for Lloyd George, even the figures submitted to the War Cabinet by the War Office while the battle was still in progress, which he claims to have been false but which as far as the BEF were concerned were broadly accurate – *and which Lloyd George accepted at the time* – made nonsense of Haig's assurances to the War Policy Committee that he would not be entering into a great offensive with heavy losses.[136] The questions now remain, what did Lloyd George do about it and what should he have done?

VIII

The Passchendaele chapters place at centre-stage one of the major themes of the *War Memoirs*: the struggle for control of the conduct and strategy of the war between the Government and the military. With Lloyd George's advent to the Prime Ministership this became more acute. Lloyd George, as he had demonstrated in 1915–16, and would demonstrate again in 1917 as Prime Minister, had his own sometimes idiosyncratic ideas on how to run the war. Throughout the *War Memoirs*, the struggle is presented as one between his dynamism and vision and the tradition bound and blinkered brotherhood of the military. At certain times, such as in Calais in February 1917 and later that year with the introduction of convoys, he was willing and able to impose his ideas on the military and naval authorities. The Passchendaele chapters, however, tell a different story. Lloyd George, having reached the apex of power, and utterly convinced that the Flanders strategy recommended by his military advisers was wrong and would end in failure, was nevertheless unable or unwilling to veto it or to call a halt when in October at the latest it was clear that it would not achieve its purpose and casualties were mounting. How does Lloyd George explain his failure to veto or to later halt the offensive?

There were, he argues, a number of reasons for his inaction. He could, for example, have followed what he called the 'Nivelle precedent'. Back in April, he relates, it became known to French ministers that certain of Nivelle's subordinates opposed his plan. The new Ministry was itself doubtful regarding Nivelle's ambitious plan, so they sought out these generals and listened to their views. Later, the Government did step in and halt operations, in the end also removing Nivelle from his command. But if the British Government had sought alternative advice from Haig's subordinates, Lloyd George asserts, unlike the French generals (though few of them actually spoke out strongly against Nivelle at the conference called to deal with the issue) they would have put their loyalty to Haig before the Government.[137] Lloyd George might have imposed a halt on Haig in October. But the 'Nivelle precedent', he argues, did not auger well for that approach. When the French Government halted operations, mutinies erupted. (What exactly is Lloyd George trying to say here? That the French soldier turned to mutiny because the offensive was halted?) Lloyd George could not take such chances with the British Army.[138]

Furthermore, Passchendaele, he argues, could not have been stopped 'without dismissing Sir Douglas Haig. Sir William Robertson would [then] have resigned.' The Government, then, would have lost its two most senior military advisers. Is this a fair assumption? And would the Government have survived? First, the Government had every right to replace Haig if it thought fit. It had already removed one Commander-in-Chief without serious repercussion. And in coming months Robertson would leave his post as CIGS without any revolt on the part of Cabinet colleagues. But would there in fact be any need to dismiss Haig? He would certainly have obeyed any order to halt operations. As Lloyd George *himself* recognised: '"Could I have stopped Passchendaele[?]" Thought of giving order – "And Haig would have obeyed it, *would not have resigned*." "But they would have said I had spoiled chance of a decisive success and of saving us from danger from the submarines."'[139] If he thought that Haig would have obeyed the order to halt the offensive, then there would have been little reason to dismiss him, unless of course a case was mounted – and this would not have been difficult – that he had so mishandled the Flanders offensive that he would have to go. After all, Sir John French was replaced for less. Moreover, by October, it was clear to any intelligent observer that there would be no decisive success – British troops were little nearer the Belgian ports than they were on 30 July.

Lloyd George elaborates on this by arguing that if Haig and/or Robertson were threatened, his political support would evaporate. At the outset, he did not have the political support within the War Policy Committee to impose a veto:

> Ought I have vetoed it? I could not have carried the Cabinet with me to that extent. On this occasion all the military and naval advisers were, in so far as we could ascertain at the time, urgent in their

insistence on the desirability and feasibility of the enterprise, and nearly half the Cabinet accepted their opinion. The majority were opposed to taking the responsibility of a veto. I am certain, therefore, that no step I was in a position personally to take would have averted that squalid catastrophe.[140]

And once the offensive was underway and failing,

I could not have done it [halted the offensive] without the assent of the Cabinet. I sounded the Members of the Cabinet individually on the subject and I also spoke to some of the Dominion representatives. They – or most of them – were under the spell of the synthetic victories at GHQ.[141]

If he was unable to persuade his colleagues, should he not have resigned rather than acquiesce in this, an operation which can only be described as a costly and bloody failure?

I have always felt there are solid grounds for criticism in that respect. My sole justification is that Haig promised not to press the attack if it became clear that he could not attain his objectives by continuing the offensive. Robertson endorsed this undertaking. Mr. Bonar Law and Lord Milner, who were as strongly opposed as I was to the whole scheme, thought we ought to be satisfied with this pledge. However, the duty of the Government in the Passchendaele affair will always be a debatable proposition.[142]

He argues that he was 'well within [his] rights and obligations as Prime Minister in placing before the generals...the reasons which convinced [him] that their plans...would end in failure', which of course he was. But it was well within his rights and obligations as Prime Minister to go much farther than placing his doubts before the generals. If he was convinced that the plan would end in failure, he was within his rights and obligations to impose a veto. He asks: '*Even if I were in a position to forbid*, ought I to have taken that responsibility? On the whole I still give the same answer to that question as I did in June 1917. The fighting of a battle is mainly a decision for the Generals.'[143]

Such arguments are largely self-serving. Although Lloyd George had no party machine behind him and his support in the House of Commons consisted of Unionists and Labour and a scattering of Liberals, his position as Prime Minister was more secure than he contends. In a great war, dependent upon mass mobilisation on both the military and industrial fronts as it had become by 1917, it was essential that the Government attract the support of all key sectors of society and economy. A Unionist Prime Minister such as Balfour or Bonar Law would not be able to attract support from organised labour as Lloyd George had by and large done, while on the other hand the spectre of a return to office by Asquith, leader of the opposition in the House of Commons, would be enough to send most Unionists running back to Lloyd George. A 'smash' of the Government over any attempt to halt Passchendaele, or even replace Haig, while not impossible, was unlikely.

Furthermore, Lloyd George asks, 'if I were in a position to forbid' either at the outset, or during the offensive. Clearly, if a Prime Minister in a liberal parliamentary political system was not in a position to impose a veto or call a halt to a major military operation likely to cost much in lives and treasure then who was? Moreover, it will be remembered that the War Policy Committee had laid down in its final report that the progress of the offensive should be monitored by the Committee and if the results were not commensurate with the losses it should be closed down. Neither the Committee nor its parent body the War Cabinet, however, displayed much interest throughout August to November in what was after all the most important military operation then under way. Most discussions in Committee meetings after July were concerned with possible operations in Italy or later in the Middle East rather than in Flanders. When the latter was addressed, there was little talk of closing the offensive down. Thus on one of the few occasions when it was raised, on 3 October, Lloyd George told the Committee that: 'He would have no hesitation in comparing the present offensive with the predictions he made about it. We had not got the Klerken Ridge, and he had always insisted that the French promised to fight but had not carried out their promise.'[144] The discussion returned to action against the Turks, with Lloyd George envisaging renewed operations on the Western Front in May the following year. Lloyd George, on more than one occasion, referred to Nivelle: in comparison with all other operations on the Western Front, he argued, including Haig's Flanders offensive, Nivelle's was the most successful. He stated that 'the effects of General Nivelle's operation had been underrated by the General Staff. Actually it had been the most successful operation this year, if measured from the point of view of captures in prisoners and guns.'[145] Lloyd George and the other members of the War Policy Committee were clearly aware of Haig's lack of progress, yet were more concerned with planning new operations in the peripheries than with complying with the provisions of the War Policy Committee's decision in August – deciding whether to halt any further losses stemming from futile operations in Flanders. The War Cabinet took little more interest in Flanders than the Committee, apart from acknowledging Robertson's regular reports and at one point asking for casualty figures, which did not unduly alarm the members.[146] This was a real failure of Lloyd George and the War Cabinet, an abdication of responsibility, for which Lloyd George flounders in trying to find a convincing explanation in the *War Memoirs*.[147]

IX

The Third Battle of Ypres was finally brought to a halt in November by the transfer of troops to Italy and the decision to launch another offensive on the Western Front at the end of December at Cambrai. What was won over three months was an indefensible salient that would be lost in days when the Germans launched their spring offensives the following year. What soon became clear, too, was that the losses meant there were few reserves available to exploit success in the Battle of Cambrai at the end of November, and that these losses and the exhaustion of the troops had their effect when the German offensive came in March 1918.[148]

The Passchendaele chapters are the most polemical and therefore the most inaccurate in the *War Memoirs* and, perhaps because of this, were the most popular. As noted earlier, they were issued as a separate pamphlet. What the *War Memoirs* reveal, however, is more Lloyd George's sense of guilt at having allowed it all to happen than an accurate record of developments in the period May–November 1917. His purpose was to indict Haig, and justify his own actions, or rather inaction, and in many instances he distorts the evidence and omits material damaging to his case.

Yet despite this, valid criticisms of Haig and his plans for the battle and his conduct of the battle are present, and Lloyd George did not need his exaggerations and personal criticisms of Haig to make a strong case against him. If he had managed to restrain himself, however, and produce a more accurate and balanced account, would these chapters have made such an impact among the general public? Probably not. By 1934 the public mood was receptive to such an impassioned denunciation of the 'incompetent' generals of the Great War, which a growing proportion of the thinking public regarded as a futile mistake which had needlessly taken so many British lives. In that respect (and paradoxically, for Lloyd George had after all as Prime Minister presided over the great slaughter) the account of Passchendaele in the *War Memoirs* can sit quite easily besides other well-known examples of the literature of 'disenchantment' which still shape the public perception of the Western Front in the First World War.

8
The Western Front in 1918

I

Lloyd George faced a tricky problem when it came to providing an account of 1918. How to narrate the events on the Western Front, particularly from July, without acknowledging the outstanding performance of the BEF, still under the command of Sir Douglas Haig? Lloyd George's solution is soon evident. First, the Allied reverses suffered during the German offensives beginning on 21 March were primarily Haig's responsibility. The BEF had been seriously weakened during the previous year's Flanders campaign, and Haig's inappropriate disposition of the BEF's divisions along the entire British line and his neglect of the Fifth Army's defences practically invited catastrophe. Second, the reversal of fortunes beginning in July and the eventual German defeat were due not so much due to Haig's abilities, but rather because the Allies had at last found a general of 'genius', Foch, who in response to the setbacks in March and April, and largely due to Lloyd George's pressure, was appointed to command Allied forces in France. Under the command of Foch, Lloyd George notes, Haig performed well, but as a 'second-in-command'. Lloyd George's third strategy is to downplay the significance of the Western Front in the defeat of Germany: rather, he points to the collapse of Germany's allies, Austria, Bulgaria and Turkey, as the main factor in bringing the Germans to seek an armistice, rather than any military defeat of the German army in France. All three arguments have their problems, as I demonstrate below. But first I examine Lloyd George's apparent victory in his struggle to gain greater control over the conduct of the war by the replacement of Robertson by Sir Henry Wilson. His account of a Robertson-led 'conspiracy' to topple the Government and install a German style military 'dictatorship' is, it must be said, one of the more fanciful passages in the *War Memoirs*.

152

II

The year 1918 opened with Haig still in place as Commander-in-Chief of the BEF and Robertson as CIGS. Despite Lloyd George's antipathy towards the Western Front strategy they espoused, both survived the military failures of 1917. There is little doubt that Lloyd George wanted to replace them, in Haig's case even by his 'promotion' to '*Generalissimo*' of all British forces.[1] The previous November he had made his dissatisfaction with the generals abundantly clear by a highly critical speech in Paris.[2] The failure of Third Ypres, the disappointment of Cambrai and long casualty lists meant that Lloyd George's critical attitude towards Haig in particular began to be shared even by some who had been the Field-Marshal's most fervent defenders.[3] Lloyd George, however, in the end, had to be content with the removal of several key members of Haig's entourage, including his Chief of Staff Kiggell and intelligence chief Charteris.[4]

How did Haig in particular survive the failures of Passchendaele and Cambrai? As briefly discussed in the previous chapter, Lloyd George, in the *War Memoirs*, offers more than one explanation. He suggests that while Haig's removal would have been greeted with relief by the whole army from one end of the front to the other, he could not obtain the consent of the War Cabinet or the Dominion representatives (though quite what weight the latter had in the appointment of the Commander-in-Chief of the BEF is not explained).[5] He also argues that because of the propaganda campaign waged by GHQ in France, the general public supported Haig and an attempt to replace him would have resulted in a public outcry.[6] Moreover, according to Lloyd George there was no one in the entire British army of sufficient calibre to take Haig's place, with the exceptions, he says, of the Canadian Currie and the Australian Monash of whose remarkable talents, he informs us, he was informed only after the war. Both of these extremely capable generals, however, were comparatively junior.[7] Finally, Haig's support in the press, the Unionist ranks in the House of Commons, and the Government, and of course the Palace (the King was one of Haig's more consistent supporters and a personal friend) meant that any attempt to replace him would be fraught with political complications.[8] Indeed, he points out that it was one of the conditions the Unionists imposed when they agreed to support him as Prime Minister and joined his Government in December 1916 that there would be no change in the military leadership.[9]

These are largely self-serving arguments, however, and possess little merit. As noted above, by the end of 1917 Haig's support was ebbing.

The removal of Robertson the following February was to show that Lloyd George's political position was such that he could quite safely contemplate and act on the replacement of even the most powerful of his generals. There was no 'crash' in February 1918 caused by the withdrawal of ministerial or backbench Unionist support. Indeed, it could be pointed out that another of the seemingly unshakeable Unionist conditions for joining Lloyd George's Coalition was the exclusion of Churchill from office, yet Lloyd George had appointed Churchill Minister of Munitions in mid-1917 without precipitating, despite some grumbling, any resignations amongst his Unionist colleagues. There were, too, worthy alternatives to Haig as Commander-in-Chief. General Sir Herbert Plumer, for example, had demonstrated at Messines, Passchendaele and most recently in Italy that he was a careful, competent and above all successful commander (by Western Front standards at least) and who moreover held the respect and loyalty of his troops.[10]

Perhaps Lloyd George simply lacked the political courage to dismiss Haig? Or, as Trevor Wilson has argued, perhaps Lloyd George sensed that further setbacks were in store for the BEF, and that Haig would be needed to deflect criticism from himself? Such criticism was of course all the more likely if the new C-in-C was his own nominee. Alternatively, it is possible that Lloyd George realised that Haig's hard-won experience should not be discarded lightly, and if the tide turned decisively in France Haig would come into his own.[11] David French has argued that, as at the end of 1917 moves were afoot to replace Jellicoe as First Sea Lord, and Lloyd George knew that to 'dismiss one senior commander might smack of firm government...to dismiss two would savour of panic'.[12] Whatever the real explanation, Haig remained at his post until the end of the war. Not so his colleague at the War Office, General Robertson.

Lloyd George writes in the *War Memoirs* that he 'ought to have foreseen that a change of strategy was impossible without a thorough change in military leadership. With Robertson and Haig, both men of an abnormally stubborn character, remaining in their commanding positions they held, a new policy was not attainable.'[13] Within the proverbial next breath, however, Lloyd George concludes that it was necessary, because of Haig's and Robertson's seemingly impregnable positions, 'to find some method of altering the war direction which would not involve the shock to public opinion resulting from the debasement of men who had won a larger measure of confidence at home than they had amongst the survivors of the men whom they had driven into the Flemish charnel-house'.[14] In other words, Lloyd George had indeed, according to the *War Memoirs*, decided to change the 'war direction' (and presumably the strategy too) *without* replacing Haig and Robertson.[15] Lloyd George writes that he never 'believed in costly frontal attacks either in war or politics, if there was a way around': the establishment in late 1917 of an inter-Allied 'Supreme War Council' turned out to be the 'way around' required. Whether the real *aim* of Lloyd George in this initiative was in fact the removal of Robertson, despite the claims in the *War Memoirs*, is another matter. Certainly the main *effect*, intended or not, of the establishment of the Supreme War Council was *not* a fundamental reorientation of Allied strategy but the removal of Robertson from his post as CIGS.

The formation of an inter-Allied Council, or an Allied 'General Staff', had been under discussion for some weeks. The French Government was receptive, as was the British War Cabinet. Predictably, neither British nor French generals were enthusiastic, perceiving the proposal as a threat to their positions. But according to Hankey, Lloyd George realised that Haig and Robertson would never give any front but the Western any serious consideration, and, coupled with the collapse in Russia, the Italian rout at Caporetto, and the weakness of the French, he determined that change was imperative.[17]

Not all British generals were averse to the idea. Lloyd George received valuable military support for an Allied Council from former Commander-in-Chief of the BEF Lord French, and the temporarily unemployed Sir Henry Wilson. In reports commissioned by the War Cabinet on 11 October,[18] and which were highly critical of Haig,[19] they recommended that an Allied 'Supreme Council' or 'Superior Direction' be established to coordinate strategy on all fronts. Lloyd George lost little time in acting upon such agreeable advice. The Italian defeat at Caporetto in October seemed to render such a body all the more necessary, and, after having secured a measure of agreement from the French, the Supreme War Council was established at the Rapallo conference in November 1917.[20]

The Supreme War Council consisted of the Allied Prime Ministers and one other representative on the political side, and a Permanent Military Representative from each Power as their military advisers. Initially the Council was to be purely advisory and was to meet monthly with a general brief to 'watch over the general conduct of the war'.[21] Despite its lack of 'teeth', however, Robertson and his allies were against it from the outset. Von Donop's successor as Master General of Ordnance, Major-General W.T. Furse, for example, protested that the scheme for a Supreme War Council 'appears to me to be unpractical and dangerous to the best interests of the Allies in the further conduct of the war'. It would not, he argued, lead to 'unity' but rather 'duality' of command, as the Government would be receiving military advice from two independent military advisers.[22] What would happen if they disagreed? It would only make for muddle and confusion.

Robertson agreed wholeheartedly with Furse. All military advice to the Allied Governments, he insisted, should be from the 'responsible military advisers', in the British case himself as CIGS. They alone had the requisite 'machinery and information' necessary to examine and test military plans and provide informed advice. Such 'duality' as represented by the Rapallo model would lead to 'delay, friction, weakening of responsibility and lack of confidence amongst the troops'. There was, however, one 'modification' Robertson made to Furse's criticism:

> Instead of an Inter-Allied Staff (a misnomer without an Allied C-in-C) I would establish a Military Secretariat to the Supreme War Council, on the same lines as the War Cabinet Secretariat. This could be made valuable. Roughly, its functions would be to co-ordinate information as to the military resources of the Allies, to summarise the military plans received from the High Commands of the Allies, noting any disagreements, discrepancies or lack of co-ordination, and to prepare agenda for the meetings of the Supreme War Council, bringing forward such matters as require decision in order to ensure co-ordination of plans and harmonious working.[23]

Such a 'Secretariat', clearly, would not be the alternative source of military advice which Lloyd George was determined to obtain, and as such he was bound to reject it. With both Robertson and Lloyd George digging in their heels ever more deeply over the following weeks, a final showdown between the two – which the CIGS was bound to lose – became inevitable.

The gulf between Lloyd George's support for the Supreme War Council and Robertson's insistence that the CIGS remain the sole source of military advice to the War Cabinet widened when in January 1918 an attempt was made to equip the military side of the Supreme War Council with rather more powers than originally envisaged. At the end of January, it was proposed that an 'Inter-Allied' or 'General' Reserve drawn from divisions from the Allied armies be placed under the control of the Permanent Military Representatives constituted as an 'Executive Committee' or Board, under the chairmanship of General

Foch. The Reserve was to be separate and independent; and 'not to be under the control of the Commanders-in-Chief'.[24]

This was a significant step on the road to unified command. No *Generalissimo* was to be appointed, but control over the disposition of the General Reserve would make Foch and his colleagues '*de facto* arbiters of military policy' as they would have the 'power to decide what part of the [General Reserve] would be released to the national commander'.[25] It also raised, however, again, and in a more acute form, what for Robertson was the crucial question of 'who was responsible for advising the War Cabinet, Wilson at Versailles or Robertson in London'.[26]

The crisis which followed and ended with Wilson replacing Robertson was, according to Lloyd George in a rather overheated passage of the *War Memoirs*, the result of a military conspiracy. Robertson, he asserted, was a leader of a military 'clique' which aimed to overthrow the Government and install a military dominated 'dictatorship' along the lines of the Hindenburg-Ludendorff régime in Germany.[27] In Lloyd George's view, the same people who

> thwarted every effort I had made during the War either to equip the Army, or to prevent a wasteful use being made of the enormous resources in men and material placed at their disposal, or to achieve... effective unity of front [sought to] enthrone a Government which would be practically the nominee and menial of this military party.[28]

Moreover, this military party and its supporters, in their desire to overthrow the Government, were willing to use almost any method to achieve their goal, not stopping at treasonous betrayal of vital military information to the enemy.

One example of this, according to Lloyd George, was the report which Charles à Court Repington, the pro-Robertson military correspondent of the *Morning Post*, filed from Paris on 8 February:

> The decisions of the recent Inter-Allied War Council regarding the control of British troops in the field are reported to be of such a strange character that Parliament should demand the fullest details and a Parliamentary Committee should examine them at once and take the opinions of our General Staff and of our Commanders in the field concerning the new arrangements.[29]

This was bad enough from Lloyd George's point of view. Repington, he writes in the *War Memoirs*, was an 'active collaborator' and a 'favoured confidant' of the General Staff, and was in frequent contact with Robertson and his Director of Military Operations, Sir Frederick Maurice. There was thus 'no secret about the origin and inspiration of the message'.[30] Worse was to come. On the same evening of the *Morning Post* article, the *Globe* called on the Asquith-led Opposition to resist the sidelining of Robertson and Haig. This, according to Lloyd George, was clear evidence that a 'formidable conspiracy' was being hatched, not only to reverse the Versailles decisions and defend Robertson's and Haig's positions, but also to 'supplant the Government, and substitute for it one which would make Robertson virtual dictator for the rest of the War, as Hindenburg was in Germany and by the same means'.[31] Still the ultimate betrayal was yet to come. On 11 February, Repington published what one historian has described as the most 'vitriolic composition of his journalistic career' and perhaps the greatest 'indiscretion' in the history of civil-military relations in Britain.[32] In his article headed 'The War Council. Paris Discussions. Remarkable Reports', Repington gave away the 'whole scheme' for the establishment of the General Reserve and the plan for a major offensive against the Turks in a bid to knock Turkey out of the war.[33]

This press campaign undoubtedly served to stiffen Robertson's resistance to Lloyd George's plans. Until the end of the crisis and his departure from the War Office, he was adamant: as he told Balfour during the latter's last ditch effort to make him see reason, the fact of his being offered either of the two most important posts in the General Staff (i.e. that of the CIGS with its traditional powers – those attached to the post prior to his own appointment in December 1915 – or of the permanent Military Representative at Versailles) was irrelevant. He objected to the proposed new system in principle. The military representative at Versailles should, he maintained, be quite definitely subordinate to and represent the CIGS. If this were so he would be happy to accept either post. The alternative proposed by the Prime Minister, he insisted, was unworkable. Despite some wavering over previous days, by this stage Lloyd George was not prepared to accept Robertson's demands, and thus in February 1918 Robertson was superseded by Sir Henry Wilson.[34]

Robertson, it should be noted, was within his rights to argue his case with the Government. But his position was ultimately untenable. Lloyd George's claims that he was the central figure in a conspiracy to topple the Government and establish a military dictatorship are clearly fantasy.[35] But Robertson *was* issuing something of a challenge to civilian control of the war. If Lloyd George had accepted Robertson's demands – as at times during the crisis he seemed about to do – then his Government would have been seen as weak and little more than a creature of the General Staff. If Robertson, after arguing his case with the Government, failed to convince, he should have resigned forthwith if he thought that its policy was wrong in principle and he could not carry it out. In contrast, Haig, who also thought the scheme unworkable, clearly did not think it an issue worth resigning over, and failed to support Robertson. In the *War Memoirs*, Lloyd George acknowledges that on this occasion Haig acted correctly, although he unfortunately did not 'continue to follow the fine example of constitutional loyalty he himself had set' when it came to implementing the Supreme War Council's decisions on the General Reserve, which in fact never saw the light of day.[36]

III

With Robertson out of the way and the more congenial Sir Henry Wilson installed as his successor, it may be thought that now the way would be clear for Lloyd George to implement those changes in Allied strategy which he thought necessary. He argued that an attack on the Turks in the Middle East in an attempt to knock that 'prop' (to use Lloyd George's terminology) from under Germany should be the first priority. For the west he advocated the adoption of an essentially defensive policy and the General Reserve plan, pending the arrival of sufficient numbers of Americans in France to make a renewal of offensive operations feasible.[37] There were several factors, however, which constrained Lloyd George's ability to achieve significant change.

A reorientation of Allied strategy meant, of course, that Britain's allies, in particular France, would have to be persuaded of its necessity. Although the French, especially the Commander-in-Chief General Pétain, were all in favour of a more defensive strategy in the west while waiting for the Americans to arrive in force, they were never likely to agree to a significant shift in emphasis to other theatres while the enemy was still in occupation of so much French territory. Second, Haig, too, was against any lessening of the effort on the Western Front. Convinced that the war would be won or lost in the west, he was eager to resume offensive operations in Flanders; as Lloyd George disparagingly puts it in the *War Memoirs*, 'the offensive was to be resumed in the same promising bog as soon as possible in the spring', evidence, to Lloyd George, of Haig's 'inebriated' state of mind.[38] In addition, Haig, in concert with Pétain, effectively killed the plans for a General Reserve by refusing to contribute any divisions.[39] Third, the new CIGS, Sir Henry Wilson, largely shared Robertson's and Haig's strategic preferences. All three were convinced, in varying degrees, that the Western Front remained the principal and crucial theatre. In this sense Wilson was a major disappointment to Lloyd George. In the *War Memoirs* he notes that Wilson 'was always a Westerner'; in the middle of 1918 he was complaining that Wilson was 'Wully *redivivus*'.[40]

The final, and the most important factor, however, in restricting Lloyd George's strategic options was that on 21 March 1918 the German offensive on the Western Front was finally launched. The attack was on such a scale and initially at least so effective that it soon placed the Allied armies in France in danger of separation and defeat. It resolved in a decisive fashion the strategic debate amongst Allied policy makers. Every available reinforcement would be poured into France, including recruits under 19; the age limits for conscription were lowered (to 17½) and raised (to 50 or even 55) and conscription was extended to Ireland (though never implemented).[41] There was no longer any doubt that the war would be won or lost on the Western Front, although, as we shall see, Lloyd George, in recounting the events of 1918 in the *War Memoirs*, would still not be fully persuaded of this.

The German offensives which so frustrated Lloyd George's strategic plans achieved their early successes due entirely, according to Lloyd George, to Haig's disastrous strategy over the previous year and his neglect of the defences in the Fifth Army sector. The Flanders campaign in the second half of 1917 had resulted in no great victory or capture of important territory, rather the exhaustion, demoralisation and depletion of British military manpower at a time when reserves were inexorably shrinking and it was becoming clear that the enemy had offensive plans of his own. Even Haig himself, unusually (as he was usually explaining to all who would listen the exhausted state of the *German* army), acknowledged the tired state of the BEF when he wrote in December 1917 that the BEF was 'at present much exhausted and much reduced in strength'.[42] Lloyd George wrote in his 'Rough Notes':

> When we come to contemplate the probability and even the certainty of a German attack in great force in spring of 1918 we realised more and more how disastrous had been the effect of the prolonged Flanders offensive.... [the] 1916 and 1917 campaigns had all been conducted on the assumption that there were no more German attacks on the Western front after the failure of Verdun. The French, after the Nivelle offensive, realising that the whole situation had

changed by the practical disintegration of Russia's military power, were able to organise their defences and train their troops. The Passchendaele offensive made it impossible for us to do either.[43]

Certainly the campaigns of 1917, especially in Flanders, had been costly. Only a small handful of the 57 divisions of the BEF had been spared participation in Third Ypres, and there is little doubt that divisions were tired and under strength.[44] According to Lloyd George, total British casualties for Third Ypres were 399,000, which made nonsense of GHQ's original estimate of 130,000. Haig and GHQ only had themselves to blame when faced with a manpower deficit in March 1918 of 100,000 men. Lloyd George's aim is clear. The weakened state of the BEF on the eve of the German onslaught, so weak as to precipitate a full-scale retreat of the Fifth Army when the attack occurred, was due to Haig's recklessness and blind ambition in pushing on with a failed offensive the previous year.[45]

I have addressed the issue of casualties in Flanders in a previous chapter – suffice it to say here that figures of that magnitude are today not accepted by most historians, and that a figure of around 270,000 is now widely accepted. That there was a deficit of men in March 1918, however, is clear. There remains the question: why were they not replaced? If there were not sufficient infantry to defend the British front when the great German attack came, and if it was so clear to both politicians and soldiers alike that a German attack was indeed coming, then it was the responsibility of the government of the day to protect its army from defeat and find replacements, as indeed it rushed to do after 21 March. That the Government did not provide for sufficient reinforcements for the BEF was the result of a deliberate policy on Lloyd George's part of denying Haig the troops requested for fear that they would only be consumed in a renewed offensive in Flanders. That this was so is acknowledged by Lloyd George.[46] In addition, it should not be forgotten that Haig persisted with his costly operations in Flanders *only with the sanction, explicit or tacit, of the Government led by Lloyd George himself.* He and the Government, therefore, were as responsible as anyone for the state of the BEF in March 1918.[47] Nowhere in the *War Memoirs* is there a hint of an acknowledgment of this responsibility.

Another of Lloyd George's criticisms of Haig is that he remained obsessed with Flanders. At the end of 1917 and in the early weeks of 1918, when he was not pushing for a resumption of the British offensive in that sector, he argued that if a German offensive did come, it would come in Flanders, threatening the Channel ports.[48] Or at least Haig behaved as if he thought this would happen:

> For climatic reasons an offensive in upper Flanders was unlikely and well-nigh impossible until April whilst an attack on the Somme was a feasible operation a month earlier. That consideration never seems to have occurred to him [Haig]. He pressed on with his Passchendaele defences with all his available resources as if an attack were imminent, whilst he attended in a leisurely fashion to the sector doomed to an early assault on an overwhelming scale.[49]

This was in spite of the fact that Haig, by the end of February at the latest (so Lloyd George tells us) knew the area of the German attack; or, at least, as Lloyd George states:

> Whatever Haig's anticipations might have been in January and [early] February as to the direction and strength of the German offensive, by the end of February there ought to have been no doubt even in his obdurate mind as to the part of the front against which the attack would be launched nor as to the scale upon which it would be made.

Immense preparations had been underway for weeks, and could not be concealed.[50]

Haig's 'obsession' with Flanders was reflected, Lloyd George argues, in the 'incomprehensible' disposition of his forces on the eve of the attack. From north to south the distribution of divisions and heavy guns was uneven (Table 8.1). The Fifth Army trenches, moreover, were only recently taken over from the French, and were ill-prepared to provide an effective defence against the imminent German onslaught.

Table 8.1 Disposition of divisions on the British front in March 1918

Army	Front	Divisions	Heavy guns
Second Army (Plumer)	23 miles	12	388
First Army (Horne)	33 miles	14	276
Third Army (Byng)	28 miles	14	461
Fifth Army (Gough)	42 miles	12*	515

* +3 Cavalry divisions.
Source: Edmonds (1951) p. 279. Cf. *War Memoirs*, V, p. 2848 and Martin Middlebrook (2000), p. 71.

Table 8.2 Disposition of Royal Engineer Companies
on the British front in March 1918

Army	Front	RE Cos
Second Army	23 miles	68
First Army	33 miles	56
Third Army	28 miles	54
Fifth Army	42 miles	56

Source: *War Memoirs*, V, p. 2845.

Work was, to be sure, proceeding to remedy this deficiency, but there would not be nearly enough time. According to Lloyd George, the distribution of Royal Engineer companies along the British front engaged in constructing defence works also demonstrated clearly Haig's priorities. Given the length of fronts, the Fifth Army's allocation was less than half than that given to the Second Army (Table 8.2).[51]

Haig, according to Lloyd George, had in effect 'written off' the Fifth Army. Why? Because, he argues, of his pique at having to extend his line and thereby abandon his offensive in Flanders. As Lloyd George writes:

It is true he was very much annoyed with the French for depriving him of his last chance of continuing his cherished Flanders plan by forcing him to extend his line. He felt he had done his duty by sending the Fifth Army to occupy their trenches. If these were attacked it was for Pétain and not for him to dispatch adequate reinforcements.[52]

At bottom, it came down to Passchendaele:

The underlying motive which dominated Haig's dispositions for the great battle was the fetter of Passchendaele.... This St Quentin Front [i.e. the Fifth Army] was not his concern. He [Haig] had another and better plan and the British and French Governments had between them thrown it over.... the responsibility was theirs and it was their business to see it through.[53]

Robertson, in preferring to leave office rather than implement a policy with which he disagreed, had acted honourably; Haig, Lloyd George implies, had not.

It will be clear from the above that, in Lloyd George's account, the effects of Passchendaele were far-reaching. In the *War Memoirs* Haig's offensive is used as a potent weapon with which Lloyd George assails Haig and other British generals for their responsibility for not just the squalid, muddy failure of the 1917 campaign, but also the alarming and costly reverses which were about to be visited upon the BEF, particularly the Fifth Army, in March–April 1918. It is easy, on the face of it, to criticise Haig's concentration on the Flanders sector and the comparative neglect of the Fifth Army front. If the BEF had found the Flanders terrain such difficult going in July, then Ludendorff would not find it much easier in March. The British front, as a consequence of Haig's dispositions, found itself weakest further south at the junction of the British and French armies, which of course was where the Germans would launch their devastating attack in March 1918 in a bid to separate them. If this indeed happened, as Ludendorff intended, it could lay the two Allies open to defeat in detail and a retreat of the BEF north to the Channel ports and the French to defend Paris.

Haig's rationale, however, for so disposing of his forces was precisely that Gough's Fifth Army was closest to the French who he expected, if an attack came, to come swiftly to his aid. This expectation rested on an informal agreement between Pétain and Haig. The great danger, of course, in such an arrangement lay in that Haig had to rely on the assumption that Pétain would view an attack on the Fifth Army sector with sufficient seriousness, and in the expectation that the French themselves would not be facing attack. This was of course, by no means certain. Indeed, both Haig and Pétain at various times prior to 21 March believed the Germans would launch offensives against both armies at two or three locations. In this context, the plan for the General Reserve, controlled by the Executive War Board independently of the two armies and their commanders, would arguably have provided more certainty, and would have been less vulnerable to the vagaries of personal perceptions and purely national rather than Allied concerns. But Haig was taking a calculated risk: as he saw it (correctly) the Fifth Army in the south could afford to give some ground in the face of a determined attack, while the Second Army in Flanders could not. If any sector of the British front had to be weak, through a combination of high casualties in 1916–17 and a cautious manpower policy on the part of the Government, it would have to be, Haig thought, the Fifth Army's.[54]

Lloyd George, however, viewed the arrangements for mutual support reached by Haig and Pétain as worthless. Throughout his discussion in the *War Memoirs* of the period immediately before the German attack

and of its first days, he repeatedly refers critically to the 'perfect arrangement worked out in every detail', opposing it to the General Reserve
plan which, he contends, would have saved the Fifth Army.[55] On the
third day of the battle, he writes, it was clear that the 'vaunted arrangement between Haig and Pétain...had failed to function'.[56] On
23 March he pointed out helpfully to the War Cabinet the advantages
the General Reserve plan had over the 'bargaining with the French in
the middle of a battle' then going on,[57] and that very evening, he and
Lord Milner, contemplating political intervention to sort out the mess,
both agreed that the General Reserve, had it been implemented, would
have quickly restored the Allied front.[58] When on 24 March Haig visited
Gough, consoling him with the words 'Well, Hubert, you cannot fight a
battle without men', Haig did not tell him, Lloyd George writes:

> that but for the Passchendaele obsession his defences would have
> been better prepared and his line more strongly held, and that had it
> not been for Haig's refusal to work the Versailles scheme for a
> General Reserve, ample reinforcements would have reached him in
> time to counter-attack the enemy and fling him back. Three weeks
> before the battle he knew where it was coming. Had he taken steps to
> rearrange his forces so as to hold the threatened sectors of the Third
> and Fifth as strongly as the two Northern (and unmenaced) sectors
> then being held, there would have been 37½ divisions to face the
> enemy, instead of 30. What an enormous difference that would have
> made to the result, even without a General Reserve.[59]

In fact, as has been noted by some historians, Pétain, far from
subjecting Haig to a display of 'cold charity',[60] had acted reasonably
promptly, sending six divisions as promised to Haig, and preparing to
provide another six. This was creditable, given the French fears of an
attack on their front, the lack of time and, not least, 'the confusing
situation with Fifth Army'.[61] Lloyd George noted elsewhere that French
reinforcements arrived on the 23 March, despite the fact that Pétain
had genuine fears of an attack somewhere on his front.[62] It is true,
however, that as the Germans advanced and the British retreated over
the first few days, the agreement between Haig and Pétain unravelled:
something more was needed.[63]

The situation on the night of 24 March was indeed serious. Lloyd
George writes in the *War Memoirs* that the Fifth Army 'was no longer an
Army. It was broken up into fragments – still fighting as it drifted
back...the zig-zag where it rested on the night of the 24th was on an

average over 16 miles behind the line which it held at dawn on the 21st and further retreats were inevitable.' The Third Army was not in a much better position. It was also in 'full retreat' and was 'miles' behind its original line. It was also anticipated by both the British and the French Headquarters that the important rail junction of Amiens would soon fall.[64] Most seriously, as Lloyd George relates, when Milner arrived in France he swiftly came to the conclusion that a breach had indeed opened up between the British right and the French left.[65]

In the face of this looming crisis, Lloyd George accuses both Pétain and Haig of being 'bewildered' and incapable of the decisive action needed to restore the situation. In contrast, Foch rose to the occasion like a 'giant' and displayed supreme courage.[66] At a conference held on 26 March at Doullens, Poincaré, Clemenceau, Pétain, Foch, Milner, Haig and Wilson conferred. Haig, according to Lloyd George, 'clearly took a desperate view of the position', revealed by his memorandum of the previous day in which he stated that it was only a matter of time before the British and French armies were separated. He called for the concentration of 20 French divisions 'astride the Somme west of Amiens' to operate 'on the flank of the English [*sic*] Army' which, he wrote, '*must fight its way slowly back covering the Channel ports*'.[67] Foch, however, called for the defence of Allied ground 'foot by foot', and at the conference it was proposed (Lloyd George does not say by who) that Foch be empowered to coordinate the operations of Allied armies on the Western Front.[68] Haig 'seemed not only quite willing but pleased'.[69] Lloyd George correctly points out that Foch was not appointed to command of the Allied armies; it was only the first step on the road to unity of command. General Bliss, the American Chief of Staff, wrote (as Lloyd George notes) that Foch had 'no power of command' under the Doullens agreement. He could only 'consult and advise. The result was what might have been expected. He had to waste precious time in travelling to one headquarters and the other, persuading Commanders to do what he should have been empowered to order.'[70]

The Doullens agreement was a step forward, in other words, but it soon turned out to be unsatisfactory. As Lloyd George points out, while Foch might 'flit' from one Headquarters to another, pressing his plans upon Haig and Pétain, all he could do was suggest and try to persuade: it was for the two Commanders-in-Chief to decide. They were 'not ready to part with any of their authority'. Foch 'could not co-ordinate' as he was supposed to do under the Doullens agreement because he was 'not in a position to command'. It was therefore decided to arrange another conference to clarify, and if possible strengthen Foch's powers.[71]

For Lloyd George, there was only 'one practical solution'. It was necessary to appoint Foch Supreme Commander of the Allied armies. What was
so clear to Lloyd George, however, was not at all clear to his Cabinet
colleagues or the British generals. Wilson was 'thoroughly hostile', and
Haig did not think Foch needed any additional powers.[72]

Another conference was held at Beauvais on 3 April, and resistance
was overcome. Foch was given authority over the 'strategic direction of
military operations'. The national commanders-in-chief were to retain
control of their armies' 'tactical employment', and each would have the
right to appeal to their respective government if in their view the safety
of their army was threatened by an order from Foch.[73] For Lloyd George
this appointment meant that the long awaited 'unity of command' had
finally arrived. It was vital, in his view, that Foch was appointed to this
role. Haig's outlook was too narrow and unimaginative, while Pétain
was too pessimistic, even defeatist.[74] Foch alone, as Lloyd George writes
in the *War Memoirs*, possessed the necessary 'vision and decision' to go
beyond the current difficulties and think of the next step: 'of the necessary preparations for fighting out to a final decision the vast battle
which had commenced'. Foch should not be hampered in his functions
as Supreme Commander by lack of authority. Lloyd George determined
to 'take all risks' to secure that authority for Foch.[75] In his view, the
disaster of 21 March had 'saved the Allies' by giving the political leaders
the opportunity to appoint the genius Foch Commander-in-Chief of the
Allied armies.[76]

Was this, however, in fact, a genuine unity of command? Was Foch
appointed to a real post with genuine authority over Haig and Pétain?
The new system was certainly an improvement on the disastrous
Nivelle experiment of the previous year. A *'Generalissimo'* figure above
both national commanders made more sense than one national
commander being also the supreme commander. But as it turned out in
practice, there were severe limitations to Foch's power. Foch himself
wrote that, even after Beauvais

> the term 'unified command' gives a false idea of the powers exercised
> by the individual in question – that is, if it is meant that he
> commanded in the military sense of the word, as he would do, for
> example, in the French Army. His orders to Allied troops could not
> have the same characteristics of absolutism, for these troops were not
> his.... But by persuasion he could stimulate or restrain their
> Commanders-in-Chief, decide upon the policy to follow, and thus
> bring about those concerted actions which result in victory.[77]

Persuasion was indeed the principal method that could be used in dealing with commanders who, importantly, and reminiscent of the Nivelle arrangement of the year before, retained the right to appeal to their own governments. Foch was also handicapped by the almost complete lack of a staff.[78]

The notion propagated by Lloyd George that the Doullens and Beauvais agreements restricted Haig's authority and placed him firmly under Foch as a second-in-command is something of a fiction. As Trevor Wilson has pointed out, the major qualification to Foch's authority of the right of appeal to London, given Lloyd George's aversion to major operations on the Western Front, meant that Foch could not insist on operations of which Haig disapproved beyond a certain point. For Foch and Haig, while they may disagree over specific operations, were united in their insistence that the war would be won on the Western Front, and from Foch's point of view, 'it was altogether wiser to bow to Haig's wishes than to let Lloyd George have the last say'. Thus the remainder of 1918 was marked not only by Haig's increasing success but also by his greater freedom from control by either Foch or London. Two masters with differing views meant that, in effect, Haig had none.[79]

IV

The initial German attacks had been enormously costly to both sides. By 4–5 April, when Ludendorff discontinued the attempt to take Amiens, Allied forces had been driven back about 40 miles. The Germans had captured 1200 square miles of territory and the BEF had lost 160,000 men and 1000 guns; the French about 80,000 men. But the Germans, who could less afford losses on such a scale, had lost perhaps 250,000, including many of the better trained 'storm troops' who had spearheaded the assault. And, while a large hole had indeed been knocked through the Allied line and an advance made which dwarfed those made by the Allies in 1916–17, the Germans had still not gained their strategic objectives (if indeed they had any). Arras and Amiens remained in Allied hands and the BEF, while bruised, had not been broken. Neither had the Allies been divided, as Ludendorff had hoped.[80]

What with the benefit of hindsight was clearly a strategic failure, however, had been, initially at least, a brilliant tactical success, and this seemed to some to call for changes in the command of the BEF. But again Haig survived, partly through Lloyd George being very wary of creating new political difficulties for himself. Two significant changes did occur, however, one on the political level and the other within the senior ranks of the BEF. The first change was at the War Office. Lord Derby, the 'soldier's friend', was sent to Paris to replace the retiring Lord Bertie as Ambassador. Milner moved from the War Cabinet to the War Office, while Unionist Austen Chamberlain was appointed to the War Cabinet.[81]

More controversially, Gough was sacked from command of the Fifth Army. As noted above, his dismissal had been considered on previous occasions, most notably following the Flanders offensive. In the wake of the retreat of the Fifth Army, the matter was raised again. Wilson recorded in his diary for 26 March: 'I discussed removal of Gough, and told Haig he could have Rawly, [Rawlinson] and Rawly's old Fourth Army staff from Versailles, to replace Gough. Haig agreed to this.'[82] And on 3 April Wilson wrote that 'Lloyd George told Haig that Gough must go'.[83] Haig also wrote that day:

> [Lloyd George] is looking out for a scapegoat for the retreat of the Fifth Army. I pointed out that 'fewer men, extended front, and increased hostile forces, were the main causes...He was very much down on Gough. I championed the latter's case...in spite of a most difficult situation, he had never really lost his head. LG said he had not held the Somme bridges, nor destroyed them and that G must not be employed. To this I said I could not condemn an officer unheard, and that if LG wishes him suspended he must send me an order to that effect.[84]

Which Derby, still Secretary of State, did the following day. Haig later indicated that his support for Gough at this time was limited. Shortly after the war he reportedly told a friend of Gough's that 'after considerable thought I decided that the public at home... demanded a scapegoat, and that the only possible ones were Hubert [Gough] or me...I was conceited enough to think that the Army could not spare me'.[85]

Gough, in his memoirs, recalled that he was told by Haig's military secretary on 28 March that Haig had decided that he was to be replaced by Rawlinson: 'in plain language, Haig decided to replace me, to get rid of me'. Several days later Haig told him personally that he was to return home immediately: 'The orders don't come from me, Hubert', Haig said, 'They come from Lloyd George and the Cabinet.'[86] On his return to Britain, Gough found little sympathy for himself or the Fifth Army, least of all from the Government. On 9 April, he relates, Lloyd George made a statement to the House which laid the blame for the military reverses on Gough and the Fifth Army, and unfairly compared the performance of the Third Army with the Fifth. Of Gough, Lloyd George stated:

> Until the whole of the circumstances which led to the retirement of the Fifth Army, and its failure to hold the line of the Somme at least till the Germans brought up their guns, and perhaps the failure adequately to destroy the bridges – until all these things are explained, it would be unfair to censure the general in command of the army – General Gough. But until those circumstances are cleared up, it would be equally unfair to the British Army to retain his services in the field.[87]

Gough was 'furious':

> It was such a cruel travesty of the facts. It was just a smoke-cloud to cover and conceal the failure of others and of the Cabinet in particular, and it was deliberately intended to divert both attention and blame from Lloyd George himself. It was, of course, very uncomfortable for him to have to admit that the fundamental reason for the failure of the Fifth Army to hold the line was that every battalion was much below strength, and yet he and the Cabinet had kept 300,000 men at home and refused to send them to Haig in spite of his urgent requests... This did not prevent Lloyd George a little later claiming and getting great credit in the House of Commons for sending these 300,000 men to Haig without delay – the height of the crisis then being over.[88]

In spite of his apparent readiness at the time to place the blame on Gough and the Fifth Army for the March retreat, in the *War Memoirs* Lloyd George presents a very different picture. The French blamed Gough for the defeat, and Haig agreed, and consequently Gough was removed from his command. Neither the War Cabinet nor himself had anything to do with this decision: it was ordered, writes Lloyd George, by Haig 'on his own initiative, without any instruction from home'.[89] This was most unfair, even 'shabby', for Gough was not responsible for Haig's dispositions. When:

> Gough had been beaten owing to conditions for which Haig alone was responsible, Haig, instead of accepting that responsibility as an 'officer and a gentleman', removed Gough from the command and left the Government to infer that the *dégommé* General was alone to blame. Not much nobility there.[90]

The Fifth Army 'never ceased fighting.... the spirit of the troops was never broken to the end'.[91] When he encountered troops of the Fifth Army on a visit to France, Lloyd George relates, there was 'no trace of dejection or despair...it was not my picture of a defeated army'.[92] Indeed, his tribute to the Fifth Army and Gough in particular enlarges upon and reinforces earlier comments in the *War Memoirs*, notably in the account of Passchendaele in which Gough is depicted as criticising GHQ plans and, without any real evidence, telling Haig that the offensive should be shut down.[93] Gough, in fact, emerges from the pages of the *War Memoirs* as one of the very few talented British generals, and unjustly treated by Haig.

Lloyd George's defence of Gough and the Fifth Army should be seen in the context of their rapprochement in the mid-1930s, just when Lloyd George was preparing the relevant volume of the *War Memoirs*. At the end of 1935, Liddell Hart found that both Lloyd George and Gough wanted to 'bury the hatchet' and arranged for them to meet for the first time at the Athenaeum Club.[94] Clearly their first meeting was a success, for a second followed in January 1936.[95] Lloyd George and Gough found much to agree on. On two crucial points in particular, they found common ground. On Haig's dispositions in March 1918, Gough agreed that [they] were due to a preconception that Arras was the right place for the Germans to strike, and so they would concentrate there. Haig was right in [the] principle of uneven distribution, but not in the distribution he actually stuck to in face of clear evidence.'[96] And in an argument which he later expanded in his memoirs and which of course Lloyd George espoused enthusiastically in the *War Memoirs*, Gough agreed that Haig neglected the Fifth Army. Liddell Hart noted: 'Gough thought Haig's attitude was one of rather welcoming a partial loss of ground, on the idea – "that'll larn'em" (the Govt) for not doing what he wanted, and for meeting the French wishes' regarding the extension of the British line.[97]

Indeed, the two hit it off so well and agreed on so much, and Gough and his old comrades from the Fifth Army were so impressed by Lloyd George's admission that he had been wrong about Gough and the Fifth Army, that Lloyd George was invited to address the Fifth Army's reunion dinner in 1936. Due to a 'chill', however, he was unable to attend, and sent Sylvester in his place. Gough expressed regret: 'I personally would have liked to express to you my appreciation and admiration in what you have said to replace the Fifth Army on its proper pedestal.'[98] Sylvester reported that at the dinner Gough had praised Lloyd George; in particular he had complimented Lloyd George's 'generosity and greatness of mind to come out into the open and say he was wrong'.[99]

By 1936, then, due partly to Liddell Hart's intervention, the resentments and accusations which had marked Lloyd George's and Gough's views of each other had given way to a mutual admiration society. The result of this was an account of March 1918 in the *War Memoirs* which shifted the blame for the Fifth Army's retreat quite firmly from Gough to Haig. The retreat of the Fifth Army became yet another weapon in Lloyd George's arsenal with which he was able to assail Haig's reputation. Recent accounts, however, conclude that responsibility for the retreat is not quite so clear cut and that the high command, including *both* Haig and Gough, must share in that responsibility.[100] 'Burying the hatchet' with Gough also resulted in Lloyd George laying the blame for Gough's disgrace unequivocally with Haig. On this issue, however, there is clear evidence that Lloyd George also wanted Gough to go and that it was the War Cabinet, not Haig, who ordered Gough home, and indeed refused him any further command and the official inquiry which he deserved.

V

By July 1918, the Germans' offensives had clearly failed. Ludendorff had gained some ground and inflicted a great many casualties in the Allied forces but failed to achieve a decisive victory. The BEF was still intact, the unity of the Allies was unbroken and given some additional substance by the appointment of Foch as Allied commander, and strategic towns such as Amiens and, more importantly Paris and the Channel ports remained in Allied hands. By July, the Germans had lost something in the order of 1 million men; the Allies, about 900,000. Symbolic of the balance tilting even more decisively in favour of the Allies, however, was that the crisis of March–April had prompted a speeding up of the transport of American troops to France. Each week thousands of fresh troops arrived at French ports and by July substantial units were in the field. Moreover, as long as the war lasted, there was the certainty of many more to come and to this the Germans had no answer. It is in this context that the Allies, in July, began their counter-offensive on the Marne.

The section of the *War Memoirs* dealing with what became known as the 'Hundred Days' from the Battle of Amiens on 8 August to the Armistice on 11 November is the culmination of Lloyd George's praise of the strategic genius Foch and of his denigration of Haig. For despite the great

British successes beginning at Amiens, Haig, according to Lloyd George, was only 'fulfilling a role for which he was admirably adapted: that of a second in command to a strategist of unchallenged genius', that is, Foch.[101] Moreover, he criticises Haig's handling of specific operations. For example, the Battle of Amiens, which Ludendorff called the 'black day of the German army'. Haig, according to Lloyd George, let the opportunity slip for an even greater victory:

> Had Haig flung his army into the gap created and pursued the broken and demoralised Germans without respite an even greater victory was within his grasp.... Haig did not press forward with relentless drive and the Germans were given time to recover and reform their lines. Both Hindenburg and Ludendorff dwell with gratitude and surprise on this welcome respite.[102]

While criticising Haig for not exploiting the success of 8 August, Lloyd George also argues, contradictorily, that the offensive of 8 August brought the Germans to the realisation 'that all hope of victory had passed' and cites German sources which indicate that the Germans themselves regarded their setback at Amiens very seriously indeed.[103] Just what did happen on 8 August 1918 and can Haig be faulted for not following up his victory more energetically?

The Battle of Amiens had its genesis in the German gains in the area in March and April. Their advance, while it had not brought that important rail junction into German control, had brought it within range of the German artillery. Thus, after the second Battle of the Marne during July had brought the French to exhaustion, it fell to the BEF to launch a follow-up operation to eliminate this threat. The initial objective in General Rawlinson's plan was the outer Amiens defence line, representing an advance of about 6500 yards, to be carried out in three stages.[104] Haig later amended Rawlinson's plan in a more ambitious direction. Less than 72 hours before the start of the offensive, Haig in effect told Rawlinson that he was being too cautious and that Fourth Army should look to capturing the line Chaulnes-Royes, and that the attack should be directed towards Ham.[105] Haig, in other words, was 'extending Rawlinson's depth of operations from seven miles to 27'.[106]

Crucial in the success of the first day's operations, which saw the Australian and Canadian Corps reach most if not all of their objectives (III Corps on their left made only limited progress) was the element of surprise, the employment of tanks on a mass scale, and the success of British counter-battery work.[107] The cost of the operation was low by

Western Front standards; some 9000 British casualties (27,000 German); the capture of some 400 German guns and an advance of eight miles on a 15,000 yard front.[108]

On the Western Front, 'even where the first day of a major attack went well, the second and subsequent days proved hazardous'.[109] A break in the enemy line would be followed by a falling back of the enemy, a consolidation of a new defensive line with new trench systems, wire and supporting artillery, and an enemy counter-offensive with the aim of recapturing lost ground. Moreover, an advance by an attacking army beyond the range of their artillery was hazardous in the extreme. The battle of Amiens would be no exception to this.

The advances made on the 9–11 August, while significant, were not, therefore, on the same scale as on the 8 August. Corps and divisional commanders realised that they were being ordered to attack against positions of stiffening resistance, and enemy trench systems and artillery support were being re-established. Moreover, the 'key element' in the success of the British advance, the maturing 'weapons system', combining infantry, aircraft, effective artillery support (particularly accurate counter-battery work) and tanks, were, especially the last two, diminishing in quantity and effectiveness.[110]

Then came, as Trevor Wilson has described it, a 'crucial moment in the war on the Western Front'.[111] In previous offensives, Haig had persisted in flinging men against enemy defences in pursuit of distant strategic goals long after it was clear, or at least long after it ought to have been clear, that he had not the resources to achieve those goals. Now, however, Haig changed his approach. Rawlinson, commander of the Fourth Army, was persuaded by Currie, commander of the Canadian Corps, that the German defences were too strong to make an early renewal of the offensive effective. Rawlinson, in turn, persuaded Haig, and the latter decided that offensive operations would be renewed, not by the Fourth Army, but by the Third Army to the north. Foch, however, urged, 'then ordered' Haig to continue with the offensive out of Amiens. Haig refused, for the enemy positions on the line Chaulnes-Roye 'could only be taken after heavy casualties in men and tanks'. Foch persisted, but Haig held firm:

> I spoke to Foch quite straightly and let him understand that *I was responsible to my Government and fellow citizens for the handling of the British forces*. F's attitude at once changed and he said all he wanted was early information of my intentions so that he might co-ordinate the operations of the other Armies.[112]

It thus became clear that Haig, by implying that he might appeal to his Government, need only follow Foch's directives if it suited him. This would be the last time that Foch tried to issue Haig an order.[113]

How does this effect the veracity of Lloyd George's account of Amiens? His accusation that Haig let slip an even greater victory is unjustified. Haig, at last, and to his credit, had come to realise that open-ended operations with distant objectives just did not work in the conditions prevailing on the Western Front. More limited operations, launched on different sectors of the front, without letting the enemy fully recover and forcing him to move his limited reserves from one sector to another, offered greater prospects for successes. A certain degree of subtlety, or at least a certain level of sophistication had finally replaced the Allied sledgehammer. Earlier, one of Lloyd George's chief accusations against Haig had been that he did not know when to stop, for example on the Somme, and at Passchendaele. During the latter offensive, in particular, either Haig or, failing that, Lloyd George and the War Cabinet should have called a halt at the latest in October. They did not. But at Amiens Haig did just that, and turned his attention to a more promising sector of his front, and thereby avoiding yet another costly Western Front offensive which failed to meet distant objectives. To criticise Haig for making this decision is unfair and unjustified.

It perhaps needs to be reiterated that due to the peculiar command relationships pertaining from April 1918 between Haig, Foch and the British Government, Haig enjoyed a much greater freedom of action than at any other time of the war. Paradoxically, however, it has been argued that his role diminished as the size and complexity of his forces expanded; that Haig 'proved far more effective as a commander once the sphere of his activities began to diminish to an extent that brought them within the limits of his capabilities'. A much greater role was played in the final months of the war by commanders at Army, Corps, Divisional and even lower levels than in previous years, as their expertise, and the size and complexity of the BEF, steadily grew.[114] Even so, by August 1918 Haig had clearly learnt from the mistakes of the past, and part of this learning curve was the fact that in the second half of 1918 he largely refrained from interfering in the plans of his Army and Corps commanders. He would not persist in attacks with prospects of great loss of life with diminishing returns; instead, he would deliver a blow, then when that had played itself out, he would switch to another sector and deliver another. Haig, finally, had 'resorted to a manner of proceeding which, if it would yield no massive victories, would produce a succession of mounting triumphs'.[115]

VI

Which brings us to the question, just what did bring Germany to sue for an armistice? Was it military defeat on the Western Front? Or was it the collapse of Germany's allies in September and October 1918, as Lloyd George would – more or less – have it? As early as December 1914, as we have seen, Lloyd George thought that an attack on Austria-Hungary could well be a way around the developing stalemate in France. Periodically, thereafter, he advocated (as outlined in the *War Memoirs*), for example, sending greater amounts of arms to the Russians, greater diversion of resources to the Salonika front, or to the Middle East, or the sending of British guns (and sometimes troops) to Italy. This was in the belief that Germany's allies were weaker and more vulnerable militarily, but, conversely, at the same time were Germany's 'props' and that, if they collapsed Germany would not be able to sustain its military effort and its defeat would soon follow. Lloyd George became the most prominent 'Easterner' in the largely make-believe 'debate' between those who urged maximum concentration on the Western Front and those who saw great opportunities on other fronts in the east. Make-believe because as far as Britain was concerned, the 'war would be fought on the Western Front or it would be abandoned'.[116] This is as true in 1918 as it was in previous years.

In 1918 there were, Lloyd George concedes, victories on the Western Front. In addition to Amiens, where as we have seen he accuses Haig of passing up the chance of an even greater victory, he cites in particular the successful assault on the Hindenburg Line in late September. It was one of the most 'brilliant performances and decisive strokes' delivered by Haig and his 'dauntless Army'.[117] But throughout the chapter, there is little sense of Haig and the BEF's achievements of the 'Hundred Days' being due to skill (on Haig's part in particular) or British military power and expertise. Rather, behind the commanders of the national forces, 'the master-mind of Foch was at work', planning each blow, and organising the 'distribution of forces and reserves to obtain the maximum effect'.[118]

In addition, the Allies, by September 1918 were pushing back a defeated foe. Not only was the German army below strength and exhausted, but German morale both at the front and at home was collapsing due to a growing realisation that the war was lost.[119] The German Army 'was melting away, while the Allies were being reinforced by the steadily rising flood of American troops'.[120] As Trevor Wilson has noted, few of these American troops were actually appearing on the 'decisive battlefields', but acknowledging this awkward fact would have spoilt a good argument.[121] The German setbacks in France, however, were not what really counted in Germany's final defeat.

What really counted in bringing Germany's leaders to a realisation that they could not go on, according to Lloyd George, was the defeat of Germany's allies. Foch's plans for new offensives in late September were overtaken by events in other theatres. In the first week of September the Austrian Government issued its first peace note, and then on 15 September Bulgaria collapsed. And by 20 September the Turks in Palestine were conclusively defeated by British forces.[122] Germany, 'before the combined assault in the West was launched by the Allies, had already been abandoned by all her allies'. The secondary theatres 'made their contribution towards the Allied triumph on the Western Front. Had Germany's allies stood firm, the loss of morale amongst the German troops which weakened their resistance and gradually disintegrated the Army would not have occurred.'[123] Such claims are faintly reminiscent of Nazi claims that the German army was not defeated in France, but that the treacherous defection of allies and the disintegration of the home front led to the Armistice and the *diktat* of Versailles. It is perhaps little wonder that Lloyd George and Hitler agreed on so much when they met over tea during the former's visit to Germany in 1936.[124]

A simple chronology of events should suffice to dispel this myth. On 8 August came the 'black day' of the German army at Amiens; on 18 August the British advance began in Flanders; on 21 August the British began their advance across the old Somme battlefields. On 12 September the Americans launched their offensive at St Mihiel; and two days later the Allies attacked the Bulgarians at Salonika. On 18 September, the British commenced their attack on the Hindenburg Line; the next day Allenby attacked the Turks in Palestine. On 25 September, the Bulgarians sought an armistice; and on the 27th the British launched their attack which within days had breached the Hindenburg Line. The next day Ludendorff informed the Kaiser that an armistice should be sought. On 30 October, Turkey concluded an armistice, and on 4 November it was Austria's turn. And on 11 November Germany itself concluded an armistice which in effect was little better than an unconditional surrender.

By 26 September, the BEF had advanced about 25 miles on a 40-mile front.[125] By the time Bulgaria decided to sue for an armistice, it was already clear that in France the German army was in retreat, and was reeling from a series of blows all along its front. In the east it is surely more plausible that the small powers like Bulgaria hung on in the war as long as Germany had any prospect of success. Only when that hope disappeared did they leave the war with celerity. In this regard the war in Italy and the Balkans, like that in the east, was always contingent on the war in the west.[126]

If any indication is needed regarding the reality or otherwise of the German military defeat in France, then the armistice terms and indeed the eventual peace terms make instructive reading. The former precluded any renewal of hostilities by requiring evacuation of all occupied territories, the surrender of huge quantities of weapons, including submarines, machine-guns, artillery and aircraft, and even the evacuation of the left bank of the Rhine. The later peace terms included terms which no German Government would have signed 'if its military situation had been anything but calamitous'.[127] Much of this military calamity for Germany had occurred on the Western Front, and a significant part of it was due to Field-Marshal Sir Douglas Haig and the BEF.

VII

In February 1918 Lloyd George successfully maneouvred Sir William Robertson out of the post of CIGS in the confident expectation that he would be able then to impose his own strategic ideas on the military. Events, however, intervened. The Germans' offensive in France forced the Government to pour reinforcements into France; it threw into stark relief the vital importance of the Western Front.

The *War Memoirs'* account of 1918 is defensive and, as Trevor Wilson has noted, 'anti-climactic'. For according to Lloyd George, the war was not won by the BEF in France, supplied by the massively expanded munitions industries of Britain which Lloyd George himself had done so much to bring about, but by the theatres where Allied forces (among which were only small British contingents) confronted Germany's allies Austria-Hungary, Bulgaria and Turkey. The 'props, seemingly, had collapsed of their own accord, and somehow taken Germany with them'.[128] Lloyd George had become so convinced of the importance of the eastern and southern theatres that in the *War Memoirs* he remains constant to the views expressed in earlier volumes. Credit is denied to the BEF and Haig for the crucial, indeed, central role they played in the defeat of the German army.

9
Russia: War and Revolution 1914–18

I

We come now to a consideration of Lloyd George's treatment of the eastern theatre of operations. To this point this book has been concerned mostly, in one way or another, with Lloyd George's account of the war in the west, and the alternatives open to the Western Powers in pursuing the war against Germany and its allies. The conduct, or rather misconduct of the war in France and Belgium certainly preoccupied Lloyd George in the *War Memoirs*. Lloyd George's narrative, however, is not confined to that theatre alone. As we have seen, at various points in the *War Memoirs* Lloyd George discusses developments in the Balkans, the Middle East and Italy, and of course the great opportunities missed by the Western Allies in those regions. There is in the *Memoirs* also a consideration of various aspects of events on the Eastern Front and in Russia, and it is to aspects of these chapters that I now turn.

II

If one of the great themes of the *War Memoirs* is the misconduct of the war on the Western Front, a subsidiary theme is the possibilities and opportunities offered to the Allies by directing greater resources to their Russian ally. In Eastern Europe vast Russian armies confronted those of Germany and Austria-Hungary, whose forces were smaller but better equipped, and along a front significantly longer and more fluid than that in France.

In August 1914 after the German invasion of France, Russia invaded East Prussia. Never one to let an opportunity to subject generals – even in this case French ones – to strong criticism, Lloyd George uses the Russian defeat at Tannenberg which resulted from the invasion to argue that the latter was little more than an act of 'chivalrous improvisation to save France from the blunders of her generals'; it came, he observes, to a bad end with...Tannenberg.[1] Lloyd George, of course, had read Churchill's *World Crisis* as preparation for the writing of the *War Memoirs*. Here is what Churchill had to say regarding the invasion of East Prussia:

> A purely Russian treatment of their military problem would have led the Russian armies into immediate withdrawals from their frontiers until the whole of their vast mobilization was completed. Instead of this, they added to a forward mobilization an *impetuous* advance not only against Austria but into Germany. The flower of the Russian army was soon to be cut down in...East Prussia. But the results of their invasion were gathered at the decisive point....On August 25 two army corps and a cavalry division of the German right were withdrawn from France.[2]

The similarity in Lloyd George's and Churchill's argument is surely not coincidental.

Hankey, however, took issue with Lloyd George's description of the offensive as a 'chivalrous improvisation':

> The Russian plan did not work out so badly in Galicia. As regards the invasion of East Prussia, Joffre shows in his Memoirs that even before the War (as he ascertained during his visit to Russia) *it was in the programme*. Nevertheless, he always seemed to have been a bit dubious about it and was very relieved when it took place. I think I should re-draft as follows:-

> The Russians had some successes against Austria. Against Germany, if they ever had a plan it never came off. The invasion of East Prussia was little more than a *brilliant* improvisation.[3]

which prompted Liddell Hart to comment:

> As regards the Russian plan, that again was originally to concentrate against Austria and leave Germany alone. It was modified because of the agreement which the French had squeezed out of General Jilinsky in 1912. The action against Germany was certainly left rather indefinite *and only took shape under French pressure in August '14*; thus the invasion of East Prussia may be called an improvised plan, but I should hardly call it a 'brilliant' one. The conception was quite good, but the execution was fantastically bad and ill-co-ordinated.[4]

Liddell Hart, then, acknowledges that while there was provision for a Russian invasion of East Prussia in the pre-war Franco-Russian military agreement, Russian action in August 1914 was indeed hastily undertaken (and badly implemented) under French pressure with the main object of drawing German forces away from the Western Front, and this view prevailed in the *War Memoirs*.

Russian strategic planning prior to 1914 indeed shifted and changed, a product of Russia's strategic dilemma, whether to concentrate against Germany or Austria-Hungary.[5] But Russia laid plans and entered into alliances 'neither in response to Allied pressures nor from altruistic motives, but from soundly perceived self interest'. Planners had a good idea of German ambitions in Russia, and there was little doubt that Germany was perceived as the most dangerous enemy.[6] A Russian attack on East Prussia, notes historian Dennis E. Showalter, would both serve Russian strategic interests and help France. East Prussia was:

Germany's most obvious geographic weak point...East Prussia's assumed cultural and political importance in the Second Empire seemed to guarantee that the German Army – or at least that portion of it left in the East – would stand, fight, and be crushed.[7]

It made sense, moreover, to strike while the bulk of the German army was busy in Belgium and France.

It has also been argued that according to the standards then prevailing, mobilisation of the Russian First and Second Armies went 'smoothly'; the troops, in addition, were well, even generously equipped. This hardly smacks of improvisation. Difficulties in the provision of munitions after the first weeks of hostilities were due to the unexpected tremendous expenditure of shells and other munitions that took place during August and which became common on both Western and Eastern Fronts.[8] The first weeks of hostilities shattered pre-war illusions in this as in many other areas.

It should be noted, too, that the Russian advance, in its early stages at least, seemed to work. The German commander, von Prittwitz, after early setbacks, panicked and urged a full-scale retreat.[9] He quickly recovered, however, and the subsequent appointment of Field Marshal Paul von Hindenburg and General Erich Ludendorff to command in the east and the transfer of two army corps from the west saw the German forces stiffened and the stage was set for Tannenberg.

What of Russian 'chivalry' and unreadiness for action which led to the disaster at Tannenberg? Perhaps some arguing this line were influenced by Russian émigré accounts in the postwar period. With a 'hindsight sharpened by exile', former participants in the campaign and officers in the Russian Imperial Army presented the attack on East Prussia as a 'sacrificial gambit made to fulfill a moral obligation to their French ally by relieving the German pressure in the west'.[10] Lieutenant General N.N. Golovine, for example, referred to the Russian GHQ's 'chivalrous readiness to fulfill the heavy obligations undertaken by Russia', and claims that in the pre-war period Russia made undertakings to France which it could not keep except at the risk of disaster.[11] Émigré officers, however, obviously had a vested interest in seeking an explanation for the Russian defeat which did not focus on themselves and which placed the blame on the senior commanders, politicians and diplomats responsible for Russian policy and strategy.

After Tannenberg the experience of war for the Russian army in 1915 seemed to be constant retreat. The Russian 'steamroller' patently failed to fulfil the high expectations held by many in the west. As Lloyd George explains, while during that year advances on the Western Front of one kilometre were hailed as a victory, on the Eastern Front during the same period the Germans

> drove the Russian armies on a front of 500 miles to a distance ranging from 90 to 300 miles from their original entrenchments. Every shell told. The price they paid in German lives for their vast conquests was not half what we sacrificed in the attainment of trivial results. They captured more great cities and provinces than we did hamlets and shell harrowed fields.[12]

Vast numbers of Russian troops could not, in the end, compensate for lack of munitions.

The Russian inferiority in munitions was, according to Lloyd George, striking. Their defeats were entirely due to their shortages of 'artillery, rifles and ammunition of all kinds'.[13] Russia could not hope to properly equip its army of millions from its own resources, as it was a 'half-primitive peasant land, unskilled in industrial arts and therefore unable to provide her gallant young defenders with adequate weapons'. Also, it had not the wealth which could command sufficient credit to purchase equipment in the United States.[14] What then should have been done?

Britain and France, he writes, could and should have organised and increased their munitions productions to the point where they could have provided Russia with sufficient supplies to properly equip its army. The Allies, in other words, should have 'pooled their resources'.

France and Britain were the industrial powerhouses of the alliance and possessed an abundance of munitions, while Russia was rich in human resources. Britain, in late 1915, could have supplied Russia with sufficient quantities for some two million Russian soldiers 'with almost as powerful an armoury of machines and missiles as that with which she sent 1,500,000 Britons into action in the summer and autumn of 1916'.[15] But British mobilisation began too late, he argues, and both British and French generals were transfixed by the Western Front – every gun, every shell, had to be concentrated in France. That Britain and France did not 'pool their resources' with the Russians was unfortunate:

history will return a true bill against the military directors of France and Britain for their selfish obtuseness in abandoning their comrades in arms to hopeless carnage, when they might so easily have saved them and in so doing rendered the most effective help to their own countries. They never could be taught to appreciate the fact that a great victory over the Germans in Poland would be a greater service to France and Belgium than a slight advance into the German lines in Champagne, or even than the capture of a molehill in Flanders.[16]

The War Office, despite massive orders with both British and American firms, and despite significant improvements in production and delivery during 1915–16, just did not possess, however, that abundance of shells and other munitions which would have allowed a genuine pooling of resources. Shell shortages troubled the BEF in France in early 1915, after all, and were at least partly the cause of Lloyd George assuming responsibility for munitions production. Abundance did not prevail until 1917. Moreover there is no evidence that in 1915–16 Lloyd George was urging that significantly more resources should be diverted to Russia rather than sent to France or wherever else British troops were deployed. Thus in 1915, for example, he told the War Office that the early delivery of the extra guns to the BEF might make all the difference for the 1916 campaign on *the Western Front* and opposed their transfer to Russia. His main focus during 1915–16, indeed throughout the war, was to supply adequately the BEF on the Western Front.[17]

III

Lloyd George, however, was indeed arguing in 1914–17 that better strategic coordination and cooperation was necessary between the Western Allies and Russia. Any sensible politician could have seen that closer coordination between east and west had the potential to pay significant dividends. As early as February 1915, Lloyd George was urging that a conference be held of the three Powers to ascertain the true situation for each and to coordinate future action.[18] It was not until February 1917, however, that a three Power Allied conference at senior ministerial level took place in Petrograd.

Some progress was made at this conference in Petrograd towards addressing problems of transport of supplies to Russia, and the conference also recommended that a 'central organ' be established of the major allies which would advise on and coordinate strategy.[19] But, as Lloyd George points out, all this came much too late for Russia. These were issues which should have been addressed in 1915, not 1917, before 'Russian nerve, patience and endurance had been exhausted and before despair and hunger had bred disaffection'.[20] Barely one week after Milner and Henry Wilson, the principal British representatives, had presented their reports to the War Cabinet, revolution had broken out in Petrograd and the Tsar was overthrown. By May Milner could write that the 'work which our mission tried to do [in Petrograd] is as dead as Queen Anne'.[21]

The decisions taken by the Petrograd conference, late in the day as they were, were one thing. But for Lloyd George the most remarkable, indeed the most inexplicable feature of the Petrograd conference was that both Milner and Wilson returned from Russia convinced that revolution would not occur, at least while the war lasted. They must, he argues, have been 'deaf and blind' to miss the many signs of the impending eruption: 'Everything they saw, most of what they heard, pointed to revolution [he asserted], and immediate revolution.'[22] This is, of course, a classic example of Lloyd George arguing with the benefit of hindsight. And it was all very well for Lloyd George to accuse Milner and Wilson of 'blindness' and 'deafness' in regard to the impending upheaval. Lloyd George was not, after all, a member of the official delegation in Petrograd. Quite clearly, not everything that Milner and Wilson saw in Russia pointed to 'immediate revolution'.

Milner wrote that there was a 'good deal of exaggeration' in the talk of revolution, while Wilson thought that the Russian army was still capable of 'great things' having recovered from the travails of 1915. He was impressed by the soldiers' readiness to salute, and thought them 'brave and patient', but 'illiterate and stupid'.[23] These impressions were reported despite interviews with many who spoke openly of the possibility of the Tsar and his wife being assassinated and warned of disaster looming unless the Tsar instituted radical reforms.

Milner and Wilson were not alone in their impression that there would be no revolution. Experienced diplomats also failed to predict the collapse. The First Secretary in Petrograd, F.O. Findlay, for example, wrote to the Foreign Office after the revolution expressing the hope that the Embassy would not be considered 'very blind' for failing to predict the fall of the monarchy, while the British Ambassador himself, Sir George Buchanan, described the Petrograd rioting in February as 'nothing serious'.[24] The initial spontaneity and undirected nature of the early rioting in the Russian capital has been noted by many.[25] Even Lieutenant-Colonel A.W. Knox, British Military Attaché, who spoke Russian and visited the front regularly, wrote at the end of January that all that needed to be done was that the King needed to write to the Tsar 'urging him to appoint a government with the confidence of the people'. He argued that most Russians supported the Allies and hated the Germans and all that was required, he asserted, was a 'dictator who would choose a strong ministry and do a little hanging'.[26] As David French has noted, the need for a strong Russia and an active Eastern Front 'blinded' many to the realities of Russia's predicament.[27]

Both Milner and Wilson, too, realised that Russia was indeed in crisis, and knew that little if anything could be expected of its army in the near future at least. Neither were under any illusions as to the chaotic state of the transport system, the deep unpopularity of the Tsar, his wife and many of their advisers, and the weakened state of the Russian army. Indeed in his report Milner wrote of the latter:

> whether . . . either now or later, her offensive power can be so much increased as to justify our counting upon her to alter the character of the war on the Eastern front, is another question. She will continue to contain a large proportion of the enemy's forces. We may reasonably hope that she will compel him to send further reinforcements to the East. And it certainly is not impossible that she may breakthrough his line at some point in such a fashion as to compel a general retreat. But, to be quite honest, I hardly hope for as much as this, and I am quite certain that we should be unwise to reckon on it.[28]

Wilson was more positive in his assessment of the Russian army, judging on the whole that the '*moral* of the Russian Army is good' and that the men were wonderful. But he also wrote that, in the end, it was luck which would be the determining factor: 'If luck is on their side, they may do really great things . . . if luck is against them, they will do very little. The Russians have neither the *matériel* nor the organisation to force the hand of Fortune.'[29] The army was incapable of a 'single massed offensive'; the most that could be hoped for were 'local and separate offensives of the separate commands', although even these were not certain to take place. Moreover, generals and their staffs were quite out of touch with conditions in the front line, and many divisions had little or no artillery.[30] If conditions were like this in the north, where the troops were better equipped and more capably led, then it is little wonder that Wilson's French counterpart, General de Castelnau, returned from a visit to the more poorly provisioned southern Front 'profoundly depressed'.[31]

Lloyd George's criticisms of Milner and Wilson were quite unfair. As with any official delegation to even a friendly country, the delegates were in the host government's hands, and at least to some extent were only able to see and hear what and who the government thought appropriate. Even so, they saw enough and heard enough to realise that on the crucial point which was of most concern to the British Government, that of the future of military operations against the Germans on the Eastern Front, that little if anything could be expected from the Russians in the immediate future.

IV

The fall of the Tsarist autocracy in early 1917, we now know, was but the prelude to the disintegration of the Russian front and the Russian army and the eventual Bolshevik *coup d'etat*. There would be one more feeble offensive under the Provisional Government before the advent of the Bolsheviks took Russia completely out of the war. This prospect was not, however, so clear at the time. While, as we have seen, some senior British military and political figures had no great expectations of the Russian army achieving anything of value in the near future, the fall of the Tsar filled some in the west with renewed hope.

For Lloyd George, the Tsarist regime fell due to its very real failures and inadequacies. In contrast to Churchill, who argued that Russia had 'victory in her grasp' but 'sank in sight of port',[32] Lloyd George argued more realistically that she may have weathered the storm but only as a

> battered hulk, with her engines neglected and out of repair, tossed about helplessly in the breakers with a feeble and foolish captain, a scratch lot of officers, and a crew some on the brink of mutiny and the rest steeped in the spirit of discontent, rapidly fermenting into mutiny.

Churchill's view could only be explained by his 'morbid detestation of the Revolution'.[33]

Reflecting the official view that the revolution would reinvigorate Russia's war effort the Provisional Government was recognised promptly by Lloyd George's Government on 16 March 1917, and Bonar Law moved a congratulatory resolution in the House of Commons. On 21 March Lloyd George sent the new Russian Premier Prince Lvov a message which concluded:

> Freedom is the only warranty of Peace, and I do not doubt that as a result of the establishment of a stable Constitutional Government within their borders the Russian people will be strengthened in their resolve to prosecute this War until the last stronghold of tyranny on the Continent of Europe is destroyed and the free peoples of all lands can unite to secure for themselves and their children the blessings of fraternity and of Peace.[34]

While it had been 'impossible' to help the old Russia, under the new regime, Lloyd George told C.P. Scott, 'all would be different'.[35]

Lloyd George, like many others when confronted by the spectacle of Russian government's collapse and revolution, liked to invoke the analogy of the earlier revolution in France. After all, it was comforting in the context of the struggle with the Central Powers to imagine that, like the French Republicans in 1793–94, the Russian democrats, after the collapse of an autocratic and thoroughly discredited monarchy, would with renewed vigour rouse the people against foreign invaders and drive them from Russian soil. The circumstances in 1917, however, were quite different and the analogy was inappropriate.[36]

This became only too clear over the coming months. Far from the Russians being reinvigorated with patriotic fervour and driving the Germans out of their country, the Provisional Government's attempts to carry on the war met with fierce opposition both inside the army and among the more radical parties, not least the Bolsheviks led by Lenin who had recently returned from exile with German help. Throughout the life of the Provisional Government the fighting ability of the Russian army steadily disintegrated, as Robertson recognised:

> There is just a chance that the Russian revolution will have a bad effect on Germany. I hope to goodness it has for it is certainly having a bad one in Russia. In the Fleet everything is disorganised, the sailors have shot their Admirals and Captains, and the discipline in

the Army is also very bad. As we feared, it has spread to the Caucasus where there has been a mutiny, and the General commanding one of the detachments...has resigned his Command because his men refused to obey him. I am fairly convinced we shall get nothing out of Russia this year anywhere.[37]

As if to underline the increasing ineffectiveness of the army, it was apparent within days that the last Russian offensive of the war, launched in early July, had failed utterly.[38]

The Bolsheviks attempted uprising the same month demonstrated the fragility of support for the Provisional Government; while General Kornilov's attempted military 'coup' soon after further demonstrated the Government's weakness. Kerensky was forced to accept the help of the Bolsheviks to survive, thereby reviving their fortunes after a failed uprising. The Government was tottering, and the only real threat now came from the extreme Left, who were determined on peace.

The failure of Kornilov's coup was, as Riddell wrote, 'a serious blow for the Allies'; Russia, Lloyd George writes in the *War Memoirs*, as a 'fighting force was falling to pieces'; divisions were melting away, and anarchy prevailed in Petrograd and Moscow.[39] The Prime Minister, Alexander Kerensky, was not a man of action and no match for the resolute Lenin, who on 7 November 'overthrew the Kerensky Government with the greatest of ease. Kerensky put up no fight. The Bolsheviks were in power.'[40]

The British Government was now faced with a 'situation of the utmost complication'.[41] The overriding policy objective for Britain was the continued prosecution of the war against the Central Powers. The Bolsheviks, however, were clearly bent on peace. The day after their coup they issued the 'Decree on Peace' calling on all belligerents to begin negotiations for a peace without 'annexations or indemnities'.[42] And despite their call for a *general* armistice, *bilateral* negotiations were soon underway between German and Soviet representatives.[43] On the other hand, the various anti-Bolshevik groupings scattered throughout the former Empire seemed to offer continued hostilities against the Germans and thus were more attractive from London's perspective, provided they were provided with the necessary material resources.

There were other considerations. The Bosheviks' authority extended to barely one-third of the former Russian Empire, and much of the population, Lloyd George writes in the *War Memoirs*, were distinctly hostile or at least indifferent to the new régime.[44] Politically the results of the elections for the Constituent Assembly revealed that by far the largest single party were the Right Social Revolutionaries, a peasant-based party; the Bolsheviks were in a distinct minority, and consequently they promptly dispersed it after its first meeting.[45] Another consideration in Lloyd George's view was the Bolsheviks revolutionary ideology. For Bolshevism was a universalist creed, opposed to private property and all 'bourgeois imperialist' governments, whether of the Central Powers or the Entente, and the Bolsheviks fully expected, and encouraged, revolution wherever they could. This made 'capitalist' statesmen and politicians jittery, some expecting that in the event of normalisation of relations between the new Russia and Britain a stream of communist agitators would enter the latter to foment revolution.[46]

Officially, however, the reason for Allied non-recognition of the new regime was that the Bolsheviks had so little authority over much of Russia: 'The Cossacks of the Don were opposed to them. The Ukraine wished a Government of its own. The Caucasus was by no means Bolshevik. Neither was Siberia. These were facts of great moment to us.'[47] These facts were of great moment because it was considered vital to prevent the Central Powers gaining control of the abundant resources to be found in these areas, principally oil and grain. Yet it is difficult, despite Lloyd George's protestations, to deny that there was some ideological basis, at least implicitly, to the British Government's decision to refuse recognition to the Bolsheviks and the later military intervention in support of anti-Bolshevik forces, initially with the aim of reconstituting an Eastern Front, but later still, with the clear purpose of providing military support to those factions whose overriding concern was to topple Lenin's government. The Provisional Government, after all, had less than perfect authority over the whole of Russia, but were recognised as the legitimate Government by all of the Allied Powers.[48]

The Treaty of Brest-Litovsk, concluded in March 1918, was a draconian peace. The Bolshevik Government was forced to cede huge swathes of territory to the Central Powers, and the latter gained the much sought after access to the resources of the Ukraine and the Caucasus. With the conclusion of hostilities in the east, Germany could, as Allied statesmen – including Lloyd George – feared, look forward to regaining the initiative on the Western Front. The way would be open for a renewed German offensive in France, with its army reinforced by men and munitions from the east. Even with these reinforcements, however, as we have seen, the German army was not able to inflict a decisive defeat on the Allies. For the German policy of conquest in the east remained a massive drain on manpower. The offensive on the Western Front beginning in

March 1918 was Germany's last throw of the dice for total victory, but strategic ineptitude, Allied technical and material superiority, and the arrival of the Americans in force doomed it to failure. Thus, as we can see now, the worst forebodings of Lloyd George and his colleagues were misplaced.

V

The most prominent of the countless victims of Russia's revolution and civil war, and in the context of Lloyd George's *War Memoirs*, a potentially explosive issue was the failure of the Allied governments to save the overthrown Tsar and his family. In Britain, the blame for many years was laid at the door of the Lloyd George and his Government. Lloyd George, of course, was determined to refute this allegation. But in doing so his account had the potential to cause offence in very high places indeed.

After the February uprising, Nicholas, his wife Alexandra, his son Alexei and four daughters, along with a small number of retainers, were placed under house arrest in the royal residence in Tsarskoe Selo, just outside Petrograd. Debate then began over their future. If one possibility was, indeed, exile, as was mooted by certain figures in the new Government, then the natural destination, given the close family links between Nicholas and the British King George V, was Britain.

That this did not in fact occur is a matter of historical record. Nicholas and his family were later moved to the more secure Tobolsk in Siberia, and then, after the Bosheviks came to power, to Ekaterinberg, where on the night of 16–17 July all were shot by the local Bolsheviks. The question addressed by Lloyd George is, what was the responsibility of the British Government which he led for this tragedy? His central argument in the *War Memoirs* is that:

> The fact is that at no time between his [the Tsar's] abdication and his murder was he free to leave Russia. An invitation to take refuge here was extended by the British Crown and Government. The Czar was unable in the event to avail himself of it, even had he been anxious to do so – and of that we had no evidence.[49]

The invitation issued to the former Tsar 'was not withdrawn' and the 'ultimate issue in the matter was decided by the action of the Russian Government'.[50] Nothing, Lloyd George writes, 'could be done about it unless the Russian Government changed their attitude'.[51] Thus, the

British Government could not be held responsible for the failure to rescue the Romanovs. Is this, however, the case?

The Provisional Government and the Soviets, indeed, played their part in the failure of Nicholas to find refuge. Radical elements in Soviets across the country in early 1917 were demanding the 'immediate arrest of the entire Romanov dynasty so that the possibility of restoring the monarchy was nipped in the bud'.[52] While internal opposition to the former monarch's exile was undoubtedly a major factor in the family remaining in Russia; it is clear that, whatever Lloyd George claims in the *War Memoirs*, the British offer *was* withdrawn after the King, George V, through his Private Secretary, Lord Stamfordham, repeatedly and insistently brought pressure to bear on Lloyd George and the Foreign Secretary, A.J. Balfour.

On 22 March 1917, the day, as Lloyd George relates in the *War Memoirs*, on which the Imperial War Cabinet would authorise an invitation to the Tsar and his family to come to Britain, Stamfordham met the Prime Minister to discuss the question.[53] Miliukov, the new Russian Foreign Minister, had told Buchanan that the former Tsar should take up residence abroad, and indicated that the Provisional Government would welcome an invitation from Britain. Both Stamfordham and Lloyd George agreed that this could not be refused.[54] Just over a week later, however, Stamfordham wrote to Balfour doubting, on account 'of the dangers of the voyage [and also] on general grounds of expediency, whether it is advisable that the Imperial family should take up residence in this country'.[55] But Balfour did not think that, as the invitation had already been extended, it was possible to withdraw it.[56] On 3 April Stamfordham replied:

> I have received and laid before His Majesty your letter...As his Majesty's Ministers are still anxious that the King should adhere to the original invitation sent on their advice His Majesty must regard the matter as settled, unless the Russian Government should come to any fresh decision on the subject.[57]

There the matter rested – briefly.

On 6 April, Stamfordham returned to the fray, noting to Balfour that the King had been receiving letters from people in all classes and walks of life expressing opposition to the former Tsar residing in Britain:

> As you know from the first the King has thought the presence of the Imperial family (especially of the Empress) in this country would

raise all kinds of difficulties, and I feel sure you appreciate how awkward it will be for our Royal Family who are closely connected both with Emperor and Empress. You are probably also aware that the subject has become more or less public property, and that people are either assuming that it has been initiated by the King, or deprecating the very unfair position in which His Majesty will be placed if the arrangement is carried out.

Stamfordham then arrived at his point:

> The King desires me to ask you whether after consulting the Prime Minister, Sir George Buchanan should not be communicated with a view to approaching the Russian Government to make some other plan for the future residence of their Imperial Majesties.[58]

In a postscript, Stamfordham added: 'Most people appear to think the invitation was initiated by the King whereas it was *his Govt.* who did so.'[59] Further and stronger representations from Stamfordham to both Balfour and Lloyd George had, in the end, the desired effect.[60] Buchanan was informed that the whole question was being reconsidered; Miliukov later recalled:

> Just before my resignation, Buchanan, with some embarrassment, informed me, in answer to my reminder about the cruiser which was expected [for the Imperial family] that his government 'no longer insists' on its invitation. From the memoirs of Buchanan's daughter we know how difficult it was for him to bear this refusal himself.[61]

If the former Tsar were to be refused asylum in Britain, where then could he go? France had been mentioned as a possible alternative place of refuge, as had Denmark, Switzerland and Spain. The Provisional Government thought Switzerland and Denmark too close to Germany, however, and Lloyd George was strongly against Denmark as the former Tsar might become a 'focus of intrigue of Germany'.[62] The War Cabinet thought that Spain might be a more suitable place of residence, but only in the event that Spain joined the Allies.[63] Spain's entry into the war, however, showed little sign of eventuating. As for France, Lord Bertie, the British Ambassador in Paris, poured cold water on this proposal; while he thought it a 'mercy' that the British invitation had been withdrawn ('for the Germans would have given out that the . . . British Government were keeping the ex-Emperor in reserve to be used for a restoration') he observed that feeling in France was also against granting the ex-Tsar refuge: Alexandra in particular was a 'Boche by birth [and] sentiment...She is regarded as a criminal or a criminal lunatic and the ex-Emperor as a criminal from his weakness and submission to her prompting.'[64] So Nicholas, Alexandra and their children, restrained by the Provisional Government and the revolution-aries in the Soviets,[65] denied assistance and asylum by their relatives and wartime Allies, remained in Russia, abandoned to their fate.

It is clear, then, that, as A.J. Sylvester put it, 'The failure to rescue [the Imperial family] did not lie at LG's door.'[66] Of all the actors in this drama, Lloyd George was among the least responsible. Whatever obstacles the Provisional Government and the radicals in Russia put in place to prevent them from leaving, it is difficult to argue with Kenneth Rose's conclusion that the King and Stamfordham, having judged that the political costs of granting asylum to the Romanovs outweighed any possible benefits,[67] made every effort to deny them their 'best, perhaps *their only means of escape'*, even if there was in reality because of the Soviets' obstruction little chance of an escape to British exile succeeding.[68]

Lloyd George's published account is misleading. That it was so was due to Hankey's objections to the proposed chapter on the 'Czar's Future Residence'. In his draft Lloyd George was not quite so circum-spect regarding the King as in the published version; another problem was that he quoted extensively from Foreign Office telegrams and War Cabinet minutes. Hankey especially took exception to the inclusion of an extract from the War Cabinet minutes of 13 April which read:

There was a strong feeling hostile to the Czar in this country, and that articles tending to associate the King with the Czar had appeared in the Press; it was felt that, if the Czar should take up his residency here, there was a danger that these tendencies might be stimulated and accentuated. It was further pointed out that, in the event of any differences of opinion between the British and Russian Governments, there would be a tendency in Russia to attribute our attitude to the Czar's presence. In these circumstances it was suggested that the South of France, or even Spain (but only in the event of Spain joining the Allies) might be a more suitable place of residence, if the Czar should be permitted to leave Russia.[69]

Telegrams which had passed to and fro between Balfour and Buchanan also contained objectionable references to anti-monarchical sentiment in Britain. Hankey was sure that the King 'would strongly resent' publication of this material. He considered the telegrams so central to the narrative that their omission would render the chapter 'meaningless'. Therefore he recommended that the whole chapter be suppressed. Hankey passed the chapter on to Sir Robert Vansittart, Permanent Under-Secretary of State at the Foreign Office, who entirely agreed.[70] While Hankey quite understood Lloyd George's desire to publish this material 'owing to the adverse comments that have been made against the refusal of your Government to give the Czar asylum in England', he reckoned that as the controversy had died down it would 'not be a great sacrifice to you to give up these seven pages'.[71]

Lloyd George finally bowed to pressure as he did not want to do anything which could be 'injurious to the monarchy and certainly not to the King', and, as Sylvester noted, the 'Court...might take the line that we must not publish anything'.[72] Two months later Sylvester noted in his diary that 'LG has decided to write another chapter about the Tsar. The other has been scrapped because of objections to it from Hankey, Baldwin and the Court. The new material is not to refer to the movements which were regarded as anti-monarchical in this country.'[73] As Kenneth Rose concluded, while the new, sanitised account of the episode was not 'strictly true', it had the virtue of saving the King's 'honour'.[74]

VI

Lloyd George's chapters on Russia differ from those on, for example, home politics and the Western Front. He was not a direct participant in these events, with the exception of the machinations surrounding the proposed offer of asylum to the Tsar. Nonetheless, in places he displays a greater realism than Churchill's account of the same events, particularly when dealing with the revolution. Churchill suffers from his visceral hatred of the Bolsheviks, while Lloyd George laboured under no such handicap. Of course, it should be noted that, generally, Churchill's views on the criminality of the Bolshevik régime have been thoroughly vindicated. But Lloyd George's account of this period is, in places, more balanced and perceptive. It is when dealing with that episode in which he was directly involved that official pressure resulted in an account which is distorted and misleading.

Conclusion

I

As Swinton had predicted, some people were waiting for Lloyd George's *War Memoirs* with 'guns and clubs'. Many ex-servicemen were outraged by his attacks on Haig.[1] Some prominent former senior officers, such as General Maurice, privately and publicly condemned the *Memoirs*. In a speech at the Albert Hall, Maurice labelled Lloyd George's denunciation of Haig a 'dastardly lie'.[2] Yet generally, the *Memoirs* were positively received, and they were praised as an important contribution to the history of the war. For many reviewers, however, the constant attacks on ex-colleagues and the refusal to admit that he himself had any faults or made any mistakes became tedious.

One feature of the *Memoirs* warmly received by all was the mass of documentary material published for the first time. This was particularly important in an age when most government records were not accessible to historians and were not likely to be for many years to come. The documents rendered the *Memoirs* invaluable as a historical source: 'The new facts which they display, the point of view of the war-time Prime Minister, the vast and varied scope of his work, all make this volume, like its forerunners, an indispensable contribution to our knowledge and to our descendents knowledge of Armageddon.'[3] In the *New Statesman and Nation*, in a review which placed the *War Memoirs* firmly with the 'literature of disenchantment' of the early 1930s, Kingsley Martin wrote that Lloyd George had presented a 'crushing array of official documents' to support his case. He regretted that Haig and Robertson were not still alive to answer Lloyd George's charges. They were fully documented and could only be refuted by other documents.[4] Harold Laski also recognised the crucial importance of the documentation: 'Most of [the volume's] validity depends on the proportionate importance of documents to which the public has only partial admission. What Mr Lloyd George reveals is devastatingly on his side.'[5]

Laski, however, offered what Egerton calls 'perhaps the most telling critique of the *War Memoirs* as history'.[6] Lloyd George, Laski wrote, still accepted 'the legendary account of the war as a struggle between right and wrong', and he still thought of history 'as primarily made by men who can will a given end and, if they have the necessary capacities, secure its triumph'. He was the man who won the war, and triumphed over evil; Russia withdrew from the war because Lenin 'was a bigger man than Kerensky'; there was, however, no appreciation or understanding of the vast, impersonal economic and social forces 'in the grip of which men so largely are'. Laski concluded that many 'have taken the view of history as the biography of great men; yet that simplicity will, I think, appear excessive to most of those who consider its implications'.[7]

The *Times Literary Supplement*, while also acknowledging Lloyd George's impressive array of documentary evidence, rightly pointed out that the book had another purpose: his aim was self vindication, to be achieved by 'blackening the repute' of his wartime colleagues who disagreed with his views. Opposition, according to Lloyd George, was 'due to deficiencies of will or brains or both: and by his unrestrained gratification of his vendettas Mr Lloyd George weakens his authority as a guide to historical truth'.[8] Nevertheless, despite its faults the *Times Literary Supplement* was 'glad to have the book as it is':

> When the high literary quality of the book is discounted, when the controversies into which it foams or rages have been adjourned to await the decision of a calmer and clearer-minded age, when the breadth and sweep of the narrative have been allowed to be offset by its occasional passion and its too frequent vindictiveness, this verdict remains sure: that there is one man of whom Mr Lloyd George tells the final truth and to whom he does unflinching, if unconscious, justice when he might have shown mercy. That man is himself.[9]

Liddell Hart was, unsurprisingly, complimentary in his reviews. He was, after all, reviewing a work which faithfully reflected his own views on the war, and into which had had some input. In the *Sunday Times* Liddell Hart wrote that the *War Memoirs* were unique in their importance and candour. They 'reveal, more clearly and authoritatively, than anything yet has done, why the Allies took so long and stumbled so often on the road to victory despite their immense resources'.[10] It was difficult, he thought, to see how Lloyd George's arguments could be contradicted. Even the more 'vivid' character sketches of his former colleagues had the ring of truth, as there was in the book abundant documentary evidence. Lloyd George was clearly not 'indulging in proverbial wisdom after the event' – during the war he was right, battling against 'blindness in authority'.[11]

Yet even Liddell Hart wrote that the factual case against Haig and Robertson was so strong that Lloyd George's 'vehement supplementary comments' were superfluous.[12] Robert Hield in the *Morning Post* went so far as to suggest that readers might come away after reading the volumes with the impression that it was written for no other purpose than 'to indulge the author's unappeasable feud against Earl Haig and Sir William Robertson'.[13] Whether approving or not of the attacks on ex-colleagues contained in the character sketches, they were recognised as a central, even 'outstanding' feature of the *Memoirs*.[14]

The *Morning Post*, while recognising Lloyd George's right to defend himself, 'he would have been less than human if he – the target of so many criticisms, accusations, reproaches and censures – had no impulse to defend himself and to return the enemy's fire', felt he had gone too far. He seized the opportunity with both hands – 'almost with teeth and claws as well'.[15] For many, a sense of the author's infallibility ran through the memoirs; that Lloyd George alone won the war, and it would have been won even sooner if his ideas and suggestions had been acted upon. As the *Morning Post* commented:

It is possible to give Mr Lloyd George full credit for the invaluable services...rendered to this country...without believing he was always right and that everybody else was always wrong....The reader is taught to conclude that if Mr Lloyd George could only have been Captain-General of the Forces, Lord High Admiral of the Fleet and absolute dictator in Downing street, everything would have gone much better, because all the tragic blunders that prolonged the struggle were due to a perverse refusal to follow his advice.[16]

The Economist drew lessons for the present day. His first volume, the reviewer wrote, had appeared at a time when his 'account of the pre-war world as it drifted into Armageddon is startlingly descriptive in almost every detail of the state of international tension, distorted psychology and confusion' that prevailed in European affairs in 1933. His account of the war itself, too, of men in power guided by 'obsolete ideas' and 'unable to control the forces they have conjured up' was a 'striking warning and a challenge to the statesmen of to-day'.[17]

The Economist thought three points especially were worth emphasising as typifying the 'mental background' of 1914. First, that the war came because the nations had prepared for war. Second, no one believed that war was coming until the last moment, and third, there were no 'giants' among the rulers and statesman of the powers. Whether or not one agreed with Lloyd George that a Clemenceau or a Bismarck would have averted war, 'in the light of other events none can doubt the supreme virtue of decisiveness and consistency of policy or fail to realise that in the past decade, as in the story of the war, the best intentioned efforts have again and again been paralysed by being "too late"'.[18] In short, Lloyd George's first volume painted a remarkable picture of the slide into war, with lessons for present day politicians and statesmen. The second volume, if anything, gained in dramatic force, for Lloyd George was writing about 1916, when 'we were in the thick of our troubles', and he succeeded in depicting, as few others had, 'the varied behaviour of those in control of affairs under the stress of great events'. Moreover

> these memoirs stand alone for the very good reason that on every great issue they record the attitude of one who not only had a clearer view of the goal and the way to attain it than any other war leader, but also had the power to influence and in the end to exercise the final decision.[19]

Lloyd George's greatest achievement, according to this reviewer, was, apart from unity of command in 1918, clearly the mobilisation of national resources to increase the output of munitions and weapons such as heavy artillery.[20]

II

Writing of Churchill's *World Crisis*, one historian recently described the 'old trick' (present too in *The Second World War*) employed throughout the multi-volume work. In order to illustrate just where the generals and politicians had gone so wrong in their conduct of the First World War, Churchill presented a complicated series of 'if onlys', or 'intuitive counter-factuals' around such issues as the Dardanelles campaign and the employment of the tank: 'In almost every case the issue was what great things might have been achieved "if only" Churchill's advice had been followed more closely, with little rigour applied to the analysis of what chances there had ever actually been for such an outcome.'[21] In the *War Memoirs*, Lloyd George employs precisely this same 'old trick'.

Thus, he argues that *if only* Grey had made Britain's position clear during the July crisis, then the knowledge that Britain would in fact intervene might have given Berlin pause for thought, and may well have averted war altogether, at least on the scale which eventuated. *If only* there had been, he further suggests, a Disraeli, a Gladstone, or a Bismarck in power, instead of mediocrities such as Grey, Bethmann-Hollweg or Nicholas II, then the crisis would never have been allowed to develop into a Europe wide, indeed world war. None of those in power, Lloyd George claims, wanted or intended war, but they were too timid or lacked the ability to control events.

Once hostilities were under way, Lloyd George argues that *if only his* advice had been followed, and the armies of a Balkan confederation, financed, armed and supported by the Allies – with British troops to boot – had invaded Austria-Hungary, then Germany's main 'prop' would have been knocked out of the war and Germany isolated. Lloyd George then explains the initial reverses and ensuing stalemate by arguing that *if only* the British military leaders had been a little more far-sighted prior to the war, and had equipped the army with more appropriate munitions for modern war, and *if only* they had had the intelligence and perception to see that, once the trench lines had settled, massive quantities of such weapons as heavy artillery and high explosive shells were required to have any chance of breaking the impasse, then the enemy's trenches as they had developed by early 1915 could have been attacked with much greater prospects of success and with fewer casualties. And, further east, *if only* Russia, rich in men but poor in resources, had been supplied more generously by the Western Allies, as Lloyd George had urged, then Russian arms would have had a much better chance of prevailing over the Germans and Austrians, and revolution might well have been averted.

Throughout, indeed, Lloyd George contends that *if only* his advice had been taken and the Allies had devoted more resources to fronts other than the Western, then the dreadful, futile bloodletting in France and Belgium would have been avoided and the war would have ended sooner (of course it seems not to matter that if this had been done in all probability the bloodletting in those other theatres would have been just as heavy – but *British* soldiers would perhaps not have been dying in such large numbers). He finally argues, when recounting the events of 1918, as if to provide final and conclusive vindication of his views, that the war was finally won not by the Allied armies in France defeating the Germans, but by the Allied forces in the eastern theatres finally knocking out Germany's 'props' – Austria, Bulgaria and Turkey – from under her. Germany finally found itself isolated and this, coupled with internal unrest and the effects of the Royal Navy's blockade, was what caused Germany's peace overtures in October and November, not defeat in the field on the Western Front.

Like Churchill, however, Lloyd George is at his least convincing when attempting to provide evidence that the results of his prescribed course of action or his contemporary advice would have been as he claims. Thus, for example, even if Grey had made clear to Berlin that British intervention would certainly follow the violation of Belgian neutrality, there is little evidence that the prospect of British military intervention weighed heavily in the minds of German strategists. France, they calculated, would be defeated quickly before the British presence would be large enough to make itself felt. Similarly, the notion that the political leaders of 1914 were altogether an inferior breed than previous generations is debatable, but the argument that none wanted war in 1914 but were over or rather *under*whelmed by their own timidity and mediocrity does not hold water, moreover as we have seen, Lloyd George's criticism of Grey in particular was provoked more by political controversies in the postwar period than any failings of his or disagreements with him prior to the war. One power at least, and the crucial one at that in the circumstances of July 1914 – Germany – wanted war in July 1914 and went into it with eyes wide open, because its leaders thought they could win. Lloyd George, through his misleading account, was a major contributor to the myth of the 'inadvertent' or 'accidental' war.

As for a Balkan confederation, such a suggestion belongs firmly in the realm of political fantasy in the conditions of 1914–15, and his proposal also ignored the immense logistical difficulties of operating effectively in the Balkans. Later, when proposing offensives in the Italian theatre, Lloyd George, true to form, ignored the equally awkward reality that the Italians themselves were understandably reluctant to bring the full force of the Austrian *and* German armies down upon their heads. And as we have seen, Lloyd George's picture of a British military refusing to recognise the new challenges of modern warfare on the Western Front and being resistant to the technological innovations introduced to cope with these challenges is a gross exaggeration. From Haig down, commanders on the whole, while there may have been disputes as to their most effective use, welcomed such innovations as the tank, and at the outset of the war Kitchener's recognition that the war would be a long one led to immense munitions orders which laid the basis for further expansion under the Ministry of Munitions. This, of course, is not to detract from Lloyd George's genuine achievements at the Ministry of Munitions in rationalising and expanding further Britain's productive capacity.

In the *War Memoirs* Lloyd George is also one of the main contributors to the myth that Britain's military and political leaders were mistaken in their concentration on the Western Front and their neglect of other theatres to the east. There were, of course, substantial Allied efforts in other theatres – the Dardanelles, Salonika, Italy, Russia and the Middle East, and of course British forces, munitions and finance played a role on all these fronts. Yet nothing can detract from the fact that the Entente's most dangerous enemy was Germany, a Germany whose main forces were deployed in northern France and Belgium, an area of prime and long-standing importance to Britain's national security. Even Lloyd George, at the time and in the *War Memoirs*, did not recommend the wholesale withdrawal of British forces from the Western Front, but rather the re-direction of a significant but still small proportion of Britain's forces and resources from the west to the eastern theatres – including Russia. He thus implicitly acknowledges the central part the Western Front played in the British war effort, a part dramatically confirmed to Lloyd George himself in March 1918 when the Germans launched their great offensive and he pushed for every available reinforcement to be shipped to France to halt the German advance. And as we have seen, Lloyd George cannot, on the one hand, hide his pride in the achievement of *his* Ministry of Munitions in supplying the British army – *most of which was deployed on the Western Front* – with an abundance of munitions of all types (in the pertinent passage of the *War Memoirs* he acknowledges the tremendous effect Haig's assault had on German morale), and on the other, acknowledge in the *War Memoirs* his reluctance during the war to provide additional munitions supplies to the Russians. To do so would flatly contradict his argument that Russia went under, and the Allied cause suffered, by the refusal of the Western Allies to pool their resources with their principal eastern ally.

Finally, what of his treatment of Haig in the *War Memoirs*? His view was that his devious methods used to subordinate Haig to Nivelle in 1917 were justified in the pursuit of unity of command. His refusal to forbid the Ypres offensive (the 'campaign of the mud') or to dismiss Haig was justified in various ways – his fragile political position, fear of criticism directed towards amateur interference with the professionals, the lack of a replacement for Haig. And his faint praise of Haig for his more than creditable performance in the campaigns of 1918 and the refusal to acknowledge the importance of the British victory in France in ending the war is explained by his determination to show that the war was won on the much derided 'peripheral' fronts rather than by Haig's army in France. His treatment of Haig in the *War Memoirs* must be seen in the context of the fact that he was in positions of Great Power and responsibility during 1916–17, precisely when Haig launched those costly offensives which Lloyd George so deplores: Secretary of State for War during the Battle of the Somme, and Prime Minister during that period when the BEF was fighting its way slowly and painfully towards Passchendaele. Lloyd George failed to impose his authority, and refused, despite his own misgivings, to avail himself of his power to either forbid the campaign to commence or to call a halt when it was clear it was not reaching its objectives. Moreover, when it was clear that Third Ypres had failed, and then the promise of Cambrai had turned into another disaster, Lloyd George failed to replace Haig as he undoubtedly wished to. No matter how Lloyd George twists and turns in his attempts to justify this failure in the *War Memoirs*, he cannot evade his full share of the responsibility for this debacle.

The *War Memoirs* then, are clearly Lloyd George's own personal view of wartime events, an attempt at self-justification and at defending his record against his many detractors. As he himself put it, he aimed to tell the 'naked truth about the war' as he saw it from the 'conning-tower at Downing Street'.[22] It was *his* truth about the war, seen moreover, from the perspective of the 1930s. As Trevor Wilson has noted, on this level the *War Memoirs* provide a 'graphic account of mighty deeds and vital accomplishments'. It is an account in which, of course, Lloyd George himself plays a central role in 'rallying the nation's will and in providing the implements of victory'.[23] But the *War Memoirs* are more than this. The *War Memoirs* are also about the paying off of old and more recent scores; the former against Haig, Robertson and the military command they represented and the latter against former political colleagues whose conduct during the war is condemned because of more recent 'offences' against Lloyd George.[24] Lloyd George, despite the appearance – through in particular the extensive use of official documentation – of an impartiality and an authority which struck many reviewers favourably, never for one moment entertained the idea of providing his readers with a genuinely authoritative and balanced account of the war years. Rather he determined to pursue his feuds and controversies and present *his case* through the careful and one-sided selection of documents, personal invective and the outright suppression of evidence where necessary. Those episodes considered in the present work give a fair indication of his methods in these respects.

Finally, the *War Memoirs* are a product of their time, particularly in terms of Lloyd George's views of his former colleagues, both political and military. By the 1930s, the conviction was clearly growing in many sections of society, and ever larger numbers of people that the Great War had been a mistake. The Great Powers had blundered into war in 1914, and the next four years saw millions of men die needlessly in futile, wasteful and incompetently directed warfare. The armies had been commanded by what many had come to regard as generals both incompetent and negligent in their care for the men under their command. And, most famously, this mood, beginning in the late 1920s, was beginning to be expressed by memoirists, novelists and poets, and in film and theatre.[25]

Among those works must be placed Lloyd George's *War Memoirs*. It contains all the elements which made up what might be described as a 'literature of disenchantment': the blundering into war, the incompetence, stubbornness and callousness of the military leadership, the valour of the ordinary soldiers and an overwhelming sense of waste, folly and blunder.[26] That such a work should come from the British Prime Minister who presided over these events, and who was therefore ultimately responsible for them, is curious and remarkable. One can only surmise that it was Lloyd George's profound sense of unease with his own role, his sense of guilt, and his genuine sense of horror at the carnage over which he presided, led him, by whatever means possible, to attempt to shift, through the *War Memoirs* (and other ways), responsibility to his military and political adversaries (his wartime colleagues). He was, after all, still, in 1932–36, a working politician with ambitions for a return to office.

Most historians now approach the *War Memoirs* with extreme caution. And rightly so. For the *War Memoirs* should not be regarded or used as a work of serious history, in the sense of a work written by one who strives for the utmost degree of objectivity in narrating and explaining the events of the past. Lloyd George himself, in his more candid moments, regarded the work as simultaneously a defence of his record in wartime government and his case for the prosecution against his many antagonists. As such the *War Memoirs* reveal much of the man and politician. And it is as such that the *War Memoirs* should be approached by students of the Great War.

Notes

Introduction

1. Anniker Mombauer, *Helmuth von Moltke and the Origins of the First World War* (Cambridge: Cambridge University Press, 2001), p. 1.
2. A line argued recently, for example, by Niall Ferguson in *The Pity of War* (London: Penguin, 1998).
3. A 'breakthrough' or 'breakout' of the type envisaged by Douglas Haig never occurred, however, even in 1918.
4. 'King Albert [of Belgium], King George, the Kaiser and Poincaré [President of France] were the only rulers who saw it through from the beginning to the end.' David Lloyd George, *War Memoirs*, 6 vols (London: Ivor Nicholson & Watson, 1933–36), VI, pp. vii–viii. Hereafter *War Memoirs* and vol. no.
5. Many reviewers of the *War Memoirs* commented critically upon Lloyd George's attacks on the generals in their reviews of earlier volumes. In reply, Lloyd George provided in the sixth and final volume a list of the generals and admirals that he had praised. Noticeably absent were the two successive British Commanders-in-Chief of the BEF, French and Haig, and any of the First Sea Lords or Commanders of the Grand Fleet. See ibid., p. xi.
6. Except in so far as he did not remove Haig or order him to stop during the latter stages of Third Ypres. A fairly big exception I will argue. See ch. 7.
7. Thus in a literal sense the question sometimes posed regarding the *War Memoirs* – was Lloyd George 'pamphleteering' rather than writing a serious contribution to history – must be answered in the affirmative.
8. Most notably by George W. Egerton, 'The Lloyd George *War Memoirs*: A Study in the Politics of Memory', *Journal of Modern History*, 60, 1, March 1988, pp. 55–94; for other studies of the *War Memoirs*, see also Thomas Jones, *Lloyd George* (London: Oxford University Press, 1951), pp. 267–73; Trevor Wilson, 'A Prime Minister Reflects: The *War Memoirs* of David Lloyd George', in John A. Moses and Christopher Pugsley (eds), *The German Empire and Britain's Pacific Dominions 1871–1919: Essays on the Role of Australia and New Zealand in an Age of Imperialism* (Claremont, CA: Regina Books, 2000), pp. 37–52. For contemporary accounts of Lloyd George's memoir writing, see the diaries by his secretaries, published as Colin Cross (ed.), *Life with Lloyd George: The Diary of A.J. Sylvester* (London: Macmillan, 1975) and A.J.P. Taylor (ed.), *Lloyd George: A Diary by Frances Stevenson* (London: Hutchinson, 1971).
9. See *War Memoirs*, III, pp. 1162–65; John Grigg, *Lloyd George: War Leader 1916–1918* (London: Allen Lane/Penguin, 2002), pp. 52–53 (the fourth and final volume of Grigg's biography of Lloyd George); Robert K. Massie, *Castles of Steel: Britain, Germany and the Winning of the Great War at Sea* (New York: Random House, 2003), pp. 730–31; Peter Rowland, *David Lloyd George: A Biography* (New York: Macmillan, 1975), pp. 396–98, 707–708.
10. Ibid., pp. 237–38.

11. *War Memoirs*, II, ch. 23; John Grigg, *Lloyd George: From Peace to War 1912–1916* (London: HarperCollins, 1997 ed.), pp. 326–41; R.J.Q. Adams, *Bonar Law* (London: John Murray, 1999), pp. 203–13.

12. See *War Memoirs*, V, ch. 80; Grigg, *Lloyd George*, IV, ch. 27; David French, *The Strategy of the Lloyd George Coalition 1916–1918* (Oxford: Clarendon Press, 1995), pp. 234–35; Adams, *Bonar Law*, pp. 268–72.

13. The important last volume of John Grigg's biography of Lloyd George was published too late to be fully taken into account in the present work.

1 Writing the *War Memoirs* 1931–36

1. For a sample of reviews, see pp. 195–98; elsewhere, for a good survey of reviewer's reception of the *War Memoirs*, see George W. Egerton, 'The Lloyd George *War Memoirs*: A Study in the Politics of Memory', *Journal of Modern History*, 60, 1, March 1988, pp. 78–86. For readers' letters, see House of Lords Record Office (HLRO) Lloyd George MSS (hereafter LG MSS) G/236–38.

2. Successively, the War Council, the Dardanelles Committee, the War Committee and the War Cabinet.

3. Winston S. Churchill, *The World Crisis*, 6 vols (London: Thornton and Butterworth, 1923–31). Churchill's *The Second World War*, 6 vols (London: Cassell, 1948–54), is, as Egerton suggests, a better comparison: '*War Memoirs*', p. 86.

4. See, for example, A.J.P. Taylor (ed.), *Lloyd George: A Diary by Frances Stevenson* (London: Hutchinson, 1971), p. 264.

5. One reviewer thought it 'amazing that a man commencing author [sic] in his seventieth year should have written a million words, every letter of them stamped with his own personality'; *Times Literary Supplement*, review of volume VI, 28 November 1936, p. 981.

6. Colin Cross (ed.), *Life with Lloyd George: The Diary of A.J. Sylvester* (London: Macmillan, 1975), p. 109.

7. For example, see Paul Johnson in the *New Statesman*, where he describes the *War Memoirs* as 'unreadable' and 'unread'; 19 September 1969.

8. Egerton, '*War Memoirs*', p. 66. Egerton's appraisal is shared by other historians, for example Kenneth Morgan: 'Lloyd George's memoirs, as source material and as literature, have stood the test of time far more successfully than have many such essays in self-justification, better than Churchill's writings on the 1914–18 war, and perhaps on the 1939–45 war as well'; Kenneth O. Morgan, *Lloyd George* (London: Weidenfeld and Nicolson, 1974), p. 211.

9. *Times Literary Supplement*, review of volume V, 26 September 1936.

10. *Daily Mail*, 26 October 1934.

11. Egerton, '*War Memoirs*', pp. 84–5.

12. Quoted in Thomas Jones, *Lloyd George* (London: Oxford University Press, 1951), pp. 269.

13. Ibid. Liddell Hart, on his experience in advising Lloyd George on the *Memoirs*, observed, 'I had arguments with LG that were almost as violent as those with his opponents, and regard him as a brilliant *prosecuting* counsel rather than a historian'; Liddell Hart Centre for Military Archives (LHCMA) Liddell Hart MSS 1/312/78: Liddell Hart to Professor Norman Gibbs, 28 January 1958.

14. Egerton, 'War Memoirs', p. 65.
15. HLRO LG MSS G/208: Mr Lloyd George's *War Memoirs*, Vol. V, Sales Manager of Ivor Nicholson and Watson (signature illegible), 22 September 1936. Frances Stevenson noted in September 1934: 'Today is published Vol. III of the War Memoirs. D. is very satisfied, as is also Ivor Nicholson – 6,000 advance copies (more than double previous vols.)', *Stevenson Diary*, p. 278.
16. Details in Egerton, 'War Memoirs', p. 79.
17. National Library of Wales (NLW) A.J. Sylvester MSS (hereafter Sylvester MSS): uncatalogued, 'Beginning', no date. At the time I consulted these papers they were uncatalogued, happily this is no longer the case.
18. Egerton, 'War Memoirs', pp. 58–61 and Peter Rowland, *Lloyd George: A Biography* (New York: Macmillan, 1975), pp. 572–73.
19. HLRO LG MSS G/216: Swinton to Fuller, 7 November 1922.
20. NLW Sylvester MSS: uncatalogued, 'Beginning', no date.
21. See Swinton's memoir *Over My Shoulder* (Oxford: George Ronald, 1951), p. 224.
22. NLW Sylvester MSS: uncatalogued, 'Beginning', no date.
23. HLRO LG MSS G/216: Swinton to Lloyd George, January 1924.
24. Thus during his first twelve months as a columnist Lloyd George earned £30,000; Rowland, *Lloyd George*, p. 593.
25. *War Memoirs*, I, pp. vii–viii.
26. Although it was probably not the 'National Government' he would have wanted; on Lloyd George and the formation of the National Government, see Philip Williamson, *National Crisis and National Government: British Politics, the Economy and Empire 1926–1932* (Cambridge: Cambridge University Press, 1992), pp. 275–76, 354–55.
27. There were, however, subsequent attempts to include Lloyd George in the Government. See, for example, the exchange of letters between Liberal candidate Captain Frederick Boult, MacDonald and Sylvester. Boult suggested to MacDonald that Lloyd George be invited to join the Government and MacDonald seemed to take him seriously: 'Do you think there is the least chance of his accepting? It would be a colossal blunder to give him the chance of boasting that he had been approached and had refused.' Lloyd George, however, was not interested, and did not reply to Boult personally. Boult concluded the exchange on an optimistic note: 'Mr Lloyd George did not see me, or reply personally to my letter. I enclose the correspondence in case you care to see it. Personally I still think that he would take on the job if he were asked'; MacDonald MSS PRO 30/69/1177: correspondence, 13 October–2 November 1932.
28. *War Memoirs*, I, p. viii.
29. HLRO LG MSS G/212: Lloyd George to Hankey 10 April 1933.
30. *From Private to Field Marshal* (London: Constable, 1921) and more importantly *Soldiers and Statesmen 1914–1918*, 2 vols (London: Cassell, 1926).
31. *Memories and Reflections*, 2 vols (London: Cassell, 1928): *The Genesis of the War* (London: Cassell, 1923).
32. *Twenty Five Years*, 2 vols (London: Hodder and Stoughton, 1925).
33. *The World Crisis*.
34. Sir George Arthur, *Life of Lord Kitchener*, 3 vols (London: Macmillan, 1920).
35. C.E. Callwell (ed.), *Field Marshal Sir Henry Wilson: His Life and Diaries*, 2 vols (London: Cassell, 1927).

36. J.H. Boraston and G.A.B. Dewar, *Sir Douglas Haig's Command, December 19th 1915 to November 11th, 1918* (London: Constable, 1922); Brigadier-General John Charteris, *Field Marshal Earl Haig* (London: Cassell, 1929). Alfred Duff Cooper's *Haig*, 2 vols (London: Faber & Faber, 1935–36), was still to come.
37. Nancy Maurice (ed.), *The Maurice Case* (London: Leo Cooper, 1972), pp. 181–207.
38. HLRO LG MSS G/212: Lloyd George to Hankey 10 April 1933. For a survey of the 'battle of the memoirs', see Ian Beckett, 'Frocks and Brasshats', in Brian Bond (ed.), *The First World War and British Military History* (Oxford: Clarendon Press, 1991), pp. 90–112.
39. HLRO LG MSS G/212: Lloyd George to Hankey, 18 April 1934.
40. LHCMA Liddell Hart MSS 1/450: 'Rough Notes by A.J. Sylvester. How L.G. Wrote his *War Memoirs*', 6 January 1965; NLW Sylvester MSS: uncatalogued, 'Beginning', no date. Sylvester recorded that 'The best war book L.G. has so far read was Prince Max of Baden [the last Imperial German Chancellor]', ibid., uncatalogued diary, 26 November 1931.
41. A.J.P. Taylor (ed.), *My Darling Pussy: The Letters of Lloyd George and Frances Stevenson 1913–41* (London: Weidenfeld and Nicolson, 1975), p. 161, Lloyd George to Frances Stevenson 3 December 1931. Cf. Churchill's tribute to Lloyd George in *The World Crisis 1916–18* (London: Thornton Butterworth, 1927), Part I, pp. 256–57.
42. Taylor (ed.), *My Darling Pussy*, 171, Lloyd George to Frances Stevenson, 31 December 1931.
43. NLW Sylvester MSS: uncatalogued diary, 1 December 1931.
44. And 'Still talking about the fact that Winston had not mentioned him in regard to Munitions and that he claimed that when he (Winston) was at the Munitions [*sic*] there were only so many shells!', ibid., diary, 3–4 December 1931.
45. HLRO LG MSS G/235: 'Jottings by Mr Lloyd George' (1931).
46. NLW Sylvester MSS: uncatalogued diary, 12 April 1933.
47. Throughout the period of the writing of the *Memoirs*, Lloyd George was also a working politician. As Sylvester noted: 'In order to show what a remarkable man LG is, whilst he was writing his War Memoirs he propounded his proposals which afterwards became known as "The New Deal Proposals"... He also visited Germany, saw Hitler, and travelled widely throughout the country. Thus, whilst he was studying movements in Germany of great magnitude, he was sucking up information like a sponge sucks up water, he was writing important phases for his book on the War'; NLW Sylvester MSS: uncatalogued, 'Beginning'.
48. Egerton, '*War Memoirs*', p. 69.
49. Ibid., p. 64 and Jones, *Lloyd George*, pp. 267–73.
50. NLW Sylvester MSS: uncatalogued diary 27 September 1932.
51. NLW Sylvester MSS: uncatalogued, 'How I Helped Lloyd George Write His Memoirs', no date. Elsewhere, Sylvester commented that Lloyd George was 'terribly concerned lest it should be thought that anybody else wrote the books for him'; ibid.: uncatalogued diary, 7 March 1933.
52. LHCMA Liddell Hart MSS 1/450: 'Rough Notes by A.J. Sylvester. How LG Wrote his War Memoirs', 6 January 1965.
53. On Sylvester, see his diaries edited by Colin Cross; on Frances Stevenson, apart from her diaries and letters edited by A.J.P. Taylor, see the biography by

her grand daughter, Ruth Longford, *Frances, Countess Lloyd-George: More than a Mistress* (Leominster, Herefordshire: Gracewing, Fowler Wright Books, 1996).

54. Egerton, 'War Memoirs', p. 62.

55. Sylvester came second to the Americans in international 'speedwriting' competitions at the Business Efficiency Exhibition at Olympia in 1910 and 1911. *Sylvester Diary*, 'Introduction', p. 11.

56. See the biographical details in *Sylvester Diary*, 'Introduction', pp. 11–12. Sylvester insisted upon the word 'principal' because of Frances Stevenson, still Lloyd George's private secretary but also his mistress, p. 12.

57. Ibid., pp. 12–13.

58. See, for example, diary entries for 28 September 1933: 'the Secretary of State had agreed for me to go to the F.[oreign] O[ffice]. and make copies of the telegrams to and from Russia ... went to the FO ... at 3 pm and worked hard dictating telegrams until 5.30'; 30 September 1933: 'Working desperately hard at the FO on the telegrams regarding the Russian Revolution'; 21 October 1933: 'Have been very busily engaged digging up documents at the War Cabinet Offices as the result of LG.'s talk with Hankey and Edmonds[the official historian]. But for my knowledge of Cabinet work I doubt if we could have got these'; 4 January 1934: 'I worked long hours down in the bowels of the Cabinet Office where the records had been removed and made a systematic search of masses of documents. My intimate knowledge of the documents, and of the Cabinet Office procedure was indispensable as a guide'. NLW Sylvester MSS: uncatalogued diary.

59. On Hankey's role in enforcing Cabinet secrecy and vetting ministerial memoirs, see John F. Naylor, *A Man and an Institution: Sir Maurice Hankey, the Cabinet Secretariat and the Custody of Official Secrecy* (Cambridge: Cambridge University Press, 1984); Egerton, 'War Memoirs', pp. 68–70; on Hankey and Lloyd George in particular, Naylor, *A Man and an Institution*, pp. 203–09; Peter Fraser, 'Cabinet Secrecy and War Memoirs', *History*, 70, 230, pp. 397–409 and Egerton, 'War Memoirs', pp. 69–71.

60. Ibid., p. 69.

61. HLRO LG MSS G/212: Hankey to Lloyd George, 16 April 1934. With the latter comment, he was undoubtedly thinking of the extra burden he and his staff at the Cabinet Office would have to bear, in addition to their normal workload. Occasionally Hankey's irritation would become apparent, as Sylvester noted: 'This morning LG asked me to find out if Hankey had read the MS ... Hankey was at a Cabinet. I ... spoke to him on the telephone at 1.40 pm. He was rather narky; he said how could LG expect him to have read such a lot during a weekend especially when he had to read it through carefully to check facts ... LG. must realise that he was a busy man ...', and two days later: 'I went to see Hankey. Found he had the whole of his office working hard for several days looking up facts. How they bless LG – especially when I told them they are just beginning', NLW Sylvester MSS: uncatalogued diary 27 and 29 March 1933.

62. HLRO LG MSS G/212: Hankey to Lloyd George, 16 April 1934 and Lloyd George to Hankey, 18 April 1934. On Lloyd George's criticisms of his former colleagues, cf. Sylvester's diary entry of 18 April 1933: 'Went to interview Lord Lee [of Fareham] at White Lodge at 10 am. ... Lord Lee was very pleased with what LG proposed to say about him in his book. He thought

LG had mellowed a great deal, especially towards his enemies. (Clearly he does not know LG!)'; NLW Sylvester MSS: uncatalogued diary.
63. See HLRO LG MSS G/212: Hankey to Lloyd George, 8 April 1933.
64. Ibid.
65. HLRO LG MSS G/212: Lloyd George to Hankey, 10 April 1933. Ironically, Hankey was prevented by successive Prime Ministers from publishing his own memoirs, based on his diaries, until 1961 as *The Supreme Command*, 2 vols (London: Allen & Unwin, 1961).
66. HLRO LG MSS G/212: Lloyd George to Hankey, 10 April 1933. It was evidently with some relief that Lloyd George chose the second option. As he said later, 'It is very lucky I did not have to go to the King, which would have meant Ramsay MacDonald. Sir Maurice Hankey: I helped you over Baldwin. Mr Lloyd George: you behaved like a brick, you were even willing to face any risk. The moment I discovered Ramsay was going to the United States I said, "You are too busy! Therefore I go to your second"'. HLRO LG MSS G/252: 'Note of a Conversation in a Private Room at the Pall Mall Club, SW1, after Dinner at 8.30 pm on 22 June 1933'.
67. NLW Sylvester MSS: uncatalogued diary 19 January 1934.
68. HLRO LG MSS G/212: Hankey to Lloyd George, 21 April 1934.
69. Ibid.
70. Ibid.
71. Egerton, *'War Memoirs'*, p. 63.
72. HLRO LG MSS G/9/18/19: Hankey to Lloyd George, 21 October 1933. A description of the breakfast appears in *War Memoirs*, III, pp. 1151–55. See also, on a separate question, HLRO LG MSS G/212: Sylvester note to Lloyd George, 20 March 1934: 'Sir Maurice Hankey says he feels that he may have a lot in his diary about his visit with you to the Front in September, 1917 . . . Hankey has promised to look up his diary and will probably be able to let you know tomorrow'. The next day Hankey wrote to Lloyd George with an extract from his diary attached.
73. HLRO LG MSS G/8/18/22: Hankey to Lloyd George, 2 April 1934.
74. HLRO LG MSS G/212: Hankey to Lloyd George, 16 April 1934.
75. HLRO LG MSS G/212: Hankey to Lloyd George, 11 April 1933. On Liddell Hart, see the biography by Alex Danchev, *Alchemist of War: The Life of Basil Liddell Hart* (London: Weidenfeld and Nicolson, 1998), also Brian Bond, *Liddell Hart: A Study of his Military Thought* (London: Cassell, 1977) and John J. Mearsheimer, *Liddell Hart and the Weight of History* (Ithaca and London: Cornell University Press, 1988).
76. Hew Strachan, '"The Real War": Liddell Hart, Cruttwell, Falls', in Brian Bond (ed.), *British Military History*, p. 49.
77. Quoted in Brian Bond, *Liddell Hart*, p. 18.
78. Quoted in ibid., p. 20. Liddell Hart's emphasis. See Mearsheimer, *Liddell Hart*, ch. 3 for an account of the evolution of Liddell Hart's thoughts on the conduct of the First World War and Strachan, 'The Real War', in Brian Bond (ed.), *British Military History*, pp. 41–67.
79. Mearsheimer comments that 'the pronouncements of Lloyd George . . . surely also worked to reinforce Liddell Hart's growing doubts about his country's military leadership', *Liddell Hart*, p. 56.

80. See Strachan, 'The Real War', in Brian Bond (ed.), *British Military History*, p. 49 and below, ch. 2 and conclusion for Lloyd George's views.
81. HLRO Beaverbrook MSS C/219: Countess Lloyd George to Lord Beaverbrook, 20 June 1950. Although the former also noted in the same letter 'It would be wrong, however, to say that he [Liddell Hart] *influenced* L.G. In my opinion very few people ever influenced L.G. He formed his own judgements and made up his own mind.' There was, in fact, little need for Liddell Hart to *influence* Lloyd George one way or the other. As an indication of the esteem with which Lloyd George regarded Liddell Hart, the latter noted in his memoirs that Lloyd George, inscribing a copy of one of the volumes of *his* memoirs, wrote: 'Captain Liddell Hart – I regard him as the highest and soundest authority on modern war whom it has been my privilege to meet', and further suggested that had Lloyd George been returned to office as Prime Minister – admittedly an extremely unlikely event – it was his intention to 'make me War Minister, or Minister of Defence'. See B.H. Liddell Hart, *Memoirs*, 2 vols (London: Cassell, 1965), I, p. 362. After Lloyd George's death, Liddell Hart considered writing Lloyd George's biography. He concluded that a major drawback was that he was regarded generally as being 'predisposed in his [Lloyd George's] favour'. Frances Stevenson in the end chose Malcolm Thomson, Lloyd George's former secretary as his official biographer. LHCMA Liddell Hart MSS, 1/450: note, 26 May 1945.
82. LHCMA Liddell Hart MSS 1/450: 'Sylvester Notes for Liddell Hart', 17 November 1964. Lloyd George at one point described MacDonald as a 'conceited, jealous fellow' who might try to 'scotch his book'; NLW Sylvester MSS: uncatalogued diary, 30 March 1933; while Frances Stevenson recorded Lloyd George's remark on MacDonald that 'in the last century there had been some Prime Ministers who were failures, and some who were hated, but he could not recall one that had been a figure of fun – until Ramsay'; *Stevenson Diary*, p. 263, 25 March 1934.
83. PRO 30/69/1179 MacDonald MSS: Hankey to MacDonald, 18 April 1934. Interestingly, Lloyd George at one point in the *War Memoirs* also refers to MacDonald as a possible Kerensky; *War Memoirs*, IV, p. 1895.
84. PRO 30/69/1179 MacDonald MSS: MacDonald to Hankey, 19 April 1934. MacDonald died in 1937 without writing his memoirs.
85. *Sylvester Diary*, pp. 107–08, 25 April 1934.
86. *Stevenson Diary*, p. 269, 24 April 1934.
87. *War Memoirs*, IV, p. 1885. See also the passages on p. 1949.
88. LHCMA Liddell Hart MSS 1/450: 'Sylvester Notes for Liddell Hart', 17 November 1964.
89. HLRO LG MSS G/216: Baldwin to Lloyd George, 19 April 1933.
90. *Sylvester Diary*, p. 107, 11 April 1934.
91. HLRO LG MSS G/252: 'Note of a Conversation in a Private Room at the Pall Mall Club, 22 June 1933'. Those present were Lloyd George, General J.C. Smuts, Hankey, Lloyd George's son Gwilym and Sylvester. This lengthy record of conversation has led one of Haig's recent biographers to suggest that Lloyd George kept an extensive diary. Denis Winter claims: 'Diaries usually offer the quickest check on the integrity of a particular collection [of private papers]. The shrewdest manipulators either re-wrote their diaries in

entirety or kept this most contemporary of records well away from public scrutiny. Lloyd George is a case in point. In a conversation minuted by the Cabinet Office [A.J. Sylvester, Lloyd George's *private secretary*, and not an official of the Cabinet Office, recorded this discussion], Hankey referred to Lloyd George's diary as even fuller than his own. . . . there is no trace of such a diary in the Lloyd George papers today', *Haig's Command: A Reassessment* (London: Penguin, 1992), p. 311. There is no trace of a diary in the Lloyd George papers in the House of Lords Record Office for the simple reason that it does not exist. In the context of the conversation it is clear that Hankey was referring to the *War Memoirs, not* a diary. The passage reads: 'General Smuts: It will be *the* Book; *the* Book that will be read afterwards. Mr Lloyd George: Until Hankey is in a position to publish his Diary. Sir Maurice Hankey: It is not as complete as yours. General Smuts: Hankey's will be much more fragmentary. Yours will be the *considered judgement* of the chief witness. Sir Maurice Hankey: And the *next two volumes* are of much more importance than what you have already written.' My emphasis.

92. HLRO LG MSS G/239: 'M. Bark on the Russian Collapse', 28 September 1933.
93. HLRO LG MSS G/252: 'Notes of a Conversation . . . at the Reform Club, 22 June 1933'.
94. See LHCMA Liddell Hart MSS 11/1935/107; 11/1936/31: Notes on meetings with Lloyd George and General Gough, 28 November 1935 and 27 January 1936.
95. See the list in NLW Sylvester MSS: uncatalogued list of interviews.
96. See Egerton, '*War Memoirs*', pp. 84–85.

2 'Pandemonium let loose': The outbreak of war 1914

1. Lloyd George told Sylvester in 1933: 'If you had had a Palmerston or Disraeli at the Foreign Office in 1914 there would have been no war'; Colin Cross (ed.), *Life with Lloyd George: The Diary of A.J. Sylvester* (London: Macmillan, 1975), p. 96.
2. Trevor Wilson, 'A Prime Minister Reflects: The *War Memoirs* of David Lloyd George', in John A. Moses and Christopher Pugsley (eds), *The German Empire and Britain's Pacific Dominions 1871–1919: Essays on the Role of Australia and New Zealand in an Age of Imperialism* (Claremont, CA: Regina Books, 2000), p. 40.
3. Ibid., pp. 42–43.
4. *War Memoirs*, I, p. 89.
5. HLRO LG MSS G/212: Hankey notes on chapters.
6. *War Memoirs*, I, pp. 91–99.
7. Ibid., pp. 46–47. Of course, Grey argued that Britain was *not* committed.
8. HLRO LG MSS G/235: 'Jottings'.
9. *War Memoirs*, I, pp. 49–51.
10. Paul Guinn, *British Strategy and Politics 1914–1918* (Oxford: Clarendon Press, 1965), p. 23. It should be noted, however, that for much of 1913–14 Lloyd George largely concentrated on domestic affairs and seemed to take little interest in foreign policy. In the 18 months up to July 1914 he attended only one meeting of the CID; John Grigg, *Lloyd George* Vol. III: *From Peace to War 1912–1916* (London: HarperCollins, 1997 ed.), p. 137.

11. On the debates over the naval estimates, see A.J.A. Morris, *The Scaremongers: The Advocacy of War and Rearmament 1896–1914* (London: Routledge and Kegan Paul, 1984), esp. pp. 164ff, David Stevenson, *Armaments and the Coming of War: Europe 1904–1914* (Oxford: Clarendon Press, 1996), pp. 165–75; D.W. Sweet, 'Great Britain and Germany', in F.H. Hinsley (ed.), *British Foreign Policy under Sir Edward Grey* (Cambridge: Cambridge University Press, 1977) pp. 227–31; Gilbert, *David Lloyd George: A Political Life* Vol. I: The Architect of Change 1863–1912 (Columbus: Ohio State University Press, 1987), and II: *Organizer of Victory 1912–1916* (Columbus: Ohio State University Press, 1992), I, pp. 364–68 and II, pp. 71–79; Michael G. Fry, *Lloyd George and Foreign Policy*, Vol. I, *The Education of a Statesman* (Montreal and London: McGill-Queen's University Press, 1977), pp. 105–29, 167–81; F.W. Wiemann, 'Lloyd George and the Struggle for the Navy Estimates of 1914', in A.J.P. Taylor, *Lloyd George: Twelve Essays* (London: Hamish Hamilton, 1971), pp. 71–91; E.L. Woodward, *Great Britain and the German Navy* (Oxford: Clarendon Press, 1935), pp. 219–39, 423–28; Grigg, *Lloyd George*, III, pp. 132–37.

12. On Lloyd George's 1908 visit to Germany and his inept 'diplomatic' initiative in pursuit of an Anglo-German naval agreement, see *War Memoirs*, pp. 28–32; Harold Spender, *The Fire of Life: A Book of Memories* (London: Hodder and Stoughton, no date) (1926), pp. 161–66; Harold Spender, *The Prime Minister* (New York: George H. Doran, 1920), ch. 12; Gilbert, *Lloyd George*, I, pp. 349–51; Grigg, *Lloyd George*, II, pp. 306–07; and Fry, *Lloyd George and Foreign Policy*, pp. 97–103.

13. Lloyd George clearly thought that his intervention had averted war. See *Sylvester Diary*, p. 96. On the Agadir crisis and the Mansion House speech, see Edward, Viscount Grey, *Twenty Five Years*, 2 vols (London: Hodder and Stoughton, 1925), I, pp. 215–18; Winston S. Churchill, *The World Crisis*, 6 vols (London: Thornton Butterworth, 1923–31), I, pp. 46–50; Earl of Oxford and Asquith (H.H. Asquith), *The Genesis of the War* (London: Cassell, 1923), pp. 92–94; Arthur C. Murray, *Master and Brother: Murrays of Elibank* (London: John Murray, 1945), pp. 84–85; Fry, *Lloyd George and Foreign Policy*, p. 137; Grigg, *Lloyd George*, II, pp. 308–10; Gilbert, *Lloyd George*, I, pp. 449–54; the same author's 'Pacifist to Interventionist: David Lloyd George in 1911 and 1914. Was Belgium an Issue?', *Historical Journal*, 28, 4, 1985, pp. 863–85; Keith Wilson, 'The Agadir Crisis, the Mansion House Speech and the Double-Edgedness of Agreements', *Historical Journal*, XV, 3, 1972, pp. 513–32; Timothy Boyle, 'New Light on Lloyd George's Mansion House Speech', *Historical Journal*, 23, 2, 1980, pp. 431–33; Richard A. Cosgrove, 'A Note on Lloyd George's Speech at the Mansion House, 21 July 1911, *Historical Journal*, xii, 4, 1969, pp. 698–701; M.L. Dockrill, 'British Policy during the Agadir Crisis of 1911', in Hinsley (ed.), *British Foreign Policy under Sir Edward Grey*, pp. 271–87. Lloyd George's notes for the speech and correspondence between Murray and William Tyrell can be found in the House of Lords Library.

14. Trevor Wilson (ed.), *The Political Diaries of C.P. Scott 1911–1928* (London: Collins, 1970), p. 86.

15. Ibid., p. 47.

16. Trevor Wilson, 'A Prime Minister Reflects', p. 42.

17. *War Memoirs*, I, pp. 94–95.
18. Ibid., pp. 59–60.
19. Murray, *Master and Brother*, pp. 121–22.
20. G. Riddell, *Lord Riddell's War Diary* (London: Ivor Nicholson & Watson, 1933), p. 3; John Morley, *Memorandum on Resignation* (London: Macmillan, 1928), p. 2; Gilbert, *Lloyd George*, II, p. 109.
21. See John C.G. Röhl, *The Kaiser and his Court: Wilhelm II and the Government of Germany* (Cambridge: Cambridge University Press, 1996), ch. 7.
22. L.L. Farrar Jr, *Arrogance and Anxiety: The Ambivalence of German Power 1848–1914* (Iowa City: University of Iowa Press, 1981), p. 171.
23. Grey died just as the first volume of the *War Memoirs* was published.
24. This sale realised £3,000,000; see J.M. McEwen, 'Lloyd George's Acquisition of the *Daily Chronicle* in 1918', *Journal of British Studies*, XXII, 1, Fall 1982, p. 143. On the Lloyd George Fund, a cause of continuing division in the Liberal Party even after the 'reunion' of 1923, see Jones, *Lloyd George*, pp. 201–03; Rowland, *David Lloyd George*, pp. 447–48, 575–77, 609–10, 631–33.
25. Cited in Jones, *Lloyd George*, p. 224; see also Mark Pottle (ed.), *Champion Redoubtable: The Diaries and Letters of Violet Bonham Carter 1914–45* (London: Weidenfeld and Nicolson, 1998), pp. 169–72.
26. Churchill's government propaganda sheet the *British Gazette* carried messages of support for the government from Asquith and Grey, while Lloyd George expressed his sympathy towards the miners; Rowland, *David Lloyd George*, p. 623; Jones, *Lloyd George*, p. 218. On Lloyd George and Labour in the 1920s, see C.J. Wrigley, 'Lloyd George and the Labour Party after 1922', in Judith Loades (ed.), *The Life and Times of David Lloyd George* (Bangor: Headstart History, 1991), pp. 49–69.
27. Rowland, *David Lloyd George*, p. 668; Murray, *Master and Brother*, p. 122.
28. HLRO LG MSS G/211: Lloyd George to William George, 28 May 1933.
29. Ibid.
30. Lord Beaverbrook, *Politicians and the War 1914–1916* (London: Oldbourne, 1960 ed.), p. 22.
31. Fry, *Lloyd George and Foreign Policy*, p. 185.
32. *War Memoirs*, I, p. 51.
33. Ibid., pp. 71–73.
34. *Scott Diaries*, p. 91. My emphasis. See also Cameron Hazlehurst, *Politicians at War July 1914 to May 1915: A Prologue to the Triumph of Lloyd George* (London: Jonathan Cape, 1971), p. 64.
35. Riddell, *Lord Riddell's War Diary* (London: Ivor Nicholson & Watson, 1933), pp. 2–4.
36. Michael and Eleonor Brock (eds), *H.H. Asquith: Letters to Venetia Stanley* (Oxford: Oxford University Press, 1985), p. 140.
37. Ibid., p. 146; Grigg, *Lloyd George*, III, p. 142.
38. *Scott Diaries*, p. 91. My emphasis.
39. Bodleian Library, Oxford, Asquith MSS 1/7: Lord Crewe (in place of Asquith) to King George V, 2 August 1914; Grigg, *Lloyd George*, III, p. 142; Hazlehurst, *Politicians at War*, p. 98.
40. *Scott Diaries*, p. 96.
41. Riddell, *Riddell Diaries*, p. 7.

42. *Scott Diaries*, p. 96. Scott's emphasis. The claim that only two members of the Cabinet were in favour of intervention up to 2 August is of course incorrect: Grey, Asquith and Churchill were all in favour of intervention from the outset.
43. Samuel R. Williamson, *The Politics of Grand Strategy: Britain and France Prepare for War 1904–1914* (London: Ashfield Press, 1990), pp. 168–70, 188–93; Fry, *Lloyd George and Foreign Policy*, I, pp. 143–45; Guinn, *British Strategy and Politics*, pp. 19–20; Gilbert, *Lloyd George*, I, pp. 454–57; the same author's 'Pacifist to Interventionist', pp. 871–73; C.E. Callwell, *Field Marshal Sir Henry Wilson: His Life and Diaries*, 2 vols (London: Cassell, 1927), I, pp. 99–101; Grigg, *Lloyd George*, III, p. 141, n. 1.
44. Quoted in Gilbert, 'Pacifist to Interventionist', pp. 873–74; also Gilbert, *Lloyd George*, I, p. 456; Hazlehurst, *Politicians at War*, p. 63.
45. *Scott Diaries*, p. 92. My emphasis.
46. See the argument in Trevor Wilson, *The Myriad Faces of War: Britain and the Great War 1914–1918* (Cambridge: Polity Press, 1986), pp. 33–34. Henry Wilson pointed out in August 1911 that British intervention, even given a limited territorial transgression against Belgium, could even up the balance of forces between France and Germany, and mean the difference between defeat and withstanding the German attack. It is reasonable to assume that this would have made some impression upon ministers at the meeting, particularly pro-French ones such as Lloyd George, and despite his hesitations in July–August 1914 regarding the extent of a German violation of Belgium that the dominant factor in 1914 remained France. And that therefore even a minor violation of Belgian territory, if it resulted in a French defeat – and remember that many in 1911 and later in 1914 were convinced that France would succumb to the German Army (as almost certainly it would have) – would have meant British entry in any event (perhaps a few days or weeks later). By that time it would have been much more difficult to intervene effectively on the Western Front. Thus, those with foresight perhaps would have concluded that early intervention was better than later, whatever the extent of the invasion of Belgium.
47. *War Memoirs*, I, pp. 74–77.
48. PRO 30/69/1753/1: MacDonald Memorandum, 23 September 1914.
49. Frances Lloyd George, *The Years that are Past* (London: Hutchinson, 1967), pp. 73–74. Frances Stevenson spent the whole of the weekend before the outbreak of war with Lloyd George at 11 Downing Street; Grigg, *Lloyd George*, III, p. 144.
50. *Scott Diaries*, p. 94.
51. See ibid., p. 102. On Nicoll, see Hazlehurst, *Politicians at War*, pp. 219–20.
52. On Lloyd George's speech at the Queen's Hall on 19 September 1914, see Lloyd George, *The Years that are Past*, pp. 74–75; McEwen (ed.), *Riddell Diaries*, p. 90, 19 September 1914; Grigg, *Lloyd George*, III, pp. 161–67; *Stevenson Diaries*, p. 2; Gilbert, *Lloyd George*, II, pp. 117–20.
53. Grigg, *Lloyd George*, III, p. 146.
54. See Riddell, *Riddell Diaries*, pp. 4–5: 'LG. strongly insisted on the danger of aggrandising Russia and on the future problems that would arise if Russia and France were successful... I [asked Lloyd George] How should we feel if we saw France overrun and annihilated? Lloyd George said, "How would you feel if you saw Germany overrun and annihilated by Russia?".'

55. Grigg, *Lloyd George*, III, p. 146. See also Gilbert, *Lloyd George*, II, pp. 112–13. The unifying force of Belgium as *casus belli* is acknowledged by Lloyd George in *War Memoirs*, I, pp. 65–66.

56. See the criticisms of Lloyd George in Keith Wilson, 'Britain', in Keith Wilson (ed.), *Decisions for War 1914* (London: UCL Press, 1995), pp. 181–82. On Lloyd George's horror at the 'pandemonium let loose' by the July crisis and the onset of war, see Kenneth O. Morgan (ed.), *Lloyd George: Family Letters 1885–1936* (Cardiff, London: University of Wales and Oxford University Presses, 1973), pp. 166–67.

57. *War Memoirs*, I, p. 55.

58. John C.G. Röhl, 'Germany', in Wilson (ed.), *Decisions for War 1914*, p. 34.

59. Ibid., pp. 34–39.

60. See Röhl, *The Kaiser and his Court*, pp. 162–89; also Fritz Fischer, *War of Illusions: German Policies from 1911 to 1914* (London: Chatto & Windus, 1975), pp. 161–64 and Annika Mombauer, *Helmuth von Moltke and the Origins of the First World War* (Cambridge: Cambridge University Press, 2001), pp. 138–43. Von Moltke stated at the meeting, 'I believe a war is unavoidable and the sooner the better and that if Germany waited the army would get into an increasingly unfavourable position, for the enemies were arming more strongly than we, as we were very short of money'. Despite the lack of money, an Army Bill was passed the next year which greatly increased the size of the army. Admiral von Tirpitz, the architect of German naval expansion, expressed the view at the same meeting that the German navy would not be ready for another one and a half years; the Kaiser ordered him to prepare another Navy Bill to speedup construction, but this did not eventuate. What prompted these bellicose sentiments was that the Kaiser had been told that Lord Haldane told Lichnowsky, the German Ambassador in London, that if Germany attacked France, Britain 'would unconditionally spring to France's aid, for England could not allow the balance of power in Europe to be disturbed. [The Kaiser] greeted this information as a desirable clarification of the situation for the benefit of those who had felt sure of England as a result of the recent friendliness of the [British] press'; *The Kaiser and his Court*, p. 162. For a different interpretation of this War Council see Hew Strachan, *The First World War*: vol. I: *To Arms* (Oxford: Oxford University Press, 2001), pp. 52–55.

61. Fritz Fellner, 'Austria-Hungary', in Wilson (ed.), *Decisions for War 1914*, p. 23.

3 Strategic dilemmas 1914–15

1. *War Memoirs*, I, p. 358.

2. Ibid., p. 82.

3. PRO CAB 42/1/2: War Council, 5 August 1914. General Sir Ian Hamilton, who was also at this meeting, did not seem to recall the Antwerp proposal at all. In a letter to Liddell Hart in 1933, he stated that 'French was quite clear and decided. He said we should embark our troops as quickly as possible and assemble them at an agreed spot on the left of the French line. The exact spot was unknown to French or anyone else as the French would not give it in the Military Operations.' When Hamilton later saw Hankey's record of

the meeting, he thought it was 'so abbreviated that it was not worth very much but no doubt it could be got hold of by an accredited historian'. HLRO LG MSS G/212: Hamilton to Liddell Hart, 19 May 1933. (Copy)

4. Robert Blake (ed.), *The Private Papers of Douglas Haig 1914–1919* (London: Eyre and Spottiswoode, 1952), pp. 68–69; C.E. Callwell (ed.), *Field Marshal Sir Henry Wilson: His Life and Diaries*, 2 vols (London: Cassell, 1927) p. 158; also Samuel R. Williamson, *The Politics of Grand Strategy: Britain and France Prepare for War 1904–1914* (London and Atlantic Highlands NJ: Ashfield Press, 1990), p. 365; Maurice Hankey, *The Supreme Command*, 2 vols (London: Allen & Unwin, 1961), I, pp. 170–71.

5. Trevor Wilson, *The Myriad Faces of War: Britain and the Great War 1914–1918* (Cambridge: Polity Press, 1986), pp. 36–37. See also Sir Llewellyn Woodward, *Great Britain and the War of 1914–1918* (London: Methuen, 1967), p. 31; George H. Cassar, *The Tragedy of Sir John French* (Newark: University of Delaware Press, 1985), p. 84.

6. Paul Guinn, *British Strategy and Politics 1914–1918* (Oxford: Clarendon Press, 1965), pp. 13–14; William J. Philpott, 'British Military Strategy on the Western Front: Independence or Alliance 1904–1918' (DPhil thesis, University of Oxford, 1991), pp. 19–28 (published in revised form as *Anglo-French Relations and Strategy on the Western Front 1914–1918* [London: Macmillan, 1996]).

7. Grierson's memorandum of 4 January 1906, quoted in Guinn, *British Strategy*, p. 12. See also Williamson, *Politics of Grand Strategy*, pp. 48–50, 86–88, 93.

8. Quoted in Guinn, *British Strategy*, p. 14.

9. Lloyd George to Churchill, 25 August 1911, quoted in Bentley B. Gilbert, 'Pacifist to Interventionist: David Lloyd George in 1911 and 1914. Was Belgium an Issue?', *Historical Journal*, 28, 4, 1984, pp. 863–85, where he argues in part that this and ensuing letters on the subject demonstrate that both men took British participation in a war against Germany for granted, and also that 'far from regarding the invasion of Belgium only as an excuse for British intervention, the two sought for a way to enforce Belgian resistance should she decide not to fight Germany.... The integrity of Belgium was an irrelevancy'; p. 874. In the circumstances of August 1914, if Gilbert's assessment is correct, then at least part of the rationale for British deployment on Belgian soil had no validity, for Belgium *did* resist, although both Lloyd George and Churchill persisted in the proposal.

10. Randolph S. Churchill, *Young Statesman: Winston S. Churchill 1901–1914*, Companion vol. II (London: Heinemann, 1969), pp. 1117–18, Churchill to Grey, 30 August 1911, Churchill to Lloyd George, 31 August 1911.

11. B.H. Liddell Hart, *History of the First World War* (London: Pan, 1970) (pbk ed. of *A History of the World War* 1934, itself was a revised edition of *The Real War*, 1930), p. 44.

12. B.H. Liddell Hart, *Strategy: The Indirect Approach* (London: Faber & Faber, 1967) (rev.ed. of *The Strategy of Indirect Approach*, 1941), p. 168.

13. Ibid., p. 176.

14. Michael Howard, *The Continental Commitment* (London: Temple Smith, 1972), p. 55.

15. LHCMA Liddell Hart MSS 11/1933/19: 'Note, Re German Plan 1914', 21 May 1933.

16. Ibid.

17. NLW Sylvester MSS: uncatalogued interview with General Wetzell on Sunday morning, 13 September 1936.
18. *War Memoirs*, VI, pp. 3411–12. Liddell Hart persisted, in his advice to Lloyd George concerning this passage, in arguing that 'it would have upset them [the Germans] more effectively if it [the BEF] had been landed on the flank of their communications through Belgium instead of in their front', but to no avail; HLRO LG MSS G/212: Liddell Hart to Frances Stevenson, 23 October 1936, 'Notes on Volume VI (latest chapters) of Mr Lloyd George's Memoirs'.
19. *War Memoirs*, I, p. 354.
20. Ibid.
21. Ibid., pp. 355–56.
22. Ibid., p. 358.
23. Ibid., p. 359.
24. Ibid., pp. 356–57.
25. Asquith was impressed with Lloyd George's effort. As he wrote to Venetia Stanley: 'I have also received to-day two long mem[oranda] – one from Winston, the other from Lloyd George (quite good, the latter) as to the... conduct of the war. They are both keen on a new objective & theatre, as soon as our new troops are ready: W, of course, for Borkum & the Baltic: Ll.G for Salonika to join in with the Serbians, & for Syria!', Michael and Eleonor Brock (eds), *H.H. Asquith: Letters to Venetia Stanley* (Oxford: Oxford University Press, 1985), pp. 357–58.
26. HLRO LG MSS C/16/1/3: 'The War. Suggestions as to the Military Situation', 1 January 1915; printed in *War Memoirs*, I, pp. 369–80.
27. *War Memoirs*, I, p. 377.
28. Ibid., pp. 377–78.
29. Ibid., p. 373. My emphasis.
30. Ibid., pp. 372–73.
31. Ibid., pp. 379–80.
32. Wilson, *Myriad Faces*, p. 105.
33. PRO CAB 42/1/16: War Council, 13 January 1915. My emphasis.
34. *War Memoirs*, I, p. 364.
35. Ibid., pp. 364–65.
36. Ibid., p. 367.
37. Ibid.
38. On the Austro-Hungarian army see Alan Sked, *The Decline and Fall of the Austro-Hungarian Empire 1815–1918* (London: Longman, 1989), pp. 258–64; Gunther E. Rothenberg, 'The Habsburg Army in the First World War: 1914–1918', in Béla K. Király and Nándor F. Dreisziger (eds), *East Central Europe in World War I* (Highland Lakes: Atlantic Research and Publications, Social Science Monographs, 1985), pp. 289–300; István Deák, 'The Habsburg Army in the First and Last Days of World War I: A Comparative Analysis', in Király and Dreisziger (eds), *East Central Europe in World War I*, pp. 301–12; cf. Geoffrey Wawro, 'Morale in the Austro-Hungarian Army: the Evidence of Habsburg Army Campaign Reports and Allied Intelligence Officers', in Hugh Cecil and Peter H. Liddle (eds), *Facing Armageddon: The First World War Experienced* (London: Leo Cooper, 1996), pp. 399–412.
39. *War Memoirs*, I, p. 373.

40. As he wrote to Kitchener, 'I am fairly confident that you will not get these Balkan states to decide until they see khaki!', HLRO LG MSS C/5/7/13: Lloyd George to Kitchener, 29 January 1915.
41. HLRO LG MSS C/16/1/2: Memorandum by Hankey, 28 December 1914. Churchill was also pushing for a Balkan Confederation, see his World Crisis, I, pp. 486–87.
42. David Stevenson (ed.), British Documents on Foreign Affairs: Reports and Papers from the Foreign Office Confidential Print, Part II Series H, The First World War 1914–1918, 12 vols (University Publications of America, 1989; General Editors Kenneth Bourne and D. Cameron Watt), p. 17, No. 38, Grey to Erskine, British Chargé d'Affaires in Athens, 11 August 1914. Venizelos a few days later told Erskine that support for a Balkan grouping was his 'personal view', and that he was anxious that the initiative should come from Russia; p. 19, No. 43, Erskine to Grey, 12 August 1914.
43. Ibid., p. 22, No. 47, Grey to Bax-Ironside, 13 August 1914; also pp. 39–40, No. 85, Grey to Bax-Ironside, 21 August 1914.
44. David French, British Strategy and War Aims 1914–1916 (London: Allen & Unwin, 1986), p. 68.
45. Balfour Add. MSS 49707: Balfour to Hankey, 2 January 1915.
46. Ibid. Emphasis mine. French points out that Balfour could have added further point, that logistical problems posed by the difficult terrain in the Balkans would be formidable; French, British Strategy, p. 68.
47. LHCMA Liddell Hart MSS 11/1934/57: 'Lloyd George and the Strategy of the War, Evidence from Documents on the Question, 1934'.
48. Ibid. For an examination of the issues of supply and communications in the Macedonian campaign, see Cyril Falls, Military Operations in Macedonia from the Outbreak of War to the Spring of 1917, Vol. I (London: HMSO, 1933), ch. 12.
49. See War Memoirs, I, p. 381.
50. Kitchener to French, 2 January 1915, quoted in ibid., p. 382. See also Sir George Arthur, Life of Lord Kitchener, 3 vols (London: Macmillan, 1920), I, pp. 85–86.
51. HLRO LG MSS C/5/7/12: Kitchener to Lloyd George, 29 January 1915.
52. War Memoirs, I, p. 383. See PRO CAB 42/1/16: War Council, 13 January 1915.
53. HLRO LG MSS G/212: Hankey notes on chapters, 'Strategy of the War. Eastern v. Western Fronts' (1933).
54. Ibid.
55. Ibid. Kitchener told the War Council that French's views were that: 'The impossibility of breaking through the German lines is not admitted.... It is largely a question of larger supplies of ammunition and especially of high explosives. Until the impossibility of breaking through on this side was proved, there could be no question of making an attempt elsewhere. Ultimate victory must be sought for in the eastern theatre of war. In the western theatre a German victory would be decisive, but a victory of the Allies, who might drive the Germans back to the Rhine, would not be decisive. A crushing defeat however of the French would be very dangerous and embarrassing to our own safety and must be made impossible'; PRO CAB 42/1/12: War Council, 8 January 1915.

56. *War Memoirs*, I, pp. 383–85. The 'unimpeachable authority' was Liddell Hart. See HLRO LG MSS G/212: Notes on chapters 'The Strategy of the War', no date.

57. Quoted in *War Memoirs*, I, p. 384.

58. Ibid., p. 385. Asquith too at this time was wary of pouring unlimited numbers of British troops into France; as he wrote, '. . . we may have a bit of a row with the French. When you remember that we have sent them 3 times the number of men they ever reckoned on . . . their demand that we should go on pouring into their theatre every available division is more than a trifle greedy – particularly as they continue to assure us that the Germans can *never* break through the present lines.' See Brock and Brock (eds), *Letters to Venetia Stanley*, p. 393.

59. *War Memoirs*, I, pp. 386–87.

60. J.F.C. Fuller, *The Conduct of War 1789–1961* (London: Eyre and Spottiswoode, 1962), pp. 161–62.

61. Ibid., p. 161. Fuller's emphasis.

62. PRO CAB 42/1/16: War Council, 13 January 1915.

63. PRO CAB 42/1/47: War Council, 26 February 1915.

64. *War Memoirs*, I, p. 390.

65. Ibid. He continues: 'A more virile and understanding treatment of the Balkan situation [on Grey's part] would have brought Greece and also Bulgaria into the War. Italy could also have been brought in sooner.' Lloyd George told his brother: 'I think he [Grey] could have averted the war and I am quite convinced he could have saved the Balkans.' HLRO LG MSS G/211: Lloyd George to William George, 28 May 1933.

66. Haig, for one, had a much better opinion of the Territorials. He commented on Kitchener's 'ignorance of the progress made by the Territorial Army towards efficiency . . . I was very intimately acquainted, of course, with what the Territorials had been doing. I was well aware how hard some units had worked and of the splendid patriotic spirit which pervaded the whole force'; *Haig Papers*, p. 69.

67. *War Memoirs*, I, pp. 390–92.

68. See the arguments on this point in Robin Prior, Churchill's '*World Crisis*' *as History* (London: Croom Helm, 1983), esp. chs 6–7; Wilson, *Myriad Faces*, esp. pp. 115–21.

69. PRO CAB 42/1/42: War Council, 24 February 1915.

70. John Grigg, *Lloyd George: From Peace to War 1912–1916* (London: HarperCollins, 1997), p. 208. See also Lloyd George's note on the Dardanelles, written sometime later: 'I was opposed to a military expedition in Gallipoli for reasons which I have stated repeatedly . . . I felt we were attacking at a disadvantage a military power which could bring greater forces to the defence than we could possibly bring to the attack during 1915 – forces moreover with a traditional reputation for putting up an obstinate defence . . . adequate forces should be used for the purpose of achieving successful results'. HLRO LG MSS G/262: notes, untitled, no date. See also his comments at the 26 February War Council meeting: 'Mr Lloyd George thought it was more probable that the Turks would make a stand, as they had done in the Russo-Turkish War and at Chatalja in the recent Balkan Wars.' PRO CAB 42/1/47: War Council, 26 February 1915.

71. Keith Robbins, 'British Diplomacy and Bulgaria 1914–1915', *Slavonic and East European Review*, XLIX, 117, October 1971, p. 566.
72. Stevenson (ed.), *British Documents on Foreign Affairs from the Confidential Print*, Part II Series H, I, p. 383, No. 670, Lord Eustace Percy, The Balkans, 1914–15, from the Outbreak of War to the Offer to Bulgaria, 9 July 1915.
73. See ibid., Edward, Viscount Grey, *Twenty Five Years*, 2 vols (London: Hodder and Stoughton, 1925), I, p. 180; G.M. Trevelyan, *Grey of Fallodon* (London: Longmans, 1937), p. 283. The latter notes that 'Grey could not alienate Russia and bring Turkey and Bulgaria into the war against us, merely for Greek aid'. This is particularly pertinent considering the state of the Greek Army. On this point, see Prior, '*World Crisis' as History*, p. 185 and Prior's comments on Churchill's discussion of the 'lost opportunity' of Greek aid, p. 44.
74. HLRO LG MSS G/212: Hankey notes on draft chapters, 'The Dardanelles Committee and the Balkans', no date.
75. *War Memoirs*, I, p. 391.
76. Grey responded by suggesting that it 'was possible that Mr Lloyd George, if he could be spared, might accomplish something'; PRO CAB 42/1/47: War Council, 26 February 1915. This suggestion was not taken up by Lloyd George.
77. Ibid.
78. PRO CAB 42/1/36: War Council, 19 February 1915.
79. A.J.P. Taylor (ed.), *Lloyd George: A Diary by Frances Stevenson* (London: Hutchinson, 1971), p. 28. See Lloyd George's nine-page letter to Grey, 7 February 1915. At the end of the letter he tacked on one line: 'The financial conference was a great success'; HLRO LG MSS: C/4/1/16.
80. Somewhat qualified support in French's case.
81. HLRO LG MSS C/4/1/16: Lloyd George to Grey, 7 February 1915, quoted in full in *War Memoirs*, I, p 409.
82. HLRO LG MSS C/4/1/16 Lloyd George to Grey, 7 February 1915.
83. Ibid. See also *Stevenson Diary*, p. 28.
84. *War Memoirs*, I, p. 411. Stevenson wrote, 'C. called on French . . . as Grey had requested him [C.] to undertake to persuade French to release two divisions for the East. French was very amenable, and consented to do so provided that Joffre consents.' *Stevenson Diary*, p. 28.
85. *War Memoirs*, I, p. 411. Lloyd George, in the *Memoirs*, gives Robertson's approval special emphasis.
86. Ibid. Robertson, Lloyd George wrote, would have gone further and sent two divisions immediately.
87. See Grigg, *Lloyd George*, II, p. 207 and Alan Palmer, *The Gardeners of Salonika* (London: Andre Deutsch, 1965), p. 28. Although as Lloyd George said one month later, 'the reason why Greece did not intervene was not the general opposition of the King, but the fact that by the most competent military judges in Greece Germany was still expected to win . . . The same impression was influencing the other neutral countries – Bulgaria, Roumania, Italy. It required a man of real imagination and insight like Venizelos to realise the immense staying power of Great Britain which in the end would determine the issue.' *Scott Diaries*, pp. 120–21.

4 Munitions 1914–16

1. For general accounts of Lloyd George and the Ministry of Munitions, see R.J.Q. Adams, *Arms and the Wizard: Lloyd George and the Ministry of Munitions 1915–1916* (London: Cassell, 1978); Chris Wrigley, 'The Ministry of Munitions: An Innovatory Department', in Kathleen Burk (ed.), *War and the State: The Transformation of British Government 1914–1919* (London: George Allen & Unwin, 1982), pp. 32–56; John Grigg, *Lloyd George: From Peace to War 1912–1916* (London: HarperCollins, 1997), ch. 11; Bentley Brinkerhoff Gilbert, *David Lloyd George, A Political Life: Organizer of Victory 1912–1916* (Columbus: Ohio State University Press, 1992), ch. 6; Hew Strachan, *The First World War*, Vol. I *To Arms* (Oxford: Oxford University Press, 2001), pp. 1065–113 and Keith Grieves, 'Lloyd George and the Management of the British War Economy', in Roger Chickering and Stig Förster (eds), *Great War, Total War: Combat and Mobilisation on the Western Front 1914–1918* (Cambridge: Cambridge University Press, 2000), pp. 369–87.
2. Quoted in *War Memoirs*, I, pp. 200–01.
3. See Michael and Eleonor Brock (eds), *H.H. Asquith: Letters to Venetia Stanley* (Oxford: Oxford University Press, 1985), p. 558; Earl of Oxford and Asquith, *Memories and Reflections*, 2 vols (London: Cassell, 1928), II, p. 77; on Lloyd George, *H.C.Deb.* 5s, col. 318, 21 April 1915, cf. *War Memoirs*, I, pp. 195–96; and PRO MUN 9/33: Draft chapters for *War Memoirs*.
4. Martin Gilbert, *The Challenge of War: Winston S. Churchill 1914–1916* (London: Minerva, 1990), pp. 452–53.
5. BL Balfour Add. MSS 49692: Asquith to Balfour, 20 May 1915. See also Asquith's daughter's account in Mark Pottle (ed.), *Champion Redoubtable: The Diaries and Letters of Violet Bonham Carter* (London: Weidenfeld and Nicolson, 1998), pp. 50–51.
6. *War Memoirs*, I, p. 225.
7. HLRO LG MSS D/18/1/4: Northcliffe to Lloyd George (postmarked 29 May 1915).
8. *War Memoirs*, I, pp. 134–38.
9. Ibid., pp. 137–45.
10. Strachan, *The First World War*, I, pp. 994–1005.
11. Chris Wrigley, 'The Ministry of Munitions: An Innovatory Department', in Kathleen Burk (ed.), *War and the State: The Transformation of British Government 1914–1919* (London: George Allen & Unwin, 1982), p. 38; a similar point is made by Strachan, *The First World War*, I, pp. 1069.
12. Ibid.
13. Grigg, *Lloyd George*, III, p. 183. Cf. Great Britain, *History of the Ministry of Munitions*, 12 vols (first published in London: 1921–22, Microfiche Ed., Hassocks, Sussex: Harvester Press, 1976), IX, Part I, p. 11.
14. George H. Cassar, *Kitchener: Architect of Victory* (London: William Kimber, 1977), pp. 333–35; Kitchener, according to Cassar, aroused Lloyd George's 'envy and hatred'; and Lloyd George saw Kitchener as blocking his path to power; the former was 'destitute of all moral qualities... [and] placed his own interests ahead of the nation'.
15. On these points see Wrigley, 'Ministry of Munitions', in Burk (ed.), *War and the State*, pp. 35–38; *Ministry of Munitions*, IX, Part I, pp. 11–12.

16. Duncan Crow, *Man of Push and Go: The Life of George Macaulay Booth* (London: Rupert Hart-Davis, 1965), pp. 114–15.
17. According to Lloyd George: 'The sole articles of furniture in the office of the new department were two tables and a chair'; and according to Lloyd George the Office of Works even wanted to take these away; *War Memoirs*, I, pp. 242–43.
18. *Ministry of Munitions*, X, Part 1, p. 5.
19. *War Memoirs*, II, pp. 551–52; cf. Grigg, *Lloyd George*, III, p. 271; Gilbert, *Lloyd George*, II, pp. 224–25.
20. *Ministry of Munitions*, II, Part 1, p. 21.
21. *War Memoirs*, II, p. 556.
22. Ibid., pp. 556–57; HLRO LG MSS D/17/6/14 (a): French to Brade (Permanent Undersecretary of State at the War Office), 25 June 1915.
23. *Ministry of Munitions*, X, Part 1, p. 10.
24. Ibid., pp. 11–13; Strachan, *The First World War*, I, p. 1082.
25. *War Memoirs*, II, p. 557; *Ministry of Munitions*, X, Part 1, p. 16.
26. Ibid.; Gilbert, *Lloyd George*, II, pp. 226–27.
27. *War Memoirs*, II, p. 557.
28. Adams, *Arms and the Wizard*, p. 168. The war did grow of course, but the British army never grew to 100 divisions.
29. *Ministry of Munitions*, X, Part I, p. 23.
30. Ibid., p. 18.
31. Ibid., p. 20.
32. Ibid., pp. 23–25.
33. *War Memoirs*, II, p. 560; *Ministry of Munitions*, X, Part 1, pp. 25–26.
34. *War Memoirs*, VI, pp. 3390–92.
35. Ibid., II, p. 565.
36. HLRO LG MSS D/17/6/16: Memorandum on the Supply of Artillery Ammunition to the Army in the Field. 10 June 1915.
37. *Ministry of Munitions*, X, Part II, p. 2.
38. Ibid., Part III, pp. 6–7.
39. *War Memoirs*, II, pp. 567–68.
40. *Ministry of Munitions*, X, Part V, p. 72.
41. Ibid., pp. 76–80.
42. Shelford Bidwell and Dominick Graham, *Fire-power: British Army Weapons and Theories of War 1904–1945* (London: George Allen & Unwin, 1982), pp. 98–99.
43. James E. Edmonds, *Military Operations: France and Belgium 1916*, Vol. I (London: Macmillan, 1932); Vol. II (London: Macmillan, 1938), I, 123, II, pp. 568–69.
44. Ibid.; Trevor Wilson, *The Myriad Faces of War: Britain and the Great War 1914–1918* (Cambridge: Polity Press, 1986), p. 238; see also Martin Middlebrook, *The First Day on the Somme* (New York: Norton, 1972), p. 69; according to War Office statistics, there were 418 heavy guns and howitzers (6 in. and over) in France on 1 July 1916, compared with 1328 just over one year later; War Office, *Statistics of the Military Effort of the British Empire during the Great War* (London: HMSO, 1922, repr. London Stamp Exchange, 1992), pp. 441–42.
45. *Military Operations 1916*, II, p. 568; Strachan, *The First World War*, I, p. 1085.
46. PRO/30/57/82 Kitchener MSS: Kitchener to Asquith, 12 July 1915.

47. *Ministry of Munitions*, II, Part I, p. 41.

48. Ibid., p. 43; Strachan, *The First World War*, I, p. 1085.

49. HLRO LG MSS D/17/16/3–4: Edwin Montagu to Lloyd George (with enc.), 31 May 1916, Lloyd George to Montagu, 5 June 1916.

50. Hew Strachan, 'The Battle of the Somme and British Strategy', *Journal of Strategic Studies*, 21, 1, March 1998, p. 85, and his *The First World War*, I, p. 1085; see also Bidwell and Graham, *Fire-power*, pp. 98–99; Middlebrook, *First Day on the Somme*, p. 69. Of course, the problem of unexploded shells was not confined to the British. Unexploded shells from 1914 to 1918 still lie in all the battlefields of northern France and Belgium; see, on Verdun, for example, Donovan Webster, *Aftermath: The Remnants of War* (New York and Toronto: Vintage, 1998), p. 18.

51. Bidwell and Graham, *Fire-power*, p. 98; PRO WO95/2368: 'Report of Preparations and Action of 32nd Divisional Artillery during Operations of July 1916'.

52. *Military Operations 1916*, I, pp. 122–23. According to one estimate, by December 1915 the rate of premature explosions in the 4.5-in howitzer was about one in 5000; Strachan, *The First World War*, I, p. 1084.

53. *Military Operations 1916*, II, p. 568. This shortage is commented upon in some of the unit diaries and accounts of action during the battle. See, for example, PRO WO95/2491: '36th Division Operations, Action during the Preliminary Bombardment'.

54. Strachan, *The First World War*, I, p. 1084; *Ministry of Munitions*, X, Part II, ch. 2.

55. Trevor Wilson, 'A Prime Minister Reflects: The *War Memoirs* of David Lloyd George', in John A. Moses and Christopher Pugsley (eds), *The German Empire and Britain's Pacific Dominions 1871–1919: Essays on the Role of Australia and New Zealand in an Age of Imperialism* (Claremont, CA: Regina Books, 2000), p. 48; Strachan, *The First World War*, I, p. 1086; Bidwell and Graham, *Fire-power*, pp. 98–99.

56. *War Memoirs*, II, p. 614.

57. Ibid., p. 606.

58. *Military Operations 1916*, II, p. 282, n. 1; see also John Terraine, *The Smoke and the Fire: Myths and Anti-Myths of War* (London: Leo Cooper, 1992 ed.), pp. 130–42 and Denis Winter, *Death's Men: Soldiers of the Great War* (London: Penguin, 1978), pp. 204–05.

59. *War Memoirs*, II, p. 600; *Ministry of Munitions*, XI, Part V, p. 3.

60. Tim Travers, *The Killing Ground: The British Army, the Western Front and the Emergence of Modern Warfare 1900–1918* (London: Allen & Unwin, 1987), pp. 63–66; David G. Hermann, *The Arming of Europe and the Making of the First World War* (Princeton: Princeton University Press, 1996), p. 20.

61. Terraine, *The Smoke and the Fire*, p. 139.

62. Hermann, *The Arming of Europe*, pp. 68–69.

63. *Ministry of Munitions*, XI, Part V, pp. 4–5.

64. *War Memoirs*, II, p. 605; cf. extracts from Geddes' 'Family Tree', in HLRO LG MSS G/240: Notes of an interview with Sir Eric Geddes, 1 October 1932; LG MSS G/252: interview with Sir Eric Geddes, 2 December 1932.

65. HLRO LG MSS G/240: 'Bible: Munitions, Machine-guns, Machine-gun Corps'. Although Geddes in his 'Family Tree' recalled that Lloyd George insisted that they should plan for 64 machine-guns per battalion; HLRO LG MSS G/252: Geddes interview, 2 December 1932.

66. Grigg, *Lloyd George*, III, pp. 278–79.
67. Terraine, *The Smoke and the Fire*, pp. 138–39.
68. *War Memoirs*, II, p. 599; *Ministry of Munitions*, XI, Part V, pp. 9–10.
69. *Statistics*, p. 473.
70. *Ministry of Munitions*, XI, Part V, pp. 4–5.
71. Ibid., p. 10.
72. Ibid.
73. Ibid., pp. 13–15.
74. Ibid., p. 27.
75. *War Memoirs*, II, p. 606; HLRO LG MSS G/240: 'Bible: Munitions, Machine-guns and Machine-gun Corps'; Grigg, *Lloyd George*, III, p. 279; Adams, *Arms and the Wizard*, pp. 173–75.
76. Grigg, *Lloyd George*, III, p. 279.
77. On the origins of the tank see Ernest D. Swinton, *Eyewitness: Being Personal Reminiscences of Certain Phases of the Great War, including the Genesis of the Tank* (London: Hodder and Stoughton, 1932); also on Swinton IWM Gwynne MSS HAG/23/2: Lord Algernon Percy (ADC to George V) to H.A. Gwynne (editor of the *Morning Post*), 19 September 1916, who emphasised E.D. Swinton's pivotal role in the conception of the tank. See however J.P. Harris, *Men, Ideas and Tanks: British Military Thought and Armoured Forces 1903–1939* (Manchester and New York: Manchester University Press, 1995), pp. 34–38, who rather downplays Swinton's role. See also Wilson, *Myriad Faces*, pp. 338–45; B.H. Liddell Hart, *The Tanks*, 2 vols (London: Cassell, 1959), I, pp. 21–26; *Ministry of Munitions*, XII, Part III, ch. 1, on Swinton esp. pp. 3–6 and Stephen Roskill, *Hankey: Man of Secrets*, vol. I (London: Collins, 1970), pp. 146–47; Terraine, *The Smoke and the Fire*, pp. 148–60 and David J. Childs, *A Peripheral Weapon? The Production and Employment of British Tanks in the First World War* (Westport, Connecticut, London: Greenwood, 1999).
78. *War Memoirs*, II, pp. 639–40.
79. Gary Sheffield, *Forgotten Victory: The First World War Myths and Realities* (London: Headline, 2001), p. 146; J.P. Harris, 'Haig and the Tank', in Brian Bond and Nigel Cave (eds), *Haig: A Reappraisal 70 Years On* (Barnsley: Leo Cooper, 1999), pp. 147–48; John Terraine, *Haig: The Educated Soldier* (London: Hutchinson, 1963), pp. 221–22; *Ministry of Munitions*, XII, Part III, pp. 33–35.
80. See Wilson, *Myriad Faces*, p. 344; Sheffield, *Forgotten Victory*, pp. 146–47; Childs, *Peripheral Weapon?*, pp. 149–50; *Military Operations 1916*, II, p. 364; J.E. Edmonds, *A Short History of World War I* (London: Oxford University Press, 1951), pp. 188–89; Terraine, *Haig*, pp. 225–26.
81. Winston S. Churchill, *The World Crisis*, 6 vols (London: Thornton Butterworth, 1923–31), II, pp. 89–90.
82. Swinton, *Eyewitness*, pp. 297–98.
83. *Military Operations, 1916*, II, pp. 365–66.
84. *War Memoirs*, II, pp. 645–46.
85. *Military Operations 1916*, II, pp. 365–66. By late 1917, if anyone in the German High Command had realised the tank's potential it was too late; the German economy was by then 'strained to capacity' and could not have produced tanks in any significant numbers; see Roger Chickering, *Imperial Germany and the Great War 1914–1918* (Cambridge: Cambridge University Press, 1998), p. 179.

86. *War Memoirs*, II, p. 647.
87. Quoted in Martin Gilbert, *World in Torment: Winston S. Churchill 1917–1922* (London: Minerva, 1990 ed.), p. 62.
88. Harris, 'Haig and the Tank', p. 151.
89. Edmonds, *Short History*, p. 265.
90. See Tim Travers, *How the War Was Won: Command and Technology in the British Army on the Western Front 1917–1918* (London and New York: Routledge, 1992), pp. 20–22; Wilson, *Myriad Faces*, pp. 486–89; Terraine, *The Smoke and the Fire*, pp. 153–54.
91. Wilson, *Myriad Faces*, pp. 583–84, 591; Edmonds, *Short History*, pp. 344–46; Terraine, *The Smoke and the Fire*, p. 154; Harris, *Men, Ideas and Tanks*, ch. 5; Childs, *Peripheral Weapon?*, ch. 8.
92. *Military Operations 1916*, II, p. 365; Robin Prior, *Churchill's 'World Crisis' as History* (London: Croom Helm, 1983), p. 239.
93. *Military Operations, 1916*, II, p. 366, and n. 1.
94. Ibid.
95. Ibid., pp. 365–66; Prior, *'World Crisis' as History*, p. 240.

5 'To a knock-out': War office and political crisis 1916

1. John Grigg, *Lloyd George: From Peace to War 1912–1916* (London: HarperCollins, 1997), p. 357.
2. *War Memoirs*, II, p. 762.
3. Ibid., p. 769.
4. Sir William Robertson, *Soldiers and Statesmen 1914–1918*, 2 vols (London: Cassell, 1926), I, p. 179.
5. Lloyd George writes of Robertson in this context: 'Sir William Robertson . . . regarded any effort to exercise authority on my part as an impingement on his special powers, so he thrust out all his prickles whenever he suspected I might be about to attempt any rash civilian interference with the sanctity of military matters', *War Memoirs*, II, p. 769.
6. Ibid.
7. Ibid., p. 802.
8. Grigg, *Lloyd George*, III, p. 367; Robertson, *Soldiers and Statesmen*, II, ch. 9; Trevor Wilson, The *Myriad Faces of War: Britain and the Great War 1914–1918* (Cambridge: Polity Press, 1986), pp. 378–81.
9. *War Memoirs*, II, p. 785. My emphasis.
10. Ibid., pp. 789–90.
11. HLRO LG MSS G/240: 'Notes of an Interview with Sir Eric Geddes about the Work of the Ministry of Munitions etc.', 1 October 1932.
12. HLRO LG MSS G/252: Sylvester to Lloyd George, 3 December 1932.
13. HLRO LG MSS G/211: Geddes' Private Secretary to Sylvester, 20 December 1932.
14. Ibid.
15. Grigg, *Lloyd George*, III, pp. 366–67; Bentley Brinkerhoff Gilbert, *David Lloyd George, A Political Life: Organizer of Victory 1912–1916* (Columbus: Ohio State University Press, 1992), pp. 378–80; Keith Grieves, 'The Transportation Mission to GHQ, 1916', in Brian Bond *et al.* (eds), *Look to Your Front: Studies*

in the First World War (Staplehurst: Spellmount, 1999), pp. 63–78; HLRO LG MSS G/252: Notes of an Interview with Sir Eric Geddes GCB at Albourne Place, Hassocks, Surrey, on Friday 2 December 1932.

16. Lloyd George cites Haig's appreciative reference to Geddes from his final Despatch; *War Memoirs.* II, p. 801.
17. Grigg, *Lloyd George*, III, p. 367.
18. *War Memoirs*, II, p. 535.
19. Ibid., p. 538. My emphasis.
20. Ibid. Haig's offensive certainly relieved the pressure on the French at Verdun; the question remains, however, whether some other less costly way could have been found to do this. See HLRO LG MSS G/212: Liddell Hart notes on chapters, 1933; also Wilson, *Myriad Faces*, pp. 348–49 and Gary Sheffield, *Forgotten Victory: The First World War Myth and Realities* (London: Headline, 2001), p. 153.
21. *War Memoirs*, II, pp. 538–39.
22. Ibid., p. 543.
23. Ibid., p. 547.
24. Ibid., IV, pp. 2110, 2130.
25. HLRO LG MSS, G/212, Liddell Hart notes on chapters, 1933; on casualties see J.E. Edmonds, *Military Operations: France and Belgium 1916*, Vol. I (London: Macmillan, 1932), pp. 496–97, II (1938), p. 553; M.J. Williams, 'Thirty Per Cent: A Study in Casualty Statistics', *Journal of the Royal United Service Institution*, 109, February 1964, pp. 51–55, and the same author's 'Treatment of the German losses on the Somme in the British Official History: "Military Operations France and Belgium, 1916" vol. II', *Journal of the Royal United Service Institution*, 111, February 1966, pp. 69–74; Robin Prior, *Churchill's 'World Crisis' as History* (London: Croom Helm, 1983), pp. 221–30; Martin Middlebrook, *The First Day on the Somme: 1 July 1916* (New York: Norton, 1972), p. 276.
26. *War Memoirs*, II, p. 651. Lloyd George's emphasis.
27. Cited in ibid., p. 652.
28. Ibid.
29. Ibid., p. 832. German achieved the furthest extent of its conquests in 1918.
30. Ibid., p. 844.
31. Ibid., pp. 851–52.
32. On the German efforts to persuade Wilson to mediate, see Trevor Wilson (ed.), *The Political Diaries of C.P. Scott 1911–1928* (London: Collins, 1970), pp. 226, 20–22 December 1916; Arthur S. Link (ed.), *The Papers of Woodrow Wilson* (Princeton: Princeton University Press, 1982), vol. 38, pp. 313–14, Robert Lansing (Secretary of State) to Wilson, 30 September 1916, with enclosure, James Gerard (US Ambassador in Berlin) to Lansing, 25 September 1916; Howard wrote later that 'I am confident Berlin officials will go to the limit to endeavour to inveigle or coerce President Wilson into advancing peace feelers', p. 496, E.M. House to Wilson, 20 October 1916, enclosure III.
33. *War Memoirs*, II, p. 853; HLRO LG MSS E/2/21/2, Northcliffe to Lloyd George, 25 September 1916; Gilbert, *Lloyd George*, II, pp. 368–69; Wilson (ed.), *Scott Diaries*, p. 236. Northcliffe later wrote to Lloyd George that he knew through a 'leading member' of the US Embassy that a 'peace squeal' was on its way, and that the American diplomat was 'so anxious about it' he

had returned home for consultations; HLRO LG MSS E/2/21/3, Northcliffe to Lloyd George, 27 September 1916.

34. *War Memoirs*, II, pp. 853–55; *The Times*, 29 September 1916; copy in HLRO LG MSS, G/262; printed almost in full in Grigg, *Lloyd George*, III, pp. 424–28.

35. John Turner, *British Politics and the Great War: Coalition and Conflict 1915–1918* (New Haven and London: Yale University Press, 1992), p. 127.

36. *War Memoirs*, II, pp. 856–57.

37. Wilson (ed.), *Scott Diaries*, p. 227–28.

38. Kathleen Burk, *Britain, America and the Sinews of War 1914–1918* (Boston: George Allen & Unwin, 1985), pp. 84–85.

39. Although when McKenna raised the issue in Cabinet on 29 November, announcing that a 'financial crisis of the greatest magnitude seemed imminent [and that] the crisis was so serious that it might involve abandonment of the gold standard', Lloyd George dismissively remarked that 'the same fears were expressed on the outbreak of war'; John Vincent (ed.), *The Crawford Papers: The Journals of David Lindsay Twenty-Seventh Earl of Crawford and Tenth Earl of Balcarres 1871–1940 during the years 1892 to 1940* (Manchester: Manchester University Press, 1984), pp. 368–69.

40. Burk, *Sinews of War*, p. 88; Gilbert, *Lloyd George*, II, pp. 371–74 and Niall Ferguson, *The Pity of War* (London: Allen Lane Penguin, 1998), pp. 326–29.

41. *War Memoirs*, II, p. 857. Regarding the official reaction in Washington, Bentley Brinkerhoff Gilbert asserts that Lansing characterised the interview as 'unfriendly'; rather, Lansing wrote that Lloyd George would regard '*any suggestion of peace from neutrals . . .* as more or less unfriendly'. See Gilbert, *Lloyd George*, II, p. 371; Link (ed.), *Wilson Papers*, 38, p. 313, Lansing to Wilson, 30 September 1916.

42. See PRO CAB 23/1/WC13: War Cabinet 21, 23 December 1916.

43. HLRO LG MSS E/3/14/13: Le Roy-Lewis to Lloyd George, 29 September, 2 October 1916. The *Manchester Guardian* reported that the interview caused 'great annoyance' in France, which led to Lloyd George protesting to Scott; see the correspondence in *Scott Diaries*, pp. 228–31, 11–23 October 1916; Lloyd George pointed out on 23 October that he had seen the British Ambassador Bertie, who told him that the French were 'delighted with the naughty interview. Briand, whom I also saw, was very grateful for it.'

44. Quoted in Gilbert, *Lloyd George*, II, p. 374.

45. Grigg, *Lloyd George*, III, pp. 415–28.

46. *War Memoirs*, II, pp. 1008–09. The death of his son Raymond at the front on 15 September was an additional blow which had a great effect on Asquith; Mark Pottle (ed.), *Champion Redoubtable: The Diaries and Letters of Violet Bonham Carter 1914–1945* (London: Wedenfeld and Nicolson, 1998), pp. 92–93.

47. Vincent (ed.), *Crawford Papers*, p. 356. See also Wilson, *Myriad Faces*, pp. 408–12, in particular the extracts from Hankey's diary quoted on pp. 410–11 and Austen Chamberlain, *Down the Years* (London: Cassell, 1935), pp. 111–16.

48. *War Memoirs*, II, ch. 32. Hankey wrote that before the conference there was a general undercurrent of dissatisfaction, while after 'the disgruntlement took a more definite form and became directed against the personnel of the War Committee', Maurice Hankey, *The Supreme Command*, 2 vols (London: Allen & Unwin, 1961), II, pp. 563–64.

49. *War Memoirs*, II, pp. 898–909.

50. Printed in ibid., pp. 913–29.
51. Grigg, *Lloyd George*, III, p. 443; *War Memoirs*, II, p. 929.
52. Ibid., pp. 913–31. See also Hankey, *Supreme Command*, II, pp. 560–61.
53. *War Memoirs*, II, pp. 949–52; *Military Operations 1916*, II, pp. 533–35.
54. David French, *British Strategy and War Aims 1914–1916* (London: Allen & Unwin, 1986), p. 233.
55. *War Memoirs*, II, pp. 959–62.
56. A.J.P. Taylor (ed.), *Lloyd George: A Diary by Frances Stevenson* (London: Hutchinson, 1971), p. 124.
57. *War Memoirs*, II, p. 963. Hankey did not record this episode in his diary, but wrote later that it 'is supported both by my recollection and by other evidence in my possession of the views I held at that time on the conduct of the war. Moreover the proposition which Lloyd George says I enunciated opposite the Vendome column corresponds very closely to a proposal I put to Asquith on December 2nd. In addition my diary for this conference records several other conversations with Lloyd George and that all this time Ll. George was intensely friendly to me and continually asking my advice about this, that and the other', Hankey, *Supreme Command*, II, p. 563.
58. Grigg, *Lloyd George*, III, p. 445.
59. Lord Beaverbrook, *Politicians and the War 1914–1916* (London: Oldbourne, 1960), p. 316.
60. J.M. McEwen, 'The Struggle for Mastery in Britain: Lloyd George versus Asquith December 1916', *Journal of British Studies*, XVIII, 1, Fall 1978, pp. 135–39.
61. Ibid., p. 135.
62. Hankey, *Supreme Command*, II, pp. 441–42, 544.
63. For perhaps the best-known account see Beaverbrook, *Politicians and the War*, Book II; but for a corrective see John O. Stubbs. 'Beaverbrook as Historian: "Politicians and the War 1914–1916" Reconsidered', *Albion*, 14, 3–4, Fall–Winter 1982, pp. 235–53. See also Grigg, Lloyd George, III, ch. 17 and for a good recent account R.J.Q. Adams, *Bonar Law* (London: John Murray, 1999), pp. 220–43.
64. Asquith clearly greatly resented the press role in the crisis – even some of the most resolute Tory papers such as the *Morning Post* supported Lloyd George in his efforts to prosecute the war more vigorously. At the Buckingham Palace conference Balfour recorded Asquith's denunciation of the press 'which he said had played a most pernicious part both before and during the crisis, and which ought to be controlled in Britain as it was controlled in France', BL, Balfour Add. MSS, Memorandum, Buckingham Palace Conference, 7 December 1916. On the press in December 1916 see J.M. McEwen, 'The Press and the Fall of Asquith', *Historical Journal*, 21, 4, 1978, pp. 863–83.
65. See *War Memoirs*, II, ch. 35 for Lloyd George's account.
66. Ibid., p. 982. Although see, for example, Herbert, Viscount Samuel, *Memoirs* (London: Cresset Press, 1945), pp. 119–20: 'Confident that his own qualities would make him a better wartime Premier than Asquith, he no doubt felt that he was not merely justified, but under a duty to overthrow his chief and replace him.'
67. Trinity College Library, Cambridge, Montagu MSS AS1/5/15(1–2), Montagu to Maurice Bonham Carter, 6 December 1916,
68. Chamberlain, *Down the Years*, p. 125.

69. Bonar Law was confident he could have formed a government, but the principal reason he did not do so was that he 'felt sure that the Unionist Party could be relied upon to support the Government with Lloyd George as Prime Minister, and that I could not rely, as the Unionist head of a Government, on receiving anything like the amount of support from the Liberal Party which there was reason to hope would be given to a Government of which a Liberal was the head by the Unionist Party'; quoted in Adams, *Bonar Law*, p. 239.
70. HLRO LG MSS G/212, Hankey notes on chapters, vol. III (1934). Lloyd George actually received his commission from the King on the evening of 6 December and 'kissed hands' on the evening of 7 December.
71. *War Memoirs*, III, pp. 1081–82.
72. Ibid., p. 1066, also II, p. 1005; Frances Stevenson noted on 6 December that a 'message had been received from the PM to the effect that his Liberal colleagues had refused in a body to serve under D. Such patriotism!', *Stevenson Diary*, pp. 133–34.
73. Trinity College Library, Cambridge, Montagu MSS AS1/5/15(2), Montagu to Maurice Bonham Carter, 6 December 1916, AS1/10/1(10), Montagu Narrative (of the events of December 1916), 9 December 1916; Samuel, *Memoirs*, pp. 126–27.
74. *War Memoirs*, III, p. 1071.
75. HLRO LG MSS G/212, Hankey notes on chapters, vol. III (1934). Churchill had been languishing on the backbenches since 1929, and would not again hold office until September 1939.
76. *War Memoirs*, III, p. 1071. My emphasis. Hankey approved of the changes; see HLRO LG MSS G/212, Hankey to Lloyd George, 19 April 1934; cf. *Stevenson Diary*, p. 264, 29 March 1934.
77. Peter Rowland, *David Lloyd George: A Biography* (New York: Macmillan, 1975), pp. 407–09; Martin Gilbert, *World in Torment: Winston S. Churchill 1917–1922* (London: Minerva, 1990 ed.), pp. 28–31; Adams, *Bonar Law*, pp. 256–58.
78. *War Memoirs*, III, p. 1072. Cf. Lloyd George's critical comments on Churchill at the Ministry of Munitions as noted above in ch. 2.
79. *War Memoirs*, III, p. 1075.
80. Ibid., p. 1076.
81. Memorandum by Herbert Samuel, 7 December 1916, in Samuel, *Memoirs*, pp. 123–24.
82. Ibid., pp. 125–26; see also Bernard Wasserstein, *Herbert Samuel: A Political Life* (Oxford: Clarendon Press, 1992), pp. 219–20, 227–29.
83. Samuel, *Memoirs*, p. 126.
84. For example, Sylvester records an outburst by Lloyd George on Samuel and Sir John Simon (who was not Jewish): 'He said that he might now be only half a man [after his prostate operation], but he was a bloody sight better than two Jews'; see Gilbert, *Lloyd George*, II, p. 82; Colin Cross (ed.), *Life with Lloyd George: The Diary of A.J. Sylvester* (London: Macmillan, 1975), p. 47, 2 November 1931; Wasserstein, *Samuel*, pp. 335–36, and n. 3.
85. Rowland, *Lloyd George*, p. 692. Sylvester wrote in his diary in September 1931: 'LG is absolutely implacable. He is dead against a general election. He says there is no need for it. He is also very insistent that the Liberal members

of the Government should threaten to resign in a body if Ramsay and the Tories insist on an election. He says that would prevent them, even now. Samuel was disappointed, because he had got the Tories so far along the road towards agreeing a formula [for the election programme] and he probably thought LG would have been pleased.' LG, describing Samuel, said: 'One day he is as firm as Mount Zion; the next he is floating about like the ark'; *Sylvester Diary*, pp. 39–40, 30 September 1931.

86. Owen's wife's sister was married to Gwilym Lloyd George.

87. Indeed, the General Election result of October 1931 is notable for reducing the Opposition as a whole – including the Lloyd George Liberals – to a rump of 61 members as against 554 Government MPs.

88. Rowland, *Lloyd George*, p. 692; *Sylvester Diary*, p. 222, 21 November 1939. After the war Lloyd George made Samuel – a Zionist – High Commissioner for Palestine, 1920–25. Of this appointment, Sylvester in his diary in 1934: 'At lunch, LG said the best thing he had ever said about Samuel had, on the advice of his friends, been cut out of his manuscript. He had written: "I planted Samuel on Mount Sinai as the lineal descendent of Pontius Pilate"'; *Sylvester Diary*, pp. 110–11, 2 August 1934.

89. *War Memoirs*, III, p. 1067.

90. Wilson (ed.), *Scott Diaries*, pp. 239, 20–22 November 1916.

91. Bodleian Library, Oxford, Asquith MSS 1/17 Reel 8, Montagu to Asquith 5 December 1916.

92. See, for example, Beaverbrook, *Politicians and the War*, pp. 498–99; Turner, *British Politics and the Great War*, p. 145; Naomi B. Levine, *Politics, Religion and Love: The Story of H. H. Asquith, Venetia Stanley and Edwin Montagu, Based on the Life and Letters of Edwin Samuel Montagu* (New York: New York University Press, 1991), p. 384.

93. Trinity College Library, Cambridge, Montagu MSS AS1/10/1(11), Montagu Narrative (of the events of December 1916), 9 December 1916.

94. Ibid.

95. *War Memoirs*, III, p. 1079. The unhappy experience (on both sides) of Chamberlain's appointment as Director and subsequent resignation was to have unfortunate long-term consequences – according to one of Chamberlain's biographers, his experience at the Ministry of National Service led him to the conclusion 'never...to serve with Lloyd George again'; Lloyd George's dislike of Chamberlain was to be one of the main reasons Lloyd George refused Churchill's offer of a post in 1940, as Chamberlain remained Lord President of the Council until late that year. For Chamberlain's time as Director of National Service, see Keith Feiling, *Life of Neville Chamberlain* (London: Macmillan, 1970), pp. 63–75 and David Dilks, *Neville Chamberlain*, vol. I (Cambridge: Cambridge University Press, 1984), pp. 199–250.

96. BL, Balfour Add. MSS 49692: Memorandum, Buckingham Palace Conference, 7 December 1916.

97. On the Cabinet Secretariat, see *War Memoirs*, III, pp. 1080–81; cf. Hankey, *Supreme Command*, II, p. 580.

98. See Wilson, *Myriad Faces*, pp. 531–33. Though the increase in efficiency should not be overstated. For an important corrective to the view that December 1916 marked a complete break with the old system, see John Turner, 'Cabinets, Committees and Secretariats: the Higher Direction of the

War', in Kathleen Burk (ed.), *War and the State: The Transformation of British Government 1914–1919* (London: George Allen & Unwin, 1982), pp. 57–83.

6 The Nivelle offensive 1917

1. *New Statesman and Nation*, 22 September 1934.
2. HLRO LG MSS G/212: Extract from Hankey memorandum, 8 December 1916.
3. Ibid.
4. *War Memoirs*, III, pp. 1432–33.
5. Ibid., pp. 1390–98.
6. Ibid., p. 1424.
7. HLRO LG MSS G/264: Extract from Secretary's Notes of an Allied Conference, held at the Consulta, Rome, 5–7 January 1917.
8. HLRO LG MSS G/238: 'Events leading up to Nivelle, commencing at Chantilly 15 November 1916'.
9. Trevor Wilson, *The Myriad Faces of War: Britain and the Great War 1914–1918* (Cambridge: Polity Press, 1986), p. 441.
10. *War Memoirs*, III, p. 1449. See also John Grigg, *Lloyd George: War Leader 1916–1918* (London: Allen Lane/Penguin, 2002), pp. 28–30.
11. See E.L. Spears, *Prelude to Victory* (London: Jonathan Cape, 1939), pp. 29–31; Alastair Horne, *The Price of Glory: Verdun 1916* (Harmondsworth: Penguin, 1964), pp. 226–27, 308, 318, 320; Anthony Clayton, 'Robert Nivelle and the French Spring Offensive of 1917', in Brian Bond (ed.), *Fallen Stars: Eleven Studies of Twentieth Century Military Disasters* (London: Brassey's, 1991), pp. 52–64.
12. Sir William Robertson, *Soldiers and Statesmen*, 2 vols (London: Cassell, 1926), II, p. 196.
13. Ibid., pp. 196–97; Spears, *Prelude to Victory*, pp. 42–43; Cyril Falls, *Military Operations: France and Belgium 1917* (London: Macmillan, 1940), I, pp. 46–51.
14. *War Memoirs*, III, p. 1473.
15. Ibid.
16. A.J.P. Taylor (ed.), *Lloyd George: A Diary by Frances Stevenson* (London: Hutchinson, 1971), p. 139.
17. Lloyd George also liked the shape of Nivelle's head: Spears notes that Lloyd George was a 'great believer in his own powers as a phrenologist. He often judged men in this way... General Nivelle's cranium found favour in his eyes'; cf. Lloyd George's comment on General 'Tim' Harington (Plumer's Chief of Staff): 'Harington, a good staff officer but "look at his head. The shape of his head shows his limits"'; *Prelude to Victory*, p. 40; LHCMA Liddell Hart MSS 11/1932/42(a): 'Talk with Lloyd George at Criccieth, 24 September 1932'.
18. See Spears, *Prelude to Victory*, 'Introduction', by Winston Churchill, 13. John Buchan in his history of the war wrote that Lloyd George 'fell in love' with Nivelle's plan and was instantly converted. Lloyd George claims that Buchan was in his 'fictional mode' and gave a 'fanciful picture' of the meeting; he was 'inventing his facts' (which Liddell Hart thought too severe). John Buchan, *A History of the Great War* (London: Nelson, 1922), p. 436; *War Memoirs*, III,

p. 1492–93; HLRO LG MSS G/212: Liddell Hart Notes on Mr Lloyd George's Memoirs 1917; Grigg, *Lloyd George*, IV, p. 36.

19. *War Memoirs*, III, pp. 1500–01.
20. David French, *The Strategy of the Lloyd George Coalition 1914–1918* (Oxford: Clarendon Press, 1995), p. 55.
21. *War Memoirs*, III, p. 1503.
22. Ibid., VI, p. 3456.
23. Ibid., III, p. 1501.
24. *Military Operations 1917*, I, pp. 54–55. Robertson was certainly of this opinion, believing that if Haig and Nivelle got together they could settle any problems between themselves without the intervention of the politicians; David R. Woodward (ed.), *The Military Correspondence of Field-Marshal Sir William Robertson, Chief of the Imperial General Staff December 1915–February 1918* (London: Bodley Head, 1989), pp. 151–52, no. 113, Robertson to Haig, 14 February 1917.
25. Spears, *Prelude to Victory*, Bertier's despatch to Generals Lyautey and Nivelle, 16 February 1917, appendix ix, p. 546; see also Lt Colonel Rousset, *La Bataille de l'Aisne (Avril–Mai 1917)* (Paris and Brussels: G. van Ouest et Cie, 1920), pp. 20–24; Commandant de Civrieux, *L'Offensive de 1917 et le Commandement du Général Nivelle* (Paris and Brussels: G. van Ouest et Cie, 1919), pp. 40–41.
26. LRO LG MSS G/238: 'Events Leading up to Nivelle, "Bible" Copy'.
27. PRO CAB 23/1/WC79: War Cabinet, 24 February 1917. The minutes of this meeting were also withheld from the King for two days, most irregularly on such a vital issue; Kenneth Rose, *King George V* (London: Phoenix, 2000 ed.), pp. 202–203.
28. PRO CAB 23/2/WC92: War Cabinet, Appendix II, Note by the Chief of the Imperial General Staff regarding the Calais Agreement of 27 February 1917; Robertson, *Soldiers and Statesmen*, II, p. 205. Robertson's claim is of course denied by Lloyd George. Indeed, the War Cabinet meeting of 20 February 1917, with Robertson present, decided to adhere to its original decision to call a conference 'so that a definite understanding might be reached and an agreement drawn up and signed by the heads of the two Governments respectively, not only so far as the railways are concerned, but also in regard to the operations of 1917'. This hardly indicates, however, the subsequent turn of events, and certainly does not authorise Lloyd George to place Haig and the BEF under Nivelle's command. *War Memoirs*, III, p. 1509; PRO CAB 23/1/WC75: War Cabinet, 20 February 1917.
29. *War Memoirs*, III, pp. 1502–503; HLRO LG MSS G/238: 'Events Leading up to Nivelle'; G/238: Untitled section (headed 'Not Yet Revised') on Nivelle.
30. Robertson, *Soldiers and Statesmen*, II, p. 205; Maurice Hankey, *The Supreme Command*, 2 vols (London: Allen & Unwin, 1961), II, p. 615; see also *Military Operations 1917*, I, p. 55; Robert Blake (ed.), *The Private Papers of Douglas Haig 1914–1919* (London: Eyre and Spottiswoode, 1952), p. 203.
31. *War Memoirs*, III, p. 1503.
32. PRO CAB 28/2/IC17(a): Notes of an Anglo-French Conference held at Hotel Terminus, Calais, on 26–27 February 1917 at 5.30 pm.
33. Hankey, *Supreme Command*, II, pp. 615–16.

34. PRO CAB 28/2/IC17(a): Notes of an Anglo-French Conference held at Hotel Terminus, Calais, on 26–27 February 1917 at 5.30 pm.
35. PRO CAB 28/2/IC17 (b): *Projet d'Organisation de l'Unité de Commandement sur le Front Occidental*; also *Military Operations France and Belgium 1917* (London: Macmillan, 1940), I, Appendices, p. 62, Appendix 18.
36. Ibid., pp. 62–63.
37. French, *Strategy of the Lloyd George Coalition*, p. 56; *Military Operations 1917*, I, p. 56; *Haig Papers*, p. 201. While Robertson's angry reaction is well documented, Terraine notes correctly that there is a 'quality of detachment about Haig's narrative' (in the diary) which he ascribes to Haig's consciousness that it was his own position which was at stake, and to a 'cultivated immobility'; whatever it was, he was certainly willing at this stage to let Robertson and the War Office do most of the work; John Terraine, *Douglas Haig: The Educated Soldier* (London: Hutchinson, 1963), p. 270.
38. Hankey, *Supreme Command*, II, p. 616.
39. Wilson, *Myriad Faces*, p. 444.
40. *Military Operations 1917*, I, p. 56; Robertson, *Soldiers and Statesmen*, II, p. 207; Spears, *Prelude to Victory*, p. 145; Hankey, *Supreme Command*, II, p. 616.
41. See the text in PRO CAB 28/2/IC17 (b): Notes of an Anglo-French Conference held at the Hotel Terminus, Calais, on 26–27 February 1917; see also *Military Operations 1917*, I, Appendices, pp. 64–65, Appendix 19; Hankey, *Supreme Command*, II, p. 617; Spears, *Prelude to Victory*, pp. 153–56; Stephen Roskill, *Hankey: Man of Secrets*, vol. I (London: Collins, 1970), pp. 363–64.
42. Woodward (ed.), *Robertson Correspondence*, p. 156, no. 118, Robertson to Haig, 3 March 1917. Robertson's emphasis.
43. Robertson, *Soldiers and Statesmen*, II, p. 210.
44. PRO CAB 23/2/WC92: War Cabinet, 9 March 1917, Appendix II; see also Robertson, *Soldiers and Statesmen*, II, pp. 211, 214–16 and Spears, *Prelude to Victory*, pp. 150–51.
45. French, *Strategy of the Lloyd George Coalition*, pp. 58–59.
46. *War Memoirs*, III, pp. 1506–12.
47. PRO CAB 23/1/WC82: War Cabinet 28 February 1917; PRO CAB 23/2/WC92: War Cabinet, 9 March 1917; Woodward (ed.), *Robertson Correspondence*, p. 155, no. 116, Robertson to Haig, 28 February 1917.
48. See HLRO LG MSS F/3/2/14: Note from French Embassy, 7 March 1917, which insisted that Haig follow Nivelle's instructions. There was another factor apart from Nivelle's 'tone' which prompted Haig to appeal to the War Cabinet. In late February the Germans began a withdrawal to the strongly fortified Hindenburg Line (or *Siegfried Stellung*). This had the effect of shortening the German line by 25 miles, and freed up several divisions for use elsewhere. Haig became convinced that the British front in Flanders and the Channel Ports were now in danger. Haig was wrong and Nivelle, in denying that the Germans had any intentions of attacking in the north, was correct. See French, *Strategy of the Lloyd George Coalition*, pp. 58–59 and 'Failures of Intelligence: The Retreat to the Hindenburg Line and the March 1918 Offensive', in Michael Dockrill and David French (eds), *Strategy and Intelligence: British Policy during the First World War* (London: Hambledon Press, 1996), pp. 80–84; Paul Guinn, *British Strategy and Politics 1914 to 1918* (Oxford: Clarendon Press, 1965), p. 215; Wilson, *Myriad Faces*, pp. 445–48.

49. *War Memoirs*, III, p. 1511.
50. Lloyd George cites his support of Haig at the conference as 'one illustration out of many of the support I invariably accorded the Commander-in-Chief on all questions where his personal authority were concerned'; *War Memoirs*, III, pp. 1509–10; PRO CAB 28/2/IC18: Notes of an Anglo-French Conference held at 10 Downing Street, 12–13 March 1917; Wilson, *Myriad Faces*, p. 445.
51. Guinn, *British Strategy and Politics*, p. 216.
52. Buchan, *History of the Great War*, p. 436. Cf. HLRO LG MSS G/238: 'Events Leading up to Nivelle', draft: the only method of establishing complete cooperation between the two armies, 'drastic as it may seem, was definitely to establish unity of command by placing one head in literal, indisputable, supreme control. This implied the subordination of the leader of the forces of one nation to the leader of the forces of another, a proverbially invidious, delicate and difficult matter even when the nations concerned are Allies, since it arouses international prejudices and jealousy and is almost certain to wound *amour propre*. But in the circumstances, it was the only thing to be done.'
53. Woodward (ed.), *Robertson Correspondence*, p. 155, no. 116, Robertson to Haig, 28 February 1917. See also Robertson, *Soldiers and Statesmen*, II, pp. 213–14.
54. *Haig Papers*, pp. 166, 264, 301. Haig's emphasis.
55. LHCMA Maurice MSS 4/5/78: Lytton to General Maurice, 12 November 1934. See also Terraine, *Haig*, p. 276 and Grigg, *Lloyd George*, IV, p. 44. On Lytton, see Keith Grieves, 'War Correspondents and Conducting Officers on the Western Front from 1915', in Hugh Cecil and Peter H. Liddle (eds), *Facing Armageddon: The First World War Experienced* (London: Leo Cooper, 1996), pp. 728–30.
56. *War Memoirs*, III, p. 1474.
57. Ibid., p. 1496.
58. HLRO LG MSS G/238: 'Events Leading up to Nivelle'.
59. Ibid.
60. Ibid.
61. On Arras see Wilson, *Myriad Faces*, pp. 449–56 and Terraine, *Haig*, pp. 284–90.
62. *War Memoirs*, III, p. 1526.
63. Quoted in ibid., pp. 1527–28.
64. Quoted in ibid., p. 1527.
65. HLRO LG MSS F/41/5/13: Murray to Lloyd George, 14 June 1918.
66. *War Memoirs*, III, pp. 1528–29.
67. Ibid., pp. 1496–97.
68. Ibid., p. 1497.
69. Ibid., p. 1500.
70. Ibid., pp. 1500–01.
71. Ibid., p. 1503.
72. Ibid., p. 1512. On this issue, see French, 'Failures of Intelligence', pp. 67–95.
73. *War Memoirs*, III, pp. 1512–13.
74. General Ludendorff, quoted in ibid., p. 1513.
75. Ibid., p. 1514.
76. Ibid., p. 1515.
77. Robin Prior and Trevor Wilson, *Passchendaele: The Untold Story* (New Haven and London: Yale University Press, 1996), p. 30.
78. *Stevenson Diary*, p. 157.

7 'The campaign of the mud': Third Ypres 1917

1. Edmonds objected to Lloyd George's title for the Passchendaele chapters: 'Mud there certainly was most of the time, but not of the degree to justify calling Third Ypres "The Campaign of the Mud". Even to call it "A Campaign in the Mud" would be little more than to call it an autumn campaign'; J.E. Edmonds, *Military Operations: France and Belgium 1917*, vol. II (London: HMSO, 1948), p. 375. Even Haig, however, wrote in his diary of the great difficulties caused by the mud.
2. Or, as Hankey noted, in Passchendaele chapter 'the book reaches its climax'; HLRO LG MSS G/212: Hankey notes on chapters (1934).
3. Ibid.
4. David French, 'Who Knew What and When? The French Army Mutinies and the British Decision to Launch the Third Battle of Ypres', in Lawrence Freedman, Paul Hayes and Robert O'Neill (eds), *War, Strategy and International Politics: Essays in Honour of Sir Michael Howard* (Oxford: Clarendon Press, 1992), p. 153.
5. Thomas Jones, *Lloyd George* (London: Oxford University Press, 1951), p. 120; Robin Prior and Trevor Wilson, *Passchendaele: The Untold Story* (New Haven and London: Yale University Press, 1996), p. xiii.
6. *Military Operations 1917*, I, Appendices, Nivelle to Haig, p. 21 December 1917, p. 6, Appendix 2; David French, *Strategy of the Lloyd George Coalition 1914–1918* (Oxford: Clarendon Press, 1995), p. 54; David R. Woodward, *Lloyd George and the Generals* (Newark: University of Nebraska Press, 1983), p. 137.
7. *War Memoirs*, IV, pp. 2117–18, 2120–25.
8. HLRO LG MSS G/212: Hankey notes on chapters (1934).
9. *Military Operations 1917*, II, pp. 1–10.
10. PRO CAB 27/6/G179: 'Report of the Cabinet Committee on War Policy, 10 August 1917'.
11. HLRO LG MSS G/212: Hankey notes on chapters (1934).
12. *Military Operations 1917*, II, p. 8; *War Memoirs*, IV, p. 2123.
13. John Terraine, *The Road to Passchendaele: The Flanders Offensive of 1917: A Study in Inevitability* (London: Leo Cooper, 1977), pp. 17–18.
14. *War Memoirs*, IV, pp. 2117–18.
15. *Military Operations 1917*, II, p. 8.
16. William J. Philpott, *Anglo-French Relations and Strategy on the Western Front 1914–18* (London: Macmillan, 1996), p. 130. Haig wrote that he regarded the Flanders operation agreed on 'at a Conference at the War Office as long ago as the 23 November, 1916'; Robert Blake (ed.), *The Private Papers of Douglas Haig 1914–1919* (London: Eyre and Spottiswoode, 1952), p. 245.
17. Ibid., p. 184; Philpott, *Anglo-French Relations*, p. 130.
18. *Military Operations 1917*, p. I, Appendices, Haig to Nivelle, 6 January 1917, pp. 13–14.
19. Ibid., London Convention of 16 January 1917, p. 16.
20. *Haig Papers*, p. 193. My emphasis.
21. Ibid., p. 212, 14 March 1917, Haig's emphasis; PRO CAB 23/2 WC96: War Cabinet, 14 March 1917.

22. John Turner, 'Lloyd George, the War Cabinet and High Politics', in Peter H. Liddle (ed.), *Passchendaele in Perspective: The Third Battle of Ypres* (London: Leo Cooper, 1997), p. 18.
23. John Terraine, *Douglas Haig: The Educated Soldier* (London: Hutchinson, 1963), pp. 319–20.
24. PRO CAB 23/13/WC128A: Minutes of the War Cabinet 1 May 1917; *War Memoirs*, IV, p. 1551. Nivelle's dismissal was imminent.
25. Quoted in *War Memoirs*, IV, p. 1541.
26. French, *Strategy of the Lloyd George Coalition*, p. 96.
27. PRO CAB 23/13/WC128A: Minutes of the War Cabinet 1 May 1917.
28. Haig noted in his diary: 'Mr Lloyd George made two excellent speeches in which he stated that he had no pretensions to being a strategist, that he left that to his military advisers, that I, as C-in-C of the British forces in France had full power to attack where and when I thought best.... His speeches were quite excellent'; *Haig Papers*, p. 228.
29. *Military Operations 1917*, II, p. 23.
30. PRO CAB 28/2/IC21: 'Summary of the Proceedings of the Anglo-French Conference held in Paris on 4–5 May 1917'; *Military Operations 1917*, II, p. 22; Woodward, *Lloyd George and the Generals*, p. 164. Lloyd George relates that at the Paris meeting, Pétain said to him, 'I suppose you think I can't fight', to which he replied 'No, General, with your record I could not make that mistake, but I am certain that for some reason or other you won't fight'; *War Memoirs*, IV, p. 2129.
31. On Lloyd George's claims that Haig and Robertson deliberately withheld news of the mutinies from the War Cabinet, see pp. 135–37.
32. French, *Strategy of the Lloyd George Coalition*, pp. 97–98.
33. PRO CAB 27/7/WP3: Haig Memorandum, 'Present Situation and Future Plans', 12 June 1917; submitted after the capture of Messines Ridge.
34. G.C. Wynne quoted in Prior and Wilson, *Passchendaele*, p. 55.
35. PRO CAB 27/7/WP3: Haig Memorandum, 'Present Situation and Future Plans', 12 June 1917.
36. Summary in Prior and Wilson, *Passchendaele*, p. 45.
37. Ibid.
38. PRO CAB 27/7/WP3: Haig Memorandum, 'Present Situation and Future Plans', 12 June 1917.
39. *War Memoirs*, IV, p. 2157
40. PRO CAB 27/7/WP3: Haig Memorandum, 'Present Situation and Future Plans', 12 June 1917.
41. PRO CAB 27/7/WP9: Haig to Robertson, 17 June 1917.
42. Terraine, *Haig*, p. 319.
43. *War Memoirs*, IV, pp. 2149–51. Ironically, in spite of Lloyd George's praise of Harington, the latter's reaction to the *War Memoirs* account of Passchendaele was scathing. See p. 141.
44. Terraine, *Haig*, p. 315.
45. Prior and Wilson, *Passchendaele*, p. 65. On Messines, see also *Military Operation 1917*, II, pp. 32–95; Leon Wolff, *In Flanders Fields: The 1917 Campaign* (Harmondsworth: Penguin, 1987 ed.), pp. 118–35; Lyn MacDonald, *They Called it Passchendaele* (London: Macmillan, 1983), pp. 3–58; Sir Charles Harington, *Plumer of Messines* (London: John Murray, 1935), pp. 85–105;

Geoffrey Powell, *Plumer: The Soldiers' General A Biography of Field-Marshal Viscount Plumer of Messines* (London: Leo Cooper, 1990), pp. 153–96; from the German point of view, see Ludendorff's comments in his *My War Memories* (London: Hutchinson, 1919), pp. 428–29; also Heinz Hagenlücke, 'The German High Command', in Liddle (ed.), *Passchendaele in Perspective*, pp. 49–50.

46. PRO CAB 23/3WC159: War Cabinet 8 June 1917.
47. *War Memoirs*, IV, pp. 2157–58.
48. Ibid., p. 2158.
49. Brian Bond, 'Soldiers and Statesmen: British Civil-Military Relations in 1917', *Military Affairs*, October 1968, p. 65.
50. PRO CAB 27/6: 7th Meeting of the Cabinet Committee on War Policy, 19 June 1917. My emphasis.
51. Ibid., 9th Meeting of the Cabinet Committee on War Policy, 20 June 1917.
52. Ibid., 7th Meeting of the Cabinet Committee on War Policy, 19 June 1917.
53. *War Memoirs*, IV, p. 2179.
54. PRO CAB 27/6: 10th Meeting of the Cabinet Committee on War Policy, 21 June 1917; *War Memoirs*, IV, p. 2199.
55. Prior and Wilson argue persuasively that these sorts of limited attacks were the 'one hopeful aspect' of operations in 1916–17; see *Passchendaele*, p. 41; Trevor Wilson, The *Myriad Faces of War: Britain and the Great War 1914–1918* (Cambridge: Polity Press, 1986), pp. 461–63.
56. Lord Esher expressed the conundrum well, writing that the Allies could not 'reconcile waiting for the American Armies with the anxiety of the masses to get a decision speedily', though he later commented that it 'may be necessary, for military reasons, to wait for America. But the transition months will have to be occupied by effective displays of force'; HLRO LG MSS F/16/1/14: Esher to Lloyd George, 5 June 1917.
57. On Austria's peace overtures in 1917, see French, *Strategy of the Lloyd George Coalition*, pp. 103–109 and David Stevenson, *The First World War and International Politics* (Oxford: Oxford University Press, 1988), pp. 139–48.
58. HLRO LG MSS G/264: Lloyd George Memorandum, 'Arguments For and Against the Plan for a Great Offensive in France', June 1917.
59. *War Memoirs*, IV, pp. 2199–201.
60. PRO CAB 27/6: 9th Meeting of the Cabinet Committee on War Policy, 20 June 1917.
61. PRO CAB27/7/WP10: 'Remarks on the Occupation of the North Coast of Belgium by the Germans, Jellicoe', 18 June 1917.
62. *Haig Papers*, p. 240; PRO CAB 27/6: 9th Meeting of the Cabinet Committee on War Policy, 20 June 1917.
63. *War Memoirs*, IV, p. 2162.
64. *Haig Papers*, p. 240.
65. Ibid., p. 221, Robertson to Haig, 26 April 1917.
66. Prior and Wilson, *Passchendaele*, p. 201, n. 7; cf. Frank E. Vandiver, 'Field Marshal Sir Douglas Haig and Passchendaele', in Liddle (ed.), *Passchendaele in Perspective*, pp. 41–42 n. 3; *Military Operations 1917*, II, p. 102; Bond, 'Soldiers and Statesmen', p. 68; Maurice Hankey, *The Supreme Command*, 2 vols (London: Allen & Unwin, 1961), II, p. 701; Paul Guinn, *British Strategy and Politics 1914 to 1918* (Oxford: Clarendon Press, 1965), pp. 250–52; Terraine, *Haig*, p. 333. See also the Final Report of the War Policy Committee,

PRO CAB 27/6/G179: 'Report of the Cabinet Committee on War Policy', 10 August 1917, which acknowledged that while the shipping situation was serious, it was not so serious as to prevent Britain from carrying on the war in 1918.

67. S.W. Roskill, 'The U-Boat Campaign of 1917 and Third Ypres', *Journal of the Royal United Service Institution*, 616, November 1959, pp. 440–42. An attempt was made in April 1918 to neutralise the port of Bruges by blocking the canal exits at Ostend and Zeebrugge, but it ended in failure: 'At no time was the movement of smaller U-boats in and out of Bruges affected'; Wilson, *Myriad Faces*, p. 632.

68. PRO CAB 27/6: 10th Meeting of the Cabinet Committee on War Policy, 21 June 1917; *War Memoirs*, IV, pp. 2193–202.

69. Ibid., p. 2193.

70. PRO CAB 27/6: 10th Meeting of the Cabinet Committee on War Policy, 21 June 1917.

71. Ibid.

72. Ibid.

73. On guns, see *Military Operations 1917*, II, p. 136; Prior and Wilson, *Passchendaele*, pp. 71–73 (on the German defence system in general); and Paddy Griffith, 'The Tactical Problem: Infantry, Artillery and the Salient', in Liddle (ed.), *Passchendaele in Perspective*, p. 69. The Allied superiority in shells was pronounced. The commander of the Fifth Army (the main attacking force), General Hubert Gough, in retrospect certainly thought that the resources employed for Third Ypres were insufficient; he wrote to the official historian J.E. Edmonds: 'where he [Haig] failed was as always in not recognising that in order to achieve the results he envisaged it was necessary to concentrate much greater forces than those he employed... [GHQ] failed to mass anything like sufficient forces to carry out so ambitious a plan'; PRO CAB 45/140: Gough to Edmonds, 18 March 1944.

74. The French First Army, under General Anthoine, participated in Third Ypres, under Haig's command, north of Gough's Fifth Army.

75. PRO CAB 27/6: 15th Meeting of the Cabinet Committee on War Policy, 6 July 1917. My emphasis.

76. PRO CAB 27/6/G179: 'Report of Cabinet Committee on War Policy', 10 August 1917.

77. Hankey, somewhat naively, could not see how Lloyd George could 'gain anything by accusing the Generals of suppressing or manipulating information'; HLRO LG MSS G/212: Hankey notes on chapters (1934).

78. PRO CAB 27/6: 1st Meeting of the Cabinet Committee on War Policy, 11 June 1917; French, 'Who Knew What and When?', p. 139 and *Strategy of the Lloyd George Coalition*, p. 113.

79. See French, 'Who Knew What and When?', pp. 149–51.

80. French, *Strategy of the Lloyd George Coalition*, pp. 117–23.

81. PRO CAB 27/6: 13th Meeting of the Cabinet Committee on War Policy.

82. PRO CAB 27/6: 'Report of the Cabinet Committee on War Policy', 10 August 1917.

83. He continued: 'For the last two years most of us soldiers have realised that Great Britain must take the necessary steps to win the war by herself, because our French Allies had already shown that they lacked both the moral

qualities and the means for gaining the victory'; *Haig Papers*, pp. 233–34. Haig's emphasis.

84. C.E. Callwell (ed.), *Field Marshal Sir Henry Wilson: His Life and Diaries*, 2 vols (London: Cassell, 1927), I, p. 355.

85. Ibid., p. 359. See also B.H. Liddell Hart, 'The Basic Truths of Passchendaele', *Journal of the Royal United Service Institution*, 616, November 1959, pp. 433–42; *Military Operations 1917*, II, p. 27; *Haig Papers*, p. 251, Robertson to Haig, 9 August 1917; French, *Strategy of the Lloyd George Coalition*, pp. 109–11.

86. *War Memoirs*, IV, pp. 2189–90, quoting Brigadier-General John Charteris, *Field-Marshal Earl Haig* (London: Cassell, 1929). Charteris wrote, however, on the following page that: 'Unfortunately, there now set in the wettest August recorded for thirty years'; pp. 272–73.

87. *War Memoirs*, IV, p. 2207.

88. Ibid.

89. John Hussey, 'The Flanders Battleground and the Weather in 1917', in Liddle (ed.), *Passchendaele in Perspective*, pp. 141–42.

90. Ibid., p. 149.

91. Terraine, *Haig*, pp. 348–49; Hussey, 'The Flanders Battleground and the Weather in 1917', in Liddle (ed.), *Passchendaele in Perspective*, p. 154.

92. Ibid., pp. 147–48.

93. As for weather earlier in 1917, when Haig would have liked to launch an offensive in Flanders but was sidetracked by Nivelle, Hussey notes that May, June and July were 'perfect' or 'good' campaigning weather; see ibid., 148–49. On the 'mud' and weather question, see also *Military Operations 1917*, II, pp. 211–12, 373–77.

94. John Charteris, *At GHQ* (London: Cassell, 1931), pp. 240–41.

95. *War Memoirs*, IV, pp. 2232–33.

96. Even Edmonds, the official historian, wrote that 'No great victory had been won' and that Haig's goal of capturing the Belgian ports remained unfulfilled; *Military Operations 1917*, II, p. 366.

97. Terraine, *Haig*, p. 370; Prior and Wilson, *Passchendaele*, p. 179. Rawlinson went further than Haig, describing the new British position as 'untenable' in the face of a serious German attack; quoted on p. 181.

98. *War Memoirs*, IV, pp. 2234–38.

99. Ibid., p. 2224.

100. Ibid., pp. 2236–37.

101. Ibid., pp. 2212–15.

102. Ibid., p. 2215.

103. *Haig Papers*, p. 250.

104. Ibid., p. 260.

105. J.H. Boraston (ed.), *Sir Douglas Haig's Despatches (December 1915–April 1919)* (London: Dent, 1919), pp. 116–17. My emphasis. Edmonds notes that Haig was 'Well informed of the miserable conditions at the front'; *Military Operations 1917*, II, p. 378.

106. Wilson, *Myriad Faces*, p. 477.

107. PRO CAB 27/7/WP3: Haig Memorandum, 'Present Situation and Future Plans', 12 June 1917; PRO CAB 27/6/G-179: Report of the Cabinet Committee on War Policy, 10 August 1917.

108. See, for example, *Haig Papers*, pp. 256–57, diary entries 2, 4 October 1917.

109. Terraine, *Haig*, p. 333; Wilson, *Myriad Faces*, p. 477.
110. On the German soldier at Ypres, see German Werth, 'Flanders 1917 and the German Soldier', in Liddle (ed.), *Passchendaele in Perspective*, pp. 324–32. The German High Command was so confident of victory even while the battle in Flanders was in progress that several divisions were transferred from the Western Front to the east; Hagenlücke, 'The German High Command', p. 55.
111. Harington, *Plumer*, pp. 111–12.
112. LHMCA, Maurice MSS, 3/2/7, Harington to Maurice, 9 November 1934. Harington also wrote (just after publication of the Passchendaele volume of the *War Memoirs*): 'I must write & say how glad I am to see that you have had a whack at that little blighter [Lloyd George] over Passchendaele.... LG's sneer at Broodseinde ['Who remembers that name now? (Try it on one of your friends)'] is wicked. I think I shd try & present a true and dignified account of Passchendaele & clear my Chief of LG's attack on his loyalty to Haig & let Duff Cooper kill him.'
113. Quoted in Powell, *Plumer*, p. 229; Harington to Edmonds, 21 November 1934.
114. C.à.C. Repington, *The First World War 1914–1918*, 2 vols (London: Constable, 1920), II, p. 99, 14 October 1917; see also Sir John Davidson, *Haig: Master of the Field* (London: Peter Nevill, 1953), p. 66.
115. Quoted in Prior and Wilson, *Passchendaele*, pp. 160–61.
116. General Sir Hubert Gough, *The Fifth Army* (London: Hodder and Stoughton, 1931), p. 205; and the same author's *Soldiering On* (London: Arthur Barker, 1954), p. 142; also Anthony Farrar-Hockley, *Goughie* (London: Hart-Davis, MacGibbon, 1975), p. 224.
117. Esher journal, quoted in Peter Fraser, *Lord Esher: A Political Biography* (London: Hart-Davis, MacGibbon, 1973), p. 367.
118. Gough, *Soldiering On*, p. 147. In March 1918 Haig, on sending Gough home, assured him there would be an enquiry. This was never held. See also Gough's criticisms of Haig in LHCMA Liddell Hart MSS 11/1935/107: Talk with Lloyd George and General Sir Hubert Gough (at the Athenaeum) 28 November 1935. Both had expressed to Liddell Hart their desire to 'bury the hatchet', which was done at two meetings at the end of 1935 and early 1936. This rapprochement is reflected in Lloyd George's sympathetic treatment of Gough in the *War Memoirs*. See ch. 8.
119. *Military Operations 1917*, II, p. 325. This is repeated in, for example, MacDonald, *They Called It Passchendaele*, p. 195.
120. Prior and Wilson, *Passchendaele*, p. 160; Gough, *The Fifth Army*, p. 213; *Soldiering On*, pp. 138–44; Charteris, *At GHQ.*, pp. 258–59.
121. *War Memoirs*, IV, p. 2219.
122. Ibid., p. 2228. Another example of GHQ's 'tactics of deception' arose when Lloyd George visited the front in September 1917. He expressed a desire to see some prisoners of war, and those he did see were a 'weedy' lot, 'deplorably inferior to the manly samples I had seen in the early stages of the War'. He learnt later that GHQ had instructed Fifth Army to remove able-bodied prisoners from the 'cage' to give the impression that the Germans were scraping the bottom of the barrel. The source for this story was a Wilfrid Greene, KC, who was during the war on the Fifth Army's staff. According to

Liddell Hart, he told Lloyd George that he 'had a message from GHQ that LG was coming to see the prisoners of war, and the Fifth Army was to remove all the able-bodied prisoners from the cage before he arrived (LG had expressed doubts whether the German prisoners were the weedy lot that GHQ argued they were). LG persuaded Greene, with some difficulty, to let him tell the story of this episode in his memoirs.' Hankey, who accompanied Lloyd George, confirmed that the prisoners they saw on that visit were 'nerve shattered, tired, unshaved and dirty' but who 'nevertheless sprang to attention as though under review by the Kaiser'; see ibid., p. 2225; LHCMA Liddell Hart MSS 11/1934/42: Memorandum (after lunch with Lloyd George at Churt), 28 June 1934; HLRO LG MSS G/212: Hankey to Lloyd George, 21 March 1934, with extract from diary 26 September 1917.

123. *War Memoirs*, IV, p. 2233.
124. War Office, *Statistics of the Military Effort of the British Empire during the Great War* (London: HMSO, 1922, repr. London Stamp Exchange, 1992), p. 324; Martin Middlebrook, *The First Day on the Somme: 1 July 1916* (New York: Norton, 1972), pp. 243–44.
125. *Military Operations 1917*, II, p. 178; Prior and Wilson, *Passchendaele*, p. 95.
126. Brian Bond, 'Passchendaele: Verdicts, Past and Present', in Liddle (ed.), *Passchendaele in Perspective*, p. 486.
127. J.E. Edmonds, *Military Operations France and Belgium 1916*, 1 (London: Macmillan, 1932), pp. 496–97.
128. *Military Operations 1917*, II, p. 88, n. 1, p. 363, n. 1, pp. 360–63.
129. Although he has his defenders. John Terraine does not fully accept Edmonds' figures, but does accept that German casualties 'at least' equalled the British and 'probably' exceeded the British; see Terraine, *Haig*, pp. 371–73; Terraine, *The Road to Passchendaele*, Appendix III, p. 351; Bond, 'Passchendaele: Verdicts, Past and Present', p. 486.
130. Liddell Hart, 'Basic Truths of Passchendaele', p. 437.
131. Ibid., pp. 437–38.
132. M.J. Williams, 'Thirty Per Cent: A Study in Casualty Statistics', *Journal of the Royal United Service Institution*, February 1964, pp. 51–55; and 'Treatment of the British Losses on the Somme in the British Official History: "Military Operations France and Belgium 1916"', *Journal of the Royal United Service Institution*, February 1966, pp. 69–74.
133. Sir William Robertson, *Soldiers and Statesmen*, 2 vols (London: Cassell, 1926), II, p. 299; War Office, *Statistics of the Military Effort*, pp. 263–64, 326.
134. Prior and Wilson, *Passchendaele*, p. 195.
135. Hagenlücke, 'The German High Command', and Vandiver, 'Field-Marshal Sir Douglas Haig and Passchendaele', in Liddle (ed.), *Passchendaele in Perspective*, pp. 38, 55.
136. See PRO CAB 23/13/WC247B: War Cabinet Minutes, 11 October 1917; PRO CAB 23/4/WC251, War Cabinet 17 October 1917; PRO CAB 23/4/WC262, War Cabinet 1 November 1917. The figures provided to the War Cabinet, while generally reliable regarding the BEF, seriously overestimated German losses.
137. The Government did in fact seek alternative advice. In October Sir Henry Wilson and Sir John French were asked to report on operations on the Western Front. Neither man had any great love for Haig, and their reports

were predictably critical. They did not, however, have any effect on military operations. Their only significance was that both called for the establishment of an 'Inter-Allied General Staff', which was in fact established soon after as the Supreme War Council; see *War Memoirs*, IV, pp. 2367–80; Prior and Wilson, *Passchendaele*, pp. 187–88; Turner, 'Lloyd George, the War Cabinet and High Politics', in Liddle (ed.), *Passchendaele in Perspective*, pp. 21–22.

138. *War Memoirs*, IV, pp. 2221–22.
139. LHCMA Liddell Hart MSS 11/1932/42(a): 'Talk with Lloyd George at Criccieth, 24 September 1932'. My emphasis. Cf. Cross, Colin (ed.), *Life with Lloyd George: The Diary of A. J. Sylvester* (London: Macmillan, 1975), p. 92, 7 March 1933; NLW, Sylvester MSS, uncatalogued diary, 7 March 1933; and ibid., uncatalogued diary, 24 September 1932: 'If he had forbid it [sic] they [Haig and Jellicoe] would have said: "Here is the politician; but for the politician we would have had Ostend; we would have recaptured the coast of Flanders; they would have claimed they would have broken the Germans and might conceivably have driven them out. I could not have disproved it." '
140. *War Memoirs*, VI, p. 13415.
141. Ibid., IV, p. 2223.
142. Ibid., VI, p. 3415
143. Ibid., pp. 3415–16. My emphasis.
144. PRO CAB 27/6: 18th Meeting of the Cabinet Committee on War Policy, 3 October 1917.
145. Ibid.
146. PRO CAB 23/13/WC247B: Minutes of the War Cabinet, 11 October 1917; PRO CAB 23/4/WC251: War Cabinet, 17 October 1917.
147. For a different view see John Grigg, *Lloyd George: War Leader 1916–1918* (London: Allen Lane/Penguin, 2002), pp. 274–81.
148. Arguably, however, a massing of reserves at Cambrai, if available, could well have meant that the element of surprise, crucial to the success of the operation, would have been lost.

8 The Western Front in 1918

1. It is difficult to imagine that, despite his strong sense of duty, Haig would have *accepted* such a 'promotion'; HLRO LG MSS F/14/4/83: Lord Derby to Lloyd George, 11 December 1917; also David French, *The Strategy of the Lloyd George Coalition 1916–1918* (Oxford: Clarendon Press, 1995), p. 167.
2. For extracts from the speech see *War Memoirs*, IV, pp. 2397–2402; see also Paul Guinn, *British Strategy and Politics 1914 to 1918* (Oxford: Clarendon Press, 1965), pp. 267–68 and French, *Strategy of the Lloyd George Coalition*, p. 165.
3. For example, Lord Northcliffe; see Trevor Wilson, *The Myriad Faces of War: Britain and the Great War 1914–1918* (Cambridge: Polity Press, 1986), p. 547; J.M. McEwen, 'Lloyd George and Northcliffe at War 1914–1918', *Historical Journal*, 24, 3, 1981, p. 669 and Keith Grieves, 'Haig and the Government 1916–1918', in Brian Bond and Nigel Cave (eds), *Haig: A Reappraisal 70 Years On* (Barnsley: Pen and Sword, 1999), p. 117.

4. John Terraine, *Douglas Haig: The Educated Soldier* (London: Hutchinson, 1963), pp. 384–88. There were also moves to remove the unpopular Gough from his command of the Fifth Army, but this would have to wait until March 1918. When Liddell Hart asked Lloyd George what part he had played in Gough's removal from Fifth Army command, Lloyd George replied that at the end of 1917 'the Cabinet had pressed for the removal of Gough along with Kiggell, Charteris etc. Haig had eventually given way towards the others but insisted on keeping Gough'; HLRO LG MSS F/14/4/85: Derby to Haig, 12 December 1917; for Lloyd George on this, see *War Memoirs*, IV, p. 2273 and LHCMA Liddell Hart MSS 11/1935/64: Memorandum 21 March 1935.
5. *War Memoirs*, IV, pp. 2222–23.
6. Ibid., pp. 2264–65.
7. Ibid., pp. 2265–68, VI, pp. 3382, 3423–24. Both Monash and Currie rose no higher during the war than corps commander. Of Lloyd George's complaint that he had not been told about Monash, Terraine comments aptly that in early 1918 there was 'not very much to tell' as his greatest achievements as GOC Australian Corps came in the last three months of the war; John Terraine, *The Smoke and the Fire: Myths and Anti-Myths of War 1861–1945* (London: Sidgwick and Jackson, 1980), p. 190. On Monash, see Geoffrey Serle, *John Monash: A Biography* (Melbourne: Melbourne University Press, 1982), esp. ch. 13.
8. *War Memoirs*, IV, p. 2274.
9. Ibid., p. 2340.
10. Wilson, *Myriad Faces*, pp. 548–49. Lloyd George himself praises Plumer 'as one of the best soldiers in the British Army'; *War Memoirs*, IV, p. 2332. It was when in tandem with his Chief of Staff, C.H. 'Tim' Harington that Plumer was especially effective; see Peter Simkins, 'Haig and the Army Commanders', in Bond and Cave (eds), *Haig: A Reappraisal*, pp. 79–82.
11. Wilson, *Myriad Faces*, p. 549; also George H. Cassar, 'Political Leaders in Wartime: Lloyd George and Churchill', in John Bourne, Peter Liddle and Ian Whitehead (eds), *The Great World War 1914–1945*, I: *Lightning Strikes Twice* (London: HarperCollins, 2000), p. 394.
12. French, *Strategy of the Lloyd George Coalition*, p. 168. Jellicoe was replaced by Sir Rosslyn Wemyss on 24 December 1917. On the failure to replace Haig, see also Harold Laski's review of Volume V, where he confesses, mystified: 'I still cannot myself understand how, granted his views of Haig, he kept him in supreme command', *New Statesman and Nation*, 3 October 1936. The question still exercises many; see, for example, Nigel Jones, 'The Summer Before Dark', *Literary Review*, September 2004, p. 5, review of David Stevenson's *1914–1918: The History of the First World War* (London: Allen Lane Penguin, 2004).
13. *War Memoirs*, IV, p. 2338.
14. Ibid., p. 2340.
15. 'I came to the conclusion . . . that the removal of Haig and Robertson would not touch the real problem, but that there must be a more thorough and essential change in the whole method of conduct of Allied strategy if we were to win'; ibid., p. 2343.
16. Ibid., p. 2274.

17. Maurice Hankey, *The Supreme Command*, 2 vols (London: Allen & Unwin, 1961), II, p. 711.
18. PRO CAB 23/13/WC247B: War Cabinet, 11 October 1917.
19. See summary in *War Memoirs*, IV, pp. 2367–84.
20. Matthew Hughes, 'Personalities in Conflict? Lloyd George, the Generals and the Italian Campaign 1917–18', in Matthew Hughes and Matthew Seligman (eds), *Leadership in Conflict 1914–1918* (London: Leo Cooper, 2000), pp. 201–202; Robin Prior and Trevor Wilson, *Passchendaele: The Untold Story* (New Haven and London: Yale University Press, 1996), p. 188; French, *Strategy of the Lloyd George Coalition*, pp. 158–62.
21. Ibid., p. 164.
22. LHCMA Robertson MSS 4/8/8: Furse Memorandum, 'The Scheme of Organisation of a Supreme War Council', 11 November 1917.
23. LHCMA Robertson MSS 4/8/11: Robertson to Derby, 15 November 1917.
24. *War Memoirs*, V, p. 2738.
25. French, *Strategy of the Lloyd George Coalition*, pp. 216–17. Lord Derby, Secretary of State for War, commented that Wilson's 'new position completely supplanted that of Robertson . . . "Sir Henry Wilson, indeed, becomes chief military advisor on what after all is the most important matter in connection with the War," the movement of British reserves on the Western Front'; quoted in Timothy Crandall Sullivan, 'The General and the Prime Minister: Sir Henry Wilson and David Lloyd George in War and Peace 1918–1922' (PhD thesis, University of Illinois at Urbana-Champaign, 1973), p. 29.
26. French, *Strategy of the Lloyd George Coalition*, pp. 216–17; Sir William Robertson, *Soldiers and Statesmen*, 2 vols (London: Cassell, 1926), I, pp. 222–37.
27. One reviewer, commenting upon this passage, wrote: 'Difficult though it is for the detached critic to credit Robertson with any such ambition, Mr Lloyd George alleges it more than once and in the most explicit terms, and it is evidently his opinion that he successfully vindicated constitutional government against a conspiracy of military Fascists', *Times Literary Supplement*, 26 September 1936.
28. *War Memoirs*, V, pp. 2785–86.
29. Quoted in ibid., pp. 2788–89.
30. Ibid., p. 2789.
31. Ibid., pp. 2793–94.
32. Guinn, *British Strategy and Politics*, p. 292.
33. *War Memoirs*, V, pp. 2794–96.
34. British Library Balfour Add MSS 49726: Balfour Memorandum, 'Notes of a Conversation I had with the CIGS on Thursday 14 February 1918 at 3.30 pm'.
35. Although see Robertson's letter to Haig of 8 March 1916: 'I am writing this with the object of saying that practically anything may happen to our boasted British Constitution before this war ends and that the great asset is the army', quoted in David Dutton, 'The "Robertson Dictatorship" and the Balkan Campaign in 1916', *Journal of Strategic Studies*, 9, 1, March 1986, pp. 76–77, n. 5; cf. John Terraine, *To Win a War: 1918 The Year Of Victory* (London: Cassell, 2000), pp. 55–56 and John Grigg's comments in *Lloyd George: War Leader 1916–1918* (London: Allen Lane/Penguin, 2002), pp. 411–12.
36. *War Memoirs*, V, pp. 2832–33; Terraine, *Haig*, p. 405. As John Grigg notes, Haig's confidence in Robertson had been fading since Third Ypres, as he had

failed to stick to the Western Front strategy espoused by Haig and had allowed resources to be diverted to other theatres. This was most unfair as Robertson had done his best to support Haig; Grigg, *Lloyd George*, IV, p. 415.

37. A good exposition of Lloyd George's preferred option can be found in PRO CAB 23/13/WC247B: War Cabinet, 11 October 1917; *Strategy of the Lloyd George Coalition*, p. 156.

38. Haig, was 'so inebriated that he was quite oblivious of change that had taken place in position that he contemplated renewing offensive in the spring', and clearly 'not in a state of mind to give us *sober* advice'; HLRO LG MSS G/224/5: 'Mr Lloyd George's Rough Notes for Volume V of War Memoirs', no date; *War Memoirs*, IV, 2364, my emphasis. See also Prior and Wilson, *Passchendaele*, p. 194; David French, 'Failures of Intelligence: The Retreat to the Hindenburg Line and the March 1918 Offensive', in Michael Dockrill and David French (eds), *Strategy and Intelligence: British Policy during the First World War* (London: Hambledon Press, 1996), p. 85; Robert Blake (ed.), *The Private Papers of Douglas Haig 1914–1919* (London: Eyre and Spottiswoode, 1952), pp. 277–78; *War Memoirs*, V, p. 2687.

39. William Philpott, 'Haig and Britain's European Allies', in Bond and Cave (eds), *Haig: A Reappraisal*, p. 136; French, *Strategy of the Lloyd George Coalition*, pp. 221–22.

40. *War Memoirs*, VI, p. 3212; French, pp. 220–21.

41. PRO CAB 23/5/WC371: War Cabinet, 23 March 1918; WC372: War Cabinet, 25 March 1918; WC373: War Cabinet, 26 March 1918; Wilson, *Myriad Faces*, pp. 565–66 and French, *Strategy of the Lloyd George Coalition*, p. 230.

42. Quoted in David R. Woodward, 'Did Lloyd George Starve the British Army of Men Prior to the German Offensive of 21 March 1918?', *Historical Journal*, 27, 1, 1984, p. 245; *War Memoirs*, V, pp. 2444–45.

43. HLRO LG MSS G/224/5: 'Rough Notes for vol. V'.

44. This, incidentally, was one reason why the decision was taken to implement in the first weeks of 1918 a major reorganisation of the BEF by reducing the number of battalions per division from 12 to 9. This inevitably produced a good deal of confusion and led to some deterioration of morale as battalions were broken up and members relocated; Terraine, *To Win a War*, pp. 49–50; James E. Edmonds, *A Short History of World War I* (London: Oxford University Press, 1951), p. 277.

45. *War Memoirs*, V, p. 2445.

46. For example, 'War Cabinet decides not to send reinforcements to France' and 'Haig had not been given the men he asked for to continue his offensive'; HLRO LG MSS G/224/5: 'Rough Notes for Vol. V'. Of course Lloyd George's line of reasoning is that Haig possessed sufficient troops, along with the greatly increased firepower, to defend his front, and that the only reason for the Fifth Army debacle was his incompetent distribution of forces along his front. Cf. LHCMA Liddell Hart MSS 11/1935/64: Memorandum 21 March 1935, where Liddell Hart recorded Lloyd George as denying that he had anything to do with withholding men from Haig, and that if it had happened it was the doing of the War Office.

47. Woodward, 'Did Lloyd George Starve the British Army?', pp. 251–52.

48. *War Memoirs*, V, p. 2844. Some intelligence reports seemed to support this view. See for example PRO CAB 23/5/WC322: War Cabinet, 15 January 1918,

at which Robertson stated that, according to information 'derived from Russia', the 'main [German] offensive would be in Flanders, and would be accompanied by a demonstration in the South'.
49. *War Memoirs*, V, p. 2844.
50. Ibid., p. 2847. Liddell Hart made the point to Lloyd George on this passage that German preparations were proceeding on other parts of the front, in particular the French front, and that there was 'more excuse than you recognise for the view that the German attack was coming on the French front as well as on the British', LHCMA Liddell Hart MSS 1/450: 'Notes on Lloyd George's War Memoirs vol. V', 4 May 1936.
51. After the war Lloyd George wrote: 'We managed to increase the numbers of the labour forces in France from 80,000 to 300,000 in January 1918. The numbers were quadrupled. Why were they not poured into the Somme area to throw up defences at the threatened point? The answer is that they were in the North, perfecting the fortifications of the Passchendaele area ... It was this extraordinary Passchendaele obsession'; cf. HLRO LG MSS G/39/2/19: 'Draft Notes for speech to [Fifth Army] Reunion Dinner', 20 March 1937.
52. *War Memoirs*, V, p. 2851. Liddell Hart commented on this passage that Haig was more annoyed with the British Government than with the French, and that by this time he had 'swing to a more defensive frame of mind'; LHCMA Liddell Hart MSS 1/450: 'Notes on Lloyd George's War Memoirs, vol. V' (1935–36).
53. *War Memoirs*, V, p. 2854. Cf. HLRO LG MSS G/224/5: 'Rough Notes for vol. V': 'Haig had not been given the men he asked for to continue his offensive. He was too sulky to do the only thing that was possible under such conditions – distribute the men he had to the best advantage. Why should he withdraw from a battlefield he had won in spite of the politicians to suit the convenience of the very men who had done their best to thwart him. Let the responsibility be theirs. Their blood be on their own heads. He would not help them out.' Lloyd George later received some support on this from Gough, see p. 171.
54. See Middlebrook, *The Kaiser's Battle*, pp. 71–73; J.P. Harris with Niall Barr, *Amiens to the Armistice: The BEF in the Hundred Days Campaign 8 August–11 November 1918* (London: Washington: Brassey's, 1998), p. 12; Gary Sheffield, *Forgotten Victory: The First World War Myths and Realities* (London: Headline, 2001), pp. 187–88; Edmonds, *A Short History*, p. 280; Wilson, *Myriad Faces*, p. 558 and John Grigg, *Lloyd George: War Leader 1916–1918* (London: Allen Lane/Penguin, 2002), p. 456. David French has stressed the effectiveness of the German deception plan in keeping Haig's eyes firmly fixed on the north in his 'Failures of Intelligence', pp. 85–95. On this latter point, see also HLRO LG MSS G/224/5: 'Rough Notes for vol. V', where note is taken of the effectiveness of German deception prior to the March offensive.
55. *War Memoirs*, V, pp. 2898–99.
56. Ibid., p. 2886.
57. Ibid., p. 2890; cf. PRO CAB 23/5/WC371: War Cabinet, 23 March 1918.
58. *War Memoirs*, V, pp. 2892–93.
59. Ibid., p. 2901.
60. Sir Henry Wilson had warned Haig on 6 March that without a General Reserve Haig 'would be living on the charity of Pétain'; Callwell, *Wilson Life and Diaries*, II, p. 77; Wilson, *Myriad Faces*, p. 562.

61. Tim Travers, *How the War Was Won: Command and Technology in the British Army on the Western Front 1917–1918* (London and New York: Routledge, 1992), p. 66; Wilson, *Myriad Faces*, p. 562.
62. HLRO LG MSS G/224/5: 'Rough Notes for vol. V'. Liddell Hart noted in reviewing vol. V that Lloyd George did 'not do full justice to Pétain for the efforts he spontaneously made before Foch's appointment to supreme charge', 'The Candour of Lloyd George', *London Mercury*, November 1936, LHCMA Liddell Hart MSS 10/1933/156a.
63. French, *Strategy of the Lloyd George Coalition*, pp. 224–25.
64. *War Memoirs*, V, p. 2903.
65. Ibid., p. 2904.
66. Ibid., p. 2905.
67. Ibid., p. 2908. Lloyd George's emphasis.
68. Haig claimed that it was he who put the proposal: 'I at once recommended that Foch should co-ordinate the action of all Allied armies on the Western Front. Both Governments agreed to this'; Blake (ed.), *Haig Papers*, p. 298. Cf. Travers, *How the War Was Won*, pp. 66–70; Wilson, *Myriad Faces*, p. 567.
69. *War Memoirs*, p. 2910; cf. Milner's account of the conference, LHCMA Maurice MSS 4/5/10: Memorandum by Lord Milner on his visit to France including the Conference at Doullens, 26 March 1918. Lloyd George clearly based his account on Milner's memorandum.
70. Quoted in *War Memoirs*, V, p. 2911.
71. Ibid., pp. 2915–17.
72. Ibid., pp. 2917–18.
73. Ibid., p. 2925.
74. Ibid., pp. 2927–30.
75. Ibid., p. 2921.
76. Ibid., p. 2927.
77. Quoted in Terraine, *Haig*, p. 426.
78. Ibid.
79. Wilson, *Myriad Faces*, pp. 568–69.
80. Edmonds, *A Short History*, pp. 273–97; Wilson, *Myriad Faces*, pp. 556–64; Sheffield, *Forgotten Victory*, pp. 188–91; Travers, *How the War Was Won*, pp. 70–91 and Erich Ludendorff, *My War Memories 1914–1918*, 2 vols (London: Hutchinson, 1919): 'What the English and French had not succeeded in doing we had accomplished, and that in the fourth year of the war'; but he conceded that strategically the Germans had not achieved what the early stages of the battle seemed to promise, II, p. 600.
81. French, *Strategy of the Lloyd George Coalition*, pp. 232–33. Lloyd George writes of Derby: 'The events of the 21 March decided me that he was not an ideal War Minister. He was not as his best in a crisis. In an emergency leaders who sweat despondency are a source of weakness. I made up my mind . . . that he would render greater service to his country in a position where it would not be obvious that his bluffness was only bluff'; *War Memoirs*, VI, p. 3406. See also David Dutton (ed.), *Paris 1918: The War Diary of the British Ambassador, the 17th Earl of Derby* (Liverpool: Liverpool University Press, 2001), 'Introduction', pp. xxiii–xxvii.
82. C.E. Callwell (ed.), *Field Marshal Sir Henry Wilson: His Life and Diaries*, 2 vols (London: Cassell, 1927), II, p. 78.

83. Ibid., p. 86.
84. *Haig Papers*, p. 301; French, *Strategy of the Lloyd George Coalition*, p. 233.
85. Edward Beddington, quoted in Peter Simkins, 'Haig and the Army Commanders', in Bond and Cave (eds), *Haig: A Reappraisal*, p. 90.
86. Hubert Gough, *Soldiering On* (London: Arthur Barker, 1954), pp. 168–69.
87. 104 *H.C. Deb*. 5s, col. 1343.
88. Gough, *Soldiering On*, pp. 178–79; a line followed by Anthony Farrar-Hockley in 'Sir Hubert Gough and the German Breakthrough, 1918', in Brian Bond (ed.), *Fallen Stars: Eleven Studies of Twentieth Century Military Disasters* (London: Brasseys, 1991), p. 83.
89. *War Memoirs*, V, p. 2913.
90. Ibid., VI, pp. 3386–87.
91. Ibid., V, pp. 2936–37.
92. Ibid., p. 2918.
93. Ibid., pp. 2206, 2212, 2245–46. Ironically, it seems that Gough was annoyed with Lloyd George's volume on Passchendaele. As Liddell Hart wrote to Gough in 1935: '...you refer to the Prime Minister's [Lloyd George's] "venomous abuse".... Then, in the *Sunday Chronicle*, you spoke of "the very evident feeling of personal animosity and jealousy which he (LG) has evinced"'. In Liddell Hart's view, even if there were no other evidence than Gough's own book (*The Fifth Army*), there were ample grounds for criticism of the British high command over Passchendaele and March 1918, which Gough seemed to be denying; LHCMA Liddell Hart MSS 1/323/1: Liddell Hart to Gough 29 March 1935.
94. LHCMA Liddell Hart MSS 11/1935/107: 'Talk with Lloyd George and General Sir Hubert Gough (at the Athenaeum)', 28 November 1935.
95. LHCMA Liddell Hart MSS 11/1936/31: 'Talk with LG and Hubert Gough at Reform Club', dinner, 27 January 1936. Frances Stevenson wrote to Liddell Hart the week after the first meeting: 'Mr Lloyd George has asked me to drop you a line to say how much he enjoyed the dinner last week. He was very delighted to meet General Gough, and greatly enjoyed the talk with him'; Lloyd George, she wrote, hoped to meet Gough again on his (Lloyd George's) return from Tangier; LHCMA Liddell Hart MSS 1/450: Stevenson to Liddell Hart, 4 December 1935.
96. LHCMA Liddell Hart MSS 11/1935/107: 'Talk with Lloyd George and Gough', 28 November 1935.
97. Ibid.
98. HLRO LG MSS G/39/2/16: Gough to Lloyd George, 20 March 1937.
99. HLRO LG MSS G/39/2/17: Gough speech summarised by Sylvester, 21 March 1937. Gough concluded his memoirs with the publication of extracts from Churchill's *World Crisis* and Lord Birkenhead's *Turning Points of History*, which praised Gough. Also published was an extract from a letter from Lloyd George to Gough which concluded: 'I need hardly say that the facts which have come to my knowledge since the War have completely changed my mind as to the responsibility for that defeat. You were completely let down and no General could have won that battle under the conditions in which you were placed', *Soldiering On*, p. 255.
100. See, for example, the account in Travers, *How the War Was Won*, ch. 3.

101. *War Memoirs*, VI, p. 3139. Cf. Liddell Hart's comment on Foch: 'And when you call Foch a "strategian [sic] of unchallenged genius", I am afraid that I must demur to the "unchallenged" '; LHCMA LH MSS 1/450: 'Notes on Lloyd George's Memoirs – Vol. V'.
102. *War Memoirs*, VI, p. 3127.
103. Ibid., pp. 3128–31. Cf. B.H. Liddell Hart, *History of the First World War* (London: Pan, 1970), pp. 423–25; John Terraine, 'Passchendaele and Amiens II: Amiens', *Journal of the Royal United Service Institution*, CIV, 615, August 1959, p. 340.
104. Robin Prior and Trevor Wilson, *Command on the Western Front: The Military Career of Sir Henry Rawlinson 1914–18* (Oxford: Blackwell, 1992), pp. 302–303.
105. Ibid., p. 305.
106. Ibid.; Travers, *How the War Was Won*, pp. 116–18.
107. Ibid.; Wilson, *Myriad Faces*, pp. 588–89. On the tanks in particular, see J.P. Harris, *Men, Ideas and Tanks: British Military Thought and Armoured Forces 1903–1939* (Manchester and New York: Manchester University Press, 1995), pp. 175–80.
108. Prior and Wilson, *Command on the Western Front*, p. 318.
109. Ibid., p. 327.
110. Ibid.; Wilson, *Myriad Faces*, p. 593; Travers, *How the War Was Won*, pp. 125–31 and Harris, *From Amiens to the Armistice*, pp. 113–16.
111. Wilson, *Myriad Faces*, p. 594.
112. Blake (ed.), *Haig Papers*, pp. 323–24. Haig's emphasis.
113. Wilson, *Myriad Faces*, p. 595; Prior and Wilson, *Command on the Western Front*, p. 336; see also Edmonds, *A Short History*, pp. 346–49; Liddell Hart, *History of the First World War*, pp. 429–31; Terraine, *Haig*, pp. 459–61 and his *To Win a War*, pp. 118–20.
114. Prior and Wilson, *Command on the Western Front*, p. 305.
115. Robin Prior and Trevor Wilson, *The First World War* (London: Cassell, 2001), p. 191.
116. Prior and Wilson, *Command on the Western Front*, p. 305.
117. *War Memoirs*, VI, p. 3146.
118. Ibid., p. 3145.
119. Ibid., pp. 3132–35.
120. Ibid., pp. 3132–33.
121. Trevor Wilson, 'A Prime Minister Reflects: The *War Memoirs* of David Lloyd George', in John A. Moses and Christopher Pugsley (eds), *The German Empire and Britain's Pacific Dominions 1871–1919: Essays on the Role of Australia and New Zealand in an Age of Imperialism* (Claremont, CA: Regina Books, 2000), p. 51.
122. *War Memoirs*, VI, p. 3144.
123. Ibid., pp. 3144–45.
124. Lloyd George was one of many seduced by Hitler's achievements and charm in the 1930s. Soon after arrival in Germany, Sylvester recorded Lloyd George's remark that Hitler, 'as far as Germany was concerned, was the resurrection and the life', later, in discussion with Joachim von Ribbentrop, newly appointed Ambassador to Britain (and later Foreign Minister) Lloyd George said that he 'could not understand why the Germans had signed the Armistice'. After his first interview with Hitler, Lloyd George (Sylvester

wrote) 'was very much struck with Hitler. "He is a very great man", said LG. "Führer is the proper name for him, for he is a born leader, yes, a statesman." He said that Hitler was not in favour of rearmament or conscription'. See Colin Cross (ed.), *Life with Lloyd George: The Diary of A.J. Sylvester* (London: Macmillan, 1975), pp. 146–54, entries for 2–13 September 1936 and Peter Rowland, *David Lloyd George: A Biography* (New York: Macmillan, 1975), pp. 732–33.
125. Sheffield, *Forgotten Victory*, p. 204.
126. Prior and Wilson, *First World War*, p. 201.
127. Wilson, *Myriad Faces*, pp. 606–607.
128. Wilson, 'A Prime Minister Reflects', p. 51.

9   Russia: War and revolution 1914–18

1. *War Memoirs*, I, p. 359.
2. Winston S. Churchill, *The World Crisis*, 6 vols (London: Thornton Butterworth, 1923–31), I, p. 276. My emphasis. Cf. his *The World Crisis*, VI, *The Eastern Front* (1931), p. 88.
3. HLRO LG MSS G/212: Hankey comments on draft chapter, The Strategy of the War Eastern v. Western Front, no date. My emphasis.
4. HLRO LG MSS G/212: Notes on chapters The Strategy of the War, no date. The passage in italics indicates a handwritten addition by Liddell Hart. Cf. Liddell Hart's *History of the First World War* (London: Pan, 1970), p. 99: '... the Russian invasion of East Prussia did not begin before the promised time [but] it began before it was ready ... The fault of this plan lay not in the conception but in the execution. Its potential value was well proved by the alarm – indeed the dislocation of mind – caused in the German headquarters when the menace was disclosed'.
5. Richard W. Harrison, 'Samsonov and the Battle of Tannenberg', in Brian Bond (ed.), *Fallen Stars: Eleven Studies of Twentieth Century Military Disasters* (London: Brasseys, 1991), p. 14.
6. Richard Pipes, *The Russian Revolution 1899–1919* (London: Collins Harvill, 1990), p. 196.
7. Dennis E. Showalter, *Tannenberg: Clash of Empires* (Hamden, Connecticut: Archon, 1991), p. 126.
8. Norman Stone, *The Eastern Front 1914–1917* (London: Hodder and Stoughton, 1975), pp. 45–48; Robin Prior, *Churchill's 'World Crisis' as History* (London: Croom Helm, 1983), pp. 39–40 and Hew Strachan, *The First World War*, vol. I: *To Arms* (Oxford: Oxford University Press, 2001), pp. 994–1005.
9. Stone, *Eastern Front*, pp. 60–61; Pipes, *The Russian Revolution*, pp. 212–13 and Roger Chickering, *Imperial Germany and the Great War 1914–1918* (Cambridge: Cambridge University Press, 1998), pp. 24–25.
10. Showalter, *Tannenberg*, p. 125.
11. N.N. Golovine, *The Russian Campaign of 1914* (Kansas: Command and General Staff School Press, 1933), p. 346 and especially ch. 3 for a full discussion of the evolution of Russia's war plans from 1893 until 1914.
12. *War Memoirs*, I, pp. 440–41.

13. Ibid., p. 441.
14. Ibid., p. 463.
15. Ibid., p. 465.
16. Ibid., p. 460.
17. *History of the Ministry of Munitions*, 12 vols (first ed. London: 1921–22, microfiche ed., Hassocks, Sussex: Harvester Press, 1976), X, Part 1, pp. 24–26; Gilbert, *Lloyd George*, II, pp. 226–30; in late November 1915 Lloyd George told Hankey that any transfer of heavy guns to Russia should have the sanction of the War Council: 'A few days ago I discovered that the War Office had given away 6 in, 8 in and 9.2 in guns to the Russia in April of next year, although at that moment we shall be far short of the minimum requirements of the War Office. Fortunately I was able to buy the Russians off with something we could more easily spare but which they were more in need of. But I am strongly of opinion that no Minister, and certainly no official in a Department, should have the power to barter away our supplies without consultation with the [War] Council ... I found on referring to the Prime Minister that he gave his sanction to parting with one-sixth of our *surplus* – a very different position'; at the end of 1915 there was little if any surplus. HLRO LG MSS D/17/3/7: Lloyd George to Hankey, 26 November 1915, Lloyd George's emphasis.
18. HLRO LG MSS C/16/1/7: 'Some Further Considerations on the Conduct of the War', 22 February 1915.
19. *War Memoirs*, III, pp. 1571–80; Maurice Hankey, *The Supreme Command*, 2 vols (London: Allen & Unwin, 1961), II, p. 631.
20. *War Memoirs*, III, p. 1579.
21. Quoted in John Marlowe, *Milner: Apostle of Empire* (London: Hamish Hamilton, 1976), p. 264. The acting British consul in Moscow thought the conference 'useless', while the French Ambassador thought it dragged on 'to no purpose'; see R.H. Bruce Lockhart, *Memoirs of a British Agent* (London: Putnam, 1934), p. 162; Maurice Paléologue, *An Ambassador's Memoirs* (London: Hutchinson, 1925), III, p. 187 and Keith Neilson, *Strategy and Supply: The Anglo-Russian Alliance 1914–1917* (London: George Allen & Unwin, 1984), ch. 6, while the official British record of the conference with appendices can be found in PRO CAB 28/21/IC16: 'Allied Conference in Petrograd, January–February 1917'.
22. *War Memoirs*, III, pp. 1588–89.
23. Quoted in ibid., pp. 1581–82. Cf. Liddell Hart's comment on Wilson and Milner: '[Wilson] also misled about morale – because they saluted well! the [*sic*] shallowness of his impressions with the shrewdness of Milner's on the war', HLRO LG MSS G/212: 'Notes on Mr Lloyd George's Memoirs. 1917' (2 May 1934).
24. See Keith E. Neilson, 'Wishful Thinking: The Foreign Office and Russia 1907–1917', in B.J.C. McKercher and D.J. Moss (eds), *Shadow and Substance in British Foreign Policy 1895–1939: Memorial Essays Honouring C.J. Lowe* (Edmonton: University of Alberta Press, 1984), p. 169; Neilson, *Strategy and Supply*, p. 250.
25. On the rioting in the capital see Pipes, *Russian Revolution*, pp. 272–75; Allan K. Wildman, *The End of the Russian Imperial Army: The Old Army and the Soldiers Revolt (March–April 1917)* (Princeton: Princeton University Press,

1980), p. 129; E.N. Burdzhalov, *Russia's Second Revolution: The February 1917 Uprising in Petrograd* (Bloomington and Indianapolis: Indiana University Press, 1987), translator's introduction, pp. xvii, and pp. 104–110 and Orlando Figes, *A People's Tragedy: The Russian Revolution 1891–1924* (London: Jonathan Cape, 1996), p. 318.

26. Quoted in David French, *The Strategy of the Lloyd George Coalition 1916–1918* (Oxford: Clarendon Press, 1995), p. 47.

27. Ibid. Even a senior Bolshevik in Petrograd told a meeting in late February, 'There is no and will be no revolution. We have to prepare for a long period of reaction'; Figes, *A People's Tragedy*, p. 323.

28. PRO CAB 28/2/IC16 (d): 'Allied Conference at Petrograd, January–February 1917': Further confidential report by Lord Milner, 13 March 1917.

29. PRO CAB 28/2 IC16 (e): 'Allied Conference at Petrograd, January–February 1917', Report by Lieutenant-General Sir H.H. Wilson, 3 March 1917.

30. Ibid.

31. Bernard Ash, *The Lost Dictator: A Biography of Field-Marshal Sir Henry Wilson* (London: Cassell, 1968), p. 221.

32. What Liddell Hart described as Churchill's 'absurd "historical" delusion'; HLRO LG MSS G/212: 'Notes on Mr Lloyd George's Memoirs 1917' (1934).

33. See *War Memoirs*, III, pp. 1605–606; Churchill, *The World Crisis*, V, *The Aftermath* (London: Thornton Butterworth, 1929), pp. 70–72; VI, *The Eastern Front*, pp. 347–50.

34. *War Memoirs*, III, 1636–37; PRO CAB 23/2/WC98: War Cabinet, 16 March 1917.

35. Wilson, Trevor (ed.), *The Political Diaries of C.P. Scott 1911–1928* (London: Collins, 1970), p. 271.

36. See *War Memoirs*, III, pp. 1617, 1637; Figes, *People's Tragedy*, pp. 357–58; French, *Strategy of the Lloyd George Coalition*, p. 49, *Scott Diaries*, pp. 270–71; David Stevenson, *The First World War and International Politics* (Oxford: Oxford University Press, 1988), pp. 148–49 and Earl Lloyd George of Dwyfor, *Lloyd George* (London: Federick Muller, 1960), p. 24.

37. Woodward, David R. (ed.), *The Military Correspondence of Field-Marshal Sir William Robertson, Chief of the Imperial General Staff December 1915–February 1918* (London: Bodley Head, 1989), pp. 168–69, Robertson to Haig, 10 April 1917.

38. See Louise E. Heenan, *Russian Democracy's Fatal Blunder: The Summer Offensive of 1917* (New York: Praeger, 1987).

39. *War Memoirs*, V, p. 2565; Lord Riddell, *Lord Riddell's War Diary 1914–1918* (London: Ivor Nicholson & Watson, 1933), p. 272.

40. *War Memoirs*, V, p. 2565.

41. Ibid., p. 2566.

42. V.I. Lenin, *Selected Works*, 3 vols (Moscow: Progress Publishers, 1977), II, pp. 419–22.

43. *War Memoirs*, V, pp. 2567–68; also Sir Alfred Knox, *With the Russian Army 1914–1917*, 2 vols (New York: E.P. Dutton, 1921), II, pp. 723–27; Ilya Somin, *Stillborn Crusade: The Tragic Failure of Western Intervention in the Russian Civil War 1918–1920* (New Brunswick: Transaction, 1996), pp. 27–28; Richard H. Ullman, *Intervention and the War* (Princeton: Princeton University Press, 1961), pp. 20–21 and John W. Wheeler-Bennett, *Brest-Litovsk: The Forgotten Peace 1918* (London: Macmillan, 1966 ed.), pp. 79–84.

44. *War Memoirs*, V, pp. 2566–67.
45. See the results of the elections in Pipes, *Russian Revolution*, p. 542 (the Bolsheviks gained 175 seats out of 715, together with their Allies, the Left SRs, 30 per cent of the vote); on the dispersal of the Assembly, pp. 545–55; on Lenin's public justification for its dispersal, Lenin, *Selected Works*, II, 'Draft decree on the Dissolution of the Constituent Assembly', published in *Pravda*, 7, 20, January 1918, pp. 478–79.
46. *War Memoirs*, V, p. 2567.
47. Ibid.
48. Somin, *Stillborn Revolution*, p. 30.
49. *War Memoirs*, III, p. 1638. This was the line also taken by the former British Ambassador in Petrograd, Sir George Buchanan, when he came to write his memoirs. See ibid., p. 1646 and Buchanan's *My Mission to Moscow and Other Diplomatic Memories*, 2 vols (London: Cassell, 1923), II, p. 106.
50. *War Memoirs*, III, p. 1644.
51. Ibid., p. 1646.
52. See Mark D. Steinberg and Vladimir M. Khrustalëv, *The Fall of the Romanovs: Political Dreams and Personal Struggles in a Time of Revolution* (New Haven and London: Yale University Press, 1995), p. 133, document 43, telegram from the Soviet of Worker's Deputies at the Konstantovsky factories to Nikolai Chkheidze, Chairman of the Petrograd Soviet, 13 March 1917. More examples of protests from Soviets regarding plans to let the Tsar and his family leave for Britain can be found in documents 47, 51, on pp. 146–47, 149–50. The Petrograd Soviet resolved on 9 March to adopt measures to prevent Nicholas from leaving Russia; document 41, pp. 130–31.
53. *War Memoirs*, III, p. 1639.
54. Andrei Maylunas and Sergei Mironenko (eds), *A Lifelong Passion: Nicolas and Alexandra Their Own Story* (London: Weidenfeld and Nicolson, 1996), pp. 559–61, Lord Stamfordham, note of meeting with Lloyd George, 22 March 1917. The editors of this volume have used the old style Russian calendar, 13 days behind the West in 1917. Thus the date for this meeting is given as 9 March.
55. Ibid., p. 562, Stamfordham to Balfour, 30 March 1917.
56. Ibid., p. 563, Balfour to Stamfordham, 2 April 1917.
57. Ibid., p. 566, Stamfordham to Balfour, 3 April 1917.
58. HLRO LG MSS F/3/2/19: Stamfordham to Balfour, 6 April 1917.
59. Ibid. Stamfordham's emphasis. This contradicts his earlier note that it 'will be made clear that this proposal was initiated by from the Russian Government [*sic*] itself and *not from us*', Maylunas and Mironenko (eds), *Lifelong Passion*, pp. 559–61, Lord Stamfordham, note of meeting with Lloyd George, 22 March 1917. My emphasis.
60. Ibid., pp. 563–70; Kenneth Rose, *George V* (London: Weidenfeld and Nicolson, 1983), pp. 212–14.
61. Paul Miliukov, *Political Memoirs 1905–1917*, ed. Arthur P. Mendel (Ann Arbor: University of Michigan Press, 1967), p. 438. Contrary to Miliukov's impression of Buchanan's feelings on the matter, the latter telegraphed Balfour after the decision was taken to reverse the invitation: 'I entirely share your view that, if there is any danger of anti-monarchist movement, it would be far better that the ex-Emperor should not come to England.'

Buchanan's daughter Meriel later recalled in her memoirs that her father was threatened with the loss of his pension rights if he revealed the truth of the affair; Rose, *George V*, p. 214 and Meriel Buchanan, *Dissolution of an Empire* (London: John Murray, 1932), pp. 192–93.

62. Steinberg and Khrustalëv, *The Fall of the Romanovs*, p. 119; Maylunas and Mironenko (eds), *Lifelong Passion*, p. 559, Lord Stamfordham, note of meeting with Lloyd George, 22 March 1917.

63. PRO CAB 23/2/WC118: War Cabinet, 13 April 1917.

64. Sir Robert Vansittart, Permanent Under-Secretary at the Foreign Office in the 1930s, commented on Bertie: 'This kind of language will not strengthen [Lloyd George's] case. It may be thought a little overpitched – in view of the subsequent tragedy.... Who would be influenced now by what the Germans might have said then? They wd have said anything of course. The ordinary reader will think Lord Bertie pusillanimous, & that we were not very courageous to listen to this.' Although Alexandra was indeed born in Germany, she was as much English as German; her mother was Queen Victoria's second daughter, Alice, and after her death Alix spent a good part of her childhood in Britain. After her marriage to Nicholas they usually spoke and wrote in English to one another. Rose, *George V*, p. 215; Steinberg and Khrustalëv, *The Fall of the Romanovs*, pp. 27–28; HLRO LG MSS G/212: Hankey to Lloyd George, 20 April 1934, with attachment, draft chapter, 'Czar's Future Residence'.

65. Kerensky, however, laid the blame squarely on Britain: 'Although, [he wrote] the government's inquiry into the doings of the Rasputin clique had cleared the Empress [of any treasonable activities] the royal family could not be sent abroad because Great Britain had refused to give hospitality, during the War, to relatives of its royal house', Alexander Kerensky, *The Catastrophe: Kerensky's Own Story of the Russian Revolution* (London, New York: D. Appleton & Co., 1927), p. 272.

66. NLW Sylvester MSS, uncatalogued, Sylvester to Earl Lloyd George, 26 October 1983.

67. Cf. Steinberg and Khrustalëv, *The Fall of the Romanovs*, p. 120: 'both the cabinet and the king came to feel that the political disadvantages of being associated with the deposed Russian emperor and empress far outweighed any potential benefits'; it would be more accurate to say that the King *persuaded* the War Cabinet that the costs outweighed the benefits.

68. Rose, *George V*, p. 215. My emphasis. See also pp. 215–17 for the King's and Stamfordham's reaction to the murder of Nicholas and entire family. After advising his monarch that it would be unwise for him to attend a memorial service for the Romanovs, Stamfordham wrote to Lord Esher in July 1918: 'Was there a crueller murder and has this country ever before displayed such callous indifference to a tragedy of this magnitude? ... I am so thankful that the King and Queen attended the memorial service. I have not yet discovered that the P.M. or the S. of S. for F.A. were even represented. Where is our national sympathy, gratitude, common decency gone to? ... Why didn't the German Emperor make the release of the Czar and family a condition of the Brest-Litovsk peace?', while the King wrote: 'May and I attended a service at the Russian church in Welbeck Street in memory of dear Nicky, who I fear was shot last month by the Bolshevists. It was a foul murder. I was devoted

to Nicky, who was the kindest of men and a thorough gentleman: loved his country and his people.'

69. HLRO LG MSS G/212: Hankey to Lloyd George, 9 April 1934; with attachment, 'Czar's Future Residence', draft chapter; cf. PRO CAB 23/2/WC118: War Cabinet, 13 April 1917.
70. See Vansittart's comments in HLRO LG MSS G/212: Hankey to Lloyd George, 9 April 1934, with attachment, 'Czar's Future Residence'.
71. HLRO LG MSS G/212: Hankey to Lloyd George, 9 April 1934; also HLRO LGMSS G/21/1/37: Sylvester to Lloyd George, 10 April 1934.
72. Cross, Colin (ed.), *Life with Lloyd George: The Diary of A. J. Sylvester* (London: Macmillan, 1975), p. 107. Although Lloyd George was earlier infuriated when he heard that the King was 'against' the memoirs. As Sylvester records: 'He then flared up: "Why should the King be against my book? Was he against Arthur's book on Kitchener, or against the book on Haig? No, he was not. He raised no objection to what was said about me, yet when I am about to defend myself he does not like it. He can go to Hell. I owe him nothing; he owes his throne to me." ' Ibid., p. 94.
73. Ibid., p. 110.
74. Rose, *George V*, p. 218.

Conclusion

1. *British Legion Journal*, 14, 6, December 1934, p. 238.
2. See ibid., p. 241. In the same issue, Major-General A. Solly-Flood (a former divisional commander) accused Lloyd George of 'half truths' and 'gross misrepresentations' in his attacks on Haig, pp. 240–41.
3. Winston Churchill in *Daily Mail*, 26 October 1934
4. *New Statesman and Nation*, 3 November 1934.
5. *New Statesman and Nation*, 3 October 1936.
6. Egerton, '*War Memoirs*', p. 84.
7. *New Statesman and Nation*, 3 October 1936. Cf. HLRO LG MSS G/235: 'Jottings by Mr. Lloyd George' (1931–32) where observed approvingly that Carlyle had written that history is the 'essence of innumerable biographies'. See also Fry, *Lloyd George and Foreign Policy*: 'If Lloyd George had a theory of history it was that personalities were the vital forces determining the unfolding of events'; p. 69.
8. *Times Literary Supplement*, 27 September 1934.
9. *Times Literary Supplement*, 28 November 1936. Cf. Jones, *Lloyd George*: 'The book is the man, and he is a man of action. The style is the man, and the man is not a judge but an advocate', p. 269.
10. *Sunday Times*, 10 September 1933.
11. Ibid.
12. Captain Liddell Hart, 'The Candour of Lloyd George', *London Mercury*, November 1936, pp. 64–66, LHCMA Liddell Hart MSS 10/1933/156a and b.
13. *Morning Post*, 26 October 1934. A reviewer for the same newspaper wrote of an earlier volume: 'It might be imagined that the immense labour of these War Memoirs was undertaken, incidentally no doubt, to exalt "the dynamic leadership" of the writer, but mainly for the purpose of assailing with sword

and fire the reputation of the professional soldier. Such vindictive vehemence is a serious blot on the value of this monumental work, whether as a contribution to historical or to biographical literature.' *Morning Post*, 19 October 1933.

14. See Egerton, '*War Memoirs*', pp. 82–83. The *Times Literary Supplement*'s reviewer wrote: 'From the literary point of view these portraits are the outstanding feature of the book. They are of the nature of silhouettes, sharp in outline but deliberately omitting detail, for Mr. Lloyd George is far too sensitive to suppose that he can apprehend the depths of another personality.... The emphasis on the importance of personal relationships even when, and perhaps most of all when, the greatest matters are at issue is characteristic of the book', 19 October 1933.
15. *Morning Post*, 7 September 1933.
16. Ibid.
17. *The Economist*, 30 September 1933.
18. Ibid.
19. *The Economist*, 28 October 1933.
20. Ibid.
21. John Ramsden, *Man of the Century: Winston Churchill and his Legend since 1945* (London: HarperCollins, 2002), p. 208. Of course this could be said too of Churchill's Second World War volumes.
22. Quoted in Brian Bond, *The Unquiet Western Front: Britain's Role in Literature and History* (Cambridge: Cambridge University Press, 2002), p. 46.
23. Trevor Wilson, 'A Prime Minister Reflects: The *War Memoirs* of David Lloyd George', in John A. Moses and Christopher Pugsley (eds), *The German Empire and Britain's Pacific Dominions 1871–1919: Essays on the Role of Australia and New Zealand in an Age of Imperialism* (Claremont, CA: Regina Books, 2000), p. 51.
24. Ibid., pp. 51–52.
25. Ibid., p. 38. On the literary side, see Hugh Cecil, *The Flower of Battle: British Fiction Writers of the First World War* (London: Secker and Warburg, 1995); also Samuel Hynes, *A War Imagined: The First World War and English Culture* (London: The Bodley Head, 1990), esp. Parts IV–V.
26. Wilson, 'A Prime Minister Reflects', pp. 38–39.

Bibliography

Primary sources

Departmental Papers, Public Record Office, Kew, London

Cabinet MSS: CAB 23 Minutes of the War Cabinet 1916–18;
CAB 28 International Conference series 1914–18;
CAB 27 War Policy Committee Minutes;
CAB 45 Post-war Official History Correspondence.
Ministry of Munitions MSS: MUN 9/31–38 Draft chapters.
War Office MSS: WO95 Operational War Diaries.

Private papers

Addison MSS, Bodleian Library, Oxford.
Asquith MSS, Bodleian Library, Oxford.
Balfour MSS, British Library.
Beaverbrook MSS, House of Lords Record Office.
H.A. Gwynne MSS, Imperial War Museum.
Hankey MSS, Churchill College, Cambridge.
Kitchener MSS, Public Record Office.
Liddell Hart MSS, Liddell Hart Centre for Military Archives, King's College, London.
Lloyd George MSS, House of Lords Record Office.
Lloyd George Mansion House Speech MSS, House of Lords Library.
Maurice MSS, Liddell Hart Centre for Military Archives, King's College, London.
Montague MSS, Trinity College, Cambridge (Memorandum on the events of December 1916 and letter to Maurice Bonham Carter 6 December 1916).
Ramsay MacDonald MSS, Public Record Office.
Robertson MSS, Liddell Hart Centre for Military Archives, King's College, London.
Sylvester MSS, National Library of Wales, Aberystwyth.
Von Donop MSS, Public Record Office.
Sir Henry Wilson MSS (Diary 1917), Imperial War Museum, London.

Official publications and documents

Great Britain, *History of the Ministry of Munitions*, 12 vols (London: 1921–22, microfiche edition, Hassocks, Sussex: Harvester Press, 1976).
House of Commons Debates 1914–18.
War Office, *Statistics of the Military Effort of the British Empire During the Great War* (London: HMSO, 1922, repr. London Stamp Exchange, 1992).

Contemporary newspapers and journals

British Legion Journal (December 1934)
Daily Mail
The Economist
Morning Post
New Statesman and Nation
Spectator
Times Literary Supplement

Published primary sources

Barnes, John and Nicholson, David (eds), *The Leo Amery Diaries*, vol. I: *1896–1929* (London: Hutchinson, 1980).
Baker-Carr, C.D., *From Chauffeur to Brigadier* (London: Ernest Benn, 1930).
Benckendorf, Count Paul, *Last Days at Tsarkoye Selo* (London: Heinemann, 1927).
Blake, Robert (ed.), *The Private Papers of Douglas Haig 1914–1919* (London: Eyre and Spottiswoode, 1952).
Bonham Carter, Violet, *Winston Churchill As I Knew Him* (London: Eyre and Spottiswoode, Collins, 1965).
Bonham Carter, Mark and Pottle, Mark (eds), *Lantern Slides: The Diaries and Letters of Violet Bonham Carter 1904–1914* (London: Phoenix, 1997).
Boraston, J.H. (ed.), *Sir Douglas Haig's Despatches (December 1915–April 1919)* (London and Toronto: Dent, 1919).
Brock, Michael and Eleonor (eds), *H.H. Asquith: Letters to Venetia Stanley* (Oxford: Oxford University Press, 1985).
Bruce Lockhart, R.H., *Memoirs of a British Agent* (London: Putnam, 1934).
Buchanan, Sir George, *My Mission to Moscow and Other Diplomatic Memories*, 2 vols (London: Cassell, 1923).
Buchanan, Meriel, *Dissolution of an Empire* (London: John Murray, 1932).
Callwell, C.E. (ed.), *Field Marshal Sir Henry Wilson: His Life and Diaries*, 2 vols (London: Cassell, 1927).
Chamberlain, Austen, *Down the Years* (London: Cassell, 1935).
——, *Politics from Inside* (London: Cassell, 1936).
Charteris, John, *At GHQ* (London: Cassell, 1931).
Churchill, Randolph S. (ed.), *Winston S. Churchill, Companion Volumes to Vol. II: Parts II–III* (London: Heinemann, 1969).
Churchill, Winston S., *The World Crisis*, 6 vols (London: Thornton Butterworth, 1923–31).
Cross, Colin (ed.), *Life with Lloyd George: The Diary of A.J. Sylvester* (London: Macmillan, 1975).
David, Edward (ed.), *Inside Asquith's Cabinet: From the Diaries of Charles Hobhouse* (London: John Murray, 1977).
Dutton, David (ed.), *Paris 1918: The War Diary of the British Ambassador, the 17th Earl of Derby* (Liverpool: Liverpool University Press, 2001).
Esher, Lord (ed.), *Journals and Letters of Reginald, Viscount Esher*, vols III–IV (London: Ivor Nicholson & Watson, 1938).

Fisher, Lord, *Memories* (London: Hodder and Stoughton, 1919).

Fitzroy, Sir Almeric, *Memoirs*, 2 vols (London: Hutchinson & Co., n.d.).

Gooch, G.P. and Temperley, Harold (eds), *British Documents on the Origins of the War* (London: HMSO, vol. VI, 1930; vol. VII, 1932; vol. XI, 1926).

Gough, Hubert, *The Fifth Army* (London: Hodder and Stoughton, 1931).

——, *Soldiering On* (London: Arthur Barker, 1954).

Grey, Viscount, *Twenty Five Years*, 2 vols (London: Hodder and Stoughton, 1925).

Hankey, Maurice, *The Supreme Command*, 2 vols (London: Allen & Unwin, 1961).

Howard, Christopher H.D. (ed.), *The Diary of Edward Goschen 1900–1914* (London: Royal Historical Society, 1980).

Jollife, John (ed.), *Raymond Asquith: Life and Letters* (London: Century, 1980).

Kerensky, Alexander, *The Catastrophe: Kerensky's Own Story of the Russian Revolution* (London, New York: D. Appleton & Co., 1927).

——, *The Kerensky Memoirs: Russia and History's Turning Point* (London: Cassell, 1965).

Knox, Sir Afred, *With the Russian Army 1914–1917*, 2 vols (New York: E.P. Dutton, 1921).

Lenin, V.I., *Selected Works*, 3 vols (Moscow: Progress Publishers, 1977).

Liddell Hart, Basil, *Memoirs*, 2 vols (London: Cassell, 1965).

Link, Arthur S. (ed.), *The Papers of Woodrow Wilson*, vol. 38 (Princeton: Princeton University Press, 1982).

Lloyd George, David, *War Memoirs*, 6 vols (London: Ivor Nicholson & Watson, 1933–36).

Lloyd George, Frances, *The Years That Are Past* (London: Hutchinson, 1967).

Lloyd George of Dwyfor, Earl, *Lloyd George* (London: Federick Muller, 1960).

Ludendorff, General Erich, *My War Memories 1914–1918*, vol. II (London: Hutchinson, 1919).

Masterman, Lucy, *C.F.G. Masterman: A Biography* (London: Nicholson and Watson, 1939).

Maurice, Nancy (ed.), *The Maurice Case* (London: Leo Cooper, 1972).

Maylunas, Andrei and Mironenko, Sergei (eds), *A Lifelong Passion: Nicholas and Alexandra, Their Own Story* (London: Weidenfeld and Nicolson, 1996).

McEwen, John (ed.), *The Riddell Diaries 1908–1923* (London: Athlone Press, 1986).

Morgan, Kenneth O. (ed.), *Lloyd George: Family Letters 1885–1936* (Cardiff, London: University of Wales and Oxford University Presses, 1973).

Morley, John, Viscount, *Memorandum on Resignation August 1914* (London: Macmillan, 1928).

Morris, A.J.A. (ed.), *The Letters of Lieutenant-Colonel Charles à Court Repington CMG Military Correspondent of 'The Times' 1903–1918* (London: Sutton Publishing Ltd for the Army Records Society, 1999).

Murray, Arthur C., *Master and Brother: Murrays of Elibank* (London: John Murray, 1945).

Oxford and Asquith, Earl of (H.H. Asquith), *The Genesis of the War* (London: Cassell, 1923).

——, *Memories and Reflections*, 2 vols (London: Cassell, 1928).

Paléologue, Maurice, *An Ambassador's Memoirs* (London: Hutchinson, 1925), vol. III.

Pares, Bernard, *My Russian Memoirs* (New York: AMS Press, 1969; repr. 1931 ed.).

——, *A Wandering Student: A Story of a Purpose* (Syracuse, NY: Syracuse University Press, 1948).

Pottle, Mark (ed.), *Champion Redoubtable: The Diaries and Letters of Violet Bonham Carter 1914–45* (London: Weidenfeld and Nicolson, 1998).

Repington, C.à. Court, *The First World War 1914–1918*, 2 vols (London: Constable, 1920).

Riddell, Lord (Sir George), *Lord Riddell's War Diary 1914–1918* (London: Ivor Nicholson & Watson, 1933).

——, *More Pages from my Diary 1908–1914* (London: Country Life, 1934).

Robertson, Field Marshal Sir William, *From Private to Field Marshal* (London: Constable, 1921).

——, *Soldiers and Statesmen*, 2 vols (London: Cassell, 1926).

Samuel, Herbert, Viscount, *Memoirs* (London: Cresset Press, 1945).

Self, Robert C. (ed.), *The Austen Chamberlain Diary Letters: The Correspondence of Sir Austen Chamberlain with His Sisters Hilda and Ida 1916–1937* (Cambridge: Cambridge University Press, 1995 for the Royal Historical Society).

Spender, Harold, *The Fire of Life: A Book of Memories* (London: Hodder and Stoughton, 1926).

Stevenson, David (ed.) (general editors Kenneth Bourne and D. Cameron Watt), *British Documents on Foreign Affairs: Reports and Papers from the Foreign Office Confidential Print*, Part II, Series H, *The First World War 1914–1918*, 12 vols (University Publications of America, 1989).

Swinton, Ernest D., *Eyewitness: Being Personal Reminiscences of Certain Phases of the Great War, Including the Genesis of the Tank* (London: Hodder and Stoughton, 1932).

——, *Over My Shoulder* (Oxford: George Ronald, 1951).

Sylvester, A.J., *The Real Lloyd George* (London: Cassell, 1947).

Taylor, A.J.P. (ed.), *Lloyd George: A Diary by Frances Stevenson* (London: Hutchinson, 1971).

—— (ed.), *My Darling Pussy: The Letters of Lloyd George and Frances Stevenson 1913–41* (London: Weidenfeld and Nicolson, 1975).

Temple Patterson, A. (ed.), *The Jellicoe Papers: Selections from the Private and Official Correspondence of Admiral of the Fleet Earl Jellicoe*, vol. II: *1916–1935* (London: Navy Records Society, 1968).

Tirpitz, Grand Admiral von, *My Memoirs*, 2 vols (London: Hurst & Blackett, 1919).

Ullswater, Viscount (J.W. Lowther), *A Speaker's Commentaries*, vol. II (London: Edward Arnold, 1925).

Vincent, John (ed.), *The Crawford Papers: The Journals of David Lindsay, Twenty Seventh Earl of Crawford and Tenth Earl of Balcarres 1871–1940, During the Years 1892–1940* (Manchester: Manchester University Press, 1984).

Wilson, Keith (ed.), *The Rasp of War: The Letters of H. A. Gwynne to the Countess Bathurst 1914–1918* (London: Sidgwick and Jackson, 1988).

Wilson, Trevor (ed.), *The Political Diaries of C. P. Scott 1911–1928* (London: Collins, 1970).

Woodward, David R. (ed.), *The Military Correspondence of Field-Marshal Sir William Robertson, Chief of the Imperial General Staff December 1915–February 1918* (London: Bodley Head, 1989).

Secondary sources

Books

Adams, R.J.Q., *Arms and the Wizard: Lloyd George and the Ministry of Munitions 1915–1916* (London: Cassell, 1978).

——, *Bonar Law* (London: John Murray, 1999).

Arthur, Sir George, *Life of Lord Kitchener*, 3 vols (London: Macmillan, 1920).

Ash, Bernard, *The Lost Dictator: A Biography of Field-Marshal Sir Henry Wilson* (London: Cassell, 1968).

Ashley, Maurice, *Churchill as Historian* (London: Secker and Warburg, 1968).

Asprey, Robert B., *The German High Command at War: Hindenburg and Ludendorff and the First World War* (London: Warner, 1994).

Bacon, Admiral Sir R.H., *The Life of Lord Fisher of Kilverstone*, 2 vols (London: Hodder and Stoughton, 1929).

Barraclough, Geoffrey, *From Agadir to Armageddon: Anatomy of a Crisis* (London: Weidenfeld and Nicolson, 1982).

Beaverbrook, Lord, *Politicians and the War 1914–1916* (London: Oldbourne, 1960).

——, *Men and Power 1917–1918* (London: Collins, 1956).

Bidwell, Shelford and Graham, Dominick, *Fire-Power: British Army Weapons and Theories of War 1904–1945* (London: George Allen & Unwin, 1982).

Bonham-Carter, Victor, *Soldier True: The Life and Times of Field Marshal Sir William Robertson* (London: Frederick Muller, 1963).

Bond, Brian, *Liddell Hart: A Study of his Military Thought* (London: Cassell, 1977).

—— (ed.), *Fallen Stars: Eleven Studies of Twentieth Century Military Disasters* (London: Brasseys, 1991).

—— (ed.), *The First World War and British Military History* (Oxford: Clarendon Press, 1991).

—— and Cave, Nigel (eds), *Haig: A Reappraisal 70 Years On* (Barnsley: Pen and Sword, 1999).

—— *et al.* (eds), *Look to Your Front: Studies in the First World War* (Staplehurst: Spellmount, 1999).

——, *The Unquiet Western Front: Britain's Role in Literature and History* (Cambridge: Cambridge University Press, 2002).

Bourne, John, Liddle, Peter and Whitehead, Ian (eds), *The Great World War 1914–1945*, vol. I: *Lightning Strikes Twice* (London: HarperCollins, 2000).

Bridge, F.R., *Great Britain and Austria-Hungary 1906–1914: A Diplomatic History* (London: Weidenfeld and Nicolson, 1972).

——, *The Habsburg Monarchy among the Great Powers 1815–1918* (New York: Berg, 1990).

Buchan, John, *A History of the Great War*, vol. III (London: Nelson, 1922).

Burdzhalov, E.N., *Russia's Second Revolution: The February 1917 Uprising in Petrograd*, trans. and ed. Donald J. Raleigh (Bloomington and Indianapolis: Indiana University Press, 1987).

Burk, Kathleen (ed.), *War and The State: The Transformation of British Government 1914–1919* (London: George Allen & Unwin, 1982).

——, *Britain, America and the Sinews of War 1914–1918* (Boston: George Allen & Unwin, 1985).

Cassar, George H., *Kitchener: Architect of Victory* (London: William Kimber, 1977).

——, *The Tragedy of Sir John French* (Newark: University of Delaware Press, 1985).

——, *Asquith as War Leader* (London: Hambledon Press, 1994).

Cecil, Hugh, *The Flower of Battle: British Fiction Writers of the First World War* (London: Secker and Warburg, 1995).

—— and Peter H. Liddle (eds), *Facing Armageddon: The First World War Experienced* (London: Leo Cooper, 1996).

Cecil, Lamar, *Wilhelm II*, vol. II: *Emperor and Exile 1900–1941* (Chapel Hill and London: University of North Carolina Press, 1996).

Charteris, John, *Field-Marshal Earl Haig* (London: Cassell, 1929).

Chickering, Roger, *Imperial Germany and the Great War 1914–1918* (Cambridge: Cambridge University Press, 1998).

—— and Förster, Stig (eds), *Great War Total War: Combat and Mobilisation on the Western Front 1914–1918* (Cambridge: Cambridge University Press, 2000).

Childs, David J., *A Peripheral Weapon? The Production and Employment of British Tanks in the First World War* (Westport, Connecticut; London: Greenwood Press, 1999).

Churchill, Randolph S., *Young Statesman*, vol. II: *Winston S. Churchill 1901–1914* (London: Heinemann, 1967).

Collier, Basil, *Brasshat: A Biography of Field-Marshal Sir Henry Wilson* (London: Secker and Warburg, 1961).

Crow, Duncan, *A Man of Push and Go: The Life of George Macaulay Booth* (London: Rupert Hart-Davis, 1965).

Crowe, Sybil and Corp, Edward, *Our Ablest Public Servant: Sir Eyre Crowe 1864–1925* (Braunton: Merlin Books, 1993).

Danchev, Alex, *Alchemist of War: A Life of Basil Liddell Hart* (London: Weidenfeld and Nicolson, 1998).

Davidson, Sir John, *Haig: Master of the Field* (London: Peter Nevill, 1953).

De Civrieux, Commandant, *L'Offensive de 1917 et le Commandement du Général Nivelle* (Paris and Brussels: G. van Ouest et Cie, 1919).

Dewar, George A.B. and Boraston, J.H., *Sir Douglas Haig's Command December 19 1915 to November 11 1918*, vol. I (London: Constable, 1923).

Dilks, David, *Neville Chamberlain*, vol. I (Cambridge: Cambridge University Press, 1984).

Dockrill, M. and McKercher, B. (eds), *Diplomacy in World Power: Studies in British Foreign Policy 1890–1950* (Cambridge: Cambridge University Press, 1996).

—— and French, David (eds), *Strategy and Intelligence: British Policy during the First World War* (London: Hambledon Press, 1996).

Duff Cooper, Alfred, *Haig*, 2 vols (London: Faber & Faber, 1935–36).

Dugdale, Blanche E.C., *Arthur James Balfour First Earl of Balfour*, vol. II (London: Hutchinson, 1936).

Edmonds, Sir James E., *Military Operations: France and Belgium 1916*, vol. I (London: Macmillan, 1932).

——, *Military Operations: France and Belgium 1916*, vol. II (London: Macmillan, 1938).

——, *Military Operations: France and Belgium 1917*, vol. II (London: HMSO, 1948).

——, *A Short History of World War I* (London: Oxford University Press, 1951).

Ellis, John, *The Social History of the Machine Gun* (London: Croom Helm, 1975).

—— and Cox, Michael, *The World War I Databook: The Essential Facts and Figures for all the Combatants* (London: Aurum Press, 2001).

Evans, R.J.W. and Pogge von Strandmann, Hartmut (eds), *The Coming of the First World War* (Oxford: Clarendon Press, 1988).

Falls, Cyril, *Military Operations: Macedonia*, vol. I (London: HMSO, 1933).

——, *Military Operations: France and Belgium*, vol. I (London: Macmillan, 1940).

Farrar, L.L., *Arrogance and Anxiety: The Ambivalence of German Power 1848–1914* (Iowa City: University of Iowa Press, 1981).

Farrar-Hockley, Anthony, *Goughie* (London: Hart-Davis, MacGibbon, 1975).

Ferguson, Niall, *The Pity of War* (London: Allen Lane/Penguin, 1998).

Feiling, Keith, *Life of Neville Chamberlain* (London: Macmillan, 1970).

Ferro, Marc, *The Great War 1914–1918* (London: Ark 1987).

Figes, Orlando, *A People's Tragedy: The Russian Revolution 1891–1924* (London: Jonathan Cape, 1996).

Fischer, Fritz, *War of Illusions: German Policies from 1911 to 1914* (London: Chatto and Windus, 1975).

Fraser, Peter, *Lord Esher: A Political Biography* (London: Hart-Davis, MacGibbon, 1973).

French, David, *British Strategy and War Aims 1914–1916* (London: Allen & Unwin, 1986).

——, *The Strategy of the Lloyd George Coalition 1916–1918* (Oxford: Clarendon Press, 1995).

Fry, Michael G., *Lloyd George and Foreign Policy*, vol. I: *The Education of a Statesman 1890–1916* (Montreal and London: McGill-Queen's University Press, 1977).

Fuller, J.F.C., *The Conduct of War 1789–1961* (London: Eyre and Spottiswoode, 1962).

George, W.R.P., *The Making of Lloyd George* (London: Faber & Faber, 1976).

Gilbert, Bentley B., *David Lloyd George: The Architect of Change 1863–1912* (Columbus: Ohio State University Press, 1987).

——, *David Lloyd George: Organizer of Victory 1912–1916* (Columbus: Ohio State University Press, 1992).

Gilbert, Martin, *The Challenge of War: Winston S. Churchill 1914–1916* (London, Minerva, 1990).

——, *World in Torment: Winston S. Churchill 1917–1922* (London: Minerva, 1990).

Gilmour, David, *Curzon* (London: John Murray, 1994).

Gollin, A.M., *Proconsul in Politics: A Study of Lord Milner in Opposition and in Power* (London: Anthony Blond, 1964).

Golovine, N.N., *The Russian Campaign 1914* (Kansas: Command and General Staff School Press, 1933).

Grieves, Keith, *Sir Eric Geddes: Business and Government in War and Peace* (Manchester and New York: Manchester University Press, 1989).

Griffith, Paddy (ed.), *British Fighting Methods in the Great War* (London, Portland: Frank Cass, 1996).

Grigg, John, *Lloyd George: The People's Champion 1902–1911* (London: Methuen, 1978).

——, *Lloyd George: From Peace to War 1912–1916* (Pbk. Ed. London: HarperCollins, 1997).

——, *Lloyd George: War Leader 1916–1918* (London: Allen Lane/Penguin, 2002).

Guinn, Paul, *British Strategy and Politics 1914 to 1918* (Oxford: Clarendon Press, 1965).

Hamilton, Keith, *Bertie of Thame: Edwardian Ambassador* (Woodbridge, Suffolk: Royal Historical Society, Boydell Press, 1990).

Harington, Sir Charles, *Plumer of Messines* (London: John Murray, 1935).

Harris, J.P., *Men, Ideas and Tanks: British Military Thought and Armoured Forces 1903–1939* (Manchester and New York: Manchester University Press, 1995).

—— (with Niall Barr), *Amiens to the Armistice: The BEF in the Hundred Days Campaign 8 August–11 November 1918* (London, Washington: Brasseys, 1998).

Hazlehurst, Cameron, *Politicians at War July 1914 to May 1915: A Prologue to the Triumph of Lloyd George* (London: Jonathan Cape, 1971).

Heenan, Louise E., *Russian Democracy's Fatal Blunder: The Summer Offensive of 1917* (New York: Praeger, 1987).

Herrmann, David G., *The Arming of Europe and the Making of the First World War* (Princeton: Princeton University Press, 1996).

Hinsley, F.H. (ed.), *British Foreign Policy Under Sir Edward Grey* (Cambridge: Cambridge University Press, 1977).

Hogg, I.V. and Thurston, L.F., *British Artillery Weapons and Ammunition 1914–1918* (London: Ian Allan, 1972).

Howard, Michael, *The Continental Commitment* (London: Temple Smith, 1972).

——, *War and the Liberal Conscience* (Oxford: Oxford University Press, 1978).

Hughes, Matthew and Seligman, Matthew (eds), *Leadership in Conflict 1914–1918* (Barnsley: Pen and Sword, 2000).

Hynes, Samuel, *A War Imagined: The First World War and English Culture* (London: The Bodley Head, 1990).

Jenkins, Roy, *Asquith* (London: Collins, 1964).

Joll, James, *The Origins of the First World War* (London and New York: Longman, 1984).

Jones, Mervyn, *A Radical Life: The Biography of Megan Lloyd George 1902–66* (London: Hutchinson, 1991).

Jones, Thomas, *Lloyd George* (London: Oxford University Press, 1951).

Kennedy, Paul M., *The Rise of the Anglo-German Antagonism 1860–1914* (London: George Allen & Unwin, 1980).

——, *The Realities Behind Diplomacy: Background Influences on British External Policy 1865–1980* (London: Fontana, 1985).

——, *The Rise and Fall of British Naval Mastery* (London, Fontana, 1991 3rd ed.).

King, Greg, *The Last Empress: The Life and Times of Alexandra Feodorovna, Tsarina of Russia* (New York: Birch Lane Press, 1994).

King, Jere Clemens, *Generals and Politicians: Conflict between France's High Command, Parliament and Government 1914–1918* (Westport Connecticut: Greenwood Press, 1951).

Király, Béla K. and Dreisziger, Nándor F. (eds), *East Central European Society in World War I* (Highland Lakes: Atlantic Research and Publications, Social Science Monographs, Boulder, 1985).

Kitchen, Martin, *The Silent Dictatorship: The Politics of the German High Command under Hindenburg and Ludendorff 1916–1918* (London: Croom Helm, 1976).

Koss, Stephen, *Lord Haldane: Scapegoat for Liberalism* (New York and London: Columbia University Press, 1969).

——, *Asquith* (London: Allen Lane, 1976).

——, *The Rise and Fall of the Political Press in Britain*, vol. II. *The Twentieth Century* (Chapel Hill and London: University of North Carolina Press, 1984).

Levine, Naomi B., *Politics, Religion and Love: The Story of H.H. Aasquith, Venetia Stanley and Edwin Montagu, Based on the Life and Letters of Edwin Samuel Montagu* (New York: New York University Press, 1991).

Liddell Hart, B.H., *Reputations* (London: John Murray, 1928).

——, *The War in Outline* (London: Faber & Faber, 1936).

——, *Through the Fog of War* (London: Faber & Faber, 1938).

——, *The Tanks: The History of the Royal Tank Regiment and Its Predecessors, Heavy Branch Machine Gun Corps, Tank Corps and Royal Tank Corps 1914–1945*, vol. I (London: Cassell, 1959).

——, *Strategy: The Indirect Approach* (London: Faber & Faber, 1967).

——, *History of the First World War* (London: Pan, 1970).

Liddle, Peter H. (ed.), *Passchendaele in Perspective: The Third Battle of Ypres* (London: Leo Cooper, 1997).

Lieven, D.C.B., *Russia and the Origins of the First World War* (London: Macmillan, 1983).

Lincoln, W. Bruce, *Passage through Armageddon: The Russians in War and Revolution 1914–1918* (New York: Simon and Schuster, 1986).

Loades, Judith (ed.), *The Life and Times of David Lloyd George* (Bangor, Gwynedd: Headstart History, 1991).

Longford, Ruth, *Frances, Countess Lloyd-George: More than a Mistress* (Leominster, Herefordshire: Gracewing, Fowler Wright Books, 1996).

Macdonald, Lyn, *They Called It Passchendaele* (London: Macmillan, 1983).

Marlowe, John, *Milner: Apostle of Empire* (London: Hamish Hamilton, 1976).

Massie, Robert K., *Castles of Steel: Britain, Germany and the Winning of the Great War at Sea* (New York: Random House, 2003).

McKercher, B.J.C. and Moss, D.J. (eds), *Shadow and Substance in British Foreign Policy 1895–1939: Memorial Essays Honouring C.J. Lowe* (Edmonton: University of Alberta Press, 1984).

Mearsheimer, John J., *Liddell Hart and the Weight of History* (Ithaca and London: Cornell University Press, 1988).

Middlebrook, Martin, *The First Day on the Somme: 1 July 1916* (New York: Norton, 1972).

——, *The Kaiser's Battle* (Harmondsworth: Penguin, 2000).

Miller, Steven E., Lynn-Jones, Sean M. and Van Evera, Stephen (eds), *Military Strategy and the Origins of the First World War*, Rev. and expanded ed. (Princeton: Princeton University Press, 1991).

Mombauer, Annika, *Helmuth von Moltke and the Origins of the First World War* (Cambridge: Cambridge University Press, 2001).

Morgan, Kenneth O., *Lloyd George* (London: Weidenfeld and Nicolson, 1974).

Morris, A.J.A., *Radicalism Against War, 1906–1914* (London: Longman, 1972).

——, *The Scaremongers: The Advocacy of War and Rearmament 1896–1914* (London: Routledge & Kegan Paul, 1984).

Naylor, John F., *A Man and an Institution: Sir Maurice Hankey, the Cabinet Secretariat and the Custody of Cabinet Secrecy* (Cambridge: Cambridge University Press, 1984).

Neilson, Keith, *Strategy and Supply: The Anglo-Russian Alliance 1914–1917* (London: George Allen & Unwin, 1984).

——, *Britain and the Last Tsar: British Policy and Russia 1894–1917* (Oxford: Clarendon Press, 1995).

Newton, Douglas, *British Policy and the Weimar Republic 1918–1919* (Oxford: Clarendon Press, 1997).

Nicholls, Jonathan, *Cheerful Sacrifice: The Battle of Arras 1917* (London: Leo Cooper, 1990).

Nicolson, Harold, *George V: His Life and Reign* (London: Constable, 1952).

Owen, Frank, *Tempestuous Journey: Lloyd George His Life and Times* (London: Hutchinson, 1954).

Palmer, Alan, *The Gardeners of Salonika* (London: Andre Deutsch, 1965).

Philpott, William J., *Anglo-French Relations and Strategy on the Western Front 1914–18* (London: Macmillan, 1996).

Pipes, Richard, *The Russian Revolution 1899–1919* (London: Collins Harvill, 1990).

Pollock, John, *Kitchener* (London: Constable, 2001).

Powell, Geoffrey, *Plumer: The Soldiers' General A Biography of Field-Marshal Viscount Plumer of Messines* (London: Leo Cooper, 1990).

Prior, Robin, *Churchill's 'World Crisis' as History* (London: Croom Helm, 1983).

—— and Wilson, Trevor, *Command on the Western Front: The Military Career of Sir Henry Wilson 1914–18* (Oxford: Blackwell, 1992).

——, *Passchendaele: The Untold Story* (New Haven and London: Yale University Press, 1996).

Pugh, Martin, *Lloyd George* (London and New York: Longman, 1988).

Radzinsky, Edvard, *The Last Tsar: The Life and Death of Nicholas II* (London: Hodder and Stoughton, 1992).

Ramsden, John, *Man of the Century: Winston Churchill and His Legend since 1945* (London: HarperCollins, 2002).

Rhodes James, Robert, *Churchill: A Study in Failure 1900–1939* (London: Weidenfeld and Nicolson, 1990).

Robbins, Keith, *Sir Edward Grey: A Biography of Lord Grey of Fallodon* (London: Cassell, 1971).

Röhl, John C.G., *The Kaiser and his Court: Wilhelm II and the Government of Germany* (Cambridge: Cambridge University Press, 1996).

Rose, Kenneth, *George V* (London: Weidenfeld and Nicolson, 1983).

Roskill, Stephen, *Hankey: Man of Secrets*, vol. I (London: Collins, 1970).

Rothwell, Victor, *British War Aims and Peace Diplomacy 1914–1918* (Oxford: Clarendon Press, 1971).

Rousset, Lt. Col., *La Bataille de l'Aisne (Avril–Mai 1917)* (Paris and Brussels: G. van Ouest et Cie, 1920).

Rowland, Peter, *Lloyd George* (New York: Macmillan, 1975).

Scally, Robert J., *The Origins of the Lloyd George Coalition: The Politics of Social Imperialism 1900–1918* (Princeton: Princeton University Press, 1975).

Serle, Geoffrey, *John Monash: A Biography* (Melbourne: Melbourne University Press, 1982).

Sheffield, Gary, *Forgotten Victory: The First World War Myths and Realities* (London: Headline, 2001).

Showalter, Dennis E., *Tannenberg: Clash of Empires* (Hamden: Connecticut, Archon Books, 1991).

Sked, Alan, *The Decline and Fall of the Habsburg Empire* (London: Longman, 1989).

Somin, Ilya, *Stillborn Crusade: The Tragic Failure of Western Intervention in the Russian Civil War 1918–1920* (New Brunswick: Transaction, 1996).

Spears, E.L., *Prelude to Victory* (London: Jonathan Cape, 1939).

Spender, Harold, *The Prime Minister* (New York: George H. Doran, 1920).

Steinberg, Mark D. and Khrustalëv, Vladimir M., *The Fall of the Romanovs: Political Dreams and Personal Struggles in a Time of Revolution* (New Haven and London: Yale University Press, 1995).

Steiner, Zara S., *The Foreign Office and Foreign Policy 1898–1914* (London: Cambridge University Press, 1969).

——, *Britain and the Origins of the First World War* (London: Macmillan, 1977).

Stevenson, David, *The First World War and International Politics* (Oxford: Oxford University Press, 1988).

——, *Armaments and the Coming of War: Europe 1904–1914* (Oxford: Clarendon Press, 1996).

Stone, Norman, *The Eastern Front 1914–1917* (London: Hodder and Stoughton, 1975).

Strachan, Hew, *The Politics of the British Army* (Oxford: Clarendon Press, 1997).

——, *The First World War*, vol. 1: *To Arms* (Oxford: Oxford University Press, 2001).

Taylor, A.J.P., *War By Time-Table: How the First World War Began* (London: Macdonald & Co., 1969).

—— (ed.), *Lloyd George: Twelve Essays* (London: Hamish Hamilton, 1971).

——, *The Struggle for Mastery in Europe 1848–1918* (Oxford: Oxford University Press, 1971).

Terraine, John, *Douglas Haig: The Educated Soldier* (London: Hutchinson, 1963).

——, *The Road to Passchendaele: The Flanders Offensive of 1917, A Study in Inevitability* (London: Leo Cooper, 1977).

——, *The Smoke and the Fire: Myths and Anti-Myths of War 1861–1945* (London: Sidgwick and Jackson, 1980).

——, *To Win a War: 1918: The Year of Victory* (London: Papermac, 1986).

Travers, Tim, *The Killing Ground: The British Army, the Western Front and the Emergence of Modern Warfare 1900–1918* (London: Allen & Unwin, 1987).

——, *How the War Was Won: Command and Technology in the British Army on the Western Front 1917–1918* (London and New York: Routledge, 1992).

Trevelyan, G.M., *Grey of Fallodon* (London, New York: Longmans, Green, 1937).

Turner, John, *British Politics and the Great War: Coalition and Conflict 1915–1918* (New Haven and London: Yale University Press, 1992).

Ullman, Richard H., *Intervention and the War* (Princeton: Princeton University Press, 1961).

Wasserstein, Bernard, *Herbert Samuel: A Political Life* (Oxford: Clarendon Press, 1992).

Watt, Richard M., *Dare Call It Treason* (London: Chatto & Windus, 1964).

Webster, Donovan, *Aftermath: The Remnants of War* (New York: Vintage, 1998).

Wheeler-Bennet, J.W., *Brest-Litovsk: The Forgotten Peace March 1918* (London: Macmillan, 1938; 1966 ed.).

Wildman, Allan K., *The End of the Russian Imperial Army: The Old Army and the Soldiers Revolt (March–April 1917)* (Princeton: Princeton University Press, 1980).

Wilson, Keith (ed.), *Decisions for War 1914* (London: UCL Press, 1995).

Wilson, Trevor, *The Downfall of the Liberal Party 1914–1935* (London: Collins, 1966).

——, *The Myriad Faces of War: Britain and the Great War 1914–1918* (Cambridge: Polity Press, 1986).

Williamson, Philip, *National Crisis and National Government: British Politics, the Economy and Empire 1926–1932* (Cambridge: Cambridge University Press, 1992).

Williamson, Samuel, R., *The Politics of Grand Strategy: Britain and France Prepare for War 1904–1914* (London: Ashfield Press, 1990).

Woodward, David R., *Lloyd George and the Generals* (Newark: University of Nebraska Press, 1983).

——, *Field Marshal Sir William Robertson: Chief of the Imperial General Staff in the Great War* (Westport Connecticut, London: Praeger, 1998).

Wolff, Leon, *In Flanders Fields: The 1917 Campaign* (Harmondsworth: Penguin, 1987 ed.).
Woodward, E. L., *Great Britain and the German Navy* (London: Frank Cass, 1964, 2nd ed.).
Wrigley, Chris, *Lloyd George* (Oxford: Blackwell, 1992).

Articles

Bailey, Jonathan, 'British Artillery in the Great War', in Griffith, Paddy (ed.), *British Fighting Methods in the Great War* (London, Portland: Frank Cass, 1996), pp. 23–49.
Beckett, Ian, 'Frocks and Brasshats', in Bond, Brian (ed.), *The First World War and British Military History* (Oxford: Oxford University Press, 1991), pp. 90–112.
Bond, Brian, 'Soldiers and Statesmen: Civil-Military Relations in 1917', *Military Affairs*, 1968, pp. 62–75.
Boyle, Timothy, 'New Light on Lloyd George's Mansion House Speech', *Historical Journal*, 23, 2, 1980, pp. 431–33.
Cassar, George H., 'Political Leaders in Wartime: Lloyd George and Churchill', in Bourne, John, Liddle, Peter and Whitehead, Ian (eds), *The Great World War 1914–1945*, vol. 1: *Lightning Strikes Twice* (London: HarperCollins, 2000), pp. 381–400.
——, 'Kitchener at the War Office', in Cecil, Hugh and Liddle, Peter H. (eds), *Facing Armageddon: The First World War Experienced* (London: Leo Cooper, 1996), pp. 37–50.
Clayton, Anthony, 'Robert Nivelle and the French Spring Offensive, 1917', in Bond, Brian (ed.), *Fallen Stars: Eleven Studies of Twentieth Century Military Disasters* (London: Brassey's, 1991), pp. 52–64.
Cosgrove, Richard A., 'A Note on Lloyd George's Speech at the Mansion House, 21 July 1911', *Historical Journal*, XII, 4, 1969, pp. 698–701.
David, Edward, 'The Liberal Party Divided 1916–1918', *Historical Journal*, XIII, 3, pp. 509–33.
Deák, István, 'The Habsburg Army in the First and Last Days of World War I: A Comparative Analysis', in Király, Béla K. and Dreisziger, Nándor F. (eds), *East Central Europe in World War I* (Highland Lakes: Atlantic Research and Publications, Social Science Monographs, 1985), pp. 301–12.
Dockrill, M.L., 'British Policy during the Agadir Crisis of 1911', in Hinsley, F.H.T. (ed.), *British Foreign Policy under Sir Edward Grey* (Cambridge: Cambridge University Press, 1977), pp. 271–87.
Dutton, David, 'The "Robertson Dictatorship" and the Balkan Campaign in 1916', *Journal of Strategic Studies*, 9, 1, March 1986, pp. 64–78.
Eckstein, 'Some Notes on Sir Edward Grey's Policy in July 1914', *Historical Journal*, XV, 2, 1972, pp. 321–24.
Egerton, George W., 'The Lloyd George *War Memoirs*: A Study in the Politics of Memory', *Journal of Modern History*, 60, 1, March 1988, pp. 55–94.
Galbraith, John S., 'British War Aims in World War I: A Commentary on "Statesmanship"', *Journal of Imperial and Commonwealth History*, XIII, 1, October 1984, pp. 25–45.
Gilbert, Bentley B., 'Pacifist to Interventionist: David Lloyd George in 1911 and 1914. Was Belgium an Issue?', *Historical Journal*, 28, 4, 1985, pp. 863–85.

Grieves Keith, 'War Correspondents and Conducting Officers on the Western Front from 1915', in Cecil, Hugh and Liddle, Peter H. (eds), *Facing Armageddon: The First World War Experienced* (London: Leo Cooper, 1996), pp. 719–35.

——, 'The Transportation Mission to GHQ, 1916', in Brian Bond *et al.* (eds), *Look to Your Front: Studies in the First World War* (Staplehurst: Spellmount, 1999), pp. 63–78.

——, 'Lloyd George and the Management of the British War Economy', in Chickering, Roger and Förster, Stig (eds), *Great War, Total War: Combat and Mobilisation on the Western Front 1914–1918* (Cambridge: Cambridge University Press, 2000), pp. 369–87.

Griffith, Paddy, 'The Tactical Problem: Infantry, Artillery and the Salient', in Liddle, Peter H. (ed.), *Passchendaele in Perspective: The Third Battle of Ypres* (London: Leo Cooper, 1997), pp. 61–72.

Fellner, Fritz, 'Austria-Hungary', in Wilson, Keith (ed.), *Decisions for War 1914* (London: UCL Press, 1995), pp. 9–26.

Fraser, Peter, 'British War Policy and the Crisis of Liberalism in May 1915', *Journal of Modern History*, 54, March 1982, pp. 1–26.

——, 'The British "Shells Scandal" of 1915', *Canadian Journal of History*, XVIII, 1983, pp. 69–86.

——, 'Cabinet Secrecy and War Memoirs', *History*, 70, 230, October 1985, pp. 397–409.

French, David, 'Who Knew What and When? The French Army Mutinies and the British Decision to Launch the Third Battle of Ypres', in Freedman, L., Hayes P. and O'Neill, R. (eds), *War, Strategy and International Politics: Essays in Honour of Sir Michael Howard* (Oxford: Clarendon Press, 1992), pp. 133–54.

——, 'The Meaning of Attrition', *English Historical Review*, CIII, 407, April 1988, pp. 385–405.

Fry, Michael, 'Political Change in Britain, August 1914 to December 1916: Lloyd George Replaces Asquith: The Issues Underlying the Drama', *Historical Journal*, 31, 3, 1988, pp. 609–27.

Hagenlücke, Heinz, 'The German High Command', in Liddle, Peter H. (ed.), *Passchendaele in Perspective: The Third Battle of Ypres* (London: Leo Cooper, 1997), pp. 45–58.

Harris, J.P., 'The Rise of Armour', in Griffith, Paddy (ed.), *British Fighting Methods in the Great War* (London, Portland: Frank Cass, 1996), pp. 113–37.

——, 'Haig and the Tank', in Bond, Brian and Cave, Nigel (eds), *Haig: A Reappraisal 70 Years On* (Barnsley: Leo Cooper, 1999), pp. 145–54.

Howard, Christopher, 'MacDonald, Henderson and the Outbreak of War, 1914', *Historical Journal*, 20, 4, 1977, pp. 871–91.

Hughes, Matthew, 'Personalities in Conflict? Lloyd George, the Generals and the Italian Campaign 1917–1918', in Hughes, Matthew and Seligman, Matthew (eds), *Leadership in Conflict 1914–1918* (Barnsley: Pen and Sword, 2000), pp. 191–206.

Hussey, John, 'The Flanders Battleground and the Weather in 1917', in Liddle, Peter H. (ed.), *Passchendaele in Perspective: The Third Battle of Ypres* (London: Leo Cooper, 1997), pp. 140–58.

Johnson, Paul, 'Lloyd George the Sound and the Fury', *New Statesman*, 19 September 1969.

Liddell Hart, B.H., 'The Basic Truths of Passchendaele', *Journal of the Royal United Service Institution*, CIV, 616, November 1959, pp. 433–39.

Lockwood, P.A., 'Milner's Entry into the War Cabinet, December 1916', *Historical Journal*, VII, 1, 1964, pp. 120–34.

McEwen, J.M., 'The Press and the Fall of Asquith', *Historical Journal*, 21, 4, 1978, pp. 863–83.

——, 'The Struggle for Mastery in Britain: Lloyd George Versus Asquith, December 1916', *Journal of British Studies*, XVIII, 1, Fall 1978, pp. 131–56.

——, 'Northcliffe and Lloyd George at War, 1914–1918', *Historical Journal*, 24, 3, 1981, pp. 651–72.

——, 'Lloyd George's Acquisition of the Daily Chronicle in 1918', *Journal of British Studies*, XXII, 1, Fall 1982, pp. 127–44.

——, ' "Brass-Hats" and the British Press during the First World War', *Canadian Journal of History*, XVIII, 1983, pp. 43–67.

McGill, Barry, 'Asquith's Predicament 1914–1918', *Journal of Modern History*, 3, 39, September 1967, pp. 283–303.

Neilson, Keith, ' "Only a d...d Marionette"? The Influence of Ambassadors on British Foreign Policy 1904–1914', in Dockrill, M. and McKercher, B. (eds), *Diplomacy in World Power: Studies in British Foreign Policy 1890–1950* (Cambridge: Cambridge University Press, 1996), pp. 56–78.

Philpott, William, 'Haig and Britain's European Allies', in Bond, Brian and Cave, Nigel (eds), *Haig: A Reappraisal 70 Years On* (Barnsley: Leo Cooper, 1999), pp. 128–44.

Pugh, Martin, 'Left in the Centre? Lloyd George and the Centrist Tradition in British Politics', in Loades, Judith (ed.), *The Life and Times of David Lloyd George* (Bangor, Gwynedd: Headstart History, 1991), pp. 17–31.

Rhodes James, R., 'Britain: Soldiers and Biographers', *Journal of Contemporary History*, 3, 1, January 1968, pp. 89–101.

Robbins, Keith, 'British Diplomacy and Bulgaria 1914–1915', *Slavonic and East European Review*, XLIX, 117. October 1971, pp. 560–85.

Röhl, John C.G., 'Germany', in Wilson, Keith (ed.), *Decisions for War 1914* (London: UCL Press, 1995), pp. 27–54.

Roskill, S. W., 'The U-Boat Campaign of 1917 and Third Ypres', *Journal of the Royal United Service Institution*, CIV, 616, November 1959, pp. 440–42.

Rothenberg, Gunther E., 'The Habsburg Army in the First World War', in Király, Béla K. and Dreisziger, Nándor F. (eds), *East Central Europe in World War I* (Highland Lakes: Atlantic Research and Publications, Social Science Monographs, 1985), pp. 289–300.

Simkins, Peter, 'Haig and the Army Commanders', in Bond, Brian and Cave, Nigel (eds), *Haig: A Reappraisal 70 Years On* (Barnsley: Leo Cooper, 1999), pp. 78–106.

Stevenson, David, 'The Failure of Peace Negotiations in 1917', *Historical Journal*, 34, 1, 1991, pp. 65–86.

Strachan, Hew, 'The Real War Liddell Hart, Cruttwell, Falls', in Bond, Brian (ed.), *The First World War and British Military History* (Oxford: Oxford University Press, 1991), pp. 41–67.

——, 'The Battle of the Somme and British Strategy', *Journal of Strategic Studies*, 21, 1, March 1998, pp. 79–95.

Stubbs, John O., 'Beaverbrook as Historian: "Politicians and the War 1914–1916" Reconsidered', *Albion*, 14, 3–4, Fall–Winter 1982, pp. 235–53.

Taylor, Philip M., 'The Foreign Office and British Propaganda during the First World War', *Historical Journal*, 23, 4, 1980, pp. 875–98.

Terraine, John, 'Passchendaele and Amiens I', *Journal of the Royal United Service Institution*, CIV, 614, May 1959, pp. 173–83.
——, 'Passchendaele and Amiens II: Amiens', *Journal of the Royal United Service Institution*, CIV, 615, August 1959, pp. 331–40.
Turner, John, 'State Purchase of the Liquor Trade in the First World War', *Historical Journal*, 23, 3, 1980, pp. 589–615.
——, 'Cabinets, Committees and Secretariats: The Higher Direction of the War', in Burk, Kathleen (ed.), *War and the State: The Transformation of British Government 1914–1919* (London: George Allen & Unwin, 1982), pp. 57–83.
——, 'Lloyd George, the War Cabinet and High Politics', in Liddle, Peter H. (ed.), *Passchendaele in Perspective: The Third Battle of Ypres* (London: Leo Cooper, 1997), pp. 14–29.
Vallone, Stephen J., ' "There Must Be Some Misunderstanding": Sir Edward Grey's Diplomacy of August 1, 1914', *Journal of British Studies*, 27, 4, October 1988, pp. 405–24.
Vandiver, Frank E., 'Field Marshal Sir Douglas Haig and Passchendaele', in Liddle, Peter H. (ed.), *Passchendaele in Perspective: The Third Battle of Ypres* (London: Leo Cooper, 1997), pp. 30–44.
Wawro, Geoffrey, 'Morale in the Austro-Hungarian Army: The Evidence of Habsburg Army Campaign Reports and Allied Intelligence Officers', in Cecil, Hugh and Liddle, Peter H. (eds), *Facing Armageddon: The First World War Experienced* (London: Leo Cooper, 1996), pp. 399–412.
Williams, M.J., 'Thirty Per Cent: A Study in Casualty Statistics', *Journal of the Royal United Service Institution*, 109, February 1964, pp. 51–55.
——, 'Treatment of the German Losses on the Somme in the British Official History: "Military Operations France and Belgium 1916" vol. II', *Journal of the Royal United Service Institution*, 111, February 1966, pp. 69–74.
Williams, Rhodri, 'Lord Kitchener and the Battle of Loos: French Politics and British Strategy in the Summer of 1915', in Freedman, Hayes and Robert, O'Neill (eds), *War, Strategy and International Politics: Essays in Honour of Sir Michael Howard* (Oxford: Clarendon Press, 1992), pp. 117–32.
Wilson, Keith, 'The Agadir Crisis, the Mansion House Speech and the Double-Edgedness of Agreements', *Historical Journal*, XV, 3, 1972, pp. 513–32.
——, 'The British Cabinet's Decision for War, 2 August 1914', *British Journal of International Studies*, I, 1975, pp. 148–59.
——, 'Britain', in Wilson, Keith (ed.), *Decisions for War 1914* (London: UCL Press, 1995), pp. 175–208.
Wilson, Trevor, 'A Prime Minister Reflects: The *War Memoirs* of David Lloyd George', in Moses, John A. and Pugsley, Christopher (eds), *The German Empire and Britain's Pacific Dominions 1871–1919: Essays on the Role of Australia and New Zealand in an Age of Imperialism* (Claremont, CA: Regina Books, 2000), pp. 39–52.
Woodward, David R., 'Did Lloyd George Starve the British Army of Men Prior to the German Offensive of 21 March 1918?', *Historical Journal*, 27, 1, 1984, pp. 241–52.
Wrigley, Chris, 'The Ministry of Munitions: An Innovatory Department', in Burk, Kathleen (ed.), *War and the State: The Transformation of British Government 1914–1919* (London: George Allen & Unwin, 1982), pp. 32–56.

——, 'Lloyd George and the Labour Party after 1922', in Loades, Judith (ed.), *The Life and Times of David Lloyd George* (Bangor, Gwynedd: Headstart History, 1991), pp. 49–69.

Young, Harry F., 'The Misunderstanding of August 1, 1914', *Journal of Modern History*, 48, December 1976, pp. 644–65.

Theses

Buchanan, Lawrence Roe, 'The Governmental Career of Sir Eric Campbell Geddes (PhD thesis, University of Virginia, 1979).

Greenhalgh, Elizabeth, 'A Study in Alliance Warfare: The Battle of the Somme 1916' (MA thesis, Australian Defence Force Academy, University of New South Wales, 1996).

Hanks, Robert J., 'How the First World War was Almost Lost: Anglo-French Relations and the March Crisis of 1918' (MA thesis, University of Calgary, 1992).

Hennes, Randolph Y., 'The March Retreat of 1918: An Anatomy of a Battle' (PhD thesis, University of Washington, 1966).

Philpott, William J., 'British Military Strategy on the Western Front: Independence or Alliance 1904–1918' (D.Phil thesis, University of Oxford, 1991).

Ryan, W. Michael, 'Lieutenant-Colonel Charles Court Repington: A Study in the Interaction of Personality. the Press and Power' (PhD thesis, University of Cincinatti, 1976).

Sullivan, Timothy Crandall, 'The General and the Prime Minister: Sir Henry Wilson and David Lloyd George in War and Peace 1918–1922' (PhD thesis, University of Illinois at Urbana-Champaign, 1973).

Thompson, J. Lee, 'Lord Northcliffe and the Great War: Politicians, the Press and Propaganda 1914–1918' (PhD thesis, Texas A&M University, 1996).

Index

Printed in the United States
104520LV00001B/65/A